CONTENTS

MOVING IMAGE AND SOUND, KNOWLEDGE AND ACCESS

The British Universities Film & Video Council (BUFVC) promotes the production, study and use of moving image and sound for teaching, learning and research. We provide access to television and radio programmes under licence, we are a centre of specialist knowledge and expertise, print reference books and publish databases online, we make available significant content across all subject disciplines and provide advice and training. We support the use of audio-visual media as an integrated and rewarding part of the teaching and learning experience.

INTRODUCTION
Murray Weston

This is the fifth edition of the British Universities Film & Video Council's Handbook, which was first published in 1991. From this edition onwards we intend to issue updates of the Handbook on an annual basis. As part of this plan we shall, from now on, include annual report information on the Council's funding and core activities.

The revised title for this fifth edition reflects the Council's mission statement and this volume aims to demonstrate our promotion of the use of moving image and sound, in their increasingly varied and complex forms, for learning and research.

This book is for students, teachers and information specialists. It offers a snapshot view of the world of audio-visual media for the higher and further education communities. Along with updates on the latest activities of the BUFVC itself, the directory section provides detailed information and guidance on a selection of blogs, discussion lists, courses and websites as well as contact details for other agencies such as the UK Higher Education Academy and the Regional Support Centres. It also offers an account of festivals and awards, information on all the main UK broadcasters, and a selection of distributors handling content which will be of interest to those involved in teaching and learning.

Marianne Open has compiled a list of all the radio and television broadcasters featured in the Television and Radio Index for Learning and Teaching (TRILT) while Cathy Grant has provided an invaluable account of the main media legislation and reports issued by government departments and selected bodies during the last twelve months.

Each edition of the Handbook features some new essays and, in this edition, these range from Joe Smith's forthright analysis of the broadcasting regulator Ofcom (in the light of its decision over Channel 4's controversial documentary, THE GREAT GLOBAL WARMING SWINDLE), to Nicholas Pronay's passionate defence of the need to establish an audio-visual equivalent for legal deposit that already exists for print publications in the UK, persuasively arguing that technological advances have made it possible to look at this merely as an extension to existing legislation. The BUFVC's Chairman John Ellis came to academia following a successful career as a media practitioner and his essay looks at some of the ways in which moving image and sound content can be employed best in learning and research.

In autumn 2008 the BUFVC's Off-Air Recording Back-up Service entered a new era. The BUFVC successfully trialled the recording and retention of BBC Radio 4 output as MP3 files to provide long term post-transmission access for the benefit of all BUFVC member institutions which are ERA licensed. The release of the Box of Broadcasts (BoB) shared service online by

Bournemouth University in association with the BUFVC and Cambridge Imaging Systems will permit licensed post-transmission access on- and off-campus to television and radio. This highly efficient service will radically improve the speed at which programmes can be made available for study.

Newsfilm Online, the result of BUFVC's work during a period of more than four years, was formally launched in October 2008 (via www.nfo.ac.uk) and has received generous praise for its work. The BUFVC also released online the Independent Local Radio Sharing archive – the Felicity Wells Memorial Archive (via http://radio.bufvc.ac.uk) – which is the first of three Independent Local Radio archive collections that shall be hosted by the BUFVC and released before the end of 2009.

We now have substantial experience in the preparation of moving image and sound content for online delivery to support learning and we intend to make use of this by preparing more content for delivery to our constituency.

In this our sixtieth anniversary year the BUFVC will extend and radically improve its services delivered online. We are building upon a track record of work, which is second to none in the UK, to promote the long-term use of moving image and sound for learning and research.

Murray Weston
Chief Executive
BUFVC

Credits
This book was compiled by the BUFVC's Information Service: Sergio Angelini, Cathy Grant and Marianne Open with assistance from Linda Kaye and Marilyn Sarmiento. Our grateful thanks go to all of them for their hard work and attention to detail. Every care has been taken to ensure the accuracy of the information in this Handbook. If errors are found, or if there is information that you wish to see in a future edition, please contact the editor at library@bufvc.ac.uk.

Note
Entries in the individual sections of the Directory are listed alphabetically by title, except for University Audio-Visual Centres, where they are listed alphabetically by university (i.e. University of Manchester files under M); HE Academy Subject Centres, where they are listed by subject; and Media Legislation and Reports, where they are listed by issuer.

ABOUT THE BUFVC

OFF-AIR RECORDING BACK-UP SERVICE

We record and retain more than 44,000 hours of UK television and radio per year. These programmes may be copied for any licensed member institution. Orders for copies can be made online.

Service

We offer a television and radio recording back-up service on behalf of UK member institutions holding a current Educational Recording Agency (ERA) licence. A member institution can request videocassettes or burned CD/DVD copies of missed programmes broadcast since June 1998 (for television) and since 18 September 2008 for BBC Radio 4. The BUFVC is one of the few bodies in Britain holding a letter of agreement permitting the post-transmission supply of copies of UK broadcasts under ERA licence and Section 35 of the Copyright, Designs and Patents Act 1988.

Coverage

BUFVC's Off-Air Television and Radio Recording Back-Up Service currently records BBC1, BBC2, BBC3, BBC4, ITV1, Channel 4, Five and BBC Radio 4. We have retained television recordings from 1998 onwards and can call on other collections to locate a requested programme as far back as 1990. We have recorded and retained more than 350,000 hours of programmes since 1998, with 44,000 hours now being added every year. Users can elect to receive their television programmes in a variety of formats: burned CD copies with compressed files in QuickTime and Windows Media variants, or the more popular VHS and DVD options. Radio broadcasts are burned as MP3 files onto CD or DVD.

Ordering

BUFVC member representatives may now order copies of programmes via TRILT online. Simply find the programme record in the TRILT database (see below) and the system will carry across all the details. Representatives can see at a glance the programmes that have already been requested and track their progress on the system.

TRILT – Television and Radio Index for Learning and Teaching

Web: www.trilt.ac.uk

TRILT is a unique database of the programmes transmitted by more than 350 UK television and radio channels since 2001. It carries more than eight million records and grows by 3,000 records per day. It also offers an e-mail alert service.

Service

TRILT delivers advance information on programmes and an e-mail alert service. It is an essential tool for all audio-visual librarians and for those wishing to identify and order specific programme content from our Off-Air Television Recording Back-Up Service.

Unlike other online electronic programme guides, TRILT retains the programme data long-term, creating an archive of broadcast information growing by more than a million records each year. With comprehensive data from 2001 and selected data from 1995 to 2001, TRILT can be used to research a topic, find programme repeats, locate a specific missed programme, or plan viewing and recording up to ten days in advance.

Features

TRILT database entries indicate which programmes are available from our Off-Air Television and Radio Recording Back-Up Service. Selected programme entries are 'enhanced' with additional information, such as longer descriptions, contributor details, production credits, links to relevant websites, tie-in books and keywords.

TRILT is accessible only to staff and students in subscribing BUFVC member institutions. To check the current membership status of your institution please telephone 020 7393 1500 or e-mail ask@bufvc.ac.uk. It is possible also to test TRILT with four weeks of data in our open-access demonstration version.

ONLINE SERVICES

We make available a huge amount of information on moving image and sound content through a number of online databases, all designed for ease of use and to serve the needs of UK higher education and research.

Researcher's Guide Online (RGO)

Web: www.bufvc.ac.uk/rgo

The RGO is an authoritative guide to accessible film, television and radio archives in the UK. It is complemented by our long-established printed reference work, *The Researcher's Guide: Film, Television, Radio and Related Documentation Collections in the UK*. It now also incorporates the *Researcher's Guide to Screen Heritage* (see opposite).

Moving Image Gateway (MIG)

Web: www.bufvc.ac.uk/gateway

The Moving Image Gateway connects you to more than 1,000 reviewed sites around the Internet which deliver valuable moving image, sound and related content online. It is fully searchable by subject discipline, and now includes references to podcasting and video podcasting sources.

HERMES

Web: www.bufvc.ac.uk/hermes

HERMES catalogues over 30,000 audio-visual programmes selected for their usefulness in higher and further education. It covers films, videotapes, DVDs, sound recordings and other media, accessible by title, production company, personality, date and subject, and gives full content and distribution details. It also contains records of the BUFVC's library holdings.

Researcher's Guide to Screen Heritage

Web: www.bufvc.ac.uk/rgo

This is a highly detailed guide to the extensive collections of screen heritage artefacts that are held in UK collections. These physical artefacts combine to represent all the key practices within screen history including the magic lantern, film, television and the digital present. They include magic lanterns and slides, optical toys, film production equipment, television & video equipment, cinema equipment & fittings, artwork for animation, sets & costumes, sound technology, toys & games and documentation (such as photographs, scripts, sheet music and personal papers).

British Universities Newsreel Database (BUND)

Web: www.bufvc.ac.uk/newsreels

The BUND is the world's leading resource for the study of cinema newsreels. The BUND offers a fully searchable database of 180,000 newsreel and cinemagazine stories, 80,000 digitised production documents and a wealth of contextual resources including audio interviews, bibliographies and links to over 40,000 downloadable film clips of British Pathe newsreels.

International Database of Shakespeare on Film, Television and Radio

Web: www.bufvc.ac.uk/shakespeare

This international database of Shakespeare on film, television and radio programmes, from 1898 to the present day, was created with funding from the Arts and Humanities Research Council. It covers film, radio, television and web-based media and includes well over 6,000 records which provide highly detailed information about the titles themselves, their links to Shakespeare and his works.

BUFVC manages four television and radio research databases on behalf of Bournemouth University:

The TVTimes Project (TVTiP)

Web: www.bufvc.ac.uk/itvdata

TVTiP provides unique online access to the programme listings of the London edition of the *TVTimes* from September 1955 to March 1985. Available without charge via authentication (Athens, Shibboleth, etc.) to all UK higher and further education institutions and subscribing BUFVC members.

This Week

Web: www.bufvc.ac.uk/itvdata

THIS WEEK was a leading ITV current affairs series from 1956-1992. This database offers detailed information, including programme descriptions and personnel. Available without charge via authentication (Athens, Shibboleth, etc.) to all UK higher and further education institutions and subscribing BUFVC members.

The Felicity Wells Memorial Archive – Independent Local Radio Programme Sharing Scheme 1983-1990

Web: http://radio.bufvc.ac.uk/

The Felicity Wells Memorial Collection is the first online archive of UK commercial radio, gathered from a nationwide source. The Programme Sharing Scheme is a unique record of a key time in the history of British Commercial Radio, one which has been largely forgotten and was in danger of being obliterated forever as the oxide on the original tapes progressively degenerates. The Archive was held in store at the National Sound Archive, consisting entirely of tapes transferred from a centralised copying facility established in 1985 which operated until 1990. A number of these stations have long-since ceased to exist. The programmes made between 1983 and 1990, covering music, religion, drama, history, news and much more are now available to download from this resource. Available without charge via authentication (Athens, Shibboleth, etc.) to all UK higher and further education institutions and subscribing BUFVC members.

The Radio Research Database (RRDb)

Web: www.bufvc.ac.uk/databases/rrdb.html

The RRDb aims to carry a record of all current radio-centred academic research in the UK, to assist all those researchers working in the new discipline of Radio Studies. The database is funded by the Radio Academy and managed by the Radio Studies Network.

INFORMATION SERVICE

Web: www.bufvc.ac.uk/services

At the heart of the BUFVC's work is our specialist Information Service. The reference library holds over 4,000 books, and ninety journal runs, with current catalogues from over 800 British and overseas distributors of audio-visual materials. We also hold an extensive archive of historical film catalogues, documenting educational and training programmes no longer in distribution. Our collection of journals and magazines includes every issue of the *Radio Times* since March 1991 when it began listing all terrestrial television channels; over twenty years of *American Cinematographer*, *Screen Digest* since 1972; thirty years of *Monthly Film Bulletin*; and every issue, including supplements, of *Sight and Sound*. Information Service staff handle a wide variety of enquiries from university lecturers, television researchers, teachers and health professionals and members of the public on audio-visual materials for teaching and learning.

The Information Service and Library is available free of charge to members. Visitors are advised to make an appointment in advance.

SPECIAL COLLECTIONS

Web: www.bufvc.ac.uk/services/specialcollections.html

The BUFVC holds a number of unique book and documentation collections of great value in moving image history and research:

- *Bert Baker book collection* – relating to television and media studies
- *British Movietone News newsreel documents* – complete set of commentary scripts (1929-1979) and photocopied set of Newsreel Association of Great Britain and Ireland papers
- *British National Film and Video Catalogue documentation* – selection of papers and index cards
- *British Pathe newsreel documents* – entire surviving paper collection for British Pathe newsreels and cinemagazines
- *Brook Associates programme data* – production material on three historical television series: THE WINDSORS (1994), THE LAST EUROPEANS (1995) and THE CHURCHILLS (1995)
- *Channel 4 press releases* – complete set of press releases, November 1982 to June 2002
- *Clem Adelman collection* – cine films, audio tapes, transcripts and slides from Professor Adelman's researches into teacher-pupil relations, 1970-76
- *David Buckingham collection* – papers covering interviews with primary school children on their television viewing habits 1989-1991 for the project 'The Development of Television Literacy in Middle Childhood and Adolescence'
- *David Samuelson papers* - papers of Movietone newsreel cameraman
- *Margaret Leahy photograph album* – belonged to winner of a newsreel competition in 1922 to star in a Hollywood feature film
- *Mark Lewisohn television papers* – collection of television and radio press releases

- *Norman Fisher collection* – newsreel cameraman's photographic collection, diaries and other memorabilia
- *Norman Roper collection* – newsreel cameraman and editor's photographs, news clippings, address books, posters and equipment
- *Reg Sutton memoirs* – newsreel sound engineer's memoirs
- *Reuters Television newsreel documentation* – substantial collection of original documents, such as shot lists, dope sheets and commentary scripts, for Gaumont-British, Paramount and Universal newsreels
- *Scientific Film Association* – paper archive of the Scientific Film Association and papers of Stanley Bowler, relating to the International Scientific Film Association.
- *Shell Film Unit papers* – collection of documentary film scripts
- *Slade Film History Register* – register of documents relating to film of value to historians, originally collated under Professor Thorold Dickinson.

COURSES

Web: www.bufvc.ac.uk/courses

The BUFVC runs regular one-day courses on topics relating to the use of moving images in learning, teaching and research. We frequently add to our range of courses and aim to address evolving user needs.

Current and forthcoming BUFVC courses include:
- *Authoring Streaming Media for the World Wide Web*
- *Copyright Clearance for Print, Broadcast & Multimedia Production*
- *Encoding Digital Video – Introduction*
- *Encoding Digital Video – Advanced*
- *Moving Image and Sound for Learning and Teaching Sources, Search Strategies, Appraisal and Use*
- *Introduction to Streaming: From Production to Delivery*
- *Shooting with HDV (High Definition Video)*

PUBLICATIONS

Web: www.bufvc.ac.uk/publications

Our magazine *Viewfinder* is published four times a year and is delivered to subscribing BUFVC member institutions. This popular publication brings you up to date on the production, study and use of film, television and related media for higher education and research, and includes subject listings of recent video and audio titles.

Current BUFVC book publications:

Shakespeare on Film, Television and Radio: The Researcher's Guide
Edited by Luke McKernan, Evemarie Oesterlen and Olwen Terris
2009. Paperback. 250 pages. ISBN 978-0-901299-79-6. Price £19.99 (£17.99 to BUFVC members). Plus £2.50 postage and packaging within the UK, £6.00 elsewhere.

The study of Shakespeare on film, television and radio has never been more active, and this practical and timely Guide is the essential reference source. It brings together compact histories of Shakespeare across the different media, descriptive guides to archives and their use, web sources, guides to the use of online media, advice on locating and using films, stills and documentation, copyright guidance, and intriguing facts and figures. Everything about the how as well as the why of studying audiovisual Shakespeare is provided here – from silent cinema to the multiplex, and from cat's whiskers to YouTube. The Guide will become a standard for anyone interested in the most filmed and the most widely broadcast of all writers.

Projecting Britain: The Guide to British Cinemagazines
Edited by Emily Crosby and Linda Kaye
2008. Paperback. 200 pages. ISBN 978-0-901299-78-9. Price £19.99 (£17.99 to BUFVC members). Plus £2.50 postage and packaging within the UK, £6.00 elsewhere.

This volume explores a film genre neglected for decades. Watched by millions, both in Britain and abroad, these fascinating 'screen magazines' reflected all aspects of popular culture from fashions and fads, to football and factories. This volume spans the history of the cinemagazine from the first known example, *Kinemacolor Fashion Gazette* released in 1913, through *Mining Review* and *Look at Life* to those still produced today, such as *Prisons Video Magazine*. A remarkably pervasive and popular form of screen entertainment, cinemagazines reveal a fascinating visual document of Britain in the twentieth century.

Moving Image Knowledge and Access: The BUFVC Handbook – Fourth Edition
Edited by Cathy Grant and Luke McKernan
2007. Paperback. 252 pages. ISBN 978-0-901299-77-2. Price £19.99 (£17.99 to BUFVC members). Plus £2.50 postage and packaging within the UK, £6.00 elsewhere.
This edition includes new essays by Peter B. Kaufman, Luke McKernan, Alistair McNaught, Seán Street and Andrew Yeates.

The Researcher's Guide: Film, Television, Radio and Related Documentation Collections in the UK

Edited by Sergio Angelini

2006. Paperback. 232 pages. ISBN 0-901299-76-6. Price £19.99 (£15.99 to BUFVC members). Plus £2.50 postage and packaging within the UK, £6.00 elsewhere.

This 2006 edition of *The Researcher's Guide: Film, Television, Radio & Related Documentation Collections in the UK* has been completely revised and updated.

Known as the film researcher's 'bible' and first published in 1981, this seventh edition now has details for over 640 audio-visual collections from the United Kingdom and Ireland. It features national and regional film and television archives as well as stockshot libraries and collections held by local authorities, museums, institutions of further and higher education, industrial companies and private individuals. *The Researcher's Guide* is now available for the first time in a new compact format. It also includes two dozen new illustrations and is fully indexed.

Cinema Before Cinema: The Origins of Scientific Cinematography (First English Edition)

By Virgilio Tosi (translated by Sergio Angelini)

2005. Paperback. 248 pages. ISBN 0-901299-75-8. Price £29.99 (£25.00 to BUFVC members). Plus £2.50 postage and packaging within the UK, £6.00 elsewhere.

This classic history of early film and photography, first published in 1984, describes the scientific impulses behind sequence photographers such as Eadweard Muybridge and E.J. Marey, whose work led directly to the birth of cinema. Now entitled *Cinema Before Cinema: The Origins of Scientific Cinematography*, the book has been updated to include recent research in the field. The BUFVC is the distributor of the English-language version of the film series THE ORIGINS OF SCIENTIFIC CINEMATOGRAPHY, which Tosi produced from 1990-1993 to complement his written researches. The BUFVC has produced a DVD edition of the films, to mark the publication of the English edition of the book (see below).

The Origins of Scientific Cinematography

Directed by Virgilio Tosi

2005. DVD Region 0. 97 minutes. Colour and black & white. English language version. Available in PAL or NTSC formats. Classification: E (Exempt). Price: £49.99 (£39.00 to BUFVC members) including postage and packing.

Virgilio Tosi's classic documentary series has been made available on DVD in English for the first time. The films complement Tosi's book *Cinema Before Cinema* (also published by the

BUFVC), using archive film and original equipment to show how cinematography had its origins not in the music hall or the fairground, but in the laboratory, as scientists of the 19th and early 20th centuries attempted to find new ways of seeing and measuring the natural world. Subjects covered include Jules Janssen's 'photographic revolver' (1873–74), Eadweard Muybridge's development of serial photography of human and animal locomotion (1878–87); Étienne-Jules Marey's 'photographic gun' (1882), and his models of the Chronophotographe (1882–93); technical advancements of scientific cinematography between 1883 and 1914 in different countries; and a compilation of sequences from twenty scientific films, made between 1895 and 1911.

Yesterday's News: The British Cinema Newsreel Reader
Edited by Luke McKernan
2002. Paperback. 330 pages. ISBN 0-901299-73-1. Price £39.00 (£29.00 to BUFVC members), Plus £2.50 postage and packaging within the UK, £6.00 elsewhere.

This Reader brings together over forty key texts on the British newsreels, from their silent beginnings to their revival as the ingredient of television documentaries. The texts come from trade papers, memoirs, parliamentary debates, newspapers articles, publicity brochures, film reviews and academic essays past and present. The Reader documents how the newsreels were produced, how they were received, and the controversies they inspired through the conflicting demands of news and entertainment. It covers filming of two World Wars, from the invasion of Belgium to the liberation of Belsen; the Spanish Civil War; the rise of television; and enduring arguments over censorship, propaganda and political bias in the news. It documents their organisation, the cameramen's experiences, and the overlooked role of women in the newsreels. It covers the academic interest they have aroused, with classic studies and the best of research taking place today.

Filming History: The Memoirs of John Turner, Newsreel Cameraman
By John Turner
2001. Paperback. 256 pages. ISBN 0-901299-72-3. Price: £35.00, (£29.00 for BUFVC members). Plus £2.50 postage and packaging within the UK, £6.00 elsewhere.
John Turner worked as a cameraman for Gaumont-British News between 1937 and 1952. As a war correspondent he was attached to the Royal Navy and filmed in the UK, North Sea, Mediterranean, Italy, North Africa, north-west Europe and the Far East. In peace time he filmed

many classic news stories, and was in India at the time of independence and Gandhi's assassination. In 1952 he became the royal rota cameraman for the Newsreel Association, filming the royal Commonwealth tours and numerous exclusive royal events. Between 1962 and 1970 he became production manager and then news editor for *Pathe News*. *Filming History* will be of importance to social, cultural and political historians, university courses on media and communication studies, and anyone interested in the history of British film and the important part played in that history by the newsreels.

Film and Television Collections in Europe: the MAP-TV Guide

Edited by Daniela Kirchner

1995. Hardback. 671 pages. ISBN 1-85713-015-4. Price £75.00 (£67.50 BUFVC members). Plus £5.50 postage and packing within the UK, £9.50 postage and packing elsewhere.

An indispensable guide to 1,900 film and television archives in over forty European countries from the Atlantic to the Urals. Includes large and well known national film archives, television companies, newsreel and stockshot libraries, as well as many small and lesser known collections held by regional and local authorities, museums, business and industry, and private individuals.

'The Story of the Century!': An International Newsfilm Conference

Edited by Clyde Jeavons, Jane Mercer and Daniela Kirchner

1998. Paperback. 170 pages. ISBN 0-901299-69-3. Price £15.00 plus £2.50 postage and packing within the UK, £9.50 postage and packing elsewhere.

The papers, presentations and proceedings of an international conference held at the National Film Theatre, London, between 2 and 4 October 1996, which brought together cameramen, editors, producers, film and television researchers and academics from many countries to celebrate 100 years of news on film and television. The book provides a lively insight into the world of the newsfilm - one of the century's most powerful forms of journalism. With its mix of formal papers, presentations and discussions, the material will inform and entertain everyone interested in news on film and television.

British Universities Newsreel Project

2005, CD-ROM. Suitable both for PC and Apple Macintosh systems. £95.00 including VAT and postage and packaging. £65.00 to all BUFVC subscriber researchers and Member institutions including VAT and postage and packaging. Note: The CD-ROM does not include the digitised documents and additional data for cinemagazines added to the online database since 2000.

The CD-ROM of the British Universities Newsreel Project database was published in March

2000, and contains details of almost 160,000 British cinema newsreel stories. Between 1910 and 1979 the newsreels, released twice a week in British cinemas, gave millions their picture of national and world events. They have now preserved an invaluable record of life and news in the twentieth century. Based on the data contained in original newsreel issue sheets, the BUNP CD-ROM contains full text and keyword search facilities, allows users to see the order in which stories were presented in each reel, and contains other details such as footage lengths, cameramen's credits, and regional variations to content.

The CD-ROM comes with a detailed booklet giving a short history of the British cinema newsreel. For film researchers, archivists, historians and students of news media, the BUNP database CD-ROM is an indispensable tool.

FACILITIES AND ROOM HIRE
Web: www.bufvc.ac.uk/facilities
We offer meeting facilities and technical services at our central London premises. We have a 25-seat seminar room with high quality video/data projection facilities. High quality videoconferencing facilities are also available. Our primary connection to JANET runs at 100 mbps, so live online moving image demonstrations can be offered. Our offline viewing facilities include a 16mm (six-plate) Steenbeck viewing table, and the facility to transfer 16mm film archive recordings to video. There are also video copying facilities for various formats and standards.

DISTRIBUTION
Web: www.bufvc.ac.uk/services/distribution
The BUFVC distributes and makes available for sale a number of specialist titles. Classic titles include Sir Lawrence Bragg's famous study of the properties of bubbles on the surface of a liquid, BUBBLE MODEL OF A METAL (1954); Professor Stanley Milgram's controversial experiments on obedience to authority, OBEDIENCE (1969); John Lowenthal's documentary on a notorious Cold War case, THE TRIALS OF ALGER HISS (1980); and the thematic compilations of British newsreels produced by the InterUniversity History Film Consortium. The full list with prices is available on our online distribution catalogue or via the HERMES database (www.bufvc.ac.uk/hermes).

CONSULTANCY
Web: www.bufvc.ac.uk/consultancy
We provide specialist consultancy services capable of addressing a wide range of issues relating to the provision of academic support services using moving image and sound. Drawing upon specialist practitioners within the Council's membership, we provide assistance in fields including copyright clearance, encoding, cataloguing, metadata construction, archiving and many areas of moving image research.

LEARNING ON SCREEN

Conference

Learning on Screen is an annual conference organised by the British Universities Film & Video Council since the BUFVC merged with the Society for Screen-Based Learning in 2004.

Learning on Screen is for those developing and using moving image and sound content in learning, teaching and research. It brings together producers, courseware creators, e-learning specialists, media librarians, academic service providers, lecturers, researchers and staff developers.

Increasing quantities of moving image and sound content are now available on demand from broadcasters and national online services, and educational establishments are rapidly taking up use of these resources in their own virtual learning environments to deliver bespoke courses.

Other Learning on Screen events, such as one-day conferences, seminars and workshops, are also organised. See the Learning on Screen website for details: www.bufvc.ac.uk/learningonscreen.

Awards

The Learning on Screen Awards celebrate excellence in the production of effective learning material which employs moving pictures, sound and graphics. Such learning material might be delivered as physical media, or online, or via broadcast media – or a combination of all three. The competition is open to allcomers involved at any level in the fields of production, publishing, broadcasting, education and research.

For information on upcoming Learning on Screen events, the Awards, or to join the mailing list, visit the Learning on Screen website at www.bufvc.ac.uk/ learningonscreen or e-mail learningonscreen@bufvc.ac.uk.

MEMBERSHIP OF THE BUFVC

Members of the BUFVC enjoy a range of benefits, from access to off-air recordings to discounts on publications, courses and conferences.

Voting rights

Representatives of Ordinary Member institutions carry voting rights to determine the management and conduct of the Council.

Off-Air Television Recording Back-up Service

Licensed Ordinary Member institutions can order copies of programmes from BBC1, BBC2, BBC3, BBC4, ITV1, Channel 4, Five from June 1998 (and earlier where possible) and BBC Radio 4 from September 2008. These are available in DVD and VHS, or as burned CD copies with compressed files in QuickTime or Windows Media Player formats.

Television and Radio Index for Learning and Teaching (TRILT)
This database is only available to staff and students in BUFVC Member institutions. It holds over eight million records, and members can order copies of off-air recordings direct from the database.

Other databases
The *TV Times* and *This Week* databases are available to BUFVC Members and UK higher education users with an Athens or Shibboleth password only. Other BUFVC databases including HERMES, Moving Image Gateway and the British Universities Newsreel Database do not require access authentication.

Technical services
Members enjoy discounts on BUFVC technical services, including viewing, copying and encoding facilities.

Information Service
Members have full use of our Information Service, which will answer queries by e-mail, telephone, letter, fax or in person. Members also have access to the BUFVC book library and special collections.

Courses and Events
Staff in BUFVC Member institutions obtain discounts on registration charges for all BUFVC courses and events.

Viewfinder/Publications

The BUFVC's quarterly magazine *Viewfinder* magazine is only available to BUFVC Members, and is supplied without further charge. One free copy of each new BUFVC book publication is supplied to institutional Members, with discounts on all other purchases.

We are constantly working to add new services and resources for the benefit of BUFVC members.

Applications for membership should be accompanied by a formal letter addressed to the Chief Executive of the BUFVC. Applications will be considered by the Executive Committee of the Council before acceptance.

For further information, including details of current rates and an application form, visit www.bufvc.ac.uk/membership.

BUFVC CONTACTS

British Universities Film & Video Council
77 Wells Street, London W1T 3QJ
Tel: 020 7393 1500 **Fax:** 020 7393 1555
E-mail: ask@bufvc.ac.uk
Web: www.bufvc.ac.uk

BUFVC staff (as of October 2008)

Murray Weston – Chief Executive
☎ 020 7393 1505 E-mail: murray@bufvc.ac.uk

Luís Carrasqueiro – Deputy Chief Executive
☎ 020 7393 1510 E-mail: luis@bufvc.ac.uk

Sergio Angelini – Information and Publication
Executive
☎ 020 7393 1506 E-mail: sergio@bufvc.ac.uk

Frazer Ash – Media and Network Technician
☎ 020 7393 1503 E-mail: frazer@bufvc.ac.uk

Lotfallah Bekhradi – Network and Content
Manager
☎ 020 7393 1509 E-mail: lotfallah@bufvc.ac.uk

Markeda Cole – Media Assistant
☎ 020 7393 1514 E-mail:
markeda@bufvc.ac.uk

Ali Fowler – Events Officer / Chief
Executive's Assistant
☎ 020 7393 1512 E-mail: pa@bufvc.ac.uk

Cathy Grant – Information Officer
☎ 020 7393 1507 E-mail: cathy@bufvc.ac.uk

Gabriel Hernández – Web Developer
☎ 020 7393 1511 E-mail: gabriel@bufvc.ac.uk

Linda Kaye – Research Executive
☎ 020 7393 1518 E-mail: linda@bufvc.ac.uk

Perri Mahmood – Head of Finance
☎ 020 7393 1515 E-mail: perri@bufvc.ac.uk

Dominic O'Brien – Media & Network
Assistant
☎ 020 7393 1513 E-mail: dominic@bufvc.ac.uk

Marianne Open – TRILT Officer
☎ 020 7393 1501 E-mail:
marianne@bufvc.ac.uk

Deborah Oritogun – Administrative Assistant
☎ 020 7393 1519 E-mail: deborah@bufvc.ac.uk

Shakespeare Project
Eve-Marie Oesterlen – Broadcast Researcher
☎ 020 7393 1502 E-mail:
evemarie@bufvc.ac.uk

Olwen Terris – Senior Researcher
☎ 020 7393 1502 E-mail: olwen@bufvc.ac.uk

The BUFVC is a Limited Company of charity status that is governed by an Executive Committee elected from the appointed member representatives of 'Ordinary Member' institutions – universities and colleges in the UK (see pages 24–27). The Executive Committee members are trustees of the charity and directors of the Company.

As of end October 2008 BUFVC had 278 members, of which 214 were ordinary members (140 Higher Education institutions and 74 Further Education colleges).

HISTORY

The British Universities Film Council was first established in 1948. The original objects for which the Council was established were:

The advancement of education in the universities and institutions of university standard in the United Kingdom by the co-ordination and development of the use and study of film and related media, materials and techniques for the purpose of university teaching and research, and in particular:

    i. to promote:

        a. the collection and dissemination of information

        b. the distribution

        c. the production of films suitable for the above purpose

    ii. to co-operate with universities and similar bodies in other countries for the performance of these objects.

The BUFVC continues to represent these interests for teachers, researchers, librarians and service providers across all faculty disciplines.

In the 1960s, during a previous period of significant expansion in UK higher education, the Council was influential in making representation to the Government's Brynmor Jones Committee and subsequently received funding as a grant-in-aid body of the British Film Institute. In May 1969 the Council was incorporated as a Limited Company without share capital and employed its first full-time member of staff. By 1975 the Council's full-time secretariat had grown to seven along with its range of services and publishing activities.

In 1983 the Council became independent of the British Film Institute and received direct funding from the Department for Education and Science. It also changed its name to the British Universities Film & Video Council.

In 1993, following re-organisation of higher education funding, the Council's PES line was transferred to the Higher Education Funding Council for England (HEFCE), and The Open University was identified as a partner through which core grant monies would be passed to the Council in future.

From 1 April 1996, following a three-year review, the BUFVC became part of the portfolio of activities of the Joint Information Systems Committee (JISC), under the JISC Committee on Electronic Information (JCEI) – now JISC Content Services (JCS).

At the end of the academic year 2005-2006 it was agreed that the funding relationship by which core grant monies came via The Open University would come to an end, and that from August 2006 the BUFVC would be funded direct by HEFCE under a new 'Related Bodies Funding Agreement' with oversight by the JISC. This became effective from 1 August 2006. The BUFVC also entered a process of strategic options review assisted by external consultants and advisors. As part of the review process, the BUFVC redefined its charitable objects, which now read:

The advancement of education by promoting the production, study and use of moving image, sound and related media within post-compulsory education and research.

The BUFVC has developed and managed many innovative projects, services, publications and events in its field. Some of the highlights since 1969 include:

- Development of two of the UK's first computerised filmographic databases – HELPIS and *Audio-Visual Materials for Higher Education* (1972, 1976)
- Acquisition and development of the Slade Film History Register (1974)
- Publication of the first *Researcher's Guide to British Film and Television Collections* (1981)
- Publication of three *Researcher's Guides to British Newsreels* (1983-1993)
- Development of The Television Index (1987-2001)
- Development of the Off-Air Recording Back-Up Service (1990)
- Development of a collaborative pilot project for the delivery of moving picture content to universities and colleges online (1998)
- Development and publication online of the British Universities Newsreel Database (2000)
- Founding the JISC-funded Managing Agent and Advisory Service for moving pictures and sound – MAAS Media Online (2001-2005)
- Development of the online Television and Radio Index for Learning and Teaching – TRILT (2001)
- Founding the JISC-funded Newsfilm Online digitisation project in partnership with ITN/Reuters (2004-2007)
- Merging with the Society for Screen-Based Learning and developing the annual Learning on Screen conference and awards (2004)

- Developing a hard disk-based recording system – the Box of Broadcasts – to provide post-transmission access to UK broadcast television programmes as encoded files (2004)
- Integrating processes for online ordering of off-air recordings via the TRILT database (2007)
- Delivering 65,000 moving image files, 10 million still pictures and associated metadata to create the Newsfilm Online service www.nfo.ac.uk (2007)
- Launching the Felicity Wells Memorial Archive (the Independent Local Radio Sharing Archive) online (2008)

BUFVC FUNDING MIX 2007–2008

The BUFVC receives a core grant from the Higher Education Funding Council for England (HEFCE), under a HEFCE Related Bodies Funding Agreement with oversight by the Joint Information Systems Committee (JISC). The core grant is made under Section 65 of the *Further and Higher Education Funding Act 1992*. The BUFVC also raises additional funds from subscriptions, sales of publications, events income, sponsorship and other grants.

In the financial year ending 31st July 2008 the Council received a total income of £968,000. BUFVC's 'core grant' for the period was £509,100 and subscription income was £128,000 (13% increase on the previous year). Income relating to other grants, projects, publications and services amounted to £331,000. Expenditure for this year again reflects that the majority of income is applied to staff costs, rent and equipment.

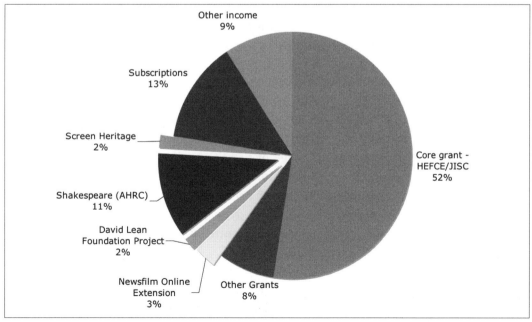

Breakdown of BUFVC income streams for 2007-2008

BUFVC CORE ACTIVITIES 2007–2008

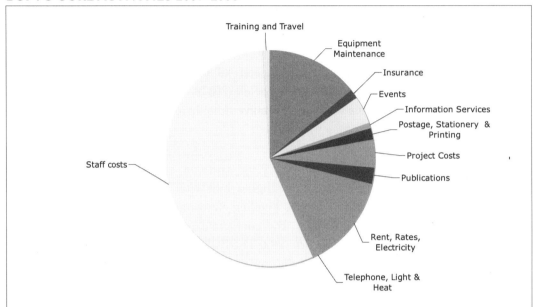

Breakdown of BUFVC expenditure for 2007-2008

Website (www.bufvc.ac.uk)

BUFVC's website is the access route to BUFVC information and services online – both those restricted to BUFVC member institutions and freely released content for general use. BUFVC databases delivered online via the website are subject to regular updating.

BUFVC Information Service (www.bufvc.ac.uk/services)

At the heart of the BUFVC lies a specialist Information Service whose activities, relationships and accumulated assets have been developed during more than thirty years of professional service to the academic community. The Information Service deals with members' enquiries; enters and amends records across the range of BUFVC databases; acquires and catalogues books, journals, catalogues and special collections; supports BUFVC courses and events; and contributes to BUFVC publications. In 2007-08 particular effort went into the re-design of *Viewfinder* and the production of three books: *Projecting Britain: The Guide to British Cine-magazines*, this edition of the *Handbook* and *Shakespeare on Film, Television and Radio: The Researcher's Guide*, due out in January 2009.

BUFVC Publications (www.bufvc.ac.uk/publications)

In 2007–2008, BUFVC's magazine *Viewfinder* continued to be published four times per year. Completely redesigned and expanded to thirty-six pages, highlights include an exclusive report on the Kreen-Akrore tribe in Brazil re-visiting their own media history by viewing THE TRIBE THAT HIDES FROM MAN on DVD; key articles on Bioethics, prison education through media, the 25th anniversary of Channel 4 and a profile of the National Video Archive of Performance; profiles of Charles Urban, experimental psychologist Chris Evans, Mike Clark – ex-BUFVC Chairman – and Professor Charles Barr, and reviews from Professor Andrew Higson, film producer Nik Powell and legal expert Richard McCracken. Some 4,500 copies of each issue were produced and circulated to subscribing member institutions and individuals.

BUFVC Off-Air Recording Back-Up Service

(www.bufvc.ac.uk/services/offair.html)
This service, operating under Section 35 of the CDPA 1988 and a letter of agreement with the licensing body, the Educational Recording Agency, delivers access to some 44,000 hours a year of UK television which the BUFVC records and retains. The service has continued to experience increasing demands, a direct result of the larger numbers of copies which are now offered to Premier Services Ordinary Member institutions, since August 2004.

In 2007/08 the service experienced an increase in demand of 31% with just over 4,000 copies of programmes sent to members. BBC2 is once again the most requested channel, with Channel 4 a close second. ITV1, Five and BBC3 together represent less than 15% of all requests.

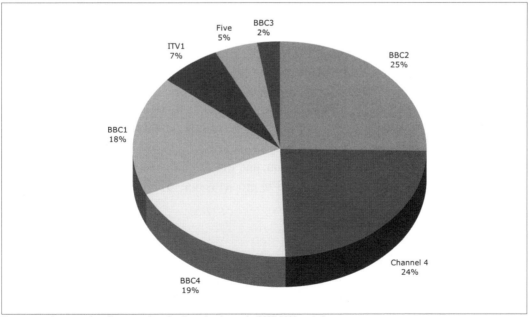

Proportion of requests for off-air recordings by channel – during the 2007-2008 period

BUFVC Courses (www.bufvc.ac.uk/courses)

The BUFVC is committed to delivering high quality courses, conferences and events to support continuing professional development. In 2007–2008 eighteen one-day courses were delivered:

Copyright Clearance for Print, Broadcast & Multimedia Production [4]

Encoding Digital Video – Introduction [4]

Encoding Digital Video – Advanced [4]

Finding and Using Audio-Visual Media in Further & Higher Education [3]

Shooting with HDV (High Definition Video) [3]

Learning on Screen (www.bufvc.ac.uk/learningonscreen)

On 18-19 March 2008 the BUFVC held its annual two-day event, this time at the University of York. This year's included a celebration of the BUFVC's sixtieth anniversary, looking at the milestones in media and education over the last six decades.

BUFVC RESEARCH PROJECTS

David Lean and Gaumont Sound News web: www.bufvc.ac.uk/databases/newsreels/about/lean.html

This six-month project was funded by the David Lean Foundation. It investigated the *Gaumont Sound News* newsreel (1929-1933), where David Lean began his film career as an editor. The project added over 2,000 story records to the British Universities Newsreel Database (BUND), as well as web pages, online video copies of *Gaumont Sound News*, and written outputs. The project began in April 2007 and concluded in April 2008.

International Database of Shakespeare on Film, Television and Radio
(www.bufvc.ac.uk/shakespeare)

This AHRC-funded research project began in September 2005 and is running for three years. It will develop an international database of Shakespeare on film, television and radio, which is being developed out of the BUFVC's HERMES database. The project is emphasising the importance of reliable distribution information, and the database will be kept up to date post-project by the BUFVC Information Service. The project is due to conclude in December 2008.

Researcher's Guide to Screen Heritage
(www.bufvc.ac.uk/rgo)

The BUFVC is a member of the Screen Heritage Network, an association of museums, archives and similar bodies working together to advance the concept of screen heritage. The Network's first collaborative project, with funding from the Museums Libraries and Archives Council, was to create a directory of moving image and screen-based artefacts in the UK, and in 2008 led to the publication online of the Researcher's Guide to Screen Heritage. The project began in April 2007 and concluded in July 2008.

JISC-FUNDED PROJECTS

Independent Radio News

One of the projects awarded funding under the second phase of the JISC Digitisation Programme is the digitisation of the LBC/Independent Radio News archive. This project is led by Bournemouth University in partnership with the BUFVC. The project was initiated in March 2007. BUFVC's involvement, to ingest metadata and sound content and to host these online, will commence after the time-frame of this report. The project is due to complete in February 2009.

OTHER ACTIVITIES

Grierson Awards (www.grierson.org)

The BUFVC was again contracted in 2008 by The Grierson Trust to assist in the processing of entries for the Grierson British Documentary Awards. Data gathered was used to enrich the TRILT and HERMES databases. The awards ceremony took place at the Royal Institution, London on 20 November 2008.

This following provides an accurate listing of all the institutions and individuals currently holding BUFVC membership, as of October 2008. This is broken down into the following categories: Ordinary members, Associate members UK, Associate members overseas as well as Schools, Corporate members, Exchange members, Honorary members and Researcher members.

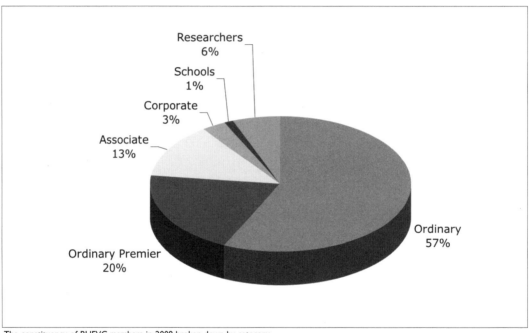

The constituency of BUFVC members in 2008 broken down by category

ORDINARY/PREMIER MEMBERS

Aberdeen College
Anglia Ruskin University
Aquinas College
Arts Institute at Bournemouth
Aston University
Barnet College

Barton Peveril College
Wellington College
Bath Spa University College
Birkbeck, University of London
Birmingham City University
Birmingham College of Food, Tourism & Creative Studies

Blackpool & the Fylde College
Boston University - London Programme
Bournemouth University
Bridgwater College
Brighton Hove & Sussex Sixth Form
 College
Brooklands College
Brunel University
Buckinghamshire Chilterns University
 College
Burton College
Canterbury Christ Church University
Cardiff University
Carmarthenshire College
Carshalton College
Central College of Commerce
Central School of Speech & Drama
Central Sussex College
Chelmsford College
City & Islington College
City College Manchester
City College Norwich
City University
Cleveland College of Art & Design
Colchester Institute
Coventry University
Cranfield University
Crossways Academy
Croydon College
Darlington College
De Montfort University
Deeside College
Dumfries and Galloway College
Dundee College
East Durham and Houghall Community
 College
Edge Hill University
Edinburgh College of Art

Enfield College
Farnborough College of Technology
Fashion Retail Academy
Filton College Bristol
Fire Service College
Glasgow Caledonian University
Glasgow School of Art
Goldsmiths' University of London
Gorseinon College
Greenwich Community College
Greenwich School of Management
Guildford College
Harper Adams University College
Henley College Coventry
Heriot Watt University
Hertford Regional College
Hillcroft College
Huddersfield New College
Hull College
Imperial College London
International Business School
Institute of Education
Keele University
King's College London
Kingston College
Kingston University
Lambeth College
Lancaster University
Leeds College of Art & Design
Leeds Metropolitan University
Leeds Trinity & All Saints College
Lewisham College
Liverpool Institute for Performing Arts
Liverpool John Moores University
London Business School
London Jewish Cultural Centre
London Metropolitan University
London School of Economics

London School of Hygiene & Tropical
   Medicine
London South Bank University
Loughborough College
Loughborough University
Macmillan Academy
Manchester Metropolitan University
Middlesbrough College
Middlesex University
Nacro (HM Prison)
Napier University
National School of Goverment
Northbrook College
Northern College
Northern Reginal College
Northumbria University
Norwich School of Art and Design
Nottingham Trent University
Open University
Oxford Brookes University
Oxford Cherwell Valley College
Perth College
Plymouth College of Art and Design
Queen Margaret University
Queen Mary, University of London
Queen's University of Belfast
Ravensbourne College of Design &
   Communication
Richmond Upon Thames College
Robert Gordon University
Roehampton University
Rose Bruford College
Rotherham College of Arts & Technology
Royal Agricultural College
Royal Holloway
Royal Marsden School of Cancer Nursing &
   Rehabilitation
Royal Military Academy

Royal Scottish Academy of Music & Drama
School of Oriental and African Studies
Sheffield Hallam University
Shrewsbury 6th Form Centre
Sixth Form College Farnborough
Solihull Sixth Form College
South Downs College
South West College
Southampton Solent University
St George's University of London
St Mary's College
Staffordshire University
Stockport College of Further & Higher
   Education
Sutton Coldfield College
Swansea Institute of Higher Education
Tavistock & Portman NHS Trust
Thames Valley University
Thurrock and Basildon College
Trinity College (Carmarthen)
Truro College
University College Falmouth
University College London
University for the Creative Arts
University of Aberdeen
University of Abertay, Dundee
University of Arts London
University of Bath
University of Bedfordshire
University of Birmingham
University of Bolton
University of Bradford
University of Brighton
University of Bristol
University of Cambridge
University of Central England
University of Central Lancashire LLRS
University of Chester

University of Chichester
University of Cumbria
University of Derby
University of Dundee
University of Durham
University of East Anglia
University of East London
University of Edinburgh
University of Essex
University of Exeter
University of Glamorgan
University of Glasgow
University of Gloucestershire
University of Hertfordshire
University of Huddersfield
University of Hull
University of Kent at Canterbury
University of Leeds
University of Leicester
University of Lincoln
University of Liverpool
University of Manchester
University of Northampton
University of Nottingham
University of Oxford
University of Plymouth
University of Portsmouth
University of Reading
University of Salford
University of Sheffield
University of Southampton
University of St Andrews
University of Stirling
University of Strathclyde
University of Sunderland
University of Surrey
University of Sussex
University of The West of Scotland

University of Teesside
University of the West of England
University of Ulster at Coleraine
University of Wales, Aberystwyth
University of Wales, Bangor
University of Wales LAMPETER
University of Wales Institute, Cardiff
University of Wales, Bangor
University of Wales, Swansea
University of Warwick
University of Westminster (Regent Campus)
University of Westminster
University of Winchester
University of Worcester
University of York
University of Wolverhampton
Waltham Forest College
West Cheshire College
West Kent College
West Thames College
Westminster Kingsway College
Wyggeston & Queen Elizabeth I College
York St John University College

ASSOCIATE MEMBERS – UK

British Medical Association Library
Imperial War Museum
National Library of Scotland
National Library of Wales
National Media Museum
North West Film Archive
Science Museum
Wellcome Trust
West Midlands Police

ASSOCIATE MEMBERS – OVERSEAS

Bibliotheque Nationale de France
City University of Hong Kong

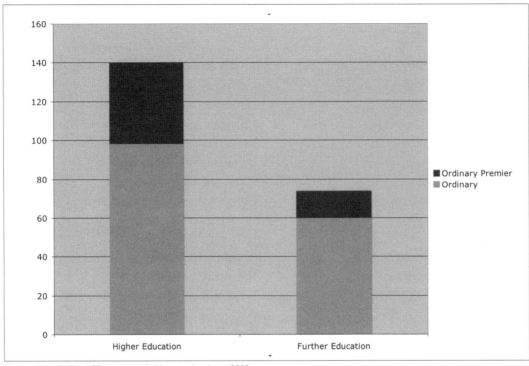

The number of HE and FE institutions holding membership in 2008.

Dartmouth College, USA
Film Institute of Ireland
Fisher Library, University of Sydney
Macquarie University, Australia
Massey University, New Zealand
National University of Singapore
Nederlands Instituut voor Beeld en Geluid
New York Public Library, USA
Ngee Ann Polytechnic, Singapore
RTE Ireland's Natinal Broadcaster
Temasek Polytechnic, Singapore
Trinity College, Dublin
Universite de Rennes 2
University College Cork
University de Montreal
University de Santiago de Compostela
The University of Auckland
University of Iowa Libraries

University of Canterbury New Zealand
University of the West Indies
University of Toronto
Vrije Universiteit
York University Libraries, Canada

OTHERS
Schools
Claremont Fan Court School
Sharnbrook Upper School & Community
  College
Shooters Hill Post 16 Campus
Wellington College

Corporate Members
BBC News and Current Affairs
The British Library
Directors & Producers Rights Society

IMG Media
ITN Archive
JVC Professional Europe Ltd
Thompson CompuMark
Twenty Twenty Television
Unique Television

Exchange Members
The British Film Institute
Federation of Commercial Audio Visual
  Libraries (FOCAL)
IVCA
Program for Art on Film Inc
Royal Anthropological Institute

Honorary Members
Mr James Ballantyne
Professor Mike Clark
Mr Geoffrey O'Brien

Miss Elizabeth Oliver
Miss Yvonne Renouf-Smith
Mrs Marilyn Sarmiento
Mr Russell Towns

Researcher Members
Ms Sheila Bailey
Ms Alana Baily
Ms Rosalind Bentley
Dr Michael Clark
Ms Claire Dunn
Ms Catriona Lewis
Mr Michael Maloney
Mr Hugh Meteyard
Ms Judy Patterson
Mr Peter Phillips
Ms Victoria Stable
Dr Vicki Wegg-Prosser
Ms Christine Whittaker

Cans of film stored at the BFI National Archive

PRESERVING THE AUDIO-VISUAL RECORD

Nicholas Pronay

From the closing decade of the 19th century, additional types of historical records came into being: moving pictures and sound recordings. These preserved, at least potentially, what people at the time saw and heard as presented by new media organisations. Almost as soon as these appeared it was recognised by some that their products would be a very important source for historians, and the first proposals for establishing archives for them appeared over 100 years ago. The relative importance of these communications media increased as the range of what was being communicated, and to whom, was rapidly and massively extended. This was partly through the development of new technologies and partly through ever-more effective forms of organisations for their production and dissemination. The synchronisation of sound and picture and then the development of electronic transmission systems, first for sound and then for sound and vision, allowed full-range communication of information and ideas – political, social and ideological.

The development of industrial-scale production and distribution organisations extended their reach to ever-larger numbers of people and to wider social, educational and age sectors of the population. This development culminated in the arrival of television, taking over from film as the primary audio-visual medium of communication. Over the same span of time the political system of the UK was gradually evolving into a popular democracy, which made the record of what the people at large were being told and shown all the more important as a historical source. Although the British Film Institute did set up what would become known as 'The National Film Archive' as early as the mid 1930s it was not ever truly that, mainly because unlike the British Library it preserved only what happened, and happens, to be donated to it. The fact is that there is still no proper comprehensive UK archive for the audio-visual record, and indeed of our audio-visual heritage.

Through serendipity, the dedication of a small legion of largely unrewarded people and the fact that they had been produced and distributed in a physical form, led to the ironical position that a far greater proportion of films, the earlier and less central communications medium, have been preserved than of television. The extent of the loss of British television output for the 1950 to 1990 period is appalling. I estimate from secondary record material that about 85% is lost and that which happens to survive does so in an unsystematic fashion. The contrast between what is available to the historian through the copyright libraries in terms of books, newspapers and periodicals – effectively a complete run – and what is available of television output, is staggering. Those who produced the radio and television part of it, the BBC and the franchised companies, enjoyed a far more privileged position and secure income than newspapers and book publishers, so the degree of irresponsibility and lack of any sense of a national obligation concerning preservation – as distinct from wanting to keep such programmes as they could for re-use or to show off with, in effect having no 'archive' at all but only a 'production library' – which had led to that loss is shaming. Explaining in 2008 on its own website why certain programmes are missing from its library, the BBC stated that such programmes which could not be repeated for copyright reasons, 'were thought to have no further use and often not kept'.[1]

And, if *that* qualifies as a justificatory explanation for why productions made on film or videotape, typically drama or other cultural programmes, were allowed to be lost, then there is no explanation at all as to why they kept no record of what went out live, which is a considerable and very important part of broadcasting. News, discussions and other forms of 'current affairs' programmes, as well as much else in the political, social and ideological spheres is wholly, or partly, 'live'. That is, it comes together, only exists, as for example the News, only at the point of transmission. It would need to be recorded for archival preservation. Such recordings – for example on videocassettes – as distinct from those which are for transmission, have long been very, very cheap, an almost invisible extra cost on the programme budget. And even though historians pointed out as early as 1970 the great significance of news, and current affairs and 'factual broadcasting' in general, as historical sources and asked for them to be kept, until the 1990s no such recordings were systematically made or retained.

To round off this horrible story, there is the final element of the inadequacy of the repositories, in terms of doctrine as well as organisation and technology, for conducting historical research where such as have survived are being kept. To be able to make proper use of record materials in today's circumstances it is essential to have searchable catalogues, rapid, copious and remote access, ready copying facilities and preferably permission for the historians to obtain their own copy of relevant extracts. The National Archives here in the UK, as well as repositories of public records in other civilised countries, provide such research facilities. The requirements to make effective use of non-written records is even greater. Attempting to work in our current film and video archives is like stepping back into Victorian England, to the days of gentleman historians with unlimited time and amanuenses. The result of haphazard preservation and the inadequacy of today's audio-visual archives for facilitating historical research is that the research is simply not being done.

The upshot is that we have lost a major dimension of our history for the second half of the 20th century. Amongst the list of sources and references of any of the major new books on the history of the period from after Second World War, the audio-visual record is conspicuous by its absence – even though the importance of the coming of television is acknowledged.

We need to find a way for ensuring that in the 21st century there will not be a repetition either of the horror stories of losses and destruction or of the valorous stories of beyond-the-call-of-duty rescues, but that the preservation of the public audio-visual records of Britain will become merely another of the routine functions of the state, as it is in respect of newspapers, books and of the records of government itself.

Just as the preservation of written and printed records required national repositories, so we need the establishment now also of a national audio-visual archive. Like the British Library and The National Archives, it needs to rest on a legal obligation placed on the 'publishers' of audio-visual materials to furnish it with a copy. As audio-visual materials, television in particular, do not come in readily preservable copies, or often in any material form at all, and need special technologies and expertise for acquisition and storage as well as for access and for making them researchable, a national audio-visual archive needs to be purpose designed. For the scale of preservation involved in a major nation's audio-visual records – over 100 television channels are operating for 20 hours or more per day in Britain, the output of which would not only have to be preserved but made researchable, which means catalogues, indices, viewing facilities – the necessary technologies had effectively not existed before. However, the 'digital revolution' that has taken place over the last 20 years and which has now substantially been completed provides *all* the technological requirements needed for a comprehensive audio-visual archive. Other countries have already established such digital archives for their own audio-visual heritage. All that is needed now is the political will, and the work of all those who would not like to see a repetition of the sad saga of the last century, to get the message across to the politicians.

The point of the changeover to digital recording technologies is not that it gives higher quality – it does not – or that it lasts longer in storage – it does not – but rather that it is re-recordable effectively without loss, is done automatically and at a much faster rate than in real time. This means that 'deposit' need not mean a physical object being deposited but a recording made of what reached the viewer

The National Archive

The National Archive in London.

together, automatically, with its 'meta data,' that is catalogue information such as its provenance and date, and in fact much else besides if desired. It allows thus the use of dynamic storage systems in which the material is being continuously re-recorded onto the next generation of recording media and formats. This overcomes the bugbear of the current archiving system that stores the actual media, plastics of various kinds on which it had been recorded at the time of production. This requires pools of legacy equipment to be maintained for the recordings to be playable, all in the knowledge that the day will come when that equipment will become unmaintainable due to lack of spare parts. However, once there is a digital archive with the equipment and systems for the continuous re-coding of output, material which originally arrived in the archive in a physical form, such as film prints, on whatever kind of plastic it was recorded on, can readily be transferred, fed into the ongoing dynamic digital recording process.

The other point of the changeover to digital affects the other end of the process – access and study. In a dynamic digital storage system viewing the material does not lead to wear and tear, for it is not done in a physical form. Viewing can therefore take place anywhere, streamed through the Internet for example, and with the inbuilt capacity for rapid scanning and selective copying which are essential research tools. In addition to manageable and affordable storage technologies and suitability for user-friendly arrangements, digital recordings are also suitable for 'data-mining'. That is the use of digital search, indexing and cataloguing techniques, much of which is carried out by high speed machines, computers, rather than expensive and slow people. This overcomes the perennial problem which has faced researchers: finding the relevant programmes, finding the relevant sections and of knowing in what other programmes were there references to the object of research – that is a subject index for pictures and sounds.

If some of this sounds like science fiction, or the voice of the ever-optimistic technophile claiming developments to be just around the corner that then take a decade or more to begin materialising, it is far from that. Today there are organisations using large scale digital storage and retrieval systems – such as GCHQ and in general in the electronic surveillance and electronic warfare organisations – which are capable of acquiring and storing quantities of digitised audio or visual material far beyond our needs. Routinely, tens of millions of telephone conversations are now recorded simultaneously and stored for extended periods of time, not in some vast, futuristic, billion-pound pile but in ordinary office buildings. High-resolution satellite images are being recorded in a continuous, 24/7 stream for intelligence gathering, security, and military and mapping purposes. Combining those storage technologies with data mining techniques allows today the retrieval of an individual telephone conversation by a key word or phrase; the retrieval of a particular image by time and location and other 'metadata', and also, increasingly by visual identifiers within the images themselves, such as a particular face or a number plate. The recording and data-mining capabilities currently available would enable the utilisation of the audio-visual record on a comparable scale, convenience and practicability as written archival materials currently available in today's archives.

Digital technologies, yes, but why compulsory deposit? For a historian that is not much of a question. No country succeeded in preserving its written heritage without a statutory requirement. All the great record collections – the Bodleian, the British Library, the Colindale Newspaper Library, and the Bibliothèque naltional de France – all rested on compulsory deposit. Of the two oldest, the Bibliothèque rests on the 1537 Ordonnance de Montpellier issued by Francis I, which ordered the deposit of a copy of everything published in print in the Royal Library. Likewise the Bodleian rests on the Elizabethan requirement for the deposit of a copy in return for the licence to print, and the subsequent transfer of these as from 1614 to the Library of Oxford University. Successive Acts of Parliament buttressed and extended compulsory deposit to cover new kinds of publications, such as newspapers, as they came along. That process in Britain stopped, alas, before the arrival of publications in the form sound-recordings and films, but it did not stop everywhere else.

One only needs to imagine what the state of our newspaper and periodicals heritage would be like without the legal requirement to deposit copies and without a national repository for preserving them, to realise the essential role compulsory deposit played. There is no need, actually, to stretch our imagination too much. It would be like the state of our broadcasting heritage. Some of that need not have happened given more of a public spirit in what was supposed to be a public service organisation resting on 'assured finance', but the more general fact is that no production organisation is institutionally or culturally inclined to preservation. They are groups of creative people seeking the new and not a group of archivists or historians bothered about the past.

If this was true before, it is so with a vengeance today. In the place of large establishments, such as the film studios in the age of the studio system, or the public service broadcasters, each with substantial bureaucracies and fixed premises, the 21st century is characterised by *ad hoc* assemblages, decentralised and distributed administrations which come together for a production and then disassemble when the production is completed and which might reassemble for another one. Expecting them to preserve their productions of their own volition would be unrealistic and unfair. The same goes for the hundred plus satellite or digital television and radio channels that also rise and disappear from time to time, and which operate on a shoestring.

In a longer perspective the same goes even for the Independent Television terrestrial franchise companies and for the BBC itself. The franchise companies and channels which came and went in the last fifty years have left nothing recognisable as an 'archive' and in the face of pressures to preserve their output, which latterly have begun to be seen as being of national value, have long happily delegated that job to whoever would do it, contributing a small sum to the running costs. Even assuming that the BBC has now come to see the light, and that the purported 'bank of computers in the basement', which it claims to run do keep a recording of output were to continue for good, can we bet for how long the BBC as such might endure? Or that it would not change its mind again? In any case, it cannot be an obligation even on the small number of franchise or licence fee based major broadcasting organisations to provide the research tools and facilities without which the material

The US National Archives in Washington DC.

is all but useless for general historical purposes. And for each to do so would be a ridiculous waste of money. As far as the digital channels are concerned it would be entirely out of the realms of the practical.

In the past at least, broadcasters and the BBC in particular, have been reluctant even to allow the recording of their output claiming 'copyright reasons'. There is an important legal and constitutional principle involved here. It is not a new one but one which the BBC had avoided acknowledging from the days of Sir John Reith. It is that a production organisation is totally free to do whatever it wishes concerning its own productions – that is *until* it has transmitted them on the public airwaves, or the 'ether' as Reith liked to call it. The airwaves – the part of the electromagnetic spectrum allocated to the UK – are owned by the nation. Individuals and organisations need to obtain a licence from the nation to put out anything on it. Once it is on the airways, it is in the public domain *ipso facto* and it is no longer for the producers to decide anything about it, except that they retain the fiduciary rights for retransmission: that is any money which might be made from re-transmitting or selling it in any form. What has been transmitted belongs to the people; to the person who it was reported would never again be able to look at a crocodile the same way having watched David Attenborough's LIFE IN COLD BLOOD (BBC, 2008), and all the others for whom what they were shown and told had significance. It *is* a historical record because it had been a historical factor: it has had an effect on whoever or whatever a generation of historians might identify as having seen it.

Although it might seem odd perhaps at first glance, in addition to those broadcasters who claim that they hold a universal copyright in what they have published, some film/television archivists have also had reservations over the introduction of compulsory deposit, and in their case with good reason. The problem with the principle of compulsory deposit for archives, in the past, was the spectre of a succession of white vans arriving at their doors and dumping assorted cans and boxes, the contents of which would require extremely expensive sorting, preservation and cataloguing, and would impose, and especially so in the case of video-recordings, even greater demands for maintaining pools of legacy equipment. Compulsory deposit could not in practice work at all for transmitted media if it were to require physical preservation. All this however only applies to the pre-digital, pre-dynamic preservation era.

It might be thought that there could be heroic legal issues involved in the proposed introduction of compulsory deposit. In fact the principle that licence to publish entails the responsibility of furnishing a copy for record purposes goes all the way back, as we have seen, to Elizabethan times and has been re-asserted many time since. So there is no need for a fundamental Act, only an amending Act or perhaps just an Order in Council, which adds any audio-visual media product which requires a licence to be publicly displayed, which covers cinema as well as television and radio, to the list of types of publications which are already covered. In the past it was by simple amending acts that new media such as newspapers were added on as they came along. There are *no* legal or structural impediments, now, to the establishment of a national audio-visual archive resting on compulsory deposit.

What should be its operational principles, its *modus operandi*? As far as the depositing of material is concerned, it is simply that all those who seek a licence for outputting audio-visual material to the *public* are required to contact the Archive and arrange for a copy to be preserved, in a manner and in a form that is to the satisfaction of the Archive. Looking at the experience of countries which already operate such a system, it would be most likely a recording made by the Archive with the cost being charged to the production or distributing company in the case of movies or to the channel in the case of transmitted material, either individually, as in the case of obtaining a certificate permitting exhibition from the British Board of Film Classification (BBFC), or collectively as an additional part of the licence fee paid by channels for the right to use a particular frequency.

The current rules about what is private and what is public would apply, the latter being the responsibility of the state and therefore of a national archive. That is: a) all such productions which have to be submitted to the BBFC, as prerequisite 'for public exhibition' in cinemas or other licensed public venues; b) everything which was transmitted by any organisation which has been granted a public licence to transmit on the air, including therefore all television and radio channels, as well as programmes made outside the UK. One might say that they are not part of our national heritage, but clearly they *were* part of what the British people saw and heard – as such they constituted part of their experience and part of the ingredients that formed their outlook. They do therefore belong in a British national archive. Any attempt to try to define a 'British' production, as distinct from a non-British production is going to suffer the same confusions as such attempts consistently suffered in the past, ever since the quota acts of 1928. The same applies to television channels produced outside the UK but which have a British licence to be beamed into the UK, such as EuroNews, Al-Jazeera, Russia Today, France 24, some Islam channels and their equivalents. All such channels contribute to the formation of views and perceptions of people in Britain. Does anyone doubt the relevance of, say, the Islam channels, when the history of our own age is going to be written?

An essential principle is that the collection should be unselective, that is take the output of channels as a whole instead of selecting particular programmes deemed to be worthy of preservation. No one is qualified today to decide what may be an important historical record in the future. The past is littered with warning examples: from the recommendation Dr Ernest Lindgren, the then curator of the British Film Institute's Archive, made to the newsreel companies that they should preserve the pictures but junk the soundtracks, because those 'were just propaganda'; to the system operated by the BBC in which a 'representative' day per month should be selected for preservation – representative of what? What would we say if we only had one copy per month of *The Times*? And selected by whom – its own editor? This does not of course mean that there should not be some selection as between channels. Some are duplicates of another or time-shifted but the selection should be only on such technical grounds, not on content or 'value'.

What about those productions that were not for public exhibition? There is a sense in which every foot of film – using film as a shorthand for moving image in

Courtesy of the Institut national de l'audio-visuel

whatever form recorded – is part of the national heritage: home movies, corporate, training, educational and advertising productions. But the collection of such, in whatever serendipitous fashion they might come into the public domain, is not to be in the brief of a National Archive any more than the records of private companies come under the Public Records rules. There is a difference between private or corporate or local or regional collections, museums or libraries or archives, and a National Archive of Audiovisual Records. They should continue to be collected through voluntary deposit or purchase and kept in the framework of local, corporate, regional or specialised collections.

Having a central point of deposit, a particular building, does not however mean a central point of access – it means both central and remote access. The central point provides viewing alongside supporting materials, indices, and reference works and exchange access with foreign archives such as at the Institut National de l'Audiovisuel (INA) of France. It should also maintain a national distributed catalogue listing of what may be held in the specialised and local collections. Here again The National Archives in the UK provides a pattern to emulate. It provides catalogue access to other collections and electronically merges them with its own catalogue and its subject and names indices. The researcher can thus identify the whole range of relevant records, or at least most of them, across the different types of collections and repositories. The increase in the productivity and the comprehensiveness of research work has been nothing short of spectacular. Access from outside the building can be accomplished remotely from anywhere. Although a delicate point, we should try to resist the national instinct for re-pioneering what some other nation has got to first, and especially the French, and rather draw lessons from them. However that may be, it is useful to at least know what it is happening there. The French had a broadly similar history of compulsory deposit for all kinds of printed publications until 1925 when the principle was extended to photographs and sound recordings; in 1977 to the cinema; in 1992 to radio and television, and in 2006 to the Internet. In 1992 the INA was established by law as the national archive, with an academic and research brief. The system adopted was that the Institut carried out the digital recording of the output of channels as broadcast, with the channels having to pay for the cost of it through an additional sum written into their licences. As of 2008 eighty-seven television and seventeen radio channels are being recorded, moving up to 100 television and twenty radio channels by 2010. The recordings are accessible for study purposes either on the premises or streamed through the Internet to registered users. The avowed academic purpose and orientation of the Institut is borne out by its users' profile. Since 1995, when it opened in purpose-designed premises, 16,000 users have registered, including those coming from some 400 Universities. 64% of users are students (57% of those being doctoral students), 10% academics and the remaining 26% are made up mainly of journalists and media professionals. The subject background of the users demonstrates that such an archive is not just for historians, or even for media studies: 23% Media Studies, 21% History, 14% Language and Literature, 10% Art and Performance, 8% Political Science and the rest ranges from Philosophy and Economics to television training and Anthropology, with a total of fourteen academic disciplines being represented. The current budget of the Institut is 10 million Euros – which shows just how economical the operation of a purpose-designed *digital* archive in a nation of comparable size and media-richness to the UK has become. And how paltry the addition to the licence fees of the broadcasters needs to be.

Nor is this a mere Gallic eccentricity. Eight European countries now operate compulsory deposit laws for their television and radio. There is even a resolution of the European Convention to that effect that about a third of the member states have ratified, though not Britain of course. The fact is that there are neither technical, nor legal, nor financial reasons, nor even 'unknowns' which should prevent or delay the setting up a national audio-visual archive.

In the USA it is possible today to access sources such as the Vanderbilt Television News Archive[2], type a subject, a name or a place into a query window and get a complete list of news broadcasts. It is possible to listen to, or get a transcript of, news stories to analyse how ABC, NBC and CBS treated them for a period going back close on forty years and also by CNN and FOX News from the time of their inception. There is a record therefore of what the American public had been shown and told through the news. That this is not so for British history for the same period is down to the BBC first and foremost – for reasons never clearly stated, but certainly not due to the technological ones put about, for how then could the Americans have done it? – and it is a grievous loss. But whatever the reasons for not keeping the record of what the British people have been shown and told in the last century were, we now certainly have the technology to be in the position to ensure that this precious material will no longer be lost for our successors in the 21st century.

Nicholas Pronay is Emeritus Professor of the Institute of Communication Studies at the University of Leeds.

Notes
1   'Why did material get lost?', www.bbc.co.uk/cult/treasurehunt/about/lost.shtml, accessed 11 October 2008.
2   http://tvnews.vanderbilt.edu/, accessed 11 October 2008.

MAKING DIGITISED FOOTAGE USEFUL

John Ellis

Digitisation will eventually open up the huge contents of audiovisual archives for everyone to use. But to what purpose? In concentrating on the means of delivery, we often neglect to ask what is being delivered and why. We can see why BUFVC spent a large amount of time and (other people's) money to make old ITN footage available through Newsfilm Online (www.nfo.ac.uk). This material demonstrably had historical significance. It was concerned with the major public events of its time; it was further sifted according to a clear set of criteria; and, perhaps most importantly, could be married with detailed paper-based metadata and even in some cases with rushes and other enriching material. The footage has scientific, political, social and even personal uses. Much news bulletin material has an enduring significance, as do many documentaries. But what about old editions of gameshows like SUPERMARKET SWEEP or DOUBLE YOUR MONEY, or such long-lived schedule fillers as the consumer affairs programme THAT'S LIFE or the low-budget soap CROSSROADS? And what of Channel 4's hugely successful BIG BROTHER or its more benign sibling, CANDID CAMERA? Surely these will remain curios at best, generating nostalgia and perhaps embarrassment for those who remember them, serving as objects of study for media students charting changing programme conventions? Such programmes, surely, are at best temporarily meaningful. They fulfil an important social role in their time, but they soon become artefacts that reward historical curiosity but have no further uses.

Anyone who believes that these are the only potential uses of this material misunderstands the potential of the digital revolution. Once digitised, these exemplary cultural artefacts take on a second life as data. They can be mined for whatever information they may contain, however incidental. They provide data on their background locations, on weather patterns, on costume, on the shape of human bodies, on their movements and voice patterns. They can be re-used for purposes that were certainly never intended, and are yet to be devised. Stephen Poliakoff's BBC drama SHOOTING THE PAST (1999) envisaged such possibilities in the resolutely analogue world of a photo archive based, perhaps, on the Camera Press archive's old premises. The archive consists of shelved boxes in which lie photos classified according to an eccentric system devised in the 1940s. In Poliakoff's drama, Timothy Spall played Oswald the archivist who had a particular skill that proved his eventual downfall. He could recall and match archived images of people from vastly different locations and periods of their lives. He could reconstruct their entire life stories from the scattered boxes of generalised 'street scenes' and highly particular occasions in which they might have played an ephemeral or background role. SHOOTING THE PAST narrates the decline of this kind of preservation-based archiving, sacrificed to the cherry-picking attitude of a new owner. To destroy the integrity of the collection was in effect to destroy Oswald himself, and the narrative leads to his suicide attempt, which fails but nevertheless leaves him incapable of the mental feats that gave meaning to his existence. This serial is a heartfelt plea for the importance of history and in particular for the preservation of the apparently ephemeral. History has now proved the importance of such an archive and made possible Oswald's imagined activities. The digitisation of visual material enables the automated searching and matching of images that, in the analogue age, the fictional Oswald carried on by prodigious mental effort and much rushing about.

Oswald's intuitive methods require three distinct operations. The first is the ability to repurpose material, ignoring its original use in order to reveal its latent potential as data. The second is the ability to combine material from diverse sources into a new combination that reveals something hitherto hidden. The third is a filtering judgement that rejects mistaken connections. Digitisation alone provides none of these. Digitised material remains inert data, waiting to be explored, but the activity of exploration is extremely difficult to undertake. The mass of audiovisual data that has accumulated in the past century requires automated searching if the non-Oswalds among us are to realise its potential as data. Yet existing search tools work with words. Picture-recognition searching remains in the earliest stages of development, and sound recognition technologies remain stalled by the seeming impossibility of reproducing the activity of sound recognition that humans routinely undertake. We can understand speech across remarkable varieties of accent, vocal tone, homonyms and the rest, but technologies cannot yet. Oswald's acts of visual recognition-across-difference remain even further in the future. Searching will rely on metadata for a long time to come.

The descriptive metadata that comes with audiovisual material (if it still exists) is notoriously varied. Newsreels and TV news material are exceptional in that they often come with detailed shot listings and even camera dope sheets that vastly enrich their potential as data. To a significant extent, we know when and where the images were created. Yet for other forms of location footage, such metadata has to be conjured up from somewhere else. Fiction films and even many documentaries actively conceal the concrete locations in which their actions took place.

Documentaries do so for the sake of confidentiality; fictions because they create their own imaginary space. Yet anyone compiling data on the history of buildings in a particular street or streets would need to have as complete a visual record as possible: the fact of having actors in the frame is supremely irrelevant to them. Instead, they might be planning a major infrastructure project like London's Crossrail which needs as much data as possible about the evolution of the sites under which it will pass in order to identify their previous uses, to reveal possible contaminants and underground hazards.

Such metadata does get created by a wide range of enthusiasts, from PhD students to fans to TV archive programme researchers and the people who actually worked on the movies. Much of this potential metadata does not get married in any durable way with the images which it elucidates. I was able to pin down the street location of the David Lean/Noel Coward film THIS HAPPY BREED (1944) from a website that since seems to have disappeared. It was clearly the work of fans, and matched 'then and now' images of the key location to within half a mile of where I live, and (which may be surprising) to the area of London where the fiction is actually set. Such data is often created as a by-product of a larger piece of work, or to satisfy one of those irritating moments of idle curiosity. Nevertheless, such data is generated in a wide variety of activities, and could be gradually accumulated by a social, wiki-type, process of knowledge accretion. Perhaps this is the only realistic way of enriching the metadata that is needed to realise the data potential of audiovisual material. The process of digitisation is expensive enough; it is hopeless to imagine that funding would be available for the mega-project of generating any metadata beyond that which is easily accessible – the wiki model is the obvious way forward.

However, any social metadata project immediately runs into two difficulties. The first is that of moderation, of eliminating inaccuracies and resolving disputes. This can be designed into the process. The second is more tricky: access to the material in the first place, as it will be subject to all the usual protections of copyright and ownership. It is clearly of use to the owners of the material to have it enhanced by the addition of richer metadata. In fact, this process might well justify the initial work of digitisation. Yet at the same time, it is not conceivable that many copyright holders will allow the kind of generalised access to their material that such a project would require. The new potential of socialised electronic media meet the existing regimes of property in a familiar impasse.

It need not be like this. BUFVC has already demonstrated, through ongoing work like TRILT, that the academic space that it inhabits can host metadata enriching projects. The privileged zone of .ac.uk is one which can be used by copyright holders in a mutually beneficial way. Serious students and researchers will need access to growing amounts of moving image material to enable their work. They would benefit from forms of electronic publishing which would link their research to the footage to which it relates. This is already standard practice for anyone who incorporates online footage into their teaching and disseminates the results. However, it should extend to the publication of research as well as to teaching. Whilst the research is being undertaken, researchers could easily participate in a social metadata enrichment project, adding information culled from their work. When material is used in a student context, the process is further enhanced, bringing the diversity of contemporary student cohorts to bear in the activity of elucidating material. The privileged zone of the academy would give crucial 'peace of mind' to copyright holders; the heterogeneity of the academic community, its links to enthusiasts and fan organisations, would add real richness to the process. The academic space is one of openness and encounter. If copyright restricted audiovisual material were more freely available within that space, the result could be a leap forward in the knowledge potential of moving image data.

John Ellis is Professor of Media Arts at Royal Holloway, University of London and author of TV FAQ *(IB Tauris, 2007),* Seeing Things *(IB Tauris, 2000) and* Visible Fictions *(Routledge, 1982). From 1982 to 1999 he ran the independent production company Large Door, which produced documentaries for Channel 4 and BBC. He is the Chairman of the BUFVC.*

OFCOM AND THE GLOBAL WARMING SWINDLE

Joe Smith

In July 2008 the broadcasting regulator Ofcom published its findings following criticism of the Channel 4 documentary THE GREAT GLOBAL WARMING SWINDLE, *originally screened 8 March 2007.*

Even in the hyperbolic world of media commentary, climate change would have good claim to being the story of the century. It promises catastrophic global change and the causes and consequences are going to reach into every household. Action on climate change carries threats and opportunities for vested interests and nails politicians across the globe to targets that few will meet.

In the period since 2006 European media portrayals of the issue have begun to take on the air of an official version, often drawing on stock phrases and images (more Polar bear anyone?). Carbon dioxide has entered the media atmosphere with mainstream reporting absorbing the notion of a scientific consensus – the IPCC position. Media storytelling has incorporated a political drama – 'will the US sign Kyoto?' and sustained some prominent sub-plots. Comment pages regularly worry about whether China's growth will cancel out 'our' carbon cuts, and the weekend features chirpily invite us all to trim our carbon footprints.

Channel 4's GREAT GLOBAL WARMING SWINDLE cut through what Ofcom termed the 'current orthodoxy' in media treatments of climate change. It had a far-reaching impact on audiences in the UK and internationally. The commissioning and broadcast of the programme, C4's ensuing decision to 'defend, defend, defend' and Ofcom's odd and nervous judgement all say something important about the difficulties broadcasters have with this enormous and complex topic. The case is of significance not just for discussion of climate change: it is relevant to a host of complex science and technology issues

In the wake of more than 250 complaints Ofcom censured C4 on a number of key points. But those areas where the regulator let the broadcaster off the hook are just as interesting. They decided that the broadcaster did not 'on balance' 'mislead the audience so as to cause harm or offence'. Ofcom did have 'concerns… as regards the portrayal of factual matters and omission of facts or views' but felt that on balance they hadn't broken the code because climate change science is now considered a 'current orthodoxy'. In other words you can't be ticked off for misleading the public if you are knocking a mainstream position. Yet recent polling shows very ambiguous responses amongst the public: large sections are demonstrably confused. Ofcom has chosen not to reprimand the broadcaster for errors in the programme that inevitably add to that confusion. This is on the grounds that it is healthy to have a wide range of views circulating on difficult topics.

SWINDLE has come to embody the dogged contrarianism that has accompanied media debates about climate change since the issue first emerged into the public consciousness at the beginning of the 1990s. The filmmakers and (most of) their interviewees project themselves as the last redoubt of plucky independent thought on the subject. The programme was a marvel of the polemicist's art. With every clause of the voiceover and every graphic the filmmaker Martin Durkin worked to set the truth free from the clutches of what he sees as a cabal of self-hating greens, featherbedded scientists and intrusive politicians.

Within the protective bubble of media commissioning it is easy to see why Swindle looked like a good idea: it was provocative and counterintuitive. It was presented as giving voice to outcast experts and promised to defy groupthink. But pop the bubble, step outside and talk to the numerous and broad climate change science and policy community and it is viewed as one of the most unhelpful pieces of programme making about a science topic that anyone can remember. Britain had established itself as a leader in the extent and quality of public debate about climate change but the Swindle programme dented that. It is a clear example of how the media's desire to appear edgy and probing can leave them exposed.

Critics of the programme wanted to know what a public service broadcaster was doing allowing such demonstrably false or dated material to be aired. From science undergraduates to leading scientists the programme won C4 an instant reputation for being crass and scientifically illiterate. One of the 250 complaints works through almost every line of script and every graphic in the film to demonstrate what they see as the factual errors and deceptions that litter the piece. In a first for Ofcom this complaint was peer reviewed. Convened by a couple of researchers and a concerned citizen, the document brought together some of the world's most experienced climate scientists, including IPCC chairs. With this simple and elegant move these complainants both reinforced their case and introduced Ofcom and any attendant media to the processes that underpin climate change science and policy. Peer review is about rigorous testing of an argument and its supporting data against the published body of scientific evidence. This and other dissections of the

© Miles Eliason / SXC

programme's failings are easily available on the Web. My purpose here is not to repeat them, but to consider what it is about the film that helped it make such an impact.

The programme's appeal lay not with the particular qualities of argument but rather in the fact that it said some things many people hope to be true. Audiences were mesmerised by a film that suggested 'climate change isn't real, and, well, if it is its natural and there's nothing useful we can do about it'.

In the media landscape the SWINDLE film is flattered by the contrast with the proper-but-dull, repetitive 'mainstream' framings of climate change. In the tight spaces of news broadcast and print stories climate change is necessarily reduced to a couple of minutes or a few hundred words. The massive human effort that is going into trying to make sense of human-biosphere-atmosphere interactions is difficult to shoehorn into these spaces with any subtlety. The programme offered a flag to rally around in response to what many see as the hectoring of greens and portentousness of scientists. Certainly there is a TV watching public that is willing to engage in intricate self-rationing through carbon budgeting. But I bet they would be outvoted by the multitude that think that one of the bonuses of finding ourselves in the Twenty First century is to be liberated from thrift and anxiety. The programme found a neglected constituency that wanted to have their emotional responses to climate change recognised.

It is tempting to respond to 'climate change sceptics' with ever-louder insistence that research on climate change is conclusively finished. This is a mistake. Public understanding will not be advanced by a mediatized branding of heretics. Indeed it will only increase the already outsized media space they currently enjoy.

And the story is so much more interesting and important than that. Geologists are now beginning to describe our entry into a new geological era – the Anthropocene – on account of the magnitude of humanity's impact on their environment. Climate change science could be said to be finishing Darwin's sentence: it confirms humans' place as inextricably part of the natural world, not dominant over it. Media treatments need to work to try to communicate something of the scale of this shift in our intellectual frame. Difficult stuff, and not a job to be done in a hurry.

The bands of uncertainty around the science are narrowing all the time, and in the short term the media needs to fill out the sense that responding to climate change isn't about acting on facts but about managing risks. Society needs to decide whether it is worth taking some sorts of risks – such as accepting the unknown economic costs of moving hard and fast towards an energy efficient economy – in the interests of reducing the unknowable risks associated with climate change.

But if the science of climate change is young the politics and economics is newborn. Developed world voters don't react well to the suggestion that climate change is their responsibility, and are not convinced that their own actions will make any difference. They want to see business and government leadership before they will take action themselves. They also seem to have a pretty keen sense that incitements to households to 'do their bit' completely ignore the ways in which successive governments have allowed ordinary lives to literally be set in concrete. Low-density car-dependent housing developments and other energy hungry planning and public provisions make low-carbon living a challenge. Governments have barely got around to cropping the much-endangered low hanging fruit of household insulation and appliance efficiency regulations let alone the much more demanding work.

People increasingly feel that climate change isn't something we need simply to be told about as a society – but that it's something we need to talk about. That would be greatly helped if mainstream politics were to halt their 'phoney peace' on the topic and worked to outbid each other with provocative ideas that could deliver a viable managed descent from a carbon economy. But they will need to be allowed the space in which to conduct that conversation amongst themselves and with the voting public. Which takes us back to media editors and commissioners. Just as they need to consider fresh tones and approaches to telling the next few years of climate science, so they need to show more ambition and imagination in their approach to climate politics.

Senior politicians have talked of needing the media to help 'create political space' within which they can work. They feel that they will be ambushed as soon as they emerge with ideas by wary publics and the bottomless cynicism of journalists. The media set a very difficult climate for public debate. News editors particularly fear being charged with 'campaigning' on an issue that they still fear is scientifically unresolved, and there are instances where they seem to over-compensate for the voice inside them that suggests they should be doing something to enable action on climate change. What kinds of risks should media leadership take? Perhaps they should recognise that in fact all they are being asked to do is extend well-established practices into a new area.

There are some simple virtues that the media need to hold close if they are to do a good job. A high quality of scrutiny will be needed across climate science, economics and politics. Editors, commissioners, journalists and producers that lack basic ecological literacy need to get their heads straight on the basics. Academics can play a significant role in these processes. At the simplest level they can be responsive and informed media consumers. Editors, programme makers, commissioners and channel controllers are sensitive to the contents of their mailbag. Well-argued critiques of media performance from authoritative sources can give pause for thought. Investing time in developing media contacts, or simply generating good press releases concerning new findings can pay off. In addition researchers are now in a position to 'broadcast themselves' in blogs, podcasts and vodcasts. In addition to assisting mainstream broadcasting's talent spotting these low cost easy-entry media platforms are ensuring that researchers can speak to and debate with new audiences directly.

The multi-channel multi-platform media environment is creating new spaces for more demanding programming. There is a risk that some of these may become genteel byways for small audiences, letting the big-audience channels off the hook of engaging with 'difficult' topics. Even if mainstream channels work to present factual content on a topic like climate change in engaging ways a significant portion of these big audiences may increasingly behave as 'consumer schedulers', screening out factual and other stretching content.

Media performance on climate change will be an interesting test of the consequences of the new media environment for the treatment of complex issues where

© Petr Kovar / SXC

science, ethics and politics intersect, and where times and places, distant and near, are threaded together. Climate change is a civil war with the future. There is widespread, if usually implicit, acceptance that the media will defend and promote notions of democracy and human rights. The very uneven distribution of hazards and harm make climate change itself an issue of human rights and democracy. But it is in the nature of the issue that most of those consequences will be experienced in the future, even if the causes lie in the present. The media – and politicians – need to do new work to try to bring the interests of the future into the present. They need to recognise that we are in new political and philosophical terrain. As a society we need to think critically and carefully about many aspects of the present, and imaginatively about how we might live differently in the future. Plenty of media producers have shown their willingness to represent the interests of the present. We need to have a good number of them embedded with the future – asking difficult questions of the present day. The research community has been slow or unforthcoming in acknowledging the normative commitments that are bundled up with 'knowing about climate change', but now need to play an active part in engaging the media in these novel webs of cause and consequence.

Taking good risks in response to what we know about climate change is one of the central challenges of our age. The media are very influential players in this game in that they set the boundaries of public debate. They need to be sure that there is sufficient scientific and policy literacy within their own ranks in order to underpin commissioning and editorial judgements. But they also need to experiment with new approaches if society is going to cope with this topic. The risk taken by the commissioners who put SWINDLE on air already feels like it comes from another age. C4's capacity for provocation and creativity now needs to be applied to a new target. Public service media have a responsibility to equip society for a long and difficult conversation about how we reduce the likelihood of dangerous climate change, and how we prepare for the environmental changes that past emissions have locked us into. Anything less and the public are being swindled.

Dr. Joe Smith is Senior Lecturer in Environment at the Open University. He peer-reviewed the media related aspects of one of the complaints to Ofcom on the Swindle programme, and has acted as academic consultant on a number of broadcast projects. He is author/editor of a number of books on environmental issues including (with Andrew Simms) Do Good Lives Have to Cost the Earth? *(Constable Robinson, 2008).*

Gerry Somers, Kinematographer and Producer, 1934.

ARCHIVES

The BUFVC maintains the Researcher's Guide Online *(www.bufvc.ac.uk/rgo), a directory of over 700 collections related to the history of moving image and sound in the UK and Ireland and which now also includes the* Researcher's Guide to Screen Heritage. *The archives listed here are all those in the public sector, whose interests are represented by the* Film Archive Forum *(www.bufvc.ac.uk/faf), of which the BUFVC is an Observer member. A number of these archives are based in higher education institutions.*

BFI NATIONAL ARCHIVE

J. Paul Getty Conservation Centre, Kingshill Way,
Berkhamsted, Hertfordshire HP4 3TP
Tel: 01442 876 301 **Fax:** 01442 289 112
London office: 21 Stephen Street,
London W1T 1LN
Tel: 020 7255 1444 (switchboard)
Web: www.bfi.org.uk/nftva/
The BFI National Archive is one of the world's greatest collections of film and television. The majority of the collection is British material but it also features internationally significant holdings from around the world. It also collects films which feature key British actors and the work of British directors. There is a wealth of material of every genre from silent newsreels to CinemaScope epics, from home movies to avant-garde experiments, from classic documentaries to vintage television, from advertisements to 3-D films, soap opera to football. The archive contains more than 50,000 fiction films, over 100,000 non-fiction titles and around 625,000 television programmes.

EAST ANGLIAN FILM ARCHIVE

The Archive Centre, Martineau Lane, Norwich
NR1 2DQ

Tel: 01603 592 664 **Fax:** 01603 458 553
E-mail: eafa@uea.ac.uk
Web: www.uea.ac.uk/eafa
The East Anglian Film Archive (EAFA) was established in 1976 to locate and preserve films and videos showing life and work in Bedfordshire, Hertfordshire, Norfolk, Suffolk, Essex and Cambridgeshire, and to provide a service of access and presentation where copyright allows. The collection spans the years from 1896 to the present day and is continuing to grow rapidly. It aims to reflect all aspects of the region – its people, society, economy, geography, history and the work of its film and video makers, both amateur and professional. EAFA is also preserving unique and growing collections of regional television output and it now houses the original film collection of the Hertfordshire Record Office. The Archive is a part of the University of East Anglia.

IMPERIAL WAR MUSEUM FILM AND VIDEO ARCHIVE

Lambeth Road, London SE1 6HZ
Tel: 020 7416 5291/2 (commercial users),
020 7416 5293/4 (non-commercial users)

Fax: 020 7416 5299
E-mail: film@iwm.org.uk
Web: http://collections.iwm.org.uk/server/show/nav.00g004

 The Imperial War Museum's Film and Video Archive is one of the foremost archives in the UK providing rich illustrations for military and social history from throughout the twentieth century. The archive holds some 120 million feet of film and 6,500 hours of video tape. A large proportion of material has been transferred to the Museum from the Services and other public bodies as the Archive is the official repository for such public record films.

LONDON'S SCREEN ARCHIVES: THE REGIONAL NETWORK

Suite 6.10, The Tea Building, 56 Shoreditch High Street, London E1 6JJ
E-mail: screen.archives@mlalondon.org.uk
Web: www.filmlondon.org.uk/screenarchives
London's Screen Archives is a new regional network supporting organisations in London that hold collections of moving image material. It helps researchers and the public find these collections and tries to ensure the preservation of important material made in or about the city.

MEDIA ARCHIVE FOR CENTRAL ENGLAND

1 Salisbury Road, University of Leicester, Leicester LE1 7RQ
Tel: 0116 252 5066 **Fax:** 0116 252 5931
E-mail: macearchive@le.ac.uk
Web: www.macearchive.org
The archive was established in 2000 as the English regional moving image archive covering the East and West Midlands. The archive exists both to collect and to be a point of reference and information about all aspects of the life, culture and history of the East and West Midlands as reflected in the moving image media. The collections of film, videotape and digital media span the entire era of moving image production from the mid-1890s to the present day and are

constantly growing. The archive is located within the University of Leicester.

NATIONAL SCREEN AND SOUND ARCHIVE OF WALES

National Library of Wales, Aberystwyth SY23 3BU
Tel: 01970 632 828 **Fax:** 01970 632 544
E-mail: agssc@llgc.org.uk
Web: http://screenandsound.llgc.org.uk/index.htm
The National Screen and Sound Archive of Wales is responsible for safeguarding and celebrating Wales' rich audio-visual heritage. The collection encompasses over 5.5m feet of film, over 250,000 hours of video, over 200,000 hours of sound recordings, and thousands of tapes, records and compact discs.

NORTH WEST FILM ARCHIVE

Manchester Metropolitan University, Minshull House, 47-49 Chorlton Street, Manchester M1 3EU
Tel: 0161 247 3097 **Fax:** 0161 247 3098
E-mail: n.w.filmarchive@mmu.ac.uk
Web: www.nwfa.mmu.ac.uk
The North West Film Archive is the professionally recognised home for moving images made in or about Cheshire, Cumbria, Greater Manchester, Lancashire and Merseyside. It is located within Manchester Metropolitan University.

NORTHERN REGION FILM AND TELEVISION ARCHIVE

School of Arts and Media, University of Teesside, Middlesbrough, Tees Valley TS1 3BA
Tel: 01642 384022 or 342923
Fax: 01642 384099
E-mail: enquires@nrfta.org.uk
Web: www.nrfta.org.uk

 The NRFTA is the public-sector moving image archive serving County Durham, Northumberland, Tees Valley and Tyne and Wear and operates from a purpose built storage facility and office at the University of Teesside in Middlesbrough.

SCOTTISH SCREEN ARCHIVE

National Library of Scotland,
39-41 Montrose Avenue, Hillington Park,
Glasgow G52 4LA
Tel: 0845 366 4600 **Fax:** 0845 366 4601
E-mail: ssaenquiries@nls.uk
Web: http://ssa.nls.uk/
The Scottish Screen Archive was established in November 1976. The film collection was inherited in part from its parent body, the Scottish Film Council, and has subsequently been enlarged through acquisitions from private and public sources in Scotland. The material dates from 1896 to the present day and concerns aspects of Scottish social, cultural and industrial history. In April 2007 Scottish Screen Archive transferred to the National Library of Scotland as a division of the Library's Collections and Research Department.

SCREEN ARCHIVE SOUTH EAST

University of Brighton, Grand Parade,
Brighton BN2 0JY
Tel: 01273 643 213 **Fax:** 01273 643 214
E-mail: screenarchive@brighton.ac.uk
Web: www.brighton.ac.uk/screenarchive/

Still taken from: KENT HOP FARMING, PART I

Screen Archive South East is a public sector moving image archive serving the South East of England. Established in 1992 at the University of Brighton as the South East Film & Video Archive, the function of this regional archive is to locate, collect, preserve, provide access to and promote screen material related to the South East and of general relevance to screen history.

SOUTH WEST FILM AND TELEVISION ARCHIVE

Melville Building, Royal William Yard,
Stonehouse, Plymouth PL1 3RP
Tel: 01752 202 650 **Fax:** 01752 205 025
E-mail: info@tswfta.co.uk
Web: www.plymouth.ac.uk/pages/
view.asp?page=20771
SWFTA is the public regional film archive for the South West of England. Its holdings are from 1898 to the present day and its core collections are the Television South West Film and Video Library (which includes all Channel 3 material for the area from 1961 to 1992) and the BBC South West Film Collection (dating from 1961 onward). In addition to the core collections the archive also holds many other amateur and professional collections.

WESSEX FILM AND SOUND ARCHIVE

Hampshire Record Office, Sussex Street,
Winchester SO23 8TH
Tel: 01962 846 154 **Fax:** 01962 878 681
E-mail: enquiries.wfsa@hants.gov.uk
Web: www3.hants.gov.uk/wfsa
 The Wessex Film and Sound Archive was set up in 1988, funded by Hampshire County Council through Hampshire Archives Trust, a registered charity. The Archive contains over 32,000 film and sound recordings relating to central southern England, including film and tapes of local TV and radio, now available to study and enjoy. We also have an 85 seat cinema for group viewing and listening.

YORKSHIRE FILM ARCHIVE

York St John University, Lord Mayor's Walk,
York YO31 7EX
Tel: 01904 876 550 **Fax:** 01904 876552
E-mail: yfa@yorksj.ac.uk
Web: www.yorkshirefilmarchive.com
The Yorkshire Film Archive finds, preserves and provides access to moving images documenting over one hundred years of life in Yorkshire. It holds over 14,000 items of film and video tape, dating from the earliest days of film making in the 1880s to the present day. It is based in York at the Fountains Learning Centre, York St John University.

Image courtesy of Scottish Screen Archive

AWARDS

A selection of regular film, television and video production awards, predominantly offered in the UK, as well as awards for writing on film and television themes.

BAF AWARDS

Web: www.nationalmediamuseum.org.uk/baf/
2007/submit.asp

Held annually as part of the Bradford Animation Festival in November, BAF awards celebrate the best in new animation from around the world. Awards are made in the following categories: student films, professional films, independent films, commercials, music videos, television series, films for children, films produced by children, and films produced using computer games software.

BBC4 WORLD CINEMA AWARDS

Web: www.bbc.co.uk/bbcfour/cinema/
worldcinema/award2007.shtml

An annual prize celebrating the best in foreign language filmmaking. A panel of judges chooses the winner from a shortlist of six films nominated by the UK's leading critics, film-school heads and festival directors.

BETTING ON SHORTS

Web: www.bettingonshorts.com

BoSs is a short-film contest held annually at the Institute of Contemporary, Arts London since 2004. Each year submissions are invited on a particular theme – in the past these have been 'playtime', 'vacancy' and 'mad or bad.' The festival audience is invited to bet on which film will win.

BRITISH ACADEMY OF FILM AND TELEVISION ARTS (BAFTA)

Web: www.bafta.org

One of the principal functions of the British Academy of Film & Television Arts is to identify and reward excellence in the art forms of the moving image. It achieves this objective by bestowing awards on those practitioners who have excelled in their chosen field of expertise. In 1947, the Academy granted three awards. Today, more than one hundred awards are bestowed annually in the fields of film, television and video games.

BRITISH ANIMATION AWARDS (BAA)

Web: www.britishanimationawards.com

The British Animation Awards covers all aspects of the UK animation scene, from student work to commercials, children's entertainment, short and experimental art films, music videos, new technologies, script-writing and craftsmanship. BAA is held every two years, most recently in 2006. The awards themselves are unique artworks (e.g. a drawing, painting, cel, collage, sculpture etc) created specially for the occasion by a leading international or UK animation artist. The 'BAAs' are exhibited for a month at the Animation Art Gallery in central London.

BRITISH ARCHAEOLOGICAL AWARDS

Web: www.britarch.ac.uk/awards

The biennial British Archaeological Awards are a

showcase for the best in British archaeology. Established in 1976 they have grown to encompass fourteen awards covering every aspect of archaeology. Among these are awards for the best Broadcast and Non-Broadcast programmes, and another for the best ICT project (website, CD-ROM, etc). These awards are sponsored by Channel 4 and are administered by the BUFVC/CBA Committee for Audiovisual Education (CAVE).

BRITISH FEDERATION OF FILM SOCIETIES – FILM SOCIETY OF THE YEAR AWARDS

Web: www.bffs.org.uk/awards.html

© 2007 Juris Kursietis / BFFS

The director Nicolas Roeg, actress Miranda Keeling and BFFS Chair David Miller present the 2007 BFFS Awards.

Each year in February, the British Federation of Film Societies invites film societies to submit applications for the prestigious Film Society of the Year Awards. Categories are The Engholm Prize for Film Society of the Year; Best film programming; Best programme; Best marketing and publicity; Best website; Community award; Best new society; Best student society; The Charles Roebuck Cup, for an individual contribution to the BFFS.

BRITISH INDEPENDENT FILM AWARDS

Web: www.bifa.org.uk
Created in 1998 and organised by Raindance, the British Independent Film Awards set out to celebrate merit and achievement in independently funded British filmmaking, to honour new talent, and to promote British films and filmmaking to a wider public.

BRITISH INTERACTIVE MEDIA ASSOCIATION (BIMA) AWARDS

Web: www.bima.co.uk/the-bimas
An annual competition looking for outstanding interactive projects in a range of categories including integrated campaign, interactive advertising, interactive television, mobile game, mobile, microsite, website, community website or campaign, outstanding achievement in accessibility, education and training, government and information, children, entertainment, arts and culture, and so on.

BROADCAST AWARDS

Web: www.broadcastnow.co.uk/awards
Annual awards rewarding excellence in television programme making.

BROADCAST DIGITAL CHANNEL AWARDS

Web: http://broadcast.hcuk.net/awards1.asp?m_pid=2511&m_nid=2506
Launched in 2005, the Broadcast Digital Channel Awards recognise and reward innovation, creativity and commercial success in the digital television industry. The categories include Best Factual Channel, Best Use of Interactive, Best News Channel, Best Specialist Channel and Best Online Community Site.

COMMONWEALTH BROADCASTING ASSOCIATION AWARDS

Web: www.cba.org.uk/awards
Annual awards for television and radio programmes from the Commonwealth. Entries may be in any language but television programmes should have English subtitles and foreign-language radio programmes must be accompanied by a text in English explaining the concept of the programme and its impact.

DEPICT!

Web: www.depict.org/competition/brief/
DepicT! seeks to uncover films from emerging filmmakers which show evidence of originality, imagination and the ability to engage the audience in 90 seconds or less. The competition is open to short films of all production techniques, including

animation, documentary, drama, experimental or artist film and hybrid work. The Award forms part of the annual Encounters Short Film Festival in Bristol.

DESCARTES PRIZE FOR SCIENCE COMMUNICATION

Web: http://ec.europa.eu/research/descartes
Launched in 2004, the Descartes Prize for Communication is an annual competition open to science communication initiatives across Europe. The competition is open to individuals and organisations that have achieved outstanding results in science communication, and have won prizes from European and/or national organisations.

ETHNOGRAPHIC FILM AWARDS

Web: www.raifilmfest.org.uk
This biennial competition is part of the international film festival sponsored by the Royal Anthropological Institute covering films on social, cultural and biological anthropology or archaeology.

EXPOSURES NATIONAL STUDENT FILM AWARDS

Web: www.exposuresfilmfestival.co.uk
Part of the Exposures Festival held in Bristol, the awards are open to student-produced films in the categories drama, documentary, experimental and animation.

FIRST LIGHT MOVIES AWARDS

Web: www.firstlightmovies.com/awards
Founded in 2001, First Light Movies funds and offers training to 5-18 year-olds throughout the UK in writing, acting, shooting, lighting, directing, and producing films, that reflect the diversity of their lives. Each year First Light holds a competition to choose the best film in each of nine categories and the awards are presented at a ceremony in the West End attended by stars and film industry executives.

FOCAL AWARDS

Web: www.focalint.org/focalawards.htm
The annual FOCAL Awards recognise productions which have used library archive and stock footage in an imaginative and innovative way and to acknowledge the work of key services involved with preservation and restoration, plus those archives and individuals who have served the industry well.

THE FREDDIE AWARDS

Web: www.thefreddies.com
MediMedia's International Health & Medical Media Awards are open to health and medical videos, DVDs, CD-ROMs or websites that address health or medical issues for consumers or health care professionals.

GRIERSON AWARDS

Web: www.griersontrust.org
The Grierson Awards commemorate the pioneering Scottish documentary filmmaker John Grierson. The awards, held in November each year, recognise and celebrate the best documentary filmmaking from Britain and abroad.

Documentary filmmaker Paul Watson, winner of two Grierson Awards in 2007.

IAMHIST PRIZE FOR A WORK IN MEDIA AND HISTORY

Web: www.iamhist.org

Biennial prize awarded for the book, radio or television programme or series, film, DVD, CD-ROM, or URL making the best contribution on the subject of media and history to have been published or shown in the preceding two years. The prize is worth $1000. The prize was awarded for the first time in 2007.

IMPERIAL WAR MUSEUM STUDENT FILM AWARDS

Web: http://london.iwm.org.uk/server/show/ConWebDoc.2310

Since 2000 the IWM has held an annual competition for students who have made films and videos incorporating archive film from the Museum's collection or about its subject matter. The awards have three categories: Best Documentary; Best Creative Response to the Subject of War; Winner of the Audience Poll.

Still from I DREAMT OF FLYING, recipient of the IWM Student Film Award for 'Best Imaginative Response to the Subject of War' in 2008.

INTERNATIONAL VISUAL COMMUNICATIONS ASSOCIATION (IVCA) AWARDS

Web: www.ivca.org/award-schemes/ivca-awards.html

Annual awards, held in London in Spring each year, which reward effective business communication in corporate video, live events, interactive media projects, business television and web sites.

JOHN BRABOURNE AWARDS

Web: www.ctbf.co.uk/johnbrabourneawards

The John Brabourne Awards are a stepping stone for young people driven to further their experiences and careers in all aspects of film and television. The CTBF awards provide cash sums of between £1,000 and £5,000 to assist with training, equipment, or the costs of travel, rent, bills or childcare. The Sponsored awards are cash sums and/or access to training, work experience, equipment or materials of a value of £1,000 to £5,000.

KRASZNA-KRAUSZ AWARDS

Web: www.editor.net/k-k

The Kraszna-Krausz Awards recognise publications about film, television and photography. Independent panels of judges select winners in all these categories and now do this annually instead of, as in the past, giving awards in alternate years to books about the still image and the moving image. The Awards are open to entries world-wide and in all languages.

LEARNING ON SCREEN

Web: www.bufvc.ac.uk/learningonscreen

The Learning on Screen Awards celebrate excellence in the production of effective learning material which employs moving pictures, sound and graphics. Such learning material might be delivered as physical media, or online, or via broadcast media – or a combination of all three. The competition is open to all-comers involved at any level in the fields of production, publishing, broadcasting, education and research.

NEW STATESMAN NEW MEDIA AWARDS

Web: www.newstatesman.com/nma/nma2008/

In 1998, New Statesman held the inaugural New Media Awards, with the aim of promoting creative and innovative use of new technology. The award categories vary, and for 2008 are: Democracy in Action, Inform and Educate, Community Activism, Campaign for Change, Innovation.

ONE WORLD MEDIA AWARDS

Web: www.owbt.org/pages/Awards/
awards_home.html

The One World Media Awards reward excellence in media coverage on issues of international development. They recognise the unique role of journalists and filmmakers in bridging the divide between different societies, and communicating the breadth of social, political and cultural experiences across the globe. The categories incorporate documentary film, radio programmes, print journalism and online media.

PANDA AWARDS

Web: www.wildscreenfestival.org

Held as part of the biennial Wildscreen Festival, The Panda Awards are the world's most prestigious awards for films about the natural world. Leading filmmakers from all over the world enter for the twenty Panda Award Categories, covering subjects as diverse as Animal Behaviour, Campaigning and Earth Sciences and skills such as Cinematography, Editing, Music Sound and Script.

PROJECTION BOX ESSAY AWARD

Web: www.pbawards.co.uk

The aims of this annual award are to encourage new research and new thinking into any historical, artistic or technical aspect of projected and moving images up to 1915; and to promote engaging, accessible, and imaginative work. The first prize of £250 is for an essay of between 5,000 and 8,000 words (including notes).

REWRITE MOBILE PHONE FILM COMPETITION

Web: www.rewritefilmfestival.co.uk/

A competition for short films produced by young people on their mobile phones, hosted by the Southwark Playhouse in London. There are of 3 categories for entrants: Remake (remake a film or a short scene from a television programme (with a twist), Reprogramme (try to change the audience's view on an issue that affects you personally), and Rewind (step into the past and change something that's been done before).

SCOTTISH STUDENTS ON SCREEN

Web: www.baftascotland.co.uk/
ScottishStudentsonScreen.htm

Annual competition designed to be a platform for the screen talent in Scotland's colleges and universities. Organised by BAFTA Scotland.

SHIERS TRUST AWARD

E-mail: clare@rts.org

The Trust awards a grant of £5,000 towards the publishing of work on any aspect of the history of television.

SONY RADIO ACADEMY AWARDS

Web: www.radioawards.org

Founded in 1983, the Sony Radio Academy Awards seek to recognise the very best of the UK radio industry, nationally, regionally and locally. Over the years the awards have set out to recognise the creative talents of journalists, writers, producers, performers and broadcasters, covering the wealth of UK radio output from speech and drama through to news, comedy and music.

STUDENT RADIO AWARDS

Web: www.studentradio.org.uk

Held as part of the Student Radio Association conference.

TELEVISUAL BULLDOG AWARDS

Web: www.televisual.com/bulldogs/

Readers of *Televisual* from the whole television production community are invited to nominate and vote for the best television programme of the year in a range of categories.

WELLCOME BROADCAST DEVELOPMENT AWARDS

Web: www.wellcome.ac.uk/

Filmmakers are offered the chance to pitch a science idea (documentary, online or games format) to a panel including television science commissioning editors as part of the Sheffield Doc/Fest. Proposals should engage the audience with issues in biomedical science. Funding will enable the winning project/s to be realised.

Student working in the Interactive Learning Centre at the University of Bradford.

BLOGS

A blog (the word is short for weblog) is a website which adds information chronologically in the form of posts, to which others can add comments. Blogs are used both as personal diaries and as commentaries on particular topics. All come with RSS (Really Simple Syndication) feeds allowing users to subscribe to favourite blogs and receive regular posts. All list posts by categories, which build up into subject-classified archives of information. A growing number of blogs contain information of relevance to the study of motion pictures and the use of motion pictures in UK higher education. The blogs listed below are some of those that the BUFVC has found useful as information sources.

There are dedicated blog search engines for pursuing particular topics, such as Technorati (www.technorati.com) and Google Blog Search (http:// blogsearch.google.com). For those interested in setting up a blog, the BBC provided a good introductory guide (www.bbc.co.uk/webwise), while some of the popular (and free) programmes for setting up a blog include Blogger (www.blogger.com), LiveJournal (www.livejournal.com) and Wordpress (www. wordpress.com).

ALTERNATIVE FILM GUIDE

Web: www.altfg.com/blog
A guide to alternative films around the world, with reviews, news and commentary.

BBC BLOG NETWORK

Web: www.bbc.co.uk/blogs
The 'home' for the wide range of blogs from across the entire BBC output. The blogs cover individual television and radio programmes, news, sport, local and international communities, and the views of editors and senior staff.

BIOETHICSBYTES

Web: http://bioethicsbytes.wordpress.com
Blog from the University of Leicester, bringing together information on multimedia resources to assist in the teaching of bioethics, with an emphasis on television programming.

THE BIOSCOPE

Web: http://bioscopic.wordpress.com
News and information on early and silent cinema, with an emphasis on research resources.

© Steve Woods / SXC

BROADCASTNOW

Web: www.broadcastnow.co.uk/
opinion_and_blogs/index.html
Opinion and discussion on matters relating to the broadcasting industry, including commissioning, multimedia, technology, news, etc

THE CENTER FOR INDEPENDENT DOCUMENTARY

Web: http://documentaries.wordpress.com
Not-for-profit American organisation collaborating with independent documentary filmmakers; a useful source of information on American documentary filmmaking in general.

DAVA – DIGITAL AUDIOVISUAL ARCHIVING

Web: http://av-archive.blogspot.com
A blog focused on the digital transformation and preservation of audio-visual materials.

DAVID BORDWELL

Web: www.davidbordwell.net/blog
Exceptional blog from one of the world's leading film theorists, providing wide-ranging observations on film art in an accessible and thought-provoking style.

DC'S IMPROBABLE SCIENCE

Web: http://dcscience.net/
A blog by David Colquhoun, Professor of Pharmacology at UCL, giving his opinion on 'bad science'. To this has now been added his idea of 'good science', centred on university politics, in particular how science should be organised to get the best results, and the invidious rise of management culture and corporatisation.

DIGITAL ETHNOGRAPHY

Web: http://mediatedcultures.net/ksudigg
Blog from a working group of Kansas State University Students and faculty exploring the possibilities of digital ethnography. Includes ongoing projects investigating the YouTube phenomenon.

DIGITAL NARRATIVES

Web: www.digitalnarratives.blogspot.com/
A blog by Ruth Page, Reader in English at Birmingham City University. In it she explores the many ways that digital media are transforming narratives, for example hypertexts, gaming, fan fiction, online archives, mash ups, digital storytelling, performance art on the web, blogging, etc.

DIGITIZATIONBLOG

Web: http://digitizationblog.interoperating.info
digitizationblog focuses on digitization and related activities (such as electronic publishing) in libraries, archives, and museums, and is intended to be a source of news relevant to people who manage and implement digitization projects.

THE DOCUMENTARY BLOG

Web: www.thedocumentaryblog.com
Enthusiastic and informative reports on the latest documentary film releases, with background features looking at documentaries thematically.

A DON'S LIFE

Web: http://timesonline.typepad.com/dons_life/
A blog by Mary Beard, Professor of Classics at Cambridge and classics editor of the TLS.

EDUPODDER

Web: http://edupodder.blogspot.com/
Advocacy site, with a well-established blog on research into the use of podcasting in education.

INFORMATION AESTHETICS

Web: http://infosthetics.com
Blog on the visualisation of information, exploring the symbiotic relationship between creative design and the field of information visualisation.

JISC DIGITISATION BLOG

Web: http://involve.jisc.ac.uk/wpmu/digitisation
The latest news on the JISC Digitisation programme, which includes major audio-visual collections such as Newsfilm Online, Archival Sound Recordings, Voices: Moving Images in the Public Sphere, and the London Broadcasting Company/Independent Radio News Archive.

MANCHESTER UNIVERSITY IR PROJECT BLOG

Web: www.irproject.manchester.ac.uk/blog/
This project aims to establish Institutional Repository Services for the University of Manchester, where members of the university can store digital copies of their scholarly work and make these materials freely and easily accessible to others. The blog provides a forum for sharing news, opinions and general information about the project.

MEDIA RESOURCES CENTER

Web: http://blogs.lib.berkeley.edu/mrc.php
Latest information from the Media Resources Center at the University of California, Berkeley, which maintains one of the best online resources guides available for film, video and broadcast references sources.

MICHAEL GEIST

Web: www.michaelgeist.ca
Well-presented blog on technology law from Dr Michael Geist, Canada Research Chair of Internet and E-commerce Law at the University of Ottawa. There is a multimedia section, with video and audio content of radio and television events in which he has taken part, plus podcasts.

NATURE NETWORK

Web: http://network.nature.com/blogs
Nature Network is a networking website for scientists around the world. It provides an online meeting place where scientists can gather, share and discuss ideas, and keep in touch. One element of the site is the blog section where scientists can give their opinion on what's going on in their particular field or in the broader world of science, either on their own blog, or by posting comments on other people's blogs.

NEW SCIENTIST

Web: www.newscientist.com/blogs/shortsharpscience/index.html
A science news blog produced by the celebrated weekly publication.

OFCOM PUBLIC SERVICE REVIEW BLOG

Web: http://comment.ofcom.org.uk/
As part of its consultation on the future of public service broadcasting in the UK, Ofcom launched

this trial blog by Rhona Parry, a member of the PSB Review team, in order to engage a broader range of people in the debate.

ORGAN GRINDER

Web: http://blogs.guardian.co.uk/organgrinder
News, discussion and opinion from *The Guardian* newspaper's Media section.

OXBLOGSTER

Web: www.oxblogster.blogspot.com/
A blog by Mike Nicholson, Director of Undergraduate Admissions at the University of Oxford. There is also a series of podcasts in which Mike Nicholson chats with students and staff from around the University about courses, colleges, what to put on the application form, and how best to prepare for the dreaded Oxford interview.

PRELINGER LIBRARY BLOG

Web: http://prelingerlibrary.blogspot.com
Reports from the Prelinger Library, putting public domain materials online through the Internet Archive (www.archive.org) and commenting on open access issues.

RESEARCHBUZZ

Web: www.researchbuzz.org
Handy information source on the world of Internet research, reporting on search engines, new data managing software, browser technology, large compendiums of information, Web directories etc.

RESTORATION TIPS & NOTES

Web: www.richardhess.com/notes
Detailed advice, in blog format, on the restoration, repair and mastering of audio formats.

SKILLSET BLOG

Web: http://blog.skillset.org/
Discussion forum for issues relating to training for the media industries.

STEPHEN'S WEB

Web: http://downes.ca
Personal site, with blogging features, of Stephen Downes of the National Research Council, Canada, investigating online learning, content syndication and new media.

STREET ANATOMY

Web: www.streetanatomy.com/blog
The past, present and future of medical visualisation.

THE TASI LIGHTBOX

Web: www.tasi.ac.uk/blog
News and views on digital imaging from the Technical Advisory Service for Digital Media.

TELEVISION ARCHIVING

Web: www.archival.tv
Jeff Ubois' well-informed blog covering online video and the future of broadcasting.

UK FILM COUNCIL

Web: www.ukfilmcouncil.org.uk/blog
Monthly blog of news topics relating to the UK Film Council and the film industry.

VIDEO ACTIVE

Web: www.videoactive.eu
The aim of the European-funded Video Active is to create access to television archives across Europe. The site is in the form of a blog, and reports on the progress of the project, which began in September 2006, and includes presentations, workplans, and news.

WARWICK BLOGS

Web: http://blogs.warwick.ac.uk/
Hundreds of blogs from staff and students at Warwick University, searchable by department and A-Z of topic. Open to non-members of the University.

BROADCASTING

Compiled by Marianne Open

The UK television and radio channels listed in this section are all of those covered by the BUFVC's database the Television and Radio Index for Learning and Teaching (TRILT) since June 2001. They are categorised as follows, then listed alphabetically within in each section:

I. Television channel recorded by the BUFVC
II. Other television channels listed on TRILT
III. Radio stations listed on TRILT (by region and nation)

The channels covered in TRILT include terrestrial, digital, cable and satellite television (with regional variations), national and local radio stations, Asian-language, Irish, Scottish Gaelic and Welsh channels and programmes. Virtually all of the British television and radio channels broadcast over this period are included. All channels that are still active on TRILT have dates of coverage, contact information and a brief description. Those channels that are no longer active on TRILT have varying levels of information; if the channel is still broadcasting, contact details are included where possible. In many cases channels have changed names since 2001. For consistency, all channels are listed under their current name, even if they appear in TRILT under their former name. Further information on all channels can be found in our channel profiles database: www.trilt.ac.uk.

I. TELEVISION AND RADIO CHANNELS RECORDED BY THE BUFVC

BBC1

Television Centre, Wood Lane, London W12 7RJ
Tel: 020 8743 8000
Web: www.bbc.co.uk/bbcone
BBC1 is a terrestrial channel available to all UK viewers. It is also available on cable, satellite and digital television. It has a diverse programming policy encompassing all genres. Most programmes are shown over the entire country but there are occasional regional opt-outs and local news and weather reports. The BUFVC records the London broadcasts of this channel.

TRILT coverage: Selective from July 1995, and comprehensive from June 2001 to date.

BBC2

Television Centre, Wood Lane, London W12 7RJ
Tel: 020 8743 8000
Web: www.bbc.co.uk/bbctwo

Michael Palin at Compiegne where the armistice was signed in November 1918 in an episode of TIMEWATCH, a BBC/Open University co-production.

BBC2 is a terrestrial channel available to all UK viewers. It is also available on digital, cable and satellite platforms. Most programmes are shown over the entire country but there are occasional regional opt-outs and local news and weather reports. The BUFVC records the London broadcasts of this channel.
TRILT coverage: Selective from July 1995, and comprehensive from June 2001 to date.

BBC3

Television Centre, Wood Lane, London W12 7RJ
Tel: 020 8743 8000
Web: www.bbc.co.uk/bbcthree
BBC3 is a digital television channel and is a re-branding of BBC Choice. BBC3 is a general entertainment channel aimed at young adults.
TRILT coverage: February 2003 to date.

BBC4

Television Centre, Wood Lane, London W12 7RJ
Tel: 020 8743 8000
Web: www.bbc.co.uk/bbcfour
BBC4 is a digital television channel and is a re-branding of BBC Knowledge. It shows a mix of documentaries, dramas and foreign language films.
TRILT coverage: March 2002 to date.

BBC RADIO 4

Broadcasting House, Portland Place, London W1A 1AA
Tel: 020 7765 5337
Web: www.bbc.co.uk/radio4
The BUFVC began recording this channel on 18 September 2008. Predominantly a speech channel, Radio 4 broadcasts a mixture of news, analysis, drama and comedy. On occasions it splits into two frequencies broadcasting different programmes on long wave and FM.
TRILT coverage: June 2001 to date.

ITV1 LONDON (weekday)

101 St Martin's Lane, London WC2N 4AZ
E-mail: london@itvlocal.com
Web: www.itvlocal.com/london
Available on digital, cable and satellite as well as terrestrially, Carlton is the ITV franchise covering London and the southeast from 6 am on Monday morning to 6 pm on Friday evening, with LWT broadcasting over the weekend period. Carlton and LWT were both re-branded ITV1 London in 2002, although they remain separate franchises.
TRILT coverage: June 2001 to date.

ITV1 LONDON (weekend)

The London Television Centre, Upper Ground, London SE1 9LT
Tel: 020 7620 1620 **Fax:** 020 7261 8163
E-mail: london@itvlocal.com
Web: www.itvlocal.com/london
London Weekend Television is the joint ITV1 franchise holder for the London region, along with Carlton. LWT broadcasts from early evening Friday to 6 am on Monday morning. LWT and

Carlton were both re-branded as ITV1 London in 2002.

TRILT coverage: June 2001 to date.

CHANNEL 4

124 Horseferry Road, London SW1P 2TX
Tel: 020 7396 4444 **Fax:** 020 7306 8366
Web: www.channel4.com
Channel 4 is a terrestrial channel available to all UK viewers. It is a general entertainment channel that is popular with younger viewers and is also strong on documentaries.
TRILT coverage: Selective from July 1995, and comprehensive from June 2001 to date.

FIVE

22 Long Acre, London WC2E 9LY
Tel: 0845 705 0505
E-mail: customerservices@five.tv
Web: www.five.tv
Five, formerly known as Channel 5, is a terrestrial television channel available in the UK. It began broadcasting at 6.00pm on 30 March 1997. It aims to provide general light entertainment, with a mix of films, sport, quiz shows, soap operas and documentaries.
TRILT coverage: Selective from March 1997, and comprehensive from June 2001 to date.

II. OTHER TELEVISION CHANNELS LISTED ON TRILT

ABC1

ABC1 has ceased broadcasting. It was part of the Disney Corporation, available on Freeview, as well as digital and cable platforms.
TRILT coverage: 31 March 2006 to 1 October 2007.

ADULT CHANNEL

Aquis House, Station Road, Hayes, Middlesex UB3 4DX
Tel: 020 8581 7000 **Fax:** 020 8581 7007
Web: www.adultchannel.co.uk
The Adult Channel broadcasts adult entertainment that is permissible within British law. Available on pay-per-view basis on cable, satellite and digital.
TRILT coverage: June 2001 to date.

ADVENTURE ONE

Shepherds Building East, 3rd Floor, Richmond Way, London W14 0DQ
Tel: 020 7751 7700 **Fax:** 020 7751 7698
E-mail: natgeoweb@bskyb.com
Web: www.natgeochannel.co.uk
Part of the National Geographic Channel, it broadcasts a wide range of programmes, including

documentaries on natural history and extreme sports. The channel has been rebranded as Nat Geo Wild. TRILT continues to carry listings under the old name.
TRILT coverage: June 2001 to date.

Anglia See **ITV1 Anglia**

ANIMAL PLANET

Discovery House, Chiswick Park,
Building 2, 566 Chiswick High Road,
London W4 5YB
Tel: 0870 050 6939 **Fax:** 020 8811 3100
E-mail: mail_us@discovery-europe.com
Web: www.animalplanet.co.uk
The Animal Planet channel is affiliated with the Discovery Channel and shows wildlife programmes. It is only available to cable, digital and satellite viewers and it is split into digital and analogue versions.
TRILT coverage: June 2001 to date.

Animal Planet Analogue See **Animal Planet**

Artsworld See **SkyArts**

ARY DIGITAL

163 Frances Road, Leyton, London E10 6NT

Tel: 020 8838 6300

Web: www.arydigitaleurope.tv/

ARY Digital, formerly known as the Pakistani Channel, is available on cable, digital and satellite platforms. TRILT continues to carry listings for the channel under the old name, Pakistani Channel.

TRILT coverage: June 2001 to date.

ASIA I TV

An Asian-language cable, satellite and digital channel. No longer active on TRILT.

ASIA I NET

An Asian-language cable, satellite and digital channel. No longer active on TRILT.

ASIANET

Asianet (Europe) Ltd, 344 High Street North, Manor Park, London E12 6PH

Tel: 020 85866511 **Fax:** 020 85866517

E-mail: website@asianetworld.tv

Web: www.asianetuk.com

An Asian-language cable, satellite and digital channel. No longer active on TRILT.

BANGLA TV

150 High Street, Stratford, London E15 2NE

Tel: 0870 005 6778 **Fax:** 02085362751

E-mail: info@banglatv.co.uk

Web: www.banglatv.co.uk

A Bengali-language channel cable, satellite and digital channel. No longer active on TRILT.

BBC Choice See BBC Three

BBC Knowledge See BBC Four

BBC NEWS 24

Television Centre, Wood Lane, London W12 7RJ

The BBC's 24-hour news service is available on digital, cable and satellite and, for a limited period each night, terrestrial BBC1.

TRILT coverage: June 2001 to date.

BBC PARLIAMENT

4 Millbank, London SW1P 3JA

Tel: 0870 010 0123

Web: http://news.bbc.co.uk/1/hi/programmes/bbc_parliament

The BBC's broadcasts of the UK parliament are available on digital, cable and satellite television.

TRILT coverage: June 2001 to date.

BBC1 See Television channels recorded by the BUFVC

BBC1 EAST

The Forum, Millennium Plain, Norwich NR2 1BH

Tel: 01603 619331

E-mail: look.east@bbc.co.uk

Web: www.bbc.co.uk/lookeast

Most BBC1 programmes are shown in all regions but there are occasional regional opt-outs and local news and weather reports.

TRILT coverage: June 2001 to date.

BBC1 LONDON

PO Box 94.9, Marylebone High St. London W1A 6FL

Tel: 020 7224 2424

E-mail: yourlondon@bbc.co.uk

Web: www.bbc.co.uk/london

TRILT coverage: June 2001 to date.

BBC1 London and South East See BBC1 London and BBC1 South East

BBC1 MIDLANDS

London Road, Nottingham NG2 4UU

Tel: 0115 955 0500

E-mail: emt@bbc.co.uk

Web: www.bbc.co.uk/eastmidlandstoday

TRILT coverage: June 2001 to date.

BBC1 North

2 St Peter's Square, Leeds LS9 8AH

Tel: 0113 244 1188

E-mail: look.north@bbc.co.uk

Web: www.bbc.co.uk/looknorthyorkslincs

TRILT coverage: June 2001 to date.

BBC1 NORTH EAST

Broadcasting Centre, Barrack Rd, Newcastle upon Tyne NE99 2NE
Tel: 0191 232 1313
E-mail: look.north.comment@bbc.co.uk
Web: www.bbc.co.uk/looknorthnecumbria
TRILT coverage: June 2001 to date.

BBC1 NORTH WEST

New Broadcasting House, Oxford Road, Manchester M60 1SJ
Telephone 0161 200 2020
E-mail: nwt@bbc.co.uk
Web: www.bbc.co.uk/northwesttonight
TRILT coverage: June 2001 to date.

BBC1 NORTHERN IRELAND

Broadcasting House, Ormeau Avenue, Belfast BT2 8HQ
Tel: 028 9033 8000
E-mail: bbcni.feedback@bbc.co.uk
Web: www.bbc.co.uk/northernireland
TRILT coverage: June 2001 to date.

BBC1 SCOTLAND

BBC Scotland, 40 Pacific Quay, Glasgow G51 1DA **Tel:** 0141 422 6000
E-mail: enquiries.scot@bbc.co.uk
Web: www.bbc.co.uk/scotland
TRILT coverage: June 2001 to date.

BBC1 SOUTH

Broadcasting House, 10 Havelock Road, Southampton SO14 7PU
Tel: 023 8022 6201
E-mail: south.today@bbc.co.uk
Web: www.bbc.co.uk/southtoday
TRILT coverage: June 2001 to date.

BBC1 SOUTH EAST

The Great Hall, Mount Pleasant Road, Tunbridge Wells TN1 1QQ
Tel: 01892 675580
E-mail: southeasttoday@bbc.co.uk
Web: www.bbc.co.uk/southeasttoday
TRILT coverage: June 2001 to date.

BBC1 SOUTH WEST

Broadcasting House, Seymour Road, Plymouth PL3 5BD
Tel: 01752 229 201
E-mail: spotlight@bbc.co.uk
Web: www.bbc.co.uk/spotlight
TRILT coverage: June 2001 to date.

© Craig Jewell / SXC

BBC1 WALES

BBC Broadcasting House, Llandaff, Cardiff CF5 2YQ
Tel: 02920 322000 **Fax:** 02920 555960
E-mail: feedback.wales@bbc.co.uk
Web: www.bbc.co.uk/wales
TRILT coverage: June 2001 to date.

BBC1 WEST

Broadcasting House, Whiteladies Road, Bristol BS8 2LR
Tel: 0117 973 2211
E-mail: pointswest@bbc.co.uk
Web: www.bbc.co.uk/pointswest
TRILT coverage: June 2001 to date.

BBC2 See **Television channels recorded by the BUFVC**

BBC2 EAST

The Forum, Millennium Plain, Norwich NR2 1BH
Tel: 01603 619331
E-mail: look.east@bbc.co.uk
Web: www.bbc.co.uk/lookeast
Most BBC2 programmes are shown in all regions but there are occasional regional opt-outs and local news and weather reports.
TRILT coverage: June 2001 to date.

BBC2 LONDON
PO Box 94.9, Marylebone High St.
London W1A 6FL
Tel: 020 7224 2424
E-mail: yourlondon@bbc.co.uk
Web: www.bbc.co.uk/london
TRILT coverage: June 2001 to date.

BBC2 MIDLANDS
London Road, Nottingham NG2 4UU
Tel: 0115 955 0500 **Fax:** 0115 902 1984
E-mail: emt@bbc.co.uk
Web: www.bbc.co.uk/eastmidlandstoday
TRILT coverage: June 2001 to date.

BBC2 NORTH
2 St Peter's Square, Leeds LS9 8AH
Tel: 0113 244 1188
E-mail: look.north@bbc.co.uk
Web: www.bbc.co.uk/looknorthyorkslincs
TRILT coverage: June 2001 to date.

BBC2 NORTH EAST
Broadcasting Centre, Barrack Rd,
Newcastle upon Tyne NE99 2NE
Tel: 0191 232 1313
E-mail: look.north.comment@bbc.co.uk
Web: www.bbc.co.uk/looknorthnecumbria
TRILT coverage: June 2001 to date.

BBC2 NORTH WEST
New Broadcasting House, Oxford Road,
Manchester M60 1SJ
Telephone 0161 200 2020
E-mail: nwt@bbc.co.uk
Web: www.bbc.co.uk/northwesttonight
TRILT coverage: June 2001 to date.

BBC2 NORTHERN IRELAND
Broadcasting House, Ormeau Avenue,
Belfast BT2 8HQ
Tel: 028 9033 8000
E-mail: bbcni.feedback@bbc.co.uk
Web: www.bbc.co.uk/northernireland
TRILT coverage: June 2001 to date.

BBC2 SCOTLAND
BBC Scotland, 40 Pacific Quay, Glasgow G51 1DA
Tel: 0141 422 6000

E-mail: enquiries.scot@bbc.co.uk
Web: www.bbc.co.uk/scotland
TRILT coverage: June 2001 to date.

BBC2 SOUTH
Broadcasting House, 10 Havelock Road,
Southampton SO14 7PU
Tel: 023 8022 6201
E-mail: south.today@bbc.co.uk
Web: www.bbc.co.uk/southtoday
TRILT coverage: June 2001 to date.

BBC2 SOUTH EAST
The Great Hall, Mount Pleasant Road,
Tunbridge Wells TN1 1QQ
Tel: 01892 675580
E-mail: southeasttoday@bbc.co.uk
Web: www.bbc.co.uk/southeasttoday
TRILT coverage: June 2001 to date.

BBC2 SOUTH WEST
Broadcasting House, Seymour Road, Plymouth
PL3 5BD
Tel: 01752 229 201
E-mail: spotlight@bbc.co.uk
Web: www.bbc.co.uk/spotlight
TRILT coverage: June 2001 to date.

BBC2 WALES
BBC Broadcasting House, Llandaff,
Cardiff CF5 2YQ
Tel: 02920 322000 **Fax:** 02920 555960
E-mail: feedback.wales@bbc.co.uk
Web: www.bbc.co.uk/wales
TRILT coverage: June 2001 to date.

BBC2 WEST
Broadcasting House, Whiteladies Road,
Bristol BS8 2LR
Tel: 0117 973 2211
E-mail: pointswest@bbc.co.uk
Web: www.bbc.co.uk/pointswest
TRILT coverage: June 2001 to date.

BID TV
Sit-up House, 179-181 The Vale, London W3 7RW
Tel: 0870 166 6667
Web: www.bid.tv

Bid TV is a digital television shopping channel featuring auctions, allowing viewers to bid on a variety of products.
TRILT coverage: March 2006 to date.

BIOGRAPHY CHANNEL

Grant Way, Isleworth, Middlesex TW7 5QD
Tel: 0870 240 3000
E-mail: contact@thebiographychannel.co.uk
Web: www.thebiographychannel.co.uk

 The Biography Channel is available on digital, satellite and cable platforms. It shows documentaries about people of note.
TRILT coverage: June 2001 to date.

BLOOMBERG TV

City Gate House, 39-45 Finsbury Square,
London EC2A 1PQ
Tel: 020 7330 7500
Web: www.bloomberg.com/tvradio/tv/
tv_index_europe.html
A finance and economics channel operated by Bloomberg LP. It is available on digital, satellite and cable platforms. Different versions of the channel are broadcast in different territories.
TRILT coverage: June 2001 to date.

BOLLYWOOD 4U (B4U)

B4U Network Europe Ltd, 19 Heather Park Drive, Transputec House, Wembley, Middlesex HA0 1SS
Tel: 020 8795 7171 **Fax:** 020 8795 7181
E-mail: enquiries@b4unetwork.com
Web: www.b4utv.com
Available on digital, B4U concentrates on South Asian films. It also shows star interviews, news and interactive programmes.
TRILT coverage: June 2001 to date.

BOOMERANG

Turner House, 16 Great Marlborough Street,
London W1F 7HS
Tel: 020 7693 1000
Web: www.boomerangtv.co.uk
A children's animation channel, available on cable and satellite. It is part of the Cartoon Network.
TRILT coverage: June 2001 to date.

Border See **ITV1 Border**

BRAVO

Virgin Media Television, 160 Great Portland Street, London W1W 5QA
Tel: 0870 043 4029
E-mail: enquiries@bravo.co.uk
Web: www.bravo.co.uk
A subscription channel available on analogue and digital cable and satellite, Aimed at male viewers, Bravo shows comedy, horror and action films and erotica.
TRILT coverage: June 2001 to date.

Bravo Analogue See **Bravo**

BRITISH EUROSPORT

Eurosport London, 55 Drury Lane,
London WC2B 5SQ
Tel: 0207 468 7777 **Fax:** 0207 468 0023
E-mail: uk@eurosport.com
Web: www.eurosport-tv.com
Sports channel available on cable, digital terrestrial and satellite. Part of the Eurosport network, which is available in over sixty countries and broadcasts in over 15 European languages.
TRILT coverage: June 2001 to date.

Carlton See **ITV1 London** (weekday)

Carlton Central See **ITV1 Carlton Central**

CARLTON CINEMA

Carlton Cinema was available to cable, digital and satellite viewers until March 2003. It showed films from the 1930s to the present. No longer active on TRILT.

Carlton West Country See **ITV1 Carlton West Country**

CARTOON NETWORK

Turner House, 16 Great Marlborough Street,
London W1F 7HS
Tel: 020 7693 1000 **Fax:** 020 7693 1001
Web: www.cartoonnetwork.co.uk

Unsurprisingly this channel is devoted to cartoons. In the UK the channel is available on cable, satellite and digital television.
TRILT coverage: June 2001 to date.

CARTOON NETWORK SATELLITE

Satellite version of Cartoon Network. See **Cartoon Network** for full details.

CBBC

Television Centre, Wood Lane, London W12 7RJ
Tel: 020 8743 8000
E-mail: cbbc.online@bbc.co.uk
Web: www.bbc.co.uk/cbbc
CBBC is a channel from the BBC, available on Freeview, cable and digital satellite platforms. The channel broadcasts from 7 am to 7 pm daily and is aimed at children aged eight to twelve.
TRILT coverage: April 2003 to date.

CBEEBIES

The Media Centre, Media Village, 201 Wood Lane, London W12 7TQ
Tel: 020 8743 8000
E-mail: cbeebies@bbc.co.uk
Web: www.bbc.co.uk/cbeebies
CBeebies is a channel from the BBC, available on Freeview, cable and digital satellite platforms. The channel broadcasts from 7 am to 7 pm daily and is aimed at children under the age of six.
TRILT coverage: April 2003 to date.

CHALLENGE

Virgin Media Television, 160 Great Portland Street, London W1W 5QA
Tel: 0870 043 4030
E-mail: enquiries@challenge.co.uk
Web: www.challenge.co.uk
Challenge is available to digital, cable and satellite viewers. Its programming consists mainly of game shows and quizzes. Both analogue and digital versions are available.
TRILT coverage: June 2001 to date.

Challenge Analogue See **Challenge**

CHANNEL

Television Centre, St Helier, Jersey JE1 3ZD
Tel: 01534 816816 **Fax:** 01534 816777
E-mail: broadcast@channeltv.co.uk
Based in Jersey with offices in Guernsey, Channel TV operates the ITV1 franchise area covering the Channel Islands. It is the smallest ITV company and produces local programmes as well as taking ITV network programmes.
TRILT coverage: June 2001 to date.

Channel 4 See **Television channels recorded by the BUFVC**

Channel 5 See **Five**

CNBC

10 Fleet Place, London EC4M 7QS
Tel: 020 7653 9300 **Fax:** 020 7653 9488
Web: www.cnbc.com
A US-based business and news channel that is available on cable.
TRILT coverage: June 2001 to date.

CNNI

Turner House, 16 Great Marlborough Street, London W1V 7HS
Tel: 020 20 7693 1000 **Fax:** 020 7693 0788
Web: http://edition.cnn.com/CNNI/
News, current affairs and business channel available on cable and satellite. There are different versions for various parts of the globe. The website carries transcripts of some programmes.
TRILT coverage: June 2001 to date.

CNX See **Toonami**

COMMUNITY CHANNEL

2nd Floor, Riverwalk House, 157-161 Millbank, London SW1P 4RR
Tel: 08708 505500
E-mail: info@communitychannel.org
Web: www.communitychannel.org
community channel The Community Channel's slogan is 'TV that gives a damn.' It is available on various digital cable and satellite platforms and runs a limited service on Freeview.
TRILT coverage: April 2003 to date.

DAVE

UKTV, 160 Great Portland Street,
London W1W 5QA
Tel: 0845 734 4355
Web: http://uktv.co.uk/dave/
Dave (formerly known as UK Gold 2) is only available to cable, digital and satellite viewers. The channel mainly shows BBC comedy and quiz show repeats.
TRILT coverage: June 2001 to date.

DISCOVERY

Discovery House, Chiswick Park, Building 2, 566 Chiswick Park Road, London W4 5YB
Tel: 020 8811 3000 **Fax:** 020 8811 3100
Web: www.discoverychannel.co.uk
The Discovery Channel is only available to cable, digital and satellite viewers. Education, with a scientific or historical slant, is a strong feature of Discovery's programming. Both analogue and digital versions are available.
TRILT coverage: June 2001 to date.

Discovery Analogue See Discovery

Discovery Civilisation See Discovery Knowledge

Discovery Health See Discovery Home & Health

DISCOVERY HOME & HEALTH

Discovery House, Chiswick Park Building 2, 566 Chiswick Park Road, London W4 5YB
Tel: 020 8811 3000 **Fax:** 020 8811 3100
Web: www.discoverychannel.co.uk/ homeandhealth/
Discovery Home & Health is available on cable, satellite and digital television. The channel started life as Discovery Health, but was re-branded in 2005, at which point it became more female oriented. TRILT continues to carry listings for the channel under the old name, Discovery Health.
TRILT coverage: June 2001 to date.

Discovery Home & Leisure See Discovery Real Time

Discovery Home & Leisure Analogue See Discovery Real Time

DISCOVERY KIDS

Discovery House, Chiswick Park Building 2, 566 Chiswick Park Road, London W4 5YB
Tel: 020 8811 3000 **Fax:** 020 8811 3100
Web: www.discoverychannel.co.uk/kids
Discovery Kids is no longer broadcasting. It was a children's channel with an educational slant available on digital cable and satellite, now some of the programmes are available on demand on the channel website.
TRILT coverage: June 2001 to March 2007.

DISCOVERY KNOWLEDGE

Discovery House, Chiswick Park Building 2, 566 Chiswick Park Road, London W4 5YB
Tel: 020 8811 3000 **Fax:** 020 8811 3100
Web: www.discoverycivilisation.co.uk
Discovery Knowledge, formerly known as Discovery Civilisation or Civilisation, is available to digital, cable and satellite customers. Its programming focuses on events and characters that made history and defined cultures. TRILT carries listings for the channel under the old name, Discovery Civilisations.
TRILT coverage: June 2001 to date.

DISCOVERY REAL TIME

Discovery House, Chiswick Park Building 2, 566 Chiswick Park Road, London W4 5YB
Tel: 020 8811 3000 **Fax:** 020 8811 3100
Web: www.discoverychannel.co.uk/web/ realtime/
Discovery Real Time is available on cable, satellite and digital television. The channel started life as Discovery Home & Leisure, but was re-branded in 2005, at which point it became more male-oriented. TRILT continues to carry listings for the channel under the old name, Discovery Home & Leisure. An analogue version of the channel is also available from some providers. This has the same programming but broadcasts for fewer hours a day.
TRILT coverage: June 2001 to date.

Discovery Science See Science

DISCOVERY SCI-TREK

Discovery House, Chiswick Park Building 2, 566 Chiswick Park Road, London W4 5YB
Tel: 020 8811 3000 **Fax:** 020 8811 3100
One of the Discovery channels, Sci-Trek was available on cable, satellite and digital television. No longer active on TRILT.

Discovery Travel & Adventure See **Travel & Living**

Discovery Wings See **Turbo**

DISNEY CHANNEL

Walt Disney Company Ltd, Building 12,
2nd Floor, 566 Chiswick High Road
London W4 5AN
Tel: 08708 80 70 80
Web: http://home.disney.co.uk/tv/
Channel aimed at children with both animated and live action programmes. The channel is available on digital, cable and satellite television and includes programmes made by companies other than Disney.
TRILT coverage: June 2001 to date.

E4 / +1

124 Horseferry Rd, London SW1P 2TX
Tel: 020 7396 4444 **Fax:** 020 7396 8368
E-mail: viewerenquiries@channel4.co.uk
Web: www.e4.com

E4 is an entertainment channel from Channel Four available on Freeview, digital, cable and satellite. Programming is geared towards young people, and the channel shows a lot of comedy, drama and reality shows. A time-shift version of this channel is also available, showing the same content an hour later.
TRILT coverage: June 2001 to date.

EUROSPORT

Eurosport London, 55 Drury Lane, London WC2B 5SQ
Tel: 020 7468 7777 **Fax:** 020 7468 0023
E-mail: info@eurosport.com
Web: www.eurosport-tv.com

Available on cable, satellite and digital in European countries, Eurosport provides sports coverage, including ones that are less commonly given coverage on terrestrial television.
TRILT coverage: June 2001 to date.

Fantasy Channel See **Television X**

Fantasy Channel Analogue See **Television X**

FILM FOUR

124-126 Horseferry Road, London SW1P 2TX
Web: www.channel4.com/film/filmontv/index.html
FilmFour is a film channel from Channel 4. It is available on Freeview and digital, satellite and cable platforms.
TRILT coverage: April 2003 to date.

Five Life See **Fiver**

FIVE US

22 Long Acre, London WC2E 9LY
Tel: 0845 705 0505
E-mail: customerservices@five.tv
Web: www.five.tv/us/
Five US is a general entertainment channel from Five. Launched in October 2006 at the same time as Five Life, the channel is available on Freeview and various digital platforms. It shows a variety of US drama and entertainment shows.
TRILT coverage: November 2007 to date.

FIVER

22 Long Acre, London WC2E 9LY
Tel: 0845 705 0505
E-mail: customerservices@five.tv
Web: www.five.tv/fiver/
Fiver, formerly known as Five Life, is a general entertainment from Five. Launched in October 2006 at the same time as Five US, the channel is available on Freeview and various digital platforms.
TRILT coverage: November 2007 to date.

Fox Kids See **Jetix**

Fox Kids Analogue See **Jetix**

FRONT ROW

Front Row is the name given to a group of pay per view channels showing films on demand on cable television. No longer active on TRILT.

FTN See **Virgin 1**

Grampian See **Scottish**

Granada See **ITV1 Granada**

GRANADA BREEZE

Granada Breeze was available on digital, cable and satellite television. It stopped broadcasting in late 2004. It was aimed at women and mostly showed lifestyle, cookery and talk shows. No longer active on TRILT.

Granada Men and Motors See **Men and Motors**

Granada Men and Motors Analogue See **Men and Motors**

GRANADA PLUS

Granada Plus was available on digital, cable and satellite television until late 2004. It showed mainly drama and comedy repeats from ITV. It was available in analogue and digital versions. No longer active on TRILT.

Granada Plus Analogue See **Granada Plus**

HALLMARK

234a King's Road, London SW3 5UA
Tel: 020 7368 9100 **Fax:** 020 7368 9101
E-mail: info@hallmarkchannel.co.uk
Web: www.hallmarkchannel.co.uk
Hallmark is available on various digital, cable and satellite platforms. It shows general entertainment programmes and films, with many US imports.
TRILT coverage: June 2001 to date.

HISTORY CHANNEL

Grant Way, Isleworth, Middlesex TW7 5QD
Tel: 0207 705 3000

E-mail: feedback@thehistorychannel.co.uk
Web: www.thehistorychannel.co.uk
The History Channel is only available to cable, digital and satellite viewers. Its programming consists of high quality factual material. Both analogue and digital versions are available.
TRILT coverage: June 2001 to date.

History Analogue See **History Channel**

HTV Wales See **ITV1 Wales**

HTV West See **ITV1 West of England**

IDEAL WORLD

Ideal Home House, Newark Road, Peterborough PE1 5WG
E-mail: customer.services@ idealshoppingdirect.co.uk
Web: www.idealworld.tv
Ideal World is a digital television shopping channel, allowing viewers to purchase a variety of products.
TRILT coverage: March 2006 to date.

ITV NEWS

ITV News was a 24 hour television news channel available in the UK on digital, cable and satellite platforms. No longer active on TRILT

ITV SPORT CHANNEL

Sports channel. No longer active on TRILT.

ITV SPORT PLUS

Sports channel. No longer active on TRILT.

ITV1 See **Television channels recorded by the BUFVC**

ITV1 ANGLIA

Anglia House Norwich, Norfolk NR1 3JG
Tel: 01603 615151
E-mail: anglia@itvlocal.com

Web: www.itvlocal.com/anglia/
Anglia Television holds the ITV franchise covering the East of England. It produces its own programmes for local broadcast.
TRILT coverage: June 2001 to date.

ITV1 BORDER

The Television Centre, Carlisle CA1 3NT
Tel: 084488 15850
E-mail: border@itvlocal.com
Web: www.itvlocal.com/border/
Border holds the ITV1 franchise for the north of England, southern Scotland and the Isle of Man. Little of its output is networked.
TRILT coverage: June 2001 to date.

ITV1 CARLTON CENTRAL

ITV Local Central, Gas Street, Birmingham B1 2JT
Tel: 0844 88 14000
E-mail: central@itvlocal.com
Web: www.itvlocal.com/central
Available on digital, cable and satellite as well as terrestrially, Carlton Central was formed in 1999 when Carlton and Central TV merged. ITV1 Carlton Central covers the Midlands. Sometimes known as ITV1 Central.
TRILT coverage: June 2001 to date.

ITV1 CARLTON WEST COUNTRY

Langage Science Park, Plymouth PL7 5BQ
Tel: 084488 14900 **Fax:** 084488 14901
E-mail: westcountry@itvlocal.com
Web: www.itvlocal.com/westcountry/
Available on digital, cable and satellite as well as terrestrially, ITV1 Carlton West Country is the ITV franchise for the South West of England. Sometimes known as ITV1 Westcountry.
TRILT coverage: June 2001 to date.

ITV1 GRANADA

Quay Street, Manchester M60 9EA
Tel: 0161 832 7211 **Fax:** 0161 827 2180
Web: www.itvlocal.com/granada/
Available on digital, cable and satellite as well as terrestrially, Granada is the ITV1 franchise for the North West region.
TRILT coverage: June 2001 to date.

ITV1 London See **Television channels recorded by the BUFVC**

ITV1 MERIDIAN

Solent Business Park, Whiteley,
Hampshire PO15 7PA
Tel: 0844 881 2000
Email: meridian@itvlocal.com
Web: www.itvlocal.com/meridian/
Available on digital, cable and satellite as well as terrestrially, Meridian is the ITV1 franchise for the South and South East of England.
TRILT coverage: June 2001 to date.

ITV1 TYNE TEES TELEVISION

Television House, The Watermark, Gateshead,
Tyne & Wear NE11 9SZ
Tel: 0844 88 15000
E-mail: tynetees@itvlocal.com
Web: www.itvlocal.com/tynetees/
Available on digital, cable and satellite as well as terrestrially, this channel holds the ITV1 franchise for the North East of England. Sometimes called ITV1 Tyne Tees.
TRILT coverage: June 2001 to date.

ITV1 WALES

The Television Centre, Culverhouse Cross, Cardiff CF5 6XJ
Tel: 084488 10100 **Fax:** 029 20 597183
Web: www.itvlocal.com/wales/
Available on digital, cable and satellite as well as terrestrially, this channel is the ITV1 franchise for Wales and was formerly known as HTV Wales.
TRILT coverage: June 2001 to date.

ITV1 WEST OF ENGLAND

Television Centre, 470 Bath Road, Bristol BS4 3HG
Tel: 0117 972 2722 **Fax:** 0117 972 2400
Web: www.itvlocal.com/west/
E-mail: west@itvlocal.com
Available on digital, cable and satellite as well as terrestrially, this channel is the ITV1 franchise for the West of England and was formerly known as HTV West. Sometimes called ITV1 West.
TRILT coverage: June 2001 to date.

© Gerard79 / SXC

ITV1 YORKSHIRE

The Television Centre, Leeds LS3 1JS
Tel: 0844 88 14150
Web: www.itvlocal.com/yorkshire/
E-mail: yorkshire@itvlocal.com
Available on digital, cable and satellite as well as terrestrially, this channel is the ITV1 franchise for Yorkshire and Lincolnshire. Sometimes called YTV.
TRILT coverage: June 2001 to date.

ITV2

Channels Department, 4th Floor,
200 Grays Inn Road, London WC1X 8HF
Tel: 020 8528 2000
Web: www.itv.com/itv2
ITV2 is a general entertainment channel. Its programming consists of ITV1 repeats, imported American shows and extended coverage of Reality TV shows.
TRILT coverage: June 2001 to date.

ITV3

Channels Department, 4th Floor, 200 Grays Inn Road, London WC1X 8HF

Tel: 020 8528 2000
Web: www.itv.com/itv3
ITV3 is a general entertainment channel. The programming consists largely of classic drama and comedy.
TRILT coverage: March 2006 to date.

ITV4

Channels Department, 4th Floor,
200 Grays Inn Road, London WC1X 8HF
Tel: 020 8528 2000
Web: www.itv.com/itv4
ITV4 is a general entertainment channel aimed at male viewers. It mainly shows sports, US dramas and comedy.
TRILT coverage: August 2006 to date.

JETIX

Jetix Europe Limited, Jetix Club, Online and Interactive, Chiswick Park, Building 12,
566 Chiswick High Road, London W4 5AN
Web: www.jetix.co.uk
Channel aimed at children, showing both animated and live action programmes. It is available on cable, satellite and digital television. Both analogue and digital versions are available. TRILT continues to carry listings for the channel under the old name, Fox Kids.
TRILT coverage: June 2001 to date.

LIBERTY TV

General entertainment channel showing a high proportion of religious programmes. No longer active on TRILT.

LIVING

Virgin Media Television,
160 Great Portland Street, London W1W 5QA
Tel: 0870 043 4028
E-mail: enquiries@livingtv.co.uk
Web: www.livingtv.co.uk
Channel available on digital, cable and satellite television, aimed at women viewers. Living shows many drama series, talk shows, soap operas and comedy programmes. Available in analogue and digital versions.
TRILT coverage: June 2001 to date.

Living Analogue See **Living**

LWT See **ITV1 London** (weekend)

MEN AND MOTORS

ITV Digital Channels Ltd, Channels Department, 4th Floor, 200 Grays Inn Road, London WC1X 8HF
Tel: 0844 88 14150
Web: www.menandmotors.co.uk
Channel available on digital, cable and satellite television. Men and Motors, formerly known as Granada Men and Motors, is a men's lifestyle channel. Both analogue and digital versions are available. TRILT continues to carry listings for the channel under the old name, Granada Men and Motors.
TRILT coverage: June 2001 to date.

Meridian See **ITV1 Meridian**

THE MONEY CHANNEL

The Money Channel ceased broadcasting in August 2001. The channel concentrated on financial programmes. No longer active on TRILT.

MORE4 /+1

124 Horseferry Road, London SW1P 2TX
E-mail: viewerenquiries@channel4.co.uk
Web: www.channel4.com/more4

Launched in October 2005, More4 is an entertainment channel from Channel 4. A time-shift version of this channel is also available, showing the same content an hour later.
TRILT coverage: October 2005 to date.

MTV

180 Oxford Street, London W1N 1DS
Tel: 020 7478 6000 **Fax:** 020 7478 6007
Web: www.mtv.co.uk
Music channel available on cable, satellite and digital television. MTV shows music videos, documentaries and entertainment series.
TRILT coverage: June 2001 to date.

MTV 2

180 Oxford Street, London W1N 1DS
Tel: 020 7478 6000 **Fax:** 020 7478 6007
Web: www.mtv.co.uk/channel/mtv2
MTV 2 specialises in alternative music. The channel is available on cable, satellite and digital television.
TRILT coverage: June 2001 to date.

MTV BASE

180 Oxford Street, London W1N 1DS
Tel: 020 7478 6000 **Fax:** 020 7478 6007
Web: www.mtv.co.uk/channel/mtvbase
Music channel available on cable, satellite and digital television. It is dedicated to urban black music from around the world.
TRILT coverage: June 2001 to date.

MTV Extra See MTV Hits

MTV HITS

180 Oxford Street, London W1N 1DS
Tel: 020 7478 6000 **Fax:** 020 7478 6007
Web: www.mtv.co.uk/channel/mtvhits
MTV Hits, formerly known as MTV Extra, plays chart hits. It is available on cable, satellite and digital television. TRILT continues to carry listings for the channel under the old name, MTV Extra.
TRILT coverage: June 2001 to date.

THE MUSIC FACTORY

180 Oxford Street, London W1D 1DS
Tel: 020 7478 6000 **Fax:** 020 7478 6007
Web: www.mtv.co.uk/channel/tmf
Music channel from MTV, available on cable, satellite and digital television. Sometimes called TMF.
TRILT coverage: March 2005 to date.

MUTV

274 Deansgate, Manchester M3 4JB
Tel: 0845 602 6899
E-mail: mutv@mutv.com
Web: www.manutd.com/mutv
Television channel devoted to Manchester United Football Club. Available on cable, satellite and digital television, MUTV shows classic and live

football matches, news about the team and magazine-type programmes.
TRILT coverage: June 2001 to date.

Nat Geo Wild See **Adventure One**

NATIONAL GEOGRAPHIC
3rd Floor, Shepherd's Building East, Richmond Way, London W14 0DQ
Tel: 020 7751 7700 **Fax:** 020 7751 7698
E-mail: natgeoweb@bskyb.com
Web: www.natgeochannel.co.uk
National Geographic is only available to cable, digital and satellite viewers. The channel shows programmes that deal with diverse aspects of the natural world. It is available in analogue and digital versions.
TRILT coverage: June 2001 to date.

National Geographic Analogue See **National Geographic**

NICK JR.
Nickelodeon UK, 15-18 Rathbone Place, London W1T 1HU
Tel: 020 7462 1000 **Fax:** 020 7462 1030
E-mail: letterbox@NickJr.co.uk
Web: www.nickjr.co.uk
The UK's first television channel aimed at very young children, Nick Jr is available on analogue and digital platforms.
TRILT coverage: June 2001 to date.

Nick Jr. Analogue See **Nick Jr.**

NICKELODEON
Nickelodeon UK, 15-18 Rathbone Place, London W1T 1HU
Tel: 020 7462 1000 **Fax:** 020 7462 1030
E-mail: letterbox@nick.co.uk
Web: www.nick.co.uk
Channel aimed at children with both animated and live action programmes. The channel is available on digital, cable and satellite television.
TRILT coverage: June 2001 to date.

Nickelodeon Analogue See **Nickelodeon**

ONSPORT1
Sports channel. No longer active on TRILT.

ONSPORT2
Sports channel. No longer active on TRILT.

Pakistani Channel See **ARY Digital**

PARAMOUNT COMEDY CHANNEL
180 Oxford Street, London W1D 1DS
Tel: 020 7478 5300 **Fax:** 020 7478 5446
Web: www.paramountcomedy.com
Channel available to cable, digital and satellite viewers. The Paramount Comedy Channel is devoted to popular television comedy series, especially American sit-coms. Both analogue and digital versions of the channel are available.
TRILT coverage: June 2001 to date.

Paramount Comedy Channel Analogue See **Paramount Comedy Channel**

PERFORMANCE
Performance has now ceased broadcasting. It was a subscription channel devoted to the arts.
TRILT coverage: June 2001 to July 2008.

PHOENIX CNE
7th Floor, The Chiswick Centre,
414 Chiswick High Road, London W4 5TF
Tel: 020 8987 4320 **Fax:** 020 8987 4333
E-mail: info@phoenixcnetv.com
Phoenix CNE (Chinese News and Entertainment) is available on digital, cable and satellite television platforms. It caters for Chinese communities in Europe.
TRILT coverage: June 2001 to date.

PLAYBOY TV
PO Box 690, Hayes, Middlesex UB3 4DX
Tel: 020 8581 7000
Web: www.playboy.co.uk
Broadcasts adult material that is permissible within British law. Available on cable and satellite, broadcasting for a limited period at night, seven days a week.
TRILT coverage: June 2001 to date.

PLAY UK

Play UK was a part of the UKTV family and its programming largely consisted of comedy and music related series. No longer active on TRILT.

QUIZ CALL

iTouch, Avalon House, 57-63 Scrutton Street, London EC2A 4PF
Web: www.quizcall.co.uk
Quiz Call is a channel available in the UK on digital, satellite, cable and Freeview. Viewers call a premium rate number for the chance to win prizes by answering quiz questions.
TRILT coverage: March 2006 to date.

QVC

Marco Polo House, 346 Queenstown Road, London SW8 4NQ
Tel: 020 7705 5600
E-mail: ukstudio@qvc.com
Web: www.qvcuk.com
QVC is a well-established general shopping channel available in the UK on Freeview, digital, cable and satellite platforms.
TRILT coverage: June 2001 to date.

RACING CHANNEL

Available on digital, cable and satellite, the Racing Channel covered racing news and meets. No longer active on TRILT.

© Brian Lary / SXC

RAPTURE TV

A UK channel dedicated to 'clubbing'. No longer active on TRILT.

RED HOT

Suite 14, Burlington House, St Saviour's Road, St Helier, Jersey JE2 4LA
Tel: 01534 703 700 **Fax:** 01534 703 760
E-mail: feedback@redhottv.co.uk
Web: www.redhottv.co.uk
Adult entertainment channel available in the UK on a pay-per-view basis.
TRILT coverage: October 2006 to date.

S4C

Parc T, Glas, Llanishen, Cardiff CF14 5DU
Tel: 0870 600 4141
Web: www.s4c.co.uk
S4C is a television channel available in Wales on analogue television. It broadcasts Welsh and English language programmes, with the majority of the English language programming being re-broadcast from Channel 4.
TRILT coverage: June 2001 to date.

S4C2

Parc Ty Glas, Llanisien, Cardiff CF4 5DU
Tel: 0870 600 4141
Web: www.s4c.co.uk
S4C2 is a partnership between S4C and BBC Wales which provides a comprehensive broadcasting service from the National Assembly for Wales. The channel is available in the UK on digital satellite, cable and Freeview.
TRILT coverage: April 2006 to date.

SCIENCE

Discovery House, Chiswick Park, Building 2, 566 Chiswick Park Road, London W4 5YB
Tel: 020 8811 3000 **Fax:** 020 8811 3100
Web: www.discoverychannel.co.uk/science
Formerly known as Discovery Science, this channel is part of the Discovery group and is available on digital, cable and satellite television. TRILT continues to carry listings under the old name, Discovery Science.
TRILT coverage: May 2003 to date.

SCI-FI

Oxford House, 76 Oxford Street, London
W1D 1BS
Tel: 0207 307 6669
E-mail: mail@uk.scifi.com
Web: www.scifi.co.uk
Sci-Fi is only available to cable, digital and satellite viewers. It generally shows feature films and reruns of science-fiction series that have previously been shown on terrestrial television.
TRILT coverage: June 2001 to date.

Sci-Fi Satellite See Sci-Fi

SCOTTISH

Pacific Quay, Glasgow G51 1PQ
Tel: 0141 300 3000 **Fax:** 0141 300 3030
Web: www.stv.tv
Scottish is the ITV franchise for Scotland. It incorporates two services, one for central Scotland and one for the north of Scotland (formerly known as Grampian). The channels are sometimes known as STV Central and STV North.
TRILT coverage: June 2001 to date.

SCREENSHOP

Sit-up House, 179-181 The Vale, London W3 7RW
Screenshop is a shopping channel available on Freeview, digital, cable and satellite television. It shows pre-recorded 'infomercials' and viewers can purchase products by phone or online.
TRILT coverage: June 2001 to date.

SHOP!

Shop! is no longer broadcasting. Shop! was a general shopping channel, available on various digital, cable and satellite platforms. No longer active on TRILT.

SIMPLY MONEY

Simply Money ceased broadcasting on 16 April 2001. Showed financial programmes. No longer active on TRILT.

SKY2

British Sky Broadcasting Ltd, Grant Way, Isleworth, Middlesex TW7 5QD
Tel: 0870 240 3000 **Fax:** 0870 240 3060
Web: www.sky.com
Originally launched as Sky One Mix, Sky2 is another BSkyB channel available on digital, cable and satellite television in the UK. Sky2 shows much of the same general entertainment content as Sky One, but at different days and times, so it can be viewed as a catch up channel (but not a time shift channel). TRILT continues to carry listings for the channel under the old name, Sky One Mix.
TRILT coverage: April 2003 to date.

SKYARTS

BSkyB, NHC 1, Grant Way, Isleworth TW7 5QD
Tel: 08702 40 40 40
E-mail: viewerr@bskyb.com
Web: www.skyarts.co.uk
SkyArts, formerly known as Artsworld, is an arts channel available on digital television, launched on 2 December 2000. TRILT continues to carry listings for the channel under the old name, Artsworld.
TRILT coverage: June 2001 to date.

SKY BOX OFFICE EVENTS

Sky Box Office Events is no longer broadcasting. It was a pay-per-view channel that screened non-regular events such as wrestling matches. No longer active on TRILT.

SKY MOVIEMAX ONDIGITAL

Movie channel. No longer active on TRILT.

SKY MOVIES ACTION/THRILLER

British Sky Broadcasting Ltd, Grant Way, Isleworth, Middlesex TW7 5QD
Web: www.skymovies.com/skymovies/actionthriller

SKYMOVIES

Part of the Sky Movies group of film channels from BSkyB. Sky Movies Action/Thriller, formerly known as Sky Movies Max, is available on digital, cable and satellite platforms in the UK. TRILT continues to carry listings for the channel under the old name, Sky Movies Max.
TRILT coverage: June 2001 to date.

Sky Movies Cinema See **Sky Movies Premiere**

SKY MOVIES CLASSICS

British Sky Broadcasting Ltd, Grant Way,
Isleworth, Middlesex TW7 5QD
Web: www.skymovies.com/skymovies/classics
Part of the Sky Movies group of film channels from
BSkyB. Sky Movies Classics, formerly known as
Sky Movies Premier 3, is available on digital, cable
and satellite platforms in the UK as part of the
Movie Mix subscription. TRILT continues to carry
listings for the channel under the old name, Sky
Movies Premier 3.
TRILT coverage: June 2001 to date.

SKY MOVIES COMEDY

British Sky Broadcasting Ltd, Grant Way,
Isleworth, Middlesex TW7 5QD
Web: www.skymovies.com/skymovies/comedy
Part of the Sky Movies group of film channels from
BSkyB. Sky Movies Comedy, formerly known as
Sky Movies Premier, is available on digital, cable
and satellite platforms in the UK as part of the
Movie Mix subscription. TRILT continues to carry
listings for the channel under the old name, Sky
Movies Premier.
TRILT coverage: June 2001 to date.

SKY MOVIES DRAMA

British Sky Broadcasting Ltd, Grant Way,
Isleworth, Middlesex TW7 5QD
Web: www.skymovies.com/skymovies/drama
Part of the Sky Movies group of film channels from
BSkyB. Sky Movies Drama, formerly known as
Sky Movies Max 5, is available on digital, cable and
satellite platforms in the UK as part of the Movie
Mix subscription. TRILT continues to carry
listings for the channel under the old name, Sky
Movies Max 5.
TRILT coverage: June 2001 to date.

SKY MOVIES FAMILY

British Sky Broadcasting Ltd, Grant Way,
Isleworth, Middlesex TW7 5QD
Web: www.skymovies.com/skymovies/family
Part of the Sky Movies group of film channels from
BSkyB. Sky Movies Family, formerly known as

Sky Movies Premier 2, is available on digital, cable
and satellite platforms in the UK as part of the
Movie Mix subscription. TRILT continues to carry
listings for the channel under the old name, Sky
Movies Premier 2.
TRILT coverage: June 2001 to date.

SKY MOVIES HD

British Sky Broadcasting Ltd, Grant Way,
Isleworth, Middlesex TW7 5QD
Web: www.skymovies.com/skymovies/hd
Part of the Sky Movies group of film channels from
BSkyB. Sky Movies HD, formerly known as Sky
Movies Max 4, is available on digital, cable and
satellite platforms in the UK as part of the Movie
Mix subscription. TRILT continues to carry
listings for the channel under the old name, Sky
Movies Max 4.
TRILT coverage: June 2001 to date.

SKY MOVIES INDIE

British Sky Broadcasting Ltd, Grant Way,
Isleworth, Middlesex TW7 5QD
Web: www.skymovies.com/skymovies/indie
Part of the Sky Movies group of film channels from
BSkyB. Sky Movies Indie, formerly known as Sky
Movies Max 3, is available on digital, cable and
satellite platforms in the UK as part of the Movie
Mix subscription. TRILT continues to carry list-
ings for the channel under the old name, Sky
Movies Max 3.
TRILT coverage: June 2001 to date.

Sky Movies Max See **Sky Movies Action/Thriller**

Sky Movies Max 2 See **Sky Movies Sci-Fi/Horror**

Sky Movies Max 3 See **Sky Movies Indie**

Sky Movies Max 4 See **Sky Movies HD**

Sky Movies Max 5 See **Sky Movies Drama**

SKY MOVIES MODERN GREATS

British Sky Broadcasting Ltd, Grant Way,
Isleworth, Middlesex TW7 5QD
Web: www.skymovies.com/skymovies/
moderngreats

Part of the Sky Movies group of film channels from BSkyB. Sky Movies Modern Greats, formerly known as Sky Movies Premier 4, is available on digital, cable and satellite platforms in the UK as part of the Movie Mix subscription. TRILT continues to carry listings for the channel under the old name, Sky Movies Premier 4.
TRILT coverage: June 2001 to date.

Sky Movies Premier See **Sky Movies Comedy**

Sky Movies Premier 2 See **Sky Movies Family**

Sky Movies Premier 3 See **Sky Movies Classics**

Sky Movies Premier 4 See **Sky Movies Modern Greats**

SKY MOVIES PREMIERE / +I

British Sky Broadcasting Ltd, Grant Way, Isleworth, Middlesex TW7 5QD
Web: www.skymovies.com/skymovies/premiere
Part of the Sky Movies group of film channels from BSkyB. Sky Movies Premiere, formerly known as Sky Movies Cinema, is available on digital, cable and satellite platforms in the UK as part of the Movie Mix subscription. A time-shift version of this channel is also available, showing the same content an hour later. TRILT continues to carry listings for the channels under the old names, Sky Movies Cinema and Sky Movies Cinema 2.
TRILT coverage: June 2001 to date.

SKY MOVIES SCI-FI/HORROR

British Sky Broadcasting Ltd, Grant Way, Isleworth, Middlesex TW7 5QD
Web: www.skymovies.com/skymovies/scifihorror
Part of the Sky Movies group of film channels from BSkyB. Sky Movies Sci-Fi/Horror, formerly known as Sky Movies Max 2, is available on digital, cable and satellite platforms in the UK as part of the Movie Mix subscription. TRILT continues to carry listings for the channel under the old name, Sky Movies Max 2.
TRILT coverage: June 2001 to date.

SKY NEWS

British Sky Broadcasting Ltd, Grant Way, Isleworth, Middlesex TW7 5QD
Tel: 0870 240 3000 **Fax:** 0870 240 3060
Web: http://news.sky.com/skynews
Sky News is a 24 hour news channel from BSkyB. It is available on Freeview, digital, cable and satellite television platforms.
TRILT coverage: June 2001 to date.

SKY ONE

British Sky Broadcasting Ltd, Grant Way, Isleworth, Middlesex TW7 5QD
Web: http://sky1.sky.com/

 Sky One is available to cable, satellite and digital viewers. It promises to be the first in the UK to deliver the best television from the United States.
TRILT coverage: June 2001 to date.

Sky One Mix See **Sky2**

SKY ONE ONDIGITAL

General entertainment channel. No longer active on TRILT.

SKY PREMIER ONDIGITAL

Movie channel. No longer active on TRILT.

SKY PREMIER WIDESCREEN

Movie channel. No longer active on TRILT.

SKY SPORTS

British Sky Broadcasting Ltd, Grant Way, Isleworth, Middlesex TW7 5QD
Tel: 0870 240 3000 **Fax:** 0870 240 3060
Web: www.skysports.com/
Sky Sports is a group of subscription sports channels from BSkyB, available on digital, cable and satellite platforms in the UK. TRILT carries listings for Sky Sports 1, 2 and 3 as well as Sky Sports Extra. These four channels are available for a monthly fee as a bundle called 'Sports Mix.'
TRILT coverage: June 2001 to date.

Skysports.comTV See **Sky Sports News**

SKY SPORTS NEWS

British Sky Broadcasting Ltd, Grant Way,
Isleworth, Middlesex W7 5QD
Tel: 0870 240 3000 **Fax:** 0870 240 3060
Web: www.skysports.com/skysports/
shows/news
Sky Sports News (formerly known as Skysports.
comTV). As suggested by the name, the channel is
devoted to sports news coverage, predominantly
football news, and broadcasts 24 hours a day in the
UK. It is owned by BSkyB. The channel is available
on Freeview and various digital, cable and satellite
platforms on the UK.
TRILT coverage: June 2001 to date.

SKY THREE

British Sky Broadcasting Ltd, Grant Way,
Isleworth, Middlesex TW7 5QD
Tel: 0870 240 3000 **Fax:** 0870 240 3060
Web: www.sky.com
Sky Three offers a mix of programming including
dramas, documentaries, lifestyle and factual enter-
tainment. It showcases programmes from Sky
One, Sky Travel and Artsworld. The channel is
available in the UK on digital satellite, cable and
Freeview.
TRILT coverage: March 2006 to date.

SKY TRAVEL

British Sky Broadcasting Ltd, Grant Way,
Isleworth, Middlesex TW7 5QD
Web: http://travel.sky.com/
Sky Travel is a channel from BSkyB with general
entertainment programming, including reality
shows relating to travel, such as AIRLINE and
CLUB REPS. There are also regular slots dedi-
cated to selling holidays. The channel is available
on various cable, satellite and digital platforms.
TRILT coverage: June 2001 to date.

TCM

Turner House, 16 Great Marlborough Street,
London W1F 7HS
Tel: 020 7693 1000
E-mail: tcmmailuk@turner.com
Web: http://tcmonline.co.uk
TCM is available to cable, digital and satellite
viewers and draws from the largest film libraries in
the world. It shows classic movies from all genres
and periods, including the silent era.
TRILT coverage: June 2001 to date.

TCM/WCW

Channel showing feature films and wrestling. No
longer active on TRILT.

TEACHERS' TV

16-18 Berners Street, London W1T 3LN
Tel: 020 7182 7430
E-mail: info@teachers.tv
Web: www.teachers.tv
Teachers' TV is a channel for everyone who
works in education.
TRILT coverage: February 2005 to date.

John Bayley filming an episode of TEACHING WITH BAYLEY.

TELEVISION X

Suite 14, Burlington House, St Saviour's Road,
St Helier, Jersey JE2 4LA
Tel: 01534 703700 **Fax:** 01534 703760
Web: www.televisionx.co.uk
Subscription channel available to digital, cable and
satellite viewers. Content consists of adult material
that is legal within the UK. The channel was
formerly known as The Fantasy Channel; TRILT
continues to carry listings under this name. Both
analogue and digital versions are available.
TRILT coverage: June 2001 to date.

THOMAS COOK TV

8 Park Place, 12 Lawn Lane, Vauxhall, London
SW8 1UD
Tel: 020 7840 7150 **Fax:** 020 7820 4471
Web: www.thomascook.com/tv/

Thomas Cook TV is a shopping channel that showcases Thomas Cook holiday destinations and packages. Viewers can phone in to book holidays. The channel is available in the UK on digital satellite, cable and Freeview.
TRILT coverage: March 2006 to date.

TOONAMI

Toonami, Turner House, 16 Great Marlborough Street, London W1F 7HS
Tel: 020 7693 1000 **Fax:** 020 7693 1001
Web: www.toonami.co.uk
CNX was re-branded as Toonami in 2003. As CNX the channel showed mostly action, adventure and anime aimed at males aged 12-34. As Toonami the channel shows more cartoons aimed at younger viewers. TRILT continues to carry listings for the channel under the old name, CNX.
TRILT coverage: April 2003 to date.

TRAVEL & LIVING

Discovery House, Chiswick Park Building 2, 566 Chiswick Park Road, London W4 5YB
Tel: 020 8811 3000 **Fax:** 020 8811 3100
Formerly known as Discovery Travel & Adventure, Travel & Living is available on digital, cable and satellite television. TRILT continues to carry listings for the channel under the old name, Discovery Travel & Adventure.
TRILT coverage: June 2001 to date.

TROUBLE

Virgin Media Television, 160 Great Portland Street, London W1W 5QA
Tel: 0870 043 4027
E-mail: enquiries@trouble.co.uk
Web: www.trouble.co.uk
Trouble TV is available to analogue and digital cable and satellite viewers. It shows programmes aimed at a teenage market, including soap operas, comedies, sit-coms and music shows.
TRILT coverage: June 2001 to date.

Trouble Analogue See **Trouble**

TURBO

Discovery House, Chiswick Park Building 2, 566 Chiswick Park Road, London W4 5YB

Tel: 020 8811 3000 **Fax:** 020 8811 3100
Turbo is available on cable, satellite and digital television. TRILT continues to carry listings for the channel under the old name, Discovery Wings.
TRILT coverage: June 2001 to date.

.TV (aka THE COMPUTER CHANNEL)

Ceased broadcasting at the end of August 2001. Concentrated on technology and IT. No longer active on TRILT.

Tyne Tees Television See **ITV1 Tyne Tees Television**

UK Bright Ideas See **UKTV Bright Ideas**

UK Drama See **UKTV Drama**

UK Food See **UKTV Food**

UK Gold See **UKTV Gold**

UK Gold 2 See **Dave**

UK Horizons See **UKTV Documentary**

UK Style See **UKTV Style**

UKTV BRIGHT IDEAS

UKTV Bright Ideas (formerly known as UK Bright Ideas) has ceased broadcasting. It mainly showed lifestyle programmes repeated from the BBC, with many home make-over and cookery shows.
TRILT coverage: April 2003 to October 2007.

UKTV DOCUMENTARY

UKTV, 160 Great Portland Street, London W1W 5QA
Tel: 0845 734 4355
Web: www.uktv.co.uk/documentary
UKTV Documentary, formerly known as UK Horizons, is part of UKTV, a joint venture between BBC Worldwide and Virgin Media. It is only available to cable, digital and satellite viewers. The channel shows factual entertainment.
TRILT coverage: June 2001 to date.

UKTV DRAMA

UKTV, 160 Great Portland Street,
London W1W 5QA
Tel: 0845 734 4355
Web: www.uktv.co.uk/drama
UKTV Drama, formerly known as UK Drama, is only available to cable, digital and satellite viewers. It is one of ten channels that make up UKTV, a joint venture between the BBC and Virgin Media.
TRILT coverage: June 2001 to date.

UKTV FOOD

UKTV, 160 Great Portland Street,
London W1W 5QA
Tel: 0845 734 4355
Web: www.uktv.co.uk/food
UKTV Food (formerly known as UK Food) is only available to cable, digital and satellite viewers. The channel mainly shows cookery shows.
TRILT coverage: April 2003 to date.

© Erik Dungan / SXC

UKTV GOLD

UKTV, 160 Great Portland Street,
London W1W 5QA
Tel: 0845 734 4355
Web: http://uktv.co.uk/gold/
UKTV Gold (formerly known as UK Gold) is only available to cable, digital and satellite viewers. The channel mainly shows repeats of BBC dramas, soap operas and comedies. TRILT continues to carry listings for the channel under the name UK Gold.
TRILT coverage: June 2001 to date.

UKTV HISTORY

UKTV, 160 Great Portland Street, London
W1W 5QA
Tel: 0845 734 4355
Web: www.uktv.co.uk/history
UKTV History is only available to cable, digital and satellite viewers. The channel shows a wide variety of light entertainment factual programmes, mostly repeated from the BBC.
TRILT coverage: June 2004 to date.

UKTV PEOPLE

UKTV, 160 Great Portland Street, London
W1W 5QA
Tel: 0845 734 4355
Web: http://uktv.co.uk/people/
UKTV People is only available to cable, digital and satellite viewers. The channel shows a wide variety of history documentaries, mostly repeated from the BBC.
TRILT coverage: May 2008 to date.

UKTV STYLE

UKTV, 160 Great Portland Street, London
W1W 5QA
Tel: 0845 734 4355
Web: http://uktv.co.uk/style/
UKTV Style (formerly known as UK Style) is only available to cable, digital and satellite viewers. The channel's programming largely consists of lifestyle shows, including DIY, property and makeover shows.
TRILT coverage: June 2001 to date.

ULSTER (UTV)

Havelock House, Ormeau Road, Belfast BT7 1EB
Tel: 028 9032 8122 **Fax:** 028 9024 6695
Web: http://u.tv
Available on digital, cable and satellite as well as terrestrially, this channel is the ITV1 franchise for Northern Ireland.
TRILT coverage: June 2001 to date.

VH1

180 Oxford Street, London W1D 1DS
Tel: 020 7478 6000 **Fax:** 020 7478 6007
Web: www.mtv.co.uk/channel/vh1

Music channel that plays classic songs from the last four decades. Also features popular documentaries about artists and groups.
TRILT coverage: June 2001 to date.

VIRGIN 1

Virgin Media Television, 160 Great Portland Street, London W1W 5QA
Tel: 0870 046 4141
E-mail: enquiries@virgin1.co.uk
Web: www.virgin1.co.uk/

 Virgin 1, formerly known as FTN, is a general entertainment channel from Virgin Media, available on Freeview and various digital, cable and satellite platforms. TRILT continues to carry listings for the channel under the old name, FTN.
TRILT coverage: April 2003 to date.

VH1 CLASSIC

180 Oxford Street, London, W1D 1DS
Tel: 020 7478 6000 **Fax:** 020 7478 6007
Web: www.mtv.co.uk/channel/vh1classic
Music channel which plays vintage hits and nostalgia from the sixties to the early nineties.
TRILT coverage: June 2001 to date.

Yorkshire See **ITV1 Yorkshire**

ZEE TV

Unit 7-9, Belvue Business Centre, Belvue Road, Northolt, Middlesex UB5 5QQ
Tel: 020 8839 4000 **Fax:** 020 8841 9550
E-mail: info@zeetv.co.uk
Web: www.zeetv.co.uk
Channel catering for the South Asian television market. Europe Zee TV broadcasts a wide variety of programmes in several languages to over a million viewers across the UK and Europe.
TRILT coverage: June 2001 to date.

III. RADIO STATIONS LISTED ON TRILT (BY REGION AND NATION)

A. NATIONAL

ABSOLUTE

1 Golden Square, London W1F 9DJ
Tel: 020 7434 1215 **Fax:** 020 7434 1197
Web: www.absoluteradio.co.uk/
Absolute, formerly known as Virgin Radio, is a commercial music radio station in the UK, playing rock and pop and available nationally and online. TRILT continues to carry listings for the channel under the old name, Virgin Radio.
TRILT coverage: June 2001 to date.

BBC RADIO 1

Yalding House, Great Portland Street, London W1N 4DJ
Tel: 020 7765 4575
Web: www.bbc.co.uk/radio1
The BBC's national popular music radio station. It broadcasts a wide range of music on disc as well as concerts, festivals and documentaries.
TRILT coverage: June 2001 to date.

BBC RADIO 2

Western House, 99 Great Portland Street, London W1A 1AA
Tel: 020 7580 4468
Web: www.bbc.co.uk/radio2
BBC Radio 2 combines popular music and culture with a diverse range of specialist music, features, documentaries, light entertainment, readings and broadcasts from concerts and festivals.
TRILT coverage: June 2001 to date.

BBC RADIO 3

Broadcasting House, Portland Place, London W1A 1AA
Tel: 020 7765 2722
Web: www.bbc.co.uk/radio3

BBC Radio 3 broadcasts a range of classical music and speech programmes. Jazz, world music, dramas and documentaries are also featured.
TRILT coverage: June 2001 to date.

BBC Radio 4 See Radio channels recorded by the BUFVC

BBC Radio 4 LW See BBC Radio 4

BBC RADIO 5

Television Centre, Wood Lane, London W12 7RJ
Tel: 03700 100 500
Web: www.bbc.co.uk/radio5
The BBC's 24-hour news and sport radio channel. Sometimes called Five Live.
TRILT coverage: June 2001 to date.

BBC RADIO 5 LIVE SPORTS EXTRA

Room 2605, Television Centre, Wood Lane, London W12 7RJ
Tel: 03700 100 500
Web: www.bbc.co.uk/fivelive/sportsextra/
BBC Radio 5 Live Sports Extra is a digital radio station that complements BBC Radio 5.
TRILT coverage: March 2006 to date.

BBC WORLD SERVICE RADIO

BBC World Service, Bush House, Strand, London WC2B 4PH
Tel: 020 7240 3456 **Fax:** 020 7557 1258
E-mail: worldservice@bbc.co.uk
Web: www.bbc.co.uk/worldservice
BBC World Service broadcasts news and programmes to many countries throughout the world. It broadcasts in thirty-three different languages and its English language programming broadcasts twenty-four hours a day.
TRILT coverage: June 2001 to date.

BBC 1XTRA

Yalding House, 152–156 Great Portland Street, London W1N 6AJ
E-mail: 1xtra@bbc.co.uk
Web: www.bbc.co.uk/1xtra
Sister channel to BBC Radio 1, playing new black music. Available on DAB digital radio, television and online.

TRILT coverage: March 2006 to date.

BBC 6 MUSIC

Western House, 99 Great Portland Street, London W1A 1AA
Tel: 020 7580 4468
Web: www.bbc.co.uk/6music
BBC 6 Music is a digital radio station from the BBC, which launched on 11th March 2002. It plays 'alternative' music. Unlike the more mainstream Radio 1 and Radio 2, 6 Music's playlist is less chart and singles focused.
TRILT coverage: March 2006 to date.

BBC 7

Room 4015, BBC Broadcasting House, London W1A 1AA
Web: www.bbc.co.uk/bbc7
BBC 7 is a digital radio station, drawing on the BBC Sound Archive's huge collection of spoken word programmes from across the decades.
TRILT coverage: March 2006 to date.

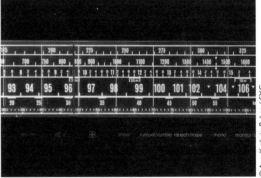

© Ann-Kathrin Rehse / SXC

BBC ASIAN NETWORK

The Mailbox, Birmingham B1 1RF
Tel: 0121 567 6000
Web: www.bbc.co.uk/asiannetwork
The BBC Asian Network is a national digital BBC radio station playing the best in new British Asian music and covering British Asian issues.
TRILT coverage: March 2006 to date.

CLASSIC FM

30 Leicester Square, London WC2H 7LA
Tel: 020 7054 8000

Web: www.classicfm.co.uk/
Classic FM is a commercial radio station devoted to classical music and owned by Gcap. It broadcasts nationally on FM and digital radio. It is also streamed online via its website.
TRILT coverage: June 2001 to date.

HEAT

Endeavour House, 189 Shaftesbury Avenue, London WC2H 8JG
Tel: 020 7437 9011
Web: www.heatradio.co.uk
Heat is a digital radio station from Emap, with the branding of the company's celebrity weekly magazine, *Heat*.
TRILT coverage: March 2006 to date.

ITN NEWS CHANNEL RADIO

200 Gray's Inn Road, London WC1X 8XZ
Tel: 020 7833 3000 **Fax:** 020 7430 4848
Digital radio news service, with news, sport, money and weather.
TRILT coverage: June 2001 to date.

KERRANG! RADIO

20 Lionel Street, Birmingham B3 1AQ
Tel: 0845 053 1052
E-mail: kerrang@kerrangradio.co.uk
Web: www.kerrangradio.co.uk
Kerrang! Radio is a digital radio station from Emap, with the branding of the company's weekly rock music magazine, *Kerrang!*
TRILT coverage: March 2006 to date.

ONEWORD

Oneword has now ceased broadcasting. It was a digital spoken word radio station available in the UK. Programming concentrated on serialisations of books, drama, comedy, interviews with authors and book and film reviews.
TRILT coverage: March 2006 to February 2008.

Q RADIO

Mappin House, 4 Winsley Street, London W1W 8HF
Tel: 020 7182 8000
Web: www.q4music.com

Q Radio is a digital radio station from Emap, with the branding of the company's monthly music and entertainment magazine, *Q*.
TRILT coverage: March 2006 to date.

RADIO ATLANTIC 252

Radio Atlantic 252 is no longer broadcasting. The commercial station transmitted from Ireland, but was available throughout the UK. No longer active on TRILT.

SMASH HITS RADIO

Mappin House, 4 Winsley Street, London W1W 8HF
Tel: 020 7182 8767
E-mail: smashhits@emap.com
Web: www.smashhits.net
Smash Hits is a digital radio station from Emap. The station took its name from the company's weekly pop magazine, which is no longer published.
TRILT coverage: March 2006 to date.

TALKSPORT

18 Hatfields, London SE1 8DJ
Tel: 08717 22 33 44
Web: http://www3.talksport.net/
TalkSPORT is a national radio station, broadcasting from London. It is also available on DAB radio and is streamed online. It is a commercial station which combines talk and sport, as its name suggests.
TRILT coverage: June 2001 to date.

Virgin Radio See **Absolute**

B. LONDON

102.2 SMOOTH FM

Smooth Radio, 26-27 Castlereagh Street, London W1H 5DL
Tel: 020 7706 4100 **Fax:** 020 7723 9742
Web: www.smoothradiolondon.co.uk/
102.2 Smooth FM, formerly known as Jazz FM 102.2, is a commercial station broadcasting in the UK, covering the Greater London area. TRILT

carries listings for the channel under the name Jazz FM 102.2.
TRILT coverage: June 2001 to date.

BBC LONDON 94.9

BBC London, PO Box 94.9, Marylebone High Street, London W1A 6FL
Tel: 020 7224 2424
E-mail: yourlondon@bbc.co.uk
Web: www.bbc.co.uk/london
BBC London 94.9, formerly known as London Live 94.9, is the BBC's local radio station for the Greater London area.
TRILT coverage: June 2001 to date.

CAPITAL FM

30 Leicester Square, London WC2H 7LA
Tel: 020 7766 6000 **Fax:** 020 7766 6100
E-mail: info@capitalradio.com
Web: www.capitalfm.co.uk
Independent local radio station serving the London area. Broadcasts popular contemporary music, classic hits, and local and national news.
TRILT coverage: June 2001 to date.

Capital Gold See Gold

CHOICE FM

GCap Media plc, 30 Leicester Square, London WC2H 7LA
Tel: 020 7054 8000 **Fax:** 020 7766 6840
E-mail: info@choice-fm.com
Web: www.choice-fm.com
Independent local radio station serving south London. Based in Brixton, it broadcasts R&B, reggae, rap, gospel and local news.
TRILT coverage: June 2001 to date.

GOLD

30 Leicester Square, London WC2H 7LA
Tel: 020 7766 6000 Fax : 020 7766 6393
Web: www.mygoldmusic.co.uk/
Gold was created after the merger of Capital Gold and the Classic Gold radio networks.
TRILT coverage: June 2001 to date.

HEART 106.2

13 Bramley Road, London W10 6SP
Tel: 020 7468 1062 **Fax:** 020 7470 1095
Web: www.heart1062.co.uk
Heart 106.2 is a commercial radio station broadcasting in the UK, covering the Greater London area.
TRILT coverage: June 2001 to date.

THE HITS RADIO

21 Holborn Viaduct, London. EC1A 2DY
E-mail: radioplayer@emap.com
Web: www.whatson.com/thehits/
The Hits Radio is a digital radio station available in London and on the internet.
TRILT coverage: March 2006 to date.

Jazz FM 102.2 See 102.2 Smooth FM

KISS 100 FM

Mappin House, 4 Winsley Street, London W1W 8HF
Tel: 020 7182 8000
Web: www.totalkiss.com
Independent local radio station serving the Greater London area. It is also available nationally on Sky digital. Broadcasts dance music, dance-related news, national and local news.
TRILT coverage: June 2001 to date.

MAGIC 105.4

Mappin House, 4 Winsley Street, London W1W 8HF
Tel: 020 7182 8233 **Fax:** 020 7975 8228
E-mail: studio@magic.fm
Web: www.magic.co.uk/

 Magic 105.4 is an independent local radio station serving Greater London. Broadcasts music, news and information.
TRILT coverage: June 2001 to date.

PARADISE FM

Broadcasts music, local news, information and community features. No longer active on TRILT.

PREMIER CHRISTIAN RADIO

PO Box 13000, London SW1P 4XP
Tel: 020 7316 1300
E-mail: response@premier.org.uk
Web: www.premier.org.uk
Premier broadcasts speech and music for the greater London area, reflecting and proclaiming the worship, thought and action of the Christian faith. It broadcasts a mixture of live and pre-recorded shows twenty-four hours a day.
TRILT coverage: March 2006 to date.

SPECTRUM 558 AM

4 Ingate Place, London SW8 3NS
Tel: 020 7627 4433 **Fax:** 020 7622 1953
Web: www.spectrumradio.net
Spectrum 558 AM claims to be the only ethnic commercial radio station aimed at London audiences. The station is available at 558AM, but is also available on DAB digital radio, various digital, cable and satellite television platforms and online. No longer active on TRILT.

SUNRISE RADIO

Sunrise House, Southall Middlesex UB2 4AT
Tel: 020 8574 6666 **Fax:** 020 8813 9700
E-mail: reception@sunriseradio.com
Web: www.sunriseradio.com
Sunrise Radio is an independent commercial radio station in the UK, covering the West London area. It is aimed at the Asian community.
TRILT coverage: June 2001 to date.

Virgin Radio See **Absolute**

XFM 104.9

30 Leicester Square, London WC2H 7LA
Tel: 020 7054 8000
Web: www.xfm.co.uk
XFM is a group of UK commercial radio stations owned by GCap Media. The channels specialise in alternative music, especially indie music.
TRILT coverage: June 2001 to date.

2CRFM

5-7 Southcote Road, Bournemouth, Dorset BH1 3LR
Tel: 01202 234900
Web: www.2crfm.co.uk/
2CR FM is a commercial station broadcasting in the UK, covering the Bournemouth area in Dorset. The station is owned by GCap Media.
TRILT coverage: June 2001 to date.

BBC RADIO BERKSHIRE

P.O Box 104.4, Reading RG4 8FH
Tel: 0118 946 4200 **Fax:** 0118 946 4555
E-mail: berkshire.online@bbc.co.uk
Web: www.bbc.co.uk/berkshire/local_radio
BBC Radio Berkshire is the BBC's local radio station for the Berkshire area.
TRILT coverage: June 2001 to date.

BBC RADIO OXFORD

269 Banbury Road, Oxford OX2 7DW
Tel: 08459 311 444
E-mail: oxford@bbc.co.uk
Web: www.bbc.co.uk/oxford/local_radio
BBC Radio Oxford is the BBC's local radio station for Oxfordshire.
TRILT coverage: June 2001 to date.

BBC RADIO SOLENT

Broadcasting House, Havelock Road, Southampton SO14 7PU
Tel: 023 8063 1311
E-mail: hampshire@bbc.co.uk
Web: www.bbc.co.uk/hampshire/local_radio
BBC Radio Solent is the BBC's local radio station for the Hampshire region.
TRILT coverage: June 2001 to date.

BBC SOUTHERN COUNTIES RADIO

Broadcasting House, Queens Road, Brighton, East Sussex BN1 3XB
Tel: 08459 570057
E-mail: southerncounties@bbc.co.uk
Web: www.bbc.co.uk/southerncounties/local_radio

BBC Southern Counties Radio is the BBC's local radio station for Surrey, Sussex and North East Hampshire.
TRILT coverage: June 2001 to date.

COUNTY SOUND RADIO

Dolphin House, North Street, Guildford GU1 4AA
Tel: 01483 300964 **Fax:** 01483 531612
E-mail: onair@countysound.co.uk
Web: www.countysound.co.uk/
Independent local radio station serving the Surrey and North East Hampshire area. Aimed at the 35+ plus age group, it broadcasts a wide range of programmes including music, speech, news and sport.
TRILT coverage: June 2001 to date.

KESTREL FM

Suite 2, Paddington House, Festival Place, Basingstoke RG21 7LJ
Tel: 01256 694000 **Fax:** 01256 694111
E-mail: Jan.ashley@kestrelfm.com
Web: www.kestrelfm.com
Kestrel FM is a commercial radio station broadcasting in the UK, covering the Basingstoke area. Listeners in this area can tune into the station at 107.6FM, but it can also be heard online.
TRILT coverage: June 2001 to date.

KICK FM

42 Bone Lane, Newbury, Berkshire RG14 5SD
Tel: 01635 841600 **Fax:** 01635 841010
E-mail: studio@kickfm.com
Web: www.kickfm.com
Independent local radio station serving the Newbury and west Berkshire area. Broadcasts soft adult contemporary music, local news and information. No longer active on TRILT.

OCEAN FM

Radio House, Apple Industrial Estate, Whittle Avenue, Fareham, PO15 5SX
Tel: 01489 589 911 **Fax:** 01489 587 739
Web: www.oceanfm.co.uk
Ocean FM, formerly known as Radio Victory, broadcasts in the Hampshire region. No longer active on TRILT.

Radio Victory See **Ocean FM**

D. SOUTH-WEST

BBC RADIO CORNWALL

BBC Cornwall, Phoenix Wharf, Truro TR1 1UA
Tel: 01872 275421
E-mail: cornwall@bbc.co.uk
Web: www.bbc.co.uk/cornwall/local_radio/index.shtml
BBC Radio Cornwall is the BBC's local radio station for the Cornwall area.
TRILT coverage: June 2001 to date.

BBC RADIO DEVON

Broadcasting House, Seymour Road, Plymouth PL3 5BD
Tel: 01752 229201
E-mail: radio.devon@bbc.co.uk
Web: www.bbc.co.uk/devon/local_radio
BBC Radio Devon is the BBC's local radio station for the Devon region.
TRILT coverage: June 2001 to date.

BBC RADIO GUERNSEY

Bulwer Avenue, St Sampsons, Guernsey GY2 4LA
Tel: 01481 200600
E-mail: guernsey@bbc.co.uk
Web: www.bbc.co.uk/guernsey/local_radio
BBC Radio Guernsey is the BBC's local radio station for the island of Guernsey.
TRILT coverage: June 2001 to date.

BBC RADIO SOMERSET SOUND

Broadcasting House, Park Street, Taunton, Somerset TA1 4DA
Tel: 01823 323956
E-mail: somerset@bbc.co.uk
Web: www.bbc.co.uk/somerset/local_radio
BBC Radio Somerset Sound is the BBC's local radio station for the Somerset region.
TRILT coverage: June 2001 to date.

BBC RADIO SWINDON

Broadcasting House, 56-58 Prospect Place, Swindon, Wiltshire SN1 3RW
Tel: 01793 513626
E-mail: wiltshire@bbc.co.uk
Web: www.bbc.co.uk/wiltshire/local_radio/radio_swindon
BBC Radio Swindon is the BBC's local radio station for the Wiltshire region.
TRILT coverage: June 2001 to date.

CLASSIC GOLD 666/954

Web: www.classicgolddigital.com
Independent local radio station covering the Exeter, mid and east Devon and Torbay areas. Broadcasts music and speech. The AM sister station of Gemini FM.
TRILT coverage: June 2001 to August 2007.

CLASSIC GOLD PLYMOUTH 1152

Earl's Acre, Plymouth, Devon PL3 4HX
Tel: 01752 275600 **Fax:** 01752 275605
Web: www.classicgolddigital.com
Independent local radio station covering the Plymouth area. Broadcasts classic hits and easy listening favourites.
TRILT coverage: June 2001 to August 2007.

Galaxy 101 See Kiss 101

GEMINI FM 97.0

Hawthorn House, Exeter Business Park, Exeter EX1 3QS
Tel: 01392 444444 **Fax:** 01392 354202
Web: www.geminiexeter.co.uk/
Independent local radio station serving the Exeter, mid and east Devon and Torbay areas on FM frequencies. Broadcasts current hits and news. Its AM sister station is Classic Gold 666/954AM.
TRILT coverage: June 2001 to date.

GWR

PO Box 2000, One Passage Street, Bristol BS99 7SN
Tel: 0117 984 3200 **Fax:** 0117 984 3202
Web: www.gwrfmbristol.co.uk/
GWR is a commercial radio station broadcasting in

the UK in the Bristol and Bath area. It is owned by GCap Media.
TRILT coverage: June 2001 to date.

ISLAND FM

12 Westerbrook, St. Sampsons, Guernsey GY2 4QQ
Tel: 01481 242000 **Fax:** 01481 249676
Web: www.islandfm.com
Island FM is a commercial radio station broadcasting in the UK, covering the Guernsey area. No longer active on TRILT.

KISS 101

Kiss 101, 26 Baldwin Street, Bristol BS1 1SE
Tel: 0117 901 0101 **Fax:** 0117 984 3204
Web: www.totalkiss.com
Independent local radio station covering the Severn estuary area, formerly known as Galaxy 101 and Vibe 101 FM. Broadcasts dance and r'n'b. TRILT continues to carry listings for the channel under the name Vibe 101 FM.
TRILT coverage: June 2001 to date.

LANTERN 96.2 FM

2b Lauder Lane, Barnstaple. EX31 3TA
Tel: 01271 366 350
Web: www.lanternfm.co.uk/
Independent local radio station serving the Barnstaple area.
TRILT coverage: June 2001 to date.

ORCHARD FM

Haygrove House, Taunton, Somerset TA3 7BT
Tel: 01823 338448
Web: www.orchardfm.co.uk/
Independent local radio station serving the Yeovil and Tauton area. Broadcasts contemporary music.
TRILT coverage: June 2001 to date.

PIRATE FM

Carn Brea Studios, Wilson Way, Redruth, Cornwall TR15 3XX
Tel: 0870 8000 007
E-mail: reception@piratefm.co.uk
Web: www.piratefm102.co.uk
Pirate FM is a commercial radio station broad-

casting in the UK, covering the Cornwall area. Listeners in this area can tune into the station at 102FM, but it can also be heard on-line. TRILT no longer carries listings for this station.

SOUTH HAMS RADIO

South Hams Business Park, Churchstow, Kingsbridge, Devon TQ7 3QR
Tel: 01548 854595
E-mail: reception@southhamsradio.com
Web: www.southhamsradio.com
South Hams Radio is a commercial station broad-casting in the UK, covering the South Hams region in Devon.
TRILT coverage: June 2001 to date.

Vibe 101 FM See **Kiss 101**

E. EAST OF ENGLAND

TRILT does not carry listings for radio stations in the East of England.

F. NORTH-EAST

3C

3C Digital Radio, 3 South Avenue, Clydebank Business Park, Glasgow G81 2RX
Tel: 0845 345 0333 or 0141 565 2307
Web: http://www3cdigital.com
3C was a radio station featuring country and western music, broadcasting in Scotland, Newcastle and Northern Ireland. No longer active on TRILT.

BBC RADIO NEWCASTLE

BBC Tyne, Broadcasting Centre, Barrack Rd, Newcastle upon Tyne NE99 1RN
Tel: 0191 232 4141
E-mail: tyne@bbc.co.uk
Web: www.bbc.co.uk/tyne/local_radio
BBC Radio Newcastle is the BBC's local radio station in the Newcastle area.
TRILT coverage: June 2001 to date.

MAGIC 1152

55 Degrees North, Pilgrim Street, Newcastle upon Tyne NE1 6BF
Tel: 0191 230 6100
Web: www.magic1152.co.uk
Independent local radio station covering the Tyne and Wear area. Broadcasts popular music, news and sport.
TRILT coverage: June 2001 to January 2008.

RADIO BORDERS

Tweedside Park, Galashiels TD1 3TD
Tel: 01896 759444 **Fax:** 0845 3457080
Web: www.radioborders.com
Radio Borders is a commercial radio station, based in the Borders region of Scotland and North Northumberland.
TRILT coverage: June 2001 to date

G. NORTH-WEST

100.4 SMOOTH FM

Laser House, Waterfront Quay, Salford Quays, Manchester, M50 3XW
Tel: 0845 0501004 **Fax:** 0845 0501005
Web: www.smoothradionorthwest.co.uk
100.4 SmoothFM, formerly known as Jazz FM 100.4, is a commercial radio station in the UK, covering the Northwest of England.
TRILT coverage: June 2001 to date.

BBC RADIO MANCHESTER

New Broadcasting House, PO Box 27, Oxford Road, Manchester, M60 1SJ
Tel: 0161 200 2020
E-mail: manchester.online@bbc.co.uk
Web: www.bbc.co.uk/manchester/local_radio/
Formerly known as GMR, BBC Radio Manchester is the BBC's local radio station for the Manchester area. TRILT continues to carry listings for the station under the old name, GMR.
TRILT coverage: June 2001 to date.

THE BAY

P.O. Box 969, St George's Quay, Lancaster LA1 3LD

Tel: 0871 2000 747
Web: www.thebay.co.uk
Independent local radio station serving the Morecambe Bay and south Lakeland areas. Broadcasts classic hits, news and community information.
TRILT coverage: June 2001 to date.

The Buzz 97.1 See **Wirral's Buzz 97.1**

BBC RADIO LANCASHIRE
Darwen Street, Blackburn, Lancashire BB2 2EA
Tel: 01254 262411
E-mail: lancashire@bbc.co.uk
Web: www.bbc.co.uk/lancashire/local_radio
BBC Radio Lancashire is the BBC's local radio station for the Lancashire region.
TRILT coverage: June 2001 to date.

BBC RADIO MERSEYSIDE
BBC Liverpool, P.O. Box 95.8, Liverpool L69 1ZJ
Tel: 0151 708 5500
E-mail: liverpool@bbc.co.uk
Web: www.bbc.co.uk/liverpool/local_radio/index.shtml
BBC Radio Merseyside is the BBC's local radio station for the Liverpool region.
TRILT coverage: June 2001 to date.

GMR See **BBC Radio Manchester**

Jazz FM 100.4 See **100.4 SmoothFM**

KEY 103FM
Castle Quay, Castlefield, Manchester M15 4PR
Tel: 0161 288 5000
Web: www.key103.co.uk
Independent local radio station for the Manchester area. No longer active on TRILT.

MAGIC 1548
St Johns Beacon, 1 Houghton Street, Liverpool L1 1RL
Tel: 0151 472 6800 **Fax:** 0151 472 6821
Web: www.magic1548.co.uk
Independent local radio station serving the Merseyside area. Aimed at the over-30s it broadcasts music, news and sport. No longer active on TRILT.

MANX RADIO
Broadcasting House, Douglas Head, Douglas, Isle of Man IM99 1SW
Tel: 01624 682600
E-mail: postbox@manxradio.com
Web: www.manxradio.com
Independent local radio station serving the Isle of Man. It broadcasts music and news. No longer active on TRILT.

RADIO CITY 96.7
St Johns Beacon, 1 Houghton Street, Liverpool L1 1RL
Tel: 0151 472 6800 **Fax:** 0151 472 6821
Web: www.radiocity.co.uk
Independent local radio station for Liverpool, the Northwest and Wales. Broadcasts popular music from the 1990s to today.
TRILT coverage: June 2001 to date.

ROCK FM
St Paul's Square, Preston PR1 1YE
Tel: 01772 477700
Web: www.rockfm.co.uk
Rock FM is a commercial radio station broadcasting in the UK, based in the Preston area.
TRILT coverage: June 2001 to date.

WIRRAL'S BUZZ 97.1
PO Box 971, Birkenhead CH41 6EY
Tel: 0151 650 1700
Web: www.wirralsbuzz.co.uk
Wirral's Buzz 97.1, formerly known as The Buzz 97.1, is an independent local radio station playing classic and current hits, and providing local and national news. No longer active on TRILT.

H. YORKSHIRE AND THE HUMBER

BBC North Yorkshire See **BBC Radio York**

BBC RADIO LEEDS

Broadcasting Centre, 2 Saint Peter's Square,
Leeds LS9 8AH
Tel: 0113 244 2131
E-mail: leeds@bbc.co.uk
Web: www.bbc.co.uk/leeds/local_radio
BBC Radio Leeds is the BBC's local radio station
for the Leeds and West Yorkshire region.
TRILT coverage: June 2001 to date.

BBC RADIO SHEFFIELD

BBC South Yorkshire, 54 Shoreham Street,
Sheffield S1 4RS
Tel: 0114 273 1177
E-mail: south.yorkshire@bbc.co.uk
Web: www.bbc.co.uk/southyorkshire/
radio_sheffield/
BBC Radio Sheffield is the BBC's local radio
station for the South Yorkshire region.
TRILT coverage: June 2001 to date.

BBC RADIO YORK

20 Bootham Row, York YO30 7BR
Tel: 01904 641351
E-mail: radio.york@bbc.co.uk
Web: www.bbc.co.uk/northyorkshire/
local_radio
BBC Radio York is the BBC's local radio station for
North Yorkshire.
TRILT coverage: June 2001 to April 2002, then
renamed as BBC North Yorkshire from April 2002
to April 2004.

HWD RADIO

The Studios, Dewsbury District Hospital,
Dewsbury, West Yorkshire WF13 4HS
Tel: 08707 469507 **Fax:** 08707 468508
E-mail: onair@hwdhospitalradio.com
HWD Radio is a hospital radio station. No longer
active on TRILT.

MAGIC 828

51 Burley Road, Leeds LS3 1LR
Tel: 0113 283 5500 **Fax:** 0113 283 5501
Web: www.magic828.co.uk
Independent local radio station serving the Leeds
area. Broadcasts popular music, and local and
national news and sport. No longer active on
TRILT.

MINSTER FM

PO Box 123, Dunnington, York YO19 5ZX
Tel: 01904 488888 **Fax:** 01904 481088
E-mail: hello@minsterfm.co.uk
Web: www.minsterfm.com
Independent local radio station covering York and
the north Yorkshire area. Broadcasts music and
local and national news.
TRILT coverage: June 2001 to date.

THE PULSE

Foster Square, Bradford, West Yorkshire BD1 5NE
Tel: 01274 203040 **Fax:** 01274 203040
Web: www.pulse.co.uk
The Pulse is a commercial radio station broad-
casting in the UK, covering the Bradford and West
Yorkshire region.
TRILT coverage: June 2001 to date

RADIO AIREDALE

Radio Airedale is a hospital radio station. No
longer active on TRILT.

I. EAST MIDLANDS

BBC RADIO DERBY

56 St Helen's Street, Derby DE1 3HY
Tel: 01332 361111
E-mail: derby@bbc.co.uk
Web: www.bbc.co.uk/derby/local_radio
BBC Radio Derby is the BBC's local radio station
for the Derbyshire region.
TRILT coverage: June 2001 to date.

PEAK 107FM

Radio House, Foxwood Road,
Chesterfield S41 9RF
Tel: 01246 269107 **Fax:** 01246 269933
E-mail: info@peak107.com

Web: www.peakfm.net

Independent local radio station covering the north Derbyshire area. It broadcasts a mix of music, and local and national news.

TRILT coverage: June 2001 to date.

J. WEST MIDLANDS

HEART 100.7

1 The Square, 111 Broad Street, Birmingham B15 1AS

Tel: 0121 695 0000 **Fax:** 0121 696 1007

E-mail: heartfm@heartfm.co.uk

Web: www.heartfm.co.uk/heart1007

Heart 100.7 is a commercial radio station broadcasting in the UK, covering the West Midlands area.

TRILT coverage: June 2001 to date.

Kix 96 See Touch FM

Radio Asia Plus See Sanskar Radio

SANSKAR RADIO

Formerly known as Radio Asia Plus, Sanskar Radio is a digital radio station that is also available online. No longer active on TRILT.

TOUCH FM

Independent local radio station, formerly known as Kix 96, serving the Coventry area. Broadcasts music news and information. No longer active on TRILT.

UCB CHRISTIAN RADIO

PO Box 255, Stoke-on-Trent ST4 8YY

Tel: 0845 6040401

E-mail: ucb@ucb.co.uk

Web: www.ucb.co.uk

UCB stands for United Christian Broadcasters. Available on DAB radio in Staffordshire and London.

TRILT coverage: June 2001 to date.

K. SCOTLAND

3C

3C Digital Radio, 3 South Avenue, Clydebank Business Park, Glasgow G81 2RX

Tel: 0845 345 0333 or 0141 565 2307

Web: http://www.3cdigital.com

3C was a radio station featuring country and western music, broadcasting in Scotland, Newcastle and Northern Ireland. No longer active on TRILT.

96.3 ROCK RADIO

PO Box 96, Parkway Court, Springhill Parkway, Glasgow G69 1AR

Tel: 0141 781 1011

Web: www.rockradioscotland.co.uk/

 96.3 Rock Radio, formerly known as Q96 FM, is a commercial station broadcasting in the UK, covering the Glasgow and Renfrewshire area. TRILT continues to carry listings for the station under the old name, Q96 FM.

TRILT coverage: June 2001 to date.

BBC RADIO NAN GAIDHEAL

Rosebank Church Street, Stornoway, Isle of Lewis HS1 2LS

Tel: 01851 705000

E-mail: alba@bbc.co.uk

Web: www.bbc.co.uk/scotland/alba/radio

BBC Radio Nan Gaidheal is the BBC's Gaelic language radio station, broadcasting in Scotland.

TRILT coverage: June 2001 to date.

BBC RADIO ORKNEY

Castle Street, Kirkwall, Orkney KW15 1DF

Tel: 01856 873939

E-mail: radio.orkney@bbc.co.uk

BBC Radio Orkney is the BBC's local radio station in the Orkney Isles. It is a local opt-out from BBC Radio Scotland.

TRILT coverage: June 2001 to date.

BBC RADIO SCOTLAND

Broadcasting House, Glasgow G12 8DG

Tel: 0870 010 0222
E-mail: enquiries.scot@bbc.co.uk
Web: www.bbc.co.uk/radioscotland/
BBC Radio Scotland is the national radio station for Scotland from the BBC.
TRILT coverage: June 2001 to date.

BBC Radio Scotland MW See **BBC Radio Scotland**

BBC RADIO SHETLAND

Pitt Lane, Lerwick, Shetland ZE1 0DW
Tel: 01595 694 747
E-mail: radio.shetland@bbc.co.uk
BBC Radio Shetland is the BBC's local radio station for the Shetland Isles. It is a local opt-out from BBC Radio Scotland.
TRILT coverage: June 2001 to date.

Beat 106 See **XFM Scotland**

CENTRAL FM

201 High Street, Falkirk FK1 1DU
Tel: 01324 611164 **Fax:** 01324 611168
E-mail: mail@centralfm.co.uk
Web: www.centralfm.co.uk
A local independent radio station covering the Stirling and Falkirk areas. It broadcasts current and past hits, local news, sport and information.
TRILT coverage: June 2001 to date.

CLYDE 1 FM

3 South Avenue, Clydebank Business Park, Glasgow G81 2RX
Tel: 0141 565 2200 **Fax:** 0141 565 2265
E-mail: info@clyde1.com
Web: www.clyde1.com
Independent local radio station serving the Glasgow area. Broadcasts popular contemporary music, sport, and local and national news. The FM sister station of the AM station Clyde 2.
TRILT coverage: June 2001 to date.

CLYDE 2 AM

3 South Avenue, Clydebank Business Park, Glasgow G81 2RX
Tel: 0141 565 2200 **Fax:** 0141 565 2265

E-mail: info@clyde2.com
Web: www.clyde2.com
Independent local radio station serving the Glasgow area. Broadcasts easy listening music, local and national news and sport. The AM sister station to Clyde1.
TRILT coverage: June 2001 to date.

Forth 1 See **Forth One**

Forth 2 See **Forth Two**

Forth AM See **Forth Two**

Forth FM See **Forth One**

FORTH ONE

Forth House, Forth Street, Edinburgh EH1 3LE
Tel: 0131 556 9255 **Fax:** 0131 558 3277
E-mail: info@forthone.com
Web: www.forthone.com
Independent local radio station, formerly known as Forth FM and Forth 1, serving the Edinburgh area. Broadcasts chart and contemporary hits, news and information.
TRILT coverage: June 2001 to date.

FORTH TWO

Forth House, Forth Street, Edinburgh EH1 3LE
Tel: 0131 556 9255 **Fax:** 0131 558 3277
E-mail: info@forth2.com
Web: www.forth2.com
Independent local radio station, formerly known as Forth AM and Forth 2, serving the Edinburgh area. Broadcasts classic hits, contemporary music, news and sport.
TRILT coverage: June 2001 to date.

KINGDOM FM

Haig House, Haig Business Park, Markinch, Fife KY7 6AQ
Tel: 01592 753 753
Web: www.kingdomfm.co.uk
Independent local radio station serving the Fife area. Broadcasts current and past hits, local news and community information.
TRILT coverage: June 2001 to date.

MORAY FIRTH RADIO

Scorguie Place, Inverness, Scotland IV3 8UJ
Tel: 01463 224433 **Fax:** 01463 243224
E-mail: mfr@mfr.co.uk
Web: www.mfr.co.uk
Independent local radio station covering the Inverness and Moray Firth area. Broadcasts a wide range of programmes including contemporary music, sport, news, entertainment and local information.
TRILT coverage: June 2001 to date.

NORTHSOUND ONE

Abbotswell Road, West Tullos, Aberdeen AB12 3AJ
Tel: 01224 337000
Web: www.northsound1.com/
Independent local radio station covering the Aberdeen area. Broadcasts contemporary hits, news, sport and information. No longer active on TRILT.

NORTHSOUND TWO

Abbotswell Road, West Tullos, Aberdeen AB12 3AJ
Tel: 01224 337000
Web: www.northsound2.com
Independent local radio station, covering the Aberdeen area. Broadcasts adult pop, news, sport and information. No longer active on TRILT.

Q96 FM See **96.3 Rock Radio**

RADIO BORDERS

Tweedside Park, Tweedside, Melrose TD1 3RS
Tel: 01896 759444 **Fax:** 0845 3457080
E-mail: programming@radioborders.com
Web: www.radioborders.com
Radio Borders is a commercial radio station, based in the Borders region of Scotland and North Northumberland.
TRILT coverage: June 2001 to date

RADIO ROYAL

Radio Royal is a hospital radio station. No longer active on TRILT.

RADIO TAY AM

6 North Isla Street, Dundee DD3 7JQ
E-mail: tayam@radiotay.co.uk

Web: www.tayam.co.uk
Tay AM is a commercial radio station broadcasting in the UK, based in the Dundee and Perth area of Scotland.
TRILT coverage: June 2001 to date.

RADIO TAY FM

PO Box 1028, Dundee DD3 7YH
Tel: 01382 200 800
E-mail: tayfm@radiotay.co.uk
Web: www.tayfm.co.uk
Tay FM is a commercial radio station broadcasting in the UK, based in the Dundee and Perth area of Scotland.
TRILT coverage: June 2001 to date.

REAL RADIO

P.O. Box 101, Parkway Court, Glasgow Business Park, Glasgow G69 6GA
Tel: 0141 7811011 **Fax:** 0141 7811112
Web: www.realradio-scotland.co.uk/
Real FM, formerly known as Scot FM, is an independent local radio covering the central Scotland area. Broadcasts adult contemporary music and speech.
TRILT coverage: June 2001 to date.

Scot FM See **Real Radio**

WESTSOUND

Radio House, 54a Holmston Road, Ayr KA7 3BE
Tel: 01292 283662 **Fax:** 01292 283665
E-mail: info@westsound.co.uk
Web: www.west-sound.co.uk

Independent local radio station based in Ayr. It plays easy listening music with local and national news plus live football.
TRILT coverage: June 2001 to date.

XFM SCOTLAND

Four Winds Pavilion, Pacific Quay,
Glasgow G51 1EB
Tel: 0141 566 6106 **Fax:** 0141 566 6110
Web: www.xfmscotland.co.uk/
An independent local radio station, formerly known as Beat 106, broadcasting a mixture of

chart and indie music to Central Scotland. The station was re-branded as XFM Scotland in 2006. No longer active on TRILT.

L. WALES

BBC RADIO CYMRU

Broadcasting House, Llantrisant Road, Llandaff, Cardiff CF5 2YQ
Tel: 08703 500 700
Web: www.bbc.co.uk/cymru/radiocymru
BBC Radio Cymru is the BBC's local radio station for the Wales area, broadcasting in the Welsh language.
TRILT coverage: June 2001 to date.

BBC RADIO WALES

Broadcasting House, Llandaff, Cardiff CF5 2YQ
Tel: 03700 100 11
E-mail: radio.wales@bbc.co.uk
Web: www.bbc.co.uk/wales/radiowales
BBC Radio Wales is the national English language radio station for Wales from the BBC.
TRILT coverage: June 2001 to date.

CLASSIC GOLD MARCHER 1260AM

Web: www.mygoldmusic.co.uk/
Local independent radio station serving the Wrexham, Chester and North Wales area. Formerly known as Marcher Gold. No longer active on TRILT.

Galaxy 101 See **Kiss 101**

KISS 101

Kiss 101, 26 Baldwin Street, Bristol BS1 1SE
Tel: 0117 901 0101 **Fax:** 0117 984 3204
Web: www.totalkiss.com/
Independent local radio station covering the Severn estuary area, formerly known as Galaxy 101 and Vibe 101 FM. Broadcasts dance and r'n'b. TRILT continues to carry listings for the channel under the name Vibe 101 FM.
TRILT coverage: June 2001 to date.

Marcher Gold See **Classic Gold Marcher 1260AM**

MARCHER SOUND

The Studios, Mold Rd, Wrexham LL11 4AF
Web: www.marchersound.co.uk/
Independent local radio station covering the Wrexham and Chester areas. Broadcasts a mix of music, and local and national news. TRILT continues to carry listings for the under the old name, MFM 103.4.
TRILT coverage: June 2001 to date.

MFM 103.4 See **Marcher Sound**

RED DRAGON FM

Red Dragon Centre Cardiff CF10 4DJ
E-mail: mail@reddragonfm.co.uk
Web: www.reddragonfm.co.uk
Red Dragon FM is a commercial radio station broadcasting in the UK, covering the Cardiff and Newport area.
TRILT coverage: June 2001 to date.

VALLEYS RADIO

PO Box 1116, Ebbw Vale, NP23 8XW
Tel: 01495 301116 **Fax:** 01495 300710
E-mail: info@valleysradio.co.uk
Web: www.valleysradio.co.uk
Valleys Radio is a commercial radio station broadcasting in the UK in the South Wales Valleys region.
TRILT coverage: June 2001 to date.

Vibe 101 FM See **Kiss 101**

M. NORTHERN IRELAND

3C

3C Digital Radio, 3 South Avenue, Clydebank Business Park, Glasgow G81 2RX
Tel: 0845 345 0333 or 0141 565 2307
Web: http://www3cdigital.com
3C was a radio station featuring country and western music, broadcasting in Scotland, Newcastle

and Northern Ireland. No longer active on TRILT.

BBC RADIO FOYLE

8 Northland Road, Derry BT48 7GD
Tel: 028 7137 8600
E-mail: radio.foyle@bbc.co.uk
Web: www.bbc.co.uk/northernireland/radiofoyle
BBC Radio Foyle is the BBC's local radio station for Derry and the North West of Northern Ireland. It runs an opt-out service from Radio Ulster.
TRILT coverage: June 2001 to date.

BBC RADIO ULSTER

Broadcasting House, Ormeau Avenue, Belfast BT2 8HQ
Tel: 028 9033 8000 **Fax:** 028 9032 6453
Web: www.bbc.co.uk/northernireland/radioulster
BBC Radio Ulster is the BBC's main local radio station for Northern Ireland.
TRILT coverage: June 2001 to date.

© Martin@parry-mania.nl / SXC

COOL FM

PO Box 974, Belfast BT1 1RT
Tel: 028 9181 7181 **Fax:** 028 9181 8913.
E-mail: music@coolfm.co.uk
Web: www.coolfm.co.uk
Independent local radio station serving Northern

Ireland. Broadcasts a mix of contemporary music and news.
TRILT coverage: June 2001 to date.

DOWNTOWN RADIO

Kiltonga Industrial Estate, Newtownards, Co. Down, Northern Ireland BT23 4ES
Tel: 028 9181 5555 **Fax:** 028 9181 8913
E-mail: programmes@downtown.co.uk
Web: www.downtown.co.uk
Independent local radio station serving Northern Ireland. Broadcasts a mix of music, news and information, and specialist music.
TRILT coverage: June 2001 to date.

Q102.9FM

The Riverview Suite, 87 Rossdowney Road, Waterside, Londonderry BT47 5SU
Tel: 02871 344449 **Fax:** 02871 311177
E-mail: requests@q102.fm
Web: www.q102.fm
Q102.9FM is a commercial station broadcasting in the UK, covering the Derry area.
TRILT coverage: June 2001 to date.

N. EIRE

RAIDIO NA GAELTACHTA

RTÉ, Donnybrook, Dublin 4, Ireland
E-mail: nag@rte.ie
Web: www.rte.ie/rnag
Raidio Na Gaeltachta is the Irish language radio channel from RTÉ.
TRILT coverage: June 2001 to date.

The Media Production Team working in the E-learning Centre at the University of Portsmouth.

COURSES AND TRAINING

The major source for information on courses and training in film, video and multimedia in the UK is the BFI/Skillset Media Courses and Multimedia Courses Directory, available at: www.bfi.org.uk/education/talkscourses/mediacourses. It is also available at: www.skillset.org/training/coursedatabase. The Directory lists details of nearly 5,000 courses across England, Northern Ireland, Scotland and Wales. Courses in film, television, video, radio and web authoring are included. The database provides comprehensive information both for those needing professional upgrading and anyone contemplating a career shift.

In addition to courses run by institutions of higher and further education, the following organisations offer relevant specialist training courses.

01ZERO-ONE, THE CREATIVE LEARNING LAB

Tel: 020 7025 1985
E-mail: info@01zero-one.co.uk
Web: www.01zero-one.co.uk
01zero-one runs a range of training and skills development courses for London's television, film, post production, interactive and new media and digital design industries. The short courses and masterclasses offered address developments in technology, creative content and business management.

4TALENT

Web: www.channel4.com/4talent/national/opportunities/events/
4Talent offers an extensive range of hands-on and practical events around the country for talented young people interested in working in the television industry. This includes workshops, showcasing, networking, pitching and funding events and opportunities in specific areas such as documentaries, comedy, drama, animation, etc.

BBC TRAINING

BBC Training & Development,
35 Marylebone High Street, London W1U 4PX
Tel: 0870 122 0216 **Fax:** 0870 122 0145
E-mail: training@bbc.co.uk
Web: www.bbctraining.com
BBC Training & Development offers an extensive range of courses in the areas of television, radio, new media, radio, journalism and broadcast technology. Some of these are subsidised by Skillset for the UK freelance community. A number of free online courses and modules are also available.

BILL CURTIS ASSOCIATES

Colpetty, Westbury Terrace, Westerham,
Kent TN16 1RP
Tel: 01959 563326
E-mail: info@bcassociates.org
Web: www.bcassociates.org
Training and production in broadcast and creative media for broadcasters, companies and freelancers, delivered by an experienced team of

practitioners in London or on site. Includes Skillset-funded courses.

BKSTS – THE MOVING IMAGE SOCIETY

Pinewood Studios, Iver Heath, Bucks SL0 0NH
Tel: 01753 656656
Web: https://nt12.orbital.net/bksts/events-and-training.asp
BKSTS offers a range of short, part-time courses, some of them supported by the Skillset freelance fund. Topics include introduction to film technologies, television technology, audio technology for television and film, projectionist training, management in the creative industries, being an effective manager, broadcast technology, from camera to screen – the technology of television, what is HD, and HD technology.

BRITISH INTERACTIVE MEDIA ASSOCIATION (BIMA)

Briarlea House, Southend Road, Billericay CM11 2PR
Tel: 01277 658107 **Fax:** 0870 051 7842
E-mail: info@bima.co.uk
Web: www.bima.co.uk/industry-insight/training-and-accreditation.asp

BIMA is the industry association representing the interactive media and digital content sector. It does not offer any courses itself but takes a proactive role to bridging the gap between the digital industry, education sector and professional development arena through encouraging student placements with its members.

BRITISH LIBRARY – LISTEN UP!

The British Library, 96 Euston Road, London NW1 2DB
Tel: 020 7412 7797
E-mail: learning@bl.uk
Web: www.bl.uk/learning/tarea/secondaryfehe/listenup/listen.html
Held on Mondays and Fridays throughout the year and aimed at students from GCSE level to higher education, this 2½-hour participatory workshop focuses on our auditory environment and explores new ways of understanding music and sound. During the session, participants hear a range of recordings from the British Library Sound Archive, which reflect the diversity of our sonic world. The workshop covers listening and interpretation skills, exploring material in the British Library Sound Archive, discussion of the shared characteristics of sound and music, engaging with live sound to develop musical ideas and compose a graphical score. The workshop is followed by an introductory talk from a member of the Sound Archive about the collection and how to access material.

BRITISH UNIVERSITIES FILM & VIDEO COUNCIL (BUFVC)

77 Wells Street, London W1T 3QJ
Tel: 020 7393 1512
E-mail: courses@bufvc.ac.uk
Web: www.bufvc.ac.uk/courses
The BUFVC offers a range of one-day courses and workshops promoting subjects related to the use of moving image in learning, teaching and research. Courses currently offered include: Copyright clearance for print, broadcast and multimedia production; Encoding digital video for streaming and network delivery (at introductory or advanced level); Moving image and sound for learning and teaching - sources, search strategies, appraisal and use; Shooting with high definition video.

CHANNEL 4 BRITISH DOCUMENTARY FILM FOUNDATION (BRITDOC)

E-mail: training @britdoc.org
Web: https://www.britdoc.org/foundation/training.php

The Foundation runs bespoke training programmes for filmmakers and organisations working to support a sustainable independent documentary filmmaking community. Specific projects and initiatives include Breakout – a year-long project and professional development scheme for black and minority ethnic writers and directors - and Lewisham Documentary Filmmakers - a pilot scheme for the London boroughs, providing an intensive training programme, which highlights alternative models of documentary funding and distribution.

CYFLE

33-35 West Bute Street, Cardiff CF10 5LH
Tel: 029 2046 5533 **Fax:** 029 2046 3344
E-mail: Cyfle@cyfle.co.uk
Web: www.cyfle.co.uk

Cyfle is the training company for the Welsh television, film and interactive media industry. In 2000 the company became a Skillset-accredited Ttraining Ppartner and a national provider for the industry across Wales. Cyfle provides a variety of training schemes covering a wide spectrum of activity from the Summer Schools for young people to Newcomer Schemes and courses for the professional seeking to update and acquire new skills.

DOCUMENTARY FILMMAKERS GROUP (DFG)

4th Floor Shacklewell Studios,
28 Shacklewell Lane, London E8 2EZ
Tel: 020 7249 6600
E-mail: info@dfgdocs.com
Web: www.dfgdocs.com/Training

DFG offers an extensive programme of short courses from one day to one month in length. These courses offer an opportunity to acquire a range of skills specifically for documentary filmmaking. In addition, DFG also runs Doclab, an intensive training course and documentary production factory in partnership with Goldsmiths, University of London. The new, ISIS documentary production and training initiative will give 16 women the opportunity, free of charge, to produce three short documentaries on human rights issues.

DV TALENT

Studio 451, Highgate Studios,
53-79 Highgate Road, London NW5 1TL
Tel: 020 7267 2300 **Fax:** 020 7428 0527
E-mail: rob@dvtalent.co.uk
Web: www.dvtalent.co.uk

DV Talent are agents, training providers and DV consultants. They offer training courses in technical and editorial skills, run by production people for production people. Some courses are subsidised by Skillset.

FILM DESIGN INTERNATIONAL

Pinewood Studios, Pinewood Road, Iver Heath, Buckinghamshire SL0 0NH
Tel: 01753 656 678
E-mail: Terry@filmdi.com
Web: www.filmdi.com

Draughtsmanship training for the film and television industry, offering initial and advanced an Art Direction and an Advanced Art Direction courses, based at Pinewood Film Studios. Skillset film skills funding is available for the cArt Direction Courses, depending on experience.

FOCAL

Pentax House, South Hill Avenue, Northolt Road, South Harrow, Middlesex HA2 0DU
Tel: 020 8423 5853 **Fax:** 020 8933 4826
E-mail: info@focalint.org
Web: www.focalint.org/training.htm

FOCAL International organises regular training events for those working in the footage industry. Several of its consultant members are professional trainers who can provide bespoke training to individuals or groups. FOCAL has also established the Jane Mercer Training Award in memory of Jane Mercer, footage researcher and Chair of FOCAL International 2000-2005. The Award is intended to provide assistance forto those wishing to further their professional development in the footage industry and its associated areas.

FT2

3rd Floor, 18-20 Southwark Street, London SE1 1TJ
Tel: 020 7407 0344 **Fax:** 020 7407 0366
E-mail: ft2@ft2.org.uk
Web: www.ft2.org.uk
FT2 is the Film and Television Freelance Training's website. FT2 is committed to assisting the film and television industry achieve a diverse workforce, which more closely represents the makeup of society as a whole. The New Entrant Technical Training Programme offers courses in all areas of the film and television industry including props, wardrobe, art department, grip, etc

INDIE TRAINING FUND

Third Floor, Procter House, 1 Procter Street, Holborn, London WC1V 6DW18-20 Southwark Street, London SE1 1TJ
Tel: 0207 7407 0454
E-mail: info@indietrainingfund.com
Web: www.indietrainingfund.com/
The Indie Training Fund is a registered charity to which UK TV and interactive media indies can contribute in return for free courses, in-house training, subsidised trainees for company placements and subsidised training for their freelance workers. Previously administered by Pact, the ITF became totally independent and took over Pact's short course programme and in.indie scheme on 1 May 2008. A separate website will be set up shortly, with online booking for the extensive range of one-day courses and seminars covering all aspects of programme production, including coping with archive clips, scheduling for drama production, negotiating music rights, and sales skills for distributors.

PACT See INDIE TRAINING FUND

Procter House, 1 Procter Street, Holborn, London WC1V 6DW
Tel: 020 7067 4367
E-mail: enquiries@pact.co.uk
Web: www.pact.co.uk/training
On 1st May 2008, the Indie Training Fund took over Pact's short course programme and in.indie scheme. A separate website, with online booking, is being set up by ITF staff but in the meantime upcoming courses are listed on the ITF website www.indietrainingfund. com/

PRAXIS FILMS

8 Clifton Road, Brighton BN1 3HP
PO Box 290, Market Rasen, Lincs LN8 6BB
Tel: 0779 111 4691
E-mail: inquiriesfo@praxisfilms.co.uk
Web: www.praxisfilms.co.uk
Praxis Films offer a variety of one and two-dayshort training courses for freelancers in-tailored to meet skills shortages identified by the television and film industry. Substantial discounts are available for courses funded by Skillset. directing, producing, research for documentary, current affairs and factual films; business, commercial and marketing courses for would-be media executives and entrepreneurs; and various 'how to handle the media' courses for business and industry executives. Courses are held in central London.

RAINDANCE

81 Berwick Street, London W1F 8TW
Tel: 020 7287 3833 **Fax:** 020 7287 3833
E-mail: courses@raindance.co.uk
Web: www.raindance.co.uk/site/
film-training-london-UK
www.raindance.co.uk/courses

Film Training Courses at Raindance
Summer 2008

Raindance offers courses aimed at directors, producers, writers, actors, agents, film and media students. All tutors are working industry professionals. Around thirty-three different one- and two-day courses are offered for those wishing to focus on particular aspects of writing, producing or directing. Other short courses run one day or evening a week. Diplomas are also offered for those taking a number of short courses to study an area in depth.

SCOTTISH SCREEN NEW ENTRANTS TRAINING SCHEME (NETS) and NEW ENTRANTS ANIMATION SCHEME GENERATING ANIMATION SKILLS PROGRAMME (GASP!NEATS)

249 West George Street, Glasgow G2 4QE
Tel: 0845 300 7300
E-mail: info@scottishscreen.com
Web: www.scottishscreen.com
Recruiting from across the UK, the NETS programme provides one-year, full-time industry-approved apprenticeships in the areas of production, technical, craft and design. Intensive three-month training is also available for those with slightly more experience, and one-day courses for runners are held at different locations in Scotland. GASP! offers the opportunity to gain hands-on experience in studios across Scotland for those wanting to work in animation. Financial assistance with courses is provided via Skillset Scotland.

SKILLSET

Focus Point, 21 Caledonian Road, London N1 9GB
Prospect House, 80-110 New Oxford Street,
London WC1A 1HB
Tel: 020 7713 9800
Fax: 020 7713 9801, 020 7520 5757 or
020 7520 5758
E-mail: info@skillset.org
Web: www.skillset.org/training/
Skillset is the national training organisation for broadcast, film, video and multimedia. It is Skillset's role to ensure that individuals and organisations can access high quality vocational training. It works with industry, training and education providers, and public agencies to make sure training provision meets industry needs. It accredits courses and approves providers on the basis of quality and relevance to industry. Skillset funds training providers who run courses for freelancers that meet a range of criteria set out by industry representatives, and eligible television freelancers can receive substantial discounts on the full course fee.

SPANNER FILMS SWOTS

Tel: 07789 862 011
E-mail: swots@spannerfilms.net

Web: www.spannerfilms.net
Spanner Films' Weekend of Techniques and Secrets (SWOTS) is an intensive two-day course, held once in year, giving more than 400 tips and secrets from every stage of making documentaries, imaginative suggestions on funding, and advice on distribution for low budget, independent productions.

TECHNICAL ADVISORY SERVICE FOR DIGITAL MEDIA (TASI)

Institute for Learning and Research Technology, University of Bristol, 8-10 Berkeley Square, Bristol BS8 1HH
Tel: 0117 331 4447
0117 928 7091
E-mail: info@tasi.ac.uk
Web: www.tasi.ac.uk/training/training.html
TASI runs a programme of full and half-day training workshops at venues around the country aimed at those involved in image digitisation projects or who wish to use digital images in learning and teaching. The small-group workshops consist of presentations and expert advice as well as practical exercises. The current programme of workshops covers four main areas: image capture and manipulation; digital imaging skills; copyright issues; building image collections. Several of the practical courses are offered at beginner, intermediate or advanced level.

TRAINING AND PERFORMANCE SHOWCASE (TAPS)

Shepperton Studios, Shepperton, Middlesex
TW17 0QD
Tel: 01932 592151 **Fax:** 01932 592233
Web: www.tapsnet.org
TAPS has become the leading training scheme for new television writers. A not-for-profit organisation with strong links to major and regional broadcasters and constant support from Skillset, TAPS seeks out talented new writers and offers professionally taught courses across the UK at accessible rates.

UNDERCURRENTS

Old Exchange, Pier Street, Swansea SA1 1RY
Tel: 01792 455900

E-mail: info@undercurrents.org
Web: www.undercurrents.org/training/index.htm

Undercurrents believes that anyone with access to equipment and the right training can effectively use video to bring about positive change in their community. Anyone wanting to be a video activist or who is part of an environmental or social justice campaign and feels that video could make a difference is invited to contact Undercurrents to discuss arranging a workshop. They also give advice on how to distribute video across the web, or even get images on to mainstream television news and current affairs programmes.

VET

Lux Building, 2-4 Hoxton Square, London N1 6US
Tel: 020 7505 4700
Fax: 020 7505 4800
E-mail: info@vet.co.uk
Web: www.vet.co.uk

VET's reputation as a leading media industry training provider is built on twenty years of training delivery. It offers regular short courses on shooting and editing with the latest equipment, and AVID certified courses. Freelance rates are available on some courses with financial support from Skillset.

DISCUSSION LISTS

The following e-mail discussion lists cover areas of audio-visual media of interest to UK higher education and research. All can be freely subscribed to and will send regular e-mails under discussion threads on topics relevant to the list. Some discussion lists are open; others have a moderator who will vet submissions before publication and may guide discussion topics or advise on 'netiquette.' Most are provided through JISCmail, the National Academic Mailing List funded by the Joint Information Systems Committee. 'Announce' lists are used to disseminate news, not for discussion of topics. All the lists below are open to all, unless indicated otherwise.

The BUFVC currently manages four JISCmail discussion lists: BUFVC-Movies, Newsreels, ShakespeareAV and TRILT-Talk.

AHDS-ALL
Web: www.jiscmail.ac.uk/lists/AHDS-ALL.html
Discussion list for disseminating news about the Arts and Humanities Data Service.

AMIA-L
Web: http://lsv.uky.edu/archives/amia-l.html
Discussion list for members of the Association of Moving Image Archivists and anyone interested in issues surrounding the archiving of motion pictures.

ARLIS-LINK
Web: www.jiscmail.ac.uk/lists/ARLIS-LINK.html
Discussion list for ARLIS/UK & Ireland, the Art Libraries Society, covering issues relating to librarianship of the visual arts.

BBC HISTORY
www.jiscmail.ac.uk/lists/BBC-HISTORY.html

Discussion list for researchers investigating the history of the BBC.

BISA
Web: www.jiscmail.ac.uk/lists/BISA.html
Discussion list for the British and Irish Sound Archives Forum.

BUFVC-MOVIES
Web: www.jiscmail.ac.uk/lists/BUFVC-MOVIES.html
BUFVC discussion list on the online delivery of moving images, also used for general BUFVC news.

CINEPHOTO
Web: www.jiscmail.ac.uk/lists/CINEPHOTO.html
An interdisciplinary mailing list for cinema and photography.

CLICKANDGOVIDEO

Web: www.jiscmail.ac.uk/lists/
CLICKANDGOVIDEO.html
Discussion on the educational value and implementation issues behind using streaming video lectures as a teaching method.

© jaylopez / SXC

CREATIVITY-IN-EDUCATION

Web: www.jiscmail.ac.uk/lists/
CREATIVITY-IN-EDUCATION.html
Designed to stimulate discussion and disseminate information on the subject of creativity in education.

ELEARNING

Web: www.jiscmail.ac.uk/lists/ELEARNING
.html
Discussion list for sharing ideas and best practice in e-learning projects in museums, libraries, archives, galleries and HE/FE organisations.

FILM-PHILOSOPHY

Web: www.jiscmail.ac.uk/lists/FILM-
PHILOSOPHY.html
Discussion 'salon' devoted to serious debate about film.

FILM-SCREENING

Web: www.jiscmail.ac.uk/lists/FILM-
SCREENING.html
Discussion list for screening films in a higher education context.

H-FILM

Web: www.h-net.org/~film
H-Film encourages scholarly discussion of cinema history and uses of the media.

HISTORY-DIGITISATION

Web: www.jiscmail.ac.uk/lists/
HISTORY-DIGITISATION.html
The application of optical character recognition (OCR) and imaging technology to historical material.

IAMS

Web: www.jiscmail.ac.uk/lists/IAMS.html
Discussion list for the International Association for Media in Science.

IASA

Web: www.nb.no/cgi-bin/wa?A0=IASALIST
Discussion list for the International Association of Sound and Audiovisual Archives.

INTUTE-ANNOUNCE

Web: www.jiscmail.ac.uk/lists/
INTUTE-ANNOUNCE.html

 Latest news from Intute, a national JISC service which provides the academic community with access to the best web resources for education and research.

JISC-ANNOUNCE

Web: www.jiscmail.ac.uk/
lists/JISC-ANNOUNCE.html
An announcement list for news from the Joint Information Systems Committee.

JISC-DEVELOPMENT

Web: www.jiscmail.ac.uk/
lists/JISC-DEVELOPMENT.html
JISC development discussion forum.

JISC-E-COLLECTIONS

Web: www.jiscmail.ac.uk/
lists/JISC-E-COLLECTIONS.html
Discussion list for electronic collection managers.

LIS-LINK

Web: www.jiscmail.ac.uk/lists/LIS-LINK.html

A general library and information science list for news and discussion.

LIS-MMIT

Web: www.jiscmail.ac.uk/lists/LIS-MMIT.html
Discussion for the CILIP Multimedia Information & Technology Group, covering issues of multimedia information and technology developments in library and information science.

LONDONSCREENARCHIVES

Web: www.mailtalk.ac.uk/lists/ londonsscreenarchives.html
Discussion list for the network of London's screen archives.

MECCSA

Web: www.jiscmail.ac.uk/lists/MECCSA.html
Discussion list for MECCSA, the Media, Communication and Cultural Studies Association, covering aspects of academic research and teaching within media.

MEDIALIB

Web: www.jiscmail.ac.uk/lists/MEDIALIB.html
Forum for media librarians and information professionals.

MEDIA-SUPPORT-SERVICES

Web: www.jiscmail.ac.uk/lists/ MEDIA-SUPPORT-SERVICES.html

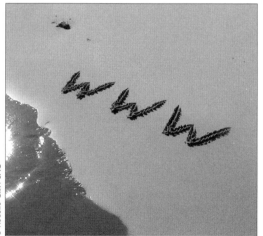

© Rodolfo Clix / SXC

Discussion list for media support departments in the UK.

MLANEWS

Web: www.jiscmail.ac.uk/lists/MLANEWS.html
News from the Museums, Libraries and Archives Council.

NEWSREELS

Web: www.jiscmail.ac.uk/lists/ NEWSREELS.html
BUFVC list for the study of cinema newsreels and their use in historical research.

PODCASTING

Web: www.jiscmail.ac.uk/lists/ PODCASTING.html
Academic podcasting and related issues.

RADIO-STUDIES

Web: www.jiscmail.ac.uk/lists/ RADIO-STUDIES.html
Debate on all issues related to radio.

SCUDD

Web: www.jiscmail.ac.uk/lists/SCUDD.html
SCUDD is the The Standing Conference of University Drama Departments, the major UK organisation of Drama (and equivalents, eg. Theatre, Performance) in Higher Education. Subscription to the List is open to SCUDD members and other interested parties.

SHAKESPEAREAV

Web: www.jiscmail.ac.uk/lists/ SHAKESPEAREAV.html
BUFVC discussion list for its audio-visual Shakespeare database project, and general issues relating to Shakespeare on film, television and radio.

SHAKSPER

Web: www.shaksper.net
Moderated list for Shakespearean researchers, instructors, students, and those who share their academic interests and concerns. Requires an application to be made before one can join the list.

STREAMING
Web: www.jiscmail.ac.uk/lists/
STREAMING.html
Discussion list for issues around streaming technology for delivering presentations.

TRILT-TALK
Web: www.jiscmail.ac.uk/lists/
TRILT-TALK.html
Broadcasting and education mailing list, managed by the BUFVC. Particularly relates to the BUFVC's Television and Radio Index for Learning and Teaching.

UK-COLLEGES
Web: www.jiscmail.ac.uk/
lists/UK-COLLEGES.html

Use of the Internet to support curriculum activity in further education colleges.

VIDEO
Web: www.jiscmail.ac.uk/lists/VIDEO.html
Issues on the use of video in education.

VISUALISATION TOOLS
Web: www.jiscmail.ac.uk/lists/
VISUALISATION-TOOLS.html
The use of visualisation tools.

VLE
Web: www.jiscmail.ac.uk/lists/VLE.html
Discussion list on all issues relating to Virtual Learning Environments.

DISTRIBUTORS

The BUFVC selects and describes audio-visual programmes available in the UK that will be of interest to UK higher education users, and publishes the details through its HERMES database (www.bufvc.ac.uk/hermes) and our quarterly publication, Viewfinder. *Below is a listing of some of the main distributors currently referred to by the BUFVC, which provide specialist content suitable for higher education and research.*

2 ENTERTAIN

33 Foley Street, London W1W 7TL
Tel: 020 7612 3000 **Fax:** 020 7612 3003
E-mail: emma.burch@2entertain.co.uk
Web: www.2entertain.co.uk
Specialises in distributing archival film and television titles, predominantly licensed from the BBC.

4 LEARNING

PO Box 400, Wetherby LS23 7LG
Tel: 08701 246 444 **Fax:** 08701 246 446
E-mail: sales@channel4learning.com
Web: www.4learningshop.co.uk/C4Shop/
The educational broadcasting arm of Channel 4. The online shop sells educational DVDs and CD-ROMs for use in primary and secondary schools.

20TH CENTURY FOX HOME ENTERTAINMENT

Twentieth Century House, 31-32 Soho Square, London W1V 6AP
Tel: 020 7753 8686 **Fax:** 020 7437 1625
Web: www.foxhome.com
Distributes films by Fox and MGM.

ACORN MEDIA UK

16 Welmar Mews, 154 Clapham Road,
London SW4 7DD
Tel: 0845 123 2312 **Fax:** 020 7627 2501
E-mail: customerservices@acornmediauk.com
Web: www.acornmedia.com
Founded in 1997, Acorn specialises in distributing archival television programmes, predominantly licensed from the BBC and ITV.

ANGEL PRODUCTIONS

8 Hillside Gardens, London N6 5ST
Tel: 020 8444 155534
E-mail: enquiries@angelproductions.co.uk
Web: www.angelproductions.co.uk

 Video tapes and DVDs for equality and HR training in the workplace. Also recent networkable resources for the education sector on viva technique and the student/supervisor relationship, produced in conjunction with Birkbeck, University of London. The company can also supply re-edited versions for specific institutions.

ARTEFACT MEDIA

1 Park View Road, Brighton, BN3 7BF
E-mail: orders@artefactmedia.com
Web: www.artefactmedia.com/
The online film store specialises in selling international documentaries on DVD and VHS, including a wide range of difficult-to-find films.

ARTIFICIAL EYE

14 King Street, London WC2E 8HR
Tel: 020 7240 5353 **Fax:** 020 7240 5242
E-mail: info@artificial-eye.com
Web: www.artificial-eye.com
Independent film and video distributor with an emphasis on foreign language titles.

AVP

School Hill Centre, Chepstow, Monmouthshire NP16 5PH
Tel: 01291 625 439 **Fax:** 01291 629 671
E-mail: info@avp.co.uk
Web: http://avp.100megs28.com
Since 1969, a major supplier of audio-visual materials in all curriculum areas to schools in the UK.

BBC ACTIVE

Mezzanine, 80 The Strand, London WC2R 0RL
Tel: 020 7010 6965 **Fax:** 020 8433 2916
E-mail: bbcactive.bbcstudies@pearson.com
Web: www.bbcactive.com

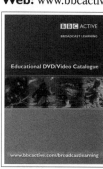

The BBC Active site, now run by Pearson Education, brings together the previously separate BBC collections covering English Language Learning (formerly BBC RLT), resources for foreign language learning, and the BBC School Shop. In addition, the Broadcast Learning section of the site (previously known as BBC Videos for Education and Training or BBC Learning) lists a selection of the general output broadcast programmes that BBC Active can supply for purchase by educational institutions. If a particular programme is not listed in this section it can be requested and supplied 'on demand'.

BBC RADIO COLLECTION

BBC Audiobooks, St James House, The Square, Lower Bristol Road, Bath BA2 3BH
Tel: 0800 136919 **Fax:** 01225 448005
E-mail: radio.collection@bbc.co.uk
Web: www.bbcworldwide.com/spokenword
BBC audio materials available commercially. The BBC Radio Collection is part of BBC Audiobooks and currently has more than 800 titles published across five main genres: Fiction and Drama, Non Fiction, Comedy, Children's and Poetry.

BFI DISTRIBUTION

21 Stephen Street, London W1P 2LN
Tel: 020 7957 8938
Web: www.bfi.org.uk
The British Film Institute is a specialist non-theatric rental distributor of international fiction and documentary films on 16mm and 35mm film, as well as VHS and DVD video.

BFI FILMSTORE

Belvedere Road, South Bank, Waterloo SE1 8XT
Tel: 020 7815 1350
E-mail: filmstore@bfi.org.uk
Web: http://filmstore.bfi.org.uk/

The British Film Institute releases its own productions as well as a variety of film and television materials made by European, American and Japanese companies. All BFI-published titles are available through the usual retail and mail order outlets, as well as via the Filmstore website. The Filmstore shop at BFI Southbank stocks many more titles as well as film books, magazines, etc.

BOLLYWOOD DVDS

DVD LTD, First Base, Beacontree Plaza, Gillette Way, Reading RG2 0BS
Tel: 08708 553385 **Fax:** 08708 553386
E-mail: info@bollywooddvds.com
Web: www.bollywooddvds.com

Online supplier of Bollywood DVDs organised by language. A number of films have English subtitles. The catalogue also has a section on religious films.

BRITISH LIBRARY ONLINE SHOP

96 Euston Road, London NW1 2DB
Tel: 020 7412 7735 **Fax:** 020 7412 7172
E-mail: bl-shop@bl.uk
Web: http://shop.bl.uk/mall/
departmentpage.cfm/BritishLibrary/87294/1/1
A range of audio publications related to the collections of the British Library's Sound Archive. Historical topics, wildlife sounds, world music, and art & literature are particularly strongly represented. There are also a few DVDs, videos and CD-ROMs based on holdings in the BL.

BRITISH UNIVERSITIES FILM & VIDEO COUNCIL

77 Wells Street, London W1T 3QJ
Tel: 020 7393 1503 **Fax:** 020 7393 1555
E-mail: services@bufvc.ac.uk
Web: www.bufvc.ac.uk/services/distribution
The BUFVC's distribution library includes Stanley Milgram's OBEDIENCE, Virgilio Tosi's THE ORIGINS OF SCIENTIFIC CINEMATOGRAPHY and two series of InterUniversity History Film Consortium films which make extensive use of archive footage.

BULLFROG FILMS

P.O. Box 149, Oley, PA 19547, USA
Tel: +1 610 779-8226 **Fax:** +1 610 370-1978
E-mail: video@bullfrogfilms.com
Web: www.bullfrogfilms.com/
Bullfrog Films is the oldest and largest publisher of videos and films about the environment in the United States. 'Environment' is defined broadly and the collection includes programmes on ecology, energy, agriculture, indigenous peoples, women's studies, genetics, marine biology, sustainable development, community regeneration, economics, ethics, and conflict resolution. In recent years they have released many films about developing countries, globalization, changing gender roles, and human rights. Styles range from animation to drama and from personal essay to investigative documentary.

CHARTBUSTERS

Premier House, Units 16-18, 8 Union Street, Luton LU1 3AN
Tel: 01582 707 172
E-mail: enquiries@findthatfilm.com
Web: www.chart-busters.co.uk/index.php
Although it confusingly also uses the trading name of *Findthatfilm.com*, Chartbusters after twenty years still offers a mail order service supplying new, rare and deleted DVDs and videos. A free Videohunt search service is available. All videos are in PAL standard and all DVDs region 2 for UK use.

CINENOVA

40 Rosebery Avenue, London EC1R 4RX
E-mail: info@cinenova.org.uk
Web: www.cinenova.org.uk
Films made by, and predominantly for, women, in the categories of experimental films, narrative feature films, artists' film and video, and documentary and educational videos.

CLASSROOM VIDEO

St Thomas Court, Thomas Lane, Redcliffe, Bristol BS1 6JG
Tel: 0117 929 1924 **Fax:** 0117 930 4345
E-mail: orders@classroomvideo.co.uk
Web: www.classroomvideo.co.uk
Educational film specialists with a library of 400 programmes in most subjects covered in primary and secondary schools. All programmes are supplied with teacher's notes and many are tailored specifically to the National Curriculum.

COACHWISE

Chelsea Close, Off Amberley Road, Armley, Leeds LS12 4HP
Tel: 0113 201 5555 **Fax:** 0113 231 9606
E-mail: enquiries@1st4sport.com
Web: www.1st4sport.com
Specialists in sports coaching, fitness training and physical education.

CONCORD MEDIA

22 Hines Rd, Ipswich IP3 9BG
Tel: 01473 726012, **Fax:** 01473 274531
E-mail: sales@concordmedia.org.uk
Web: www.concordvideo.co.uk
A long-established, not-for-profit organisation with a large collection of videos, specialising in the sectors of general and mental health, child care, race relations, war and peace, addictions, the third world, ecology, civil rights, personal relationships and social work training. Concord also handles titles made by the Arts Council. Formerly known as Concord Video and Film Council.

CONSTRUCTION INDUSTRY TRAINING BOARD PUBLICATIONS BOOKSHOP

CITB-ConstructionSkills, Bircham Newton, Kings Lynn, Norfolk PE31 6RH
Tel: 01485 577577
E-mail: information.centre@citb.co.uk
Web: www.cskills.org/workinconstr/publications/index.aspx
Films made for health and safety training within the construction industry.

CONTEMPORARY ARTS MEDIA

213 Park Street, South Melbourne, Victoria 3205, Australia
Tel: +61 8 9336 1587 **Fax:** +61 8 9335 3198
E-mail: order@artfilms.com.au
Web: www.artfilms.com.au/
A major distributor of videos relating to all aspects of the visual and performing arts. Based in Australia and formerly known as Hush Video.

CONTENDER ENTERTAINMENT

120 New Cavendish Street, London W1W 6XX
Tel: 020 7907 3773 **Fax:** 020 7907 3777
E-mail: gchurch@contendergroup.com
Web: www.contendergroup.com
Distributes contemporary film and television titles, many licensed from the BBC. Focuses particularly on long running series and one-off dramas released directly after transmission.

CULTURESHOP.ORG

10/12 Picton Street, Bristol BS6 5QA
Tel: 0117 942 7813
Web: www.cultureshop.org/contactus.php?
An online distributor of independent videos, aiming to bring the work of campaigning or video activist groups to a wider audience.

DANCE BOOKS

The Old Bakery, 4 Lenten Street, Alton, Hampshire GU34 1HG
Tel: 01420 86138 **Fax:** 01420 86142
E-mail: www.dancebooks.co.uk/contact.asp
Web: www.dancebooks.co.uk
Catalogue of about 2,500 international videos, DVDs, CDs and books relating to all types of dance.

DAVIDSON FILMS

735 Tank Farm Road, Ste 210, San Luis Obispo, California 94301, USA
Tel: +1 805 594 0422 **Fax:** +1 805 594 0532
E-mail: dfi@davidsonfilms.com
Web: www.davidsonfilms.com/
A US-based production and distribution company specialising in films relating to psychology, gerontology, child development, and neuroscience. Many of these feature footage or interviews with eminent scientists.

DOCUMENTARY EDUCATIONAL RESOURCES

101 Morse Street, Watertown, MA 02472 USA
Tel: +1 617 926 0491 **Fax:** +1 617 926 9519
E-mail: docued@der.org
Web: www.der.org

American company with an extensive catalogue of documentary films from around the world on ethnology, anthropology, world cultures, religion, women's studies and human rights. Preview clips of many titles can always be seen on YouTube.

EARTHSTATION1.COM

J.C. Kaelin, PO Box 1432, Bayonne, NJ 07002-6432, USA
E-mail: jckaelin@prosperohouse.com

Web: www.earthstation1.com

Specialises in US archive films, particularly vintage radio and public service films and broadcasts that have been digitally restored.

EDUCATIONAL BROADCASTING SERVICES TRUST

EBST online, Hamlin Way, Hardwick Narrows, Kings Lynn, Norfolk PE30 4NG

Tel: 08450 523948

E-mail: www.ebst.co.uk/shop/ index.php?main_page=contact_us

Web: www.ebst.co.uk/shop/

Educational materials that can be re-edited and customised for specific institutional use, produced in collaboration with consortia of university and college academics and media departments. The series include Maths for Engineers, Shotlist, and the Skillbank vocational skills training programmes. For sale on DVD or via download.

EINSTEIN NETWORK

67-74 Saffron Hill, London EC1N 8QX

Tel: 020 7693 7777 **Fax:** 020 7693 7788

E-mail: info@einstein-network.com

Web: www.einstein-network.com

An annual subscription service supplying regular professional development programmes, produced in-house, to subscribers of its sector-specific channels - accountancy, business, law, architecture, civil engineering, planning, surveying. An online portal service gives access to new and archived programmes and is taking over from the original video/DVD, CD-ROM delivery system.

ELECTRIC SKY

1 Clifton Mews, Clifton Hill, Brighton BN1 3HR

Tel: 01273 224440 **Fax:** 01273 224250

E-mail: info@electricsky.com

Web: www.electricsky.com/shop_results.aspx

A distributor specialising in quality factual television programmes, some of which are available for sale on DVD.

EUREKA ENTERTAINMENT

Unit 9 Ironbridge Close, Great Central Way, London NW10 0UF UK

Tel: 020 8459 8054 **Fax:** 020 8459 5162

E-mail: info@eurekavideo.co.uk

Web: http://eurekavideo.co.uk/

An independent distributor specialising in releasing classic and early/silent films on DVD, including the MASTERS OF CINEMA collection.

FACETS MULTI MEDIA

1517 W. Fullerton Avenue, Chicago, Illinois 60614, USA

Tel: +1 773 281 9075 **Fax:** +1 773 929 5437

E-mail: sales@facets.org

Web: www.facets.org/asticat

A pioneering US distributor and archive of over 65,000 independent, art, classic, documentary, silent, experimental and children's films on DVD.

FENMAN TRAINING

28 St Thomas Place, Cambridgeshire Business Park, Ely CB7 4EX

Tel: 01353 665533 **Fax:** 01353 663644

E-mail: service@fenman.co.uk

Web: www.fenman.co.uk

DVDs with accompanying study materials covering all aspects of workplace and management training.

FILM EDUCATION

21-22 Poland Street, London W1F 8QQ

Tel: 020 7851 9450 **Fax:** 020 7439 3218

E-mail: postbox@filmeducation.org

Web: www.filmeducation.org

Producer of film-specific DVD and CD-ROM materials and online resources for students studying Media Studies within the National Curriculum. Most of the resources are free to schools.

FILM VAULT

Oxford OX44 9EJ

Tel: 0845 500 57 57 **Fax:** 01865 327600

E-mail: mail@filmvault.co.uk

Web: www.filmvault.co.uk

A well-established service specialising in finding deleted and hard-to-find videos and DVDs from around the world in PAL format. Secondhand films are all checked for technical quality before despatch.

FILMBANK DISTRIBUTORS

Warner House, 98 Theobalds Road, London WC1X 8WB
Tel: 020 7984 5957/8 **Fax:** 020 7984 5951
E-mail: info@filmbank.co.uk
Web: www.filmbank.co.uk
The main source in the UK for non-theatrical presentations of feature films, available on 16mm as well as VHS and DVD video.

FILMS FOR THE HUMANITIES & SCIENCES

PO Box 2053, Princeton NJ 08543-2053, USA
Tel: +1 609 671 1000 **Fax:** +1 609 671 0266
E-mail: custserv@films.com
Web: http://ffh.films.com/
American company specialising in video materials aimed at the HE and FE education market.

GOWER PUBLISHING

Direct Sales, Bookpoint Ltd, 130 Milton Park, Oxon OX14 4SB
Tel: 01235 827730 **Fax:** 01235 400454
E-mail: gower@bookpoint.co.uk
Web: www.ashgate.com/default.aspx?page=2564
Gower publishes two main video and DVD training series: the People Skills series of 20 programmes for training and developing communication skills; the Takeaway Training series of short, practical training films providing managers, supervisors and staff with techniques, advice and ideas on some of the key areas of their job.

GRANT AND CUTLER

55-57 Great Marlborough Street, London W1F 7AY
Tel: 020 7734 2012 **Fax:** 020 7734 9272
E-mail: contactus@grantandcutler.com
Web: www.grantandcutler.com
An important source of foreign language VHS and DVD releases covering more than 30 languages.

HEALTH AND SAFETY EXECUTIVE VIDEOS

HSE Bookfinder, PO Box 1999, Sudbury Suffolk CO10 2WA.
Tel: 01787 881165

E-mail: hsebooks@hse.gsi.gov.uk
Web: www.hsebooks.com
Videos and DVDs, along with printed publications, produced by the government's Health & Safety Executive to help protect people against risks to health or safety arising out of work activities.

HOWARD HUGHES MEDICAL INSTITUTE

4000 Jones Bridge Road, Chevy Chase, MD 20815-2789, USA
Tel: +1 301 215 8500
E-mail: webmaster@hhmi.org
Web: www.hhmi.org/catalog/main?action=home
A number of programmes on topics including evolution, human weight regulation, RNA, genetic aspects of cardiovascular disease, and laboratory skills are available free on DVD. Other resources are available online.

HUMAN KINETICS EUROPE

107 Bradford Road, Stanningley, Leeds LS28 6AT
Tel: 0113 255 5665 **Fax:** 0113 255 5885
E-mail: custserv@hkeurope.com
Web: www.humankinetics.com
A US company with a UK affiliate specialising in productions dealing with physical activity including health and sport.

I. A. RECORDINGS

PO Box 476, Telford, Shropshire TF7 4RB
Tel: 01907 224509
E-mail: info@iarecordings.org
Web: www.iarecordings.org
I.A. Recordings specialises in industrial archaeology and is dedicated to recording past and present industry on film and High Definition video, recording working industry as well as the remains of past industries.

ILLUMINATIONS

19-20 Rheidol Mews, Rheidol Terrace, Islington London N1 8NU
Tel: 020 7288 8400 **Fax:** 020 7288 8488
E-mail: cat@illuminationsmedia.co.uk
Web: www.illuminationsmedia.co.uk/
Illuminations produces and distributes programmes on arts-related subjects, some of which

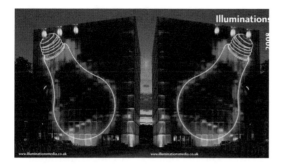

are made for television, and others in conjunction with cultural institutions.

IMPERIAL WAR MUSEUM

Online Store, Distribution Centre, IWM Duxford, Duxford, Cambs CB2 4QR
Tel: 01223 499 345 **Fax:** 01223 839 688
E-mail: iwmshop@iwm.org.uk
Web: www.iwmshop.org.uk
A range of CD and DVD titles covering the two World Wars. Many are compilations of films from the IWM's film collection.

INSIGHT MEDIA

2162 Broadway, New York, NY 10024-0621, USA
Tel: +1 212 721 6316 **Fax:** +1 212 799 5309
E-mail: custserv@insight-media.com
Web: www.insight-media.com
US-based distributor of an extensive range of DVD, video and CD-ROM titles for university, secondary and vocational education. Catalogue divided into the following sections: Art, Architecture & Design; Business & Economics; Communication; Education; Engineering; Nursing & Allied Health; Physical Education; Science & Agriculture; Social Sciences.

INSTITUTE OF CONTEMPORARY ARTS

ICA, The Mall, London SW1Y 5AH
Tel: 020 7930 0493
Web: www.ica.org.uk/?lid=49
The ICA bookshop sells a range of DVDs on and by film theorists, compilations of short experimental and animated works, documentaries, as well as DVDs on video and performance art and installations. Also an eclectic collection of audio CDs.

INSTITUTION OF CIVIL ENGINEERS

Library, 1 Great George Street, London SW1P 3AA
Tel: 020 7665 2251 **Fax:** 020 7976 7610
E-mail: library@ice.org.uk
Web: www.ice.org.uk/knowledge/knowledge_library.asp
The ICE library has hundreds of videos and a growing collection of DVDs for loan to members.

IWF - WISSEN UND MEDIEN GMBH

Nonnenstieg 72, D-37075 Göttingen, Germany
Tel: +49 551 5024-0
E-mail: iwf-goe@iwf.de
Web: www.iwf.de/iwf/default_en.htm
The Infoteque contains details of 8,500 films for use in university-level teaching and research. The collection is strong in scientific and ethnographic films. Programmes are for sale on DVD, video or CD-ROM and some can be previewed free online. Many films have English commentaries.

KULTUR FILMS

195 Highway 36, West Long Branch, NJ 07764-1304, USA
Tel: +1 932 229 2243 **Fax:** +1 732 229 0066
E-mail: info@kultur.com
Web: http://estore.websitepros.com/1652646/StoreFront.bok
Kultur distributes over 1000 of the world's greatest performing arts and cultural programming titles on DVD, featuring the legends of opera, ballet and classical music. It also offers a large collection of art, literature, and history programmes, as seen on US public television, The Discovery Channel, The History Channel and other networks.

LEEDS ANIMATION WORKSHOP

45 Bayswater Row, Leeds LS8 5LF
Tel: 0113 248 4997 **Fax:** 0113 248 4997
E-mail: info@leedsanimation.org.uk
Web: www.leedsanimation.org.uk
Maker and distributor of animated films and videos on social and education issues.

LONDON MATHEMATICAL SOCIETY

De Morgan House, 57-58 Russell Square, London WC1B 4HS

Tel: 020 7637 3686 **Fax:** 020 7323 3655
Email: lms@lms.ac.uk
Web: www.lms.ac.uk/
Video and DVD recordings of twice-yearly London Mathematical Society Popular Lectures, which aim to present exciting topics and interesting applications in mathematics to a wide audience, including those studying A-level mathematics.

LUX

18 Shacklewell Lane, London E8 2EZ
Tel: 020 7503 3980 **Fax:** 020 7503 1606
E-mail: info@lux.org.uk
Web: www.lux.org.uk
The premier UK source for non-theatrical video and film materials made by video artists and experimental filmmakers, including the London Film-makers' Co-op.

MEDIA EDUCATION FOUNDATION

60 Masonic Street, Northampton, Massachusetts 01060, USA
Tel: +1 413 584 8500 **Fax:** +1 413 586 8398
E-mail: info@mediaed.org
Web: www.mediaed.org/
The MEF produces and distributes documentary films and other educational resources to inspire critical reflection on the social, political and cultural impact of the mass media, particularly in the US.

MENTAL HEALTH SHOP

28 Castle Street, Kingston Upon Thames, Surrey, KT1 1SS
Tel: 0845 456 0455
E-mail: queries@mentalhealthshop.org
Web: www.mentalhealthshop.org/
 Distributor of video tapes, DVDs and printed materials relating to severe mental illness and other mental health problems, produced by Mental Health Media and Rethink. Materials are aimed at health professionals, people using mental health services and their carers.

METRODOME DISTRIBUTION

3rd Floor, 72-74 Dean Street, London W1D 3SG
Tel: 020 7534 2060 **Fax:** 020 7534 2062
Web: www.metrodomegroup.com/
Specialist distributor of independent, art house films, both theatrically and then on DVD.

NASA

Central Operation of Resources for Educators (CORE), Lorain County JVS-CORE, 15181 Route 58 South Oberlin, OH 44074, USA
Tel: +1 440 775-1400 **Fax:** +1 440 775-1460
E-mail: NASA_order@lcjvs.net
Web: http://education.nasa.gov/edprograms/core/home/index.html
CORE is a worldwide distribution centre for NASA's educational multimedia materials, selling DVDs at low cost. Audio and video podcasts as well as streamed videos are also available on the multimedia section of the main NASA website: www.nasa.gov/multimedia/index.html.

NATIONAL THEATRE BOOKSHOP

National Theatre, South Bank, London SE1 9PX
Tel: 020 7452 3456 **Fax:** 020 7452 3457
E-mail: bookshop@nationaltheatre.org.uk
Web: www.nationaltheatre.org.uk/24979/online-bookshop/bookshop.html
A mail order service supplying videos, DVDs and sound recordings of stage performances and film or television adaptations of plays.

OLD POND PUBLISHING

Dencora Business Centre, 36 White House Road, Ipswich IP1 5LT
Tel: 01473 238200 **Fax:** 01473 23821
E-mail: enquiries@oldpond.com
Web: www.oldpond.com
Titles relating to agriculture and farming as well as specialised machinery and vehicles.

ONEDOTZERO

Unit 212C Curtain House, 134-146 Curtain Road, London EC2A 3AR
Fax: 020 7729 0057
E-mail: info@onedotzero.com
Web: www.onedotzero.com/home.php

Distributes DVD compilations of some of the best and most innovative talent in moving image work from around the world, much of which has been showcased at Onedotzero festivals.

OPEN UNIVERSITY

Open University Worldwide, Walton Hall, Milton Keynes MK7 6AA
Tel: 01908 858793 **Fax:** 01908 858787
E-mail: ouw-customer-services@open.ac.uk
Web: www.ouw.co.uk

Marcus Du Sautoy in THE STORY OF MATHS, an Open University production for BBC4.

Materials created as part of Open University courses. Also programmes such as COAST, NATION ON FILM and THE MONEY PROGRAMME broadcast as general BBC output and produced jointly by the BBC and OU.

OXFORD EDUCATIONAL RESOURCES

PO Box 106, Kidlington, Oxon OX5 1HY
Tel: 01865 842552 **Fax:** 01865 842551
E-mail: enquiries@oer.co.uk
Web: www.oer.co.uk

OER's audio-visual medical library consists of over 6000 health-related programmes, from basic school health education through to the most advanced techniques. They include training and education programmes for doctors & surgeons, nurses, healthcare personnel and managers as well as patients. Produced in conjunction with internationally recognised medical experts, mainly from the UK, USA and Canada.

PAVILION PUBLISHING

Richmond House, Richmond Road, Brighton, East Sussex BN2 3RL
Tel: 01273 623222 **Fax:** 01273 625526
E-mail: info@pavpub.com
Web: www.pavpub.com
Print and video/DVD-based training materials on topics in health and social care. Areas covered include learning disability, mental health, young people and children, adult protection, and older people.

PIDGEON DIGITAL

World Microfilms, Microworld House, PO Box 35488, London NW8 6WD
Tel: 020 7586 4499 **Fax:** 020 7722 1068
E-mail: microworld@ndirect.co.uk
Web: www.pidgeondigital.com
Originally a series of tape-slide talks in which leading architects and designers discuss their life and work. The 200+ programmes have now been digitised and are delivered online.

QUANTUM LEAP

1A Great Northern Street, Huntingdon, Cambridgeshire PE29 7HJ
Tel: 01480 450006 **Fax:** 01480 456686
E-mail: customerservices@qleap.co.uk
Web: www.qleap.co.uk
Distributor of many non-fiction titles on a wide variety of subjects, also available through retail outlets.

REVOLVER ENTERTAINMENT

10 Lambert Place, London W11 2SH
Tel: 020 7243 4300 **Fax:** 020 7243 4302
E-mail: info@revolutiongroup.com

Web: www.revolvergroup.com
Distributor of a collection of arty and edgy DVDs in all genres, including documentary.

ROLAND COLLECTION OF FILMS AND VIDEOS ON ART

Peasmarsh, East Sussex TN31 6XJ
Tel: 01797 230421 **Fax:** 01797 230677
E-mail: info@rolandcollection.com
Web: www.rolandcollection.com
Sizeable collection of international documentaries covering all aspects of art including architecture, archaeology, art appreciation and restoration, as well as some programmes on literature and creative writing, on a pay-per-view basis.

ROYAL ANTHROPOLOGICAL INSTITUTE

50 Fitzroy Street, London W1T 5BT
Tel: 020 7387 0455 **Fax:** 020 7388 8817
E-mail: film@therai.org.uk
Web: www.therai.org.uk/film/video_sales.html

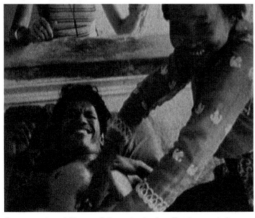

From a series of films on Balinese healer Jero Tapakan made by anthropologists Timothy Asch, Linda Connor and Patsy Asch.

Distributor of a large collection of internationally produced films, videos and DVDs on anthropology and ethnography.

SAFETY MEDIA

5a Kinmel Park, Abergele Road, Bodelwyddan, Rhyl LL18 5TX
Tel: 0845 3451703 **Fax:** 01745 536195
E-mail: sales@safetymedia.co.uk

Web: www.safetymedia.co.uk
Producer of DVD and video materials covering aspects of health and safety at work.

ST GEORGE'S HOSPITAL MEDICAL SCHOOL

Academic Services Dept, Cranmer Terrace, London SW17 0RE
Tel: 020 8725 2701 **Fax:** 020 8725 0075
E-mail: d.cleverly@sghms.ac.uk
Web: http://gp.sghms.ac.uk/depts/academic-services/productions/productions_home.cfm

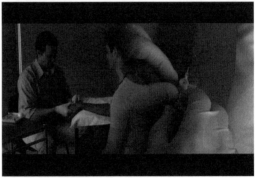

Still from CANNULATION (2007).

A range of programmes produced by St George's Media Services for use in medical training.

SCHUMACHER COLLEGE

The Old Postern, Dartington, Devon, TQ9 6EA
Tel: 01803 860057 **Fax:** 01803 866899
E-mail: captainw@zoom.co.uk
Web: www.captainw.com/webvidm.ht
Videotapes of lectures given at Schumacher College by leading thinkers on topics including ecology, spiritual enrichment, the ethics of globalisation, cosmology, philosophy, business, renewable energy, technology, economics, and sustainable development.

SECOND SIGHT FILMS

Tel: 020 8977 0553 **Fax:** 020 8977 1470
E-mail: info@secondsightfilms.co.uk
Web www.secondsightfilms.co.uk
A UK DVD distributor of celebrated classics and cult cinema from around the world, as well as some television titles.

SECONDRUN

E-mail: info@secondrundvd.com
Web: www.secondrundvd.com/
A niche-market video label and distributor, specialising in being the first to release important and award-winning films from around the world.

TEACHERS' TV

6-18 Berners Street, London W1T 3LN
Tel: 020 7182 7430
E-mail: info@teachers.tv
Web: www.teachers.tv

John Humphrys presents THE TEACHING CHALLENGE (2006).

An important producer and supplier of material for teachers across the curriculum to use in the classroom, as well as providing advice on best educational practice and management issues. Programmes available via digital television or online viewing.

TRUMEDIA

PO Box 316, Kidlington, Oxon OX5 2ZY
Tel: 01865 847837 **Fax:** 01865 847837
E-mail: sales@trumedia.co.uk
Web: www.trumedia.co.uk
Trumedia supplies videos and DVDs to UK schools, colleges and universities and is geared up to take official orders from educational institutions. The catalogue highlights programmes likely to be of use in the curriculum, but the company can supply any video in current UK distribution, as well as some deleted titles. Particularly strong in the areas of English literature and drama, as well history, natural history, business studies and foreign language films.

TRUST FOR THE STUDY OF ADOLESCENCE

23 New Road, Brighton BN1 1WZ
Tel: 01273 693311 **Fax:** 01273 679907
E-mail: info@tsa.uk.com
Web: www.tsa.uk.com
Creates and distributes resources for professionals working with young people, as well as for parents of teenagers and teenagers themselves.

TV CHOICE

PO Box 597, Bromley, Kent BR2 0YB
Tel: 020 8464 7402 **Fax:** 020 8464 7845
E-mail: tvchoiceuk@aol.com
Web: www.tvchoice.uk.com
A producer and distributor of educational videos and DVDs, most with support materials, designed for use in UK schools, colleges and universities. Wide coverage across the curriculum.

TVE

21 Elizabeth Street London SW1W 9RP
Tel: 020 7901 8855 **Fax:** 020 7901 8856
E-mail: distribution@tve.org.uk
Web: www.tve.org/
TVE's Moving Pictures Online is a searchable catalogue of over 600 documentary, drama and animation films on environment, development, health and human rights issues. DVDs sold for educational use only.

UNDERCURRENTS

Old Exchange, Pier Street, Swansea SA1 1RY
Tel: 01792 455900
E-mail: info@undercurrents.org
Web: www.undercurrents.org
A not-for-profit producer and distributor of UK and global counter-culture content. Working with video makers and communities who have been marginalised or overlooked by TV broadcasters, Undercurrents focuses on social and environmental justice issues and has some unique footage of campaigns and video activism.

UNIVERSITY OF LEEDS

Media Services, Leeds LS2 9JT
Tel: 0113 343 2660 **Fax:** 0113 343 2669
E-mail: mediaservices@leeds.ac.uk
Web: http://mediant.leeds.ac.uk/vtcatalogue/

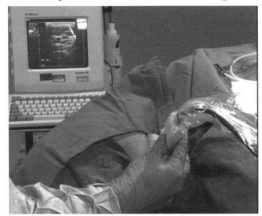

Still from LOCATION AND CANNULATION OF CENTRAL VEIN USING ULTRASOUND (Leeds TV).

Programmes produced for use in university teaching. Particularly strong in the areas of medical and nurse training, science, engineering, surveying, and French and Russian language and literature.

UNIVERSITY OF NEWCASTLE

Television Services, Information Systems & Services, The Medical Centre, Framlington Place, Newcastle-upon-Tyne NE2 4HH
Tel: 0191 222 6633
E-mail: television@ncl.ac.uk
Web: www.ncl.ac.uk/iss/tvservices/
otherservices/video_sales.php
Programmes produced for use in teaching and research. A wide range of subjects are covered, but the collection is particularly strong in the areas of medicine (surgery, obstetrics and gynaecology), education, and Dorothy Heathcote's world-famous drama workshops.

UNIVERSITY OF SHEFFIELD

Learning & Teaching Services, 5 Favell Road, Sheffield S3 7QX
Tel: 0114 222 0400 **Fax:** 0114 222 4069
E-mail: lets@shef.ac.uk

Web: www.shef.ac.uk/lets/techno/catalogue
LeTS holds a large back catalogue of high quality educational video programmes it has produced, all of which are available in DVD format. The 100+ titles cover most academic subject areas and contain valuable sequences in the form of animations and demonstrations.

UNIVERSITY OF THE WEST OF ENGLAND: THE VIDEO PROJECT

School of the Built & Natural Environment, UWE Bristol, Frenchay Campus, Coldharbour Lane, Bristol BS16 1QY
Tel: 0117 328 3008
E-mail: Duncan.Marshall@uwe.ac.uk
Web: http://environment.uwe.ac.uk/video/
index.htm
A series of videos on domestic building construction and another on building history and conservation.

UNIVIEW WORLDWIDE

PO Box 20, Hoylake, Wirral, Cheshire CH48 7HY
Tel: 0151 625 3453 **Fax:** 0151 625 3707
E-mail: sales@uniview.co.uk
Web: www.uniview.co.uk
Distributor for a wide range of educational materials with particular strengths in psychology as well as biology, sociology, sports science, health and child studies.

VEGA SCIENCE TRUST

Sussex Innovation Centre, Science Park Square, Brighton BN1 9SB
Tel: 01273 678726
E-mail: vega@vega.org.uk
Web: www.vega.org.uk
Well-established maker and distributor of more than 200 programmes on science, technology, engineering and mathematics, many of which have been broadcast. Separate series consist of interviews with eminent scientists, issues of current scientific concern, the Royal Institution Discourses, scientific master classes, and recent research projects. Most programmes are for sale on video and DVD, as well as for free viewing via the website.

Still from CAREERS IN SCIENCE, from the *Snapshots* series. (Courtesy of Vega Science Trust)

VIDEO ARTS

6-7 St Cross Street, London EC1N 8UA
Tel: 0845 601 2531 **Fax:** 0207 400 4900
E-mail: info@videoarts.co.uk
Web: www.videoarts.com
Maker of highly regarded films for business training and education management, well known for featuring such celebrities as John Cleese, who co-founded the company in 1972. Now owned by Tinopolis.

VIDEOS FOR PATIENTS

The Production Tree, Unit G16, Shepherd's Building, Rockley Road, London W14 0DA
Tel: 020 7610 5599 **Fax:** 020 7610 5333
E-mail: sales@productiontree.co.uk
Web: www.videosforpatients.co.uk
Sister company to Video Arts, which makes programmes dealing with improving the experience of patients by giving essential information on medical conditions.

VIDEOTEL INTERNATIONAL

84 Newman Street, London W1T 3EU
Tel: 020 7299 1800 **Fax:** 020 7299 1818
E-mail: mail@videotelmail.com
Web: www.videotel.co.uk
Originally a maker and distributor of training products for the marine industry, focusing on onboard training, shipping and legislation. The range has extended to include specialist programmes for oil, gas and chemical tankers, container, refrigerated cargo, passenger and RO-RO ships, offshore operations, pilots, surveyors, port and terminal operators.

VIEWTECH EDUCATIONAL MEDIA

7-8 Falcons Gate, Northavon Business Centre, Dean Road, Yate, Bristol BS37 5HN
Tel: 01454 858055 **Fax:** 01454 858056
E-mail: mail@viewtech.co.uk
Web: www.viewtech.co.uk
For over 25 years Viewtech has been distributing programmes from leading specialist educational producers. All subjects within the primary and secondary curriculum are covered, and there is also a range of material to support further/higher education and vocational training courses.

WELLCOME TRUST: MOVING IMAGE AND SOUND COLLECTIONS

183 Euston Road, London NW1 2BE
Tel: 020 7611 8766
E-mail: mfac@wellcome.ac.uk
Web: http://library.wellcome.ac.uk/misc.html
The collection consists of more than 2000 films, video productions and television programmes. The broadcast material relates largely or wholly to contemporary or near-contemporary aspects of health and medicine, and the remainder to historical aspects. There are nearly 600 non-broadcast videos and films, mainly of specialist-medical or archival interest. Viewing on Wellcome premises only.

WOMEN MAKE MOVIES

462 Broadway, Suite 500WS (at Grand Street), New York NY 10013, USA
Tel: +1 212 925 0606 **Fax:** +1 212 925 2052
E-mail: info@wmm.com
Web: www.wmm.com
US company distributing films made by, and predominantly for, women. The collection consists of more than 500 documentary, experimental, animation, dramatic and mixed-genre titles. The films and videotapes represent a diversity of styles, subjects and perspectives in women's lives.

WOODHEAD PUBLISHING

Abington Hall, Abington, Cambridge CB1 6AH
Tel: 01223 891358 **Fax:** 01223 893694
E-mail: wp@woodheadpublishing.com
Web: www.woodheadpublishing.com
Established in 1989, the company has a number of videos and DVDs in the fields of process engineering, metallurgy, timber processing, and materials.

WORLD MICROFILMS

PO Box 35488, St John's Wood, London NW8 6WD
Tel: 020 7586 4499 **Fax:** 020 722 1068
E-mail: microworld@ndirect.co.uk
Web: www.microworld.uk.com/
World Microfilms distributes the architecture programmes of Pidgeon Audiovisual, the Audio Forum collection of CDs for language learning, and the Sussex Tapes library of video and audio material for sixth form and undergraduate teaching. The Sussex Tapes collection is particularly strong in the fields of English, history and music.

YORK FILMS OF ENGLAND

23 Bradstone Avenue, Folkestone, Kent CT19 5AQ
Tel: 01303 226 234 **Fax:** 01303 858 196
E-mail: office@yorkfilms.com
Web: www.yorkfilms.com
York Films specialises in producing science programming for television, particularly space and astronomy. Several series are available for sale on DVD, as well as programmes on Nobel prizewinners, bee breeding and six programmes on the bicycle.

Image from the library of York Films.

FESTIVALS

This is a select listing of film festivals in the UK and overseas. The major source of information on film festivals worldwide is the British Council's Directory of International Film and Video Festivals, *listing over 600 international events. It is available at www.britfilms.com/ festivals.*

15-SECOND FILMS FESTIVAL

Web: www.15secondfilmfestival.com/
This festival's fifteen second silms are exactly twenty-five seconds in length – five seconds of opening titles, fifteen seconds for main body of film and five seconds of closing credits. Films can run picture and sound under the titles and end credits. Films must be presented on disc as an uncompressed Quicktime Movie

AFRICA IN MOTION

Web: www.africa-in-motion.org.uk
An annual festival, first held in 2006, that showcases classic and contemporary films from Africa as well as holding complementary events. Held in Edinburgh.

ANIMATED EXETER

Web: www.animatedexeter.co.uk
Films must be from the South West of England or South Wales.

AURORA FESTIVAL

Web: www.aurora.org.uk
Aurora is the new name for the Norwich International Animation Festival, which challenges the boundaries of animation. An art-focused, progressive event, it fuses artist retrospectives and thematic film programmes with debate, live performance and installations, alongside a selection of new work from across the world in wide-ranging competition programmes.

AV FESTIVAL

Web: www.avfest.co.uk

 A biennial international festival of electronic arts first held across venues in Newcastle, Gateshead, Sunderland and Middlesbrough in 2003. It showcases film, digital arts, music, games and new media, including many specially commissioned works. The programme features concerts, performances, film screenings, exhibitions and installations, and outdoor projections.

BABELGUM ONLINE FILM FESTIVAL

Web: www.babelgum.com/online-film-festival
This online festival was first held in 2007. Filmmakers are invited to upload their videos to the Babelgum website and enter one of four

categories: short film, mini masterpiece, animation, and documentary. Winners are decided by votes received from online viewers.

BACUP FILM FESTIVAL

Web: www.bacupfilmfestival.co.uk
Launched in 2007 in Lancashire, the short film festival (fiction titles must be longer than fifteen minutes, documentaries not more than twenty-five minutes) encourages entries from anyone for a modest £5 entry fee.

BELFAST FILM FESTIVAL

Web: www.belfastfilmfestival.org
Belfast Film Festival has a defined 'socio-political' focus on films, complemented by a commitment to bring the best of new international documentaries to Ireland in the Maysles Documentary Competition. Each year a range of films, speakers and seminars focussing on a selected theme provides a platform for debate and engagement between diverse sections of the audience.

BERWICK FILM AND MEDIA ARTS FESTIVAL

Web: www.berwickfilm-artsfest.com
Started in 2005, this festival at Berwick-upon-tweed is unusual in that part of its remit is to transform historical venues in the region into viewing centres for the duration of the Festival. It is a Biennale and the next is due in September 2009. In between there is a smaller scale Minifest, which takes places in November.

BEYOND TV

Web: www.undercurrents.org/beyondtv
BeyondTV is a week-long festival presented by Undercurrents, consisting of short movies, documentaries, music videos & animation. All films have a theme of social or environmental activism. Hosted in Swansea Marina, all proceeds from the festival go to supporting the charity work of Undercurrents.

BIRDS EYE VIEW FILM FESTIVAL

Web: www.birds-eye-view.co.uk
Begun in 2005, the Birds Eye View film festival showcases the best features, shorts and documen-taries from women filmmakers around the world, alongside special multi-media events and discussions. The festival is held in London across three venues: the ICA, BFI Southbank and the Curzon. Awards are presented for the best short, animation, documentary, with a special award for innovation.

BITE THE MANGO FILM FESTIVAL

Web: www.nationalmediamuseum.org.uk/btm/ 2008/index.asp
A festival of world cinema, including many premieres, held at the National Media Museum, Bradford. An eclectic mix of features, shorts, documentaries, masterclasses, seminars and star guests.

BLACK INTERNATIONAL FILM FESTIVAL

Web: http://www.vtelevision.co.uk/biff/
The Birmingham Black International Film Festival launched in 2007 and includes film, music, 'live' arts, and various education events in the form of seminars, exhibitions and master-classes. It also awards the Music, Video and Screen Awards (MVSA).

BRADFORD ANIMATION FESTIVAL

Web: www.nationalmediamuseum.org.uk/baf
This annual animation festival, which has been running since 1994, also hosts masterclasses, seminars, workshops, screenings and special

events led by some of the industry's top names. The festival culminates in the annual BAF Awards, which celebrate the very best in new animation from around the world.

BRADFORD INTERNATIONAL FILM FESTIVAL

Web: www.nationalmediamuseum.org.uk/bff
The Bradford International Film Festival, held every March since its launch in 1995, screens classics in the form of retrospectives as well a selection of ground-breaking, unusual and obscure new films. The festival includes a number of diverse strands, such as Cinefile, which features documentaries about films and film-makers, and Uncharted States of America, featuring emerging talent in the US independent film sector.

BRITDOC

Web: https://www.britdoc.org/festival/
Held in Oxford in July, Britdoc is a three-day annual festival showcasing short and feature-length documentaries from the UK. It provides a venue for leading international film producers, distributors and financiers to meet British film-makers face to face at structured networking events and pitching fora.

CAMBRIDGE FILM FESTIVAL

Web: www.cambridgefilmfestival.org.uk
Running for almost thirty years, the annual Cambridge Film Festival moved in 2008 from July to September and now has some outdoor screenings. Its programme includes new features, shorts, revivals and documentaries from around the world. In addition, the festival offers visits from actors and directors, fora, conferences, workshops and education events.

CAN FILM FESTIVAL

Web: www.lineout.org/index.cfm?page=canfest
The Leicester International Short Film Festival started in 1996 under the banner title of 'Seconds Out' and was intended as a means to exhibit work created by the east midlands filmmaking community. The CAN Festival has been an annual event since 2002.

CPH:DOX COPENHAGEN INTERNATIONAL DOCUMENTARY FILM FESTIVAL

Web: www.cphdox.dk
The largest international documentary festival in Scandinavia. Since 2003 CPH:DOX has issued an annual call for entries from worldwide independent, innovative and experimental cinema and visual arts projects. Devoted to supporting independent filmmaking from around the globe, the festival aims to break away from the mainstream, cross over artistic boundaries and discover new approaches to documentary filmmaking.

DEAFFEST

Web: www.deaffest.co.uk/Deaffest/index.html
Deaffest, the Deaf-led Film and Television Festival celebrates the talents of Deaf filmmakers and media artists. Events include screenings of films produced by UK and International Deaf filmmakers, Young Deaffest which showcases work produced by young Deaf filmmakers and panel discussions, networking opportunities and social events. Deaffest 2008 will be the tenth festival to be held in Wolverhampton since 1998.

DOCUMENT 6 INTERNATIONAL HUMAN RIGHTS DOCUMENTARY FILM FESTIVAL

Web: www.variant.randomstate.org/Doc6/doc6.html
Held annually in Glasgow, Document 6 presents a platform for both established and emerging documentary filmmakers to screen their work at the only UK festival dedicated to raising awareness of international human rights issues.

DOK.FEST

Web: www.dokfest-muenchen.de
This annual festival, founded in 1985 by the Munich documentary filmmakers association, showcases documentaries from around the world. There are various categories of award, some for international films and some for those made in Bavaria.

EAT OUR SHORTS

Web: www.nahemi.org/pages/index2.html

Annual two-day festival bringing together student filmmakers from all over the UK and Ireland to see each other's work and share experiences. This non-competitive festival is organised by the National Association for Higher Education in the Moving Image (NAHEMI). Twenty member schools from the UK and Ireland including all the Skillset Screen Academies are represented at the event.

EDINBURGH INTERNATIONAL FILM FESTIVAL

Web: www.edfilmfest.org.uk

An international film festival forming part of the annual Edinburgh Arts Festival. Categories include features, shorts, documentary, animation, music promos, experimental and young person's films.

EDINBURGH INTERNATIONAL TELEVISION FESTIVAL

Web: www.mgeitf.co.uk

The wide ranging programme of this major television event deals with key issues of the day and involves keynote lectures, preview screenings, masterclasses, interviews and networking parties. Founded in 1976 the Festival is held annually over the August bank holiday weekend and is attended by UK and international delegates representing the full spectrum of the industry including controllers, commissioners, producers, directors, marketers, new media companies, distributors and press.

ENCOUNTERS SHORT FILM FESTIVAL

Web: www.encounters-festival.org.uk

The Encounters Short Film Festival was brought about by the merger of the Brief Encounters International Short Film Festival with the Animated Encounters International Animation Festival. It is open to short films (less than 30 minutes in length) from around the world, including animation, documentary, drama, experimental or artists film and hybrid work. It provides a forum for emerging talent and established industry alike, designed to nurture creativity and innovation.

© Piotrek H. / SXC

EXPOSURES UK STUDENT FILM FESTIVALS

Web: www.exposuresfilmfestival.co.uk
A four-day festival of student films held annually in Manchester. Open to any moving image work on any platform, as long as it is less than 30 minutes long and made by a student at a UK educational institution. As well as featuring the best new filmmaking in categories – drama, documentary, animation, experimental and music video – Exposures hosts a range of masterclasses, premieres, workshops and discussions with key figures from film and television.

FOYLE FILM FESTIVAL

Web: www.foylefilmfestival.org
The Northern Ireland International Film Festival in now in its twenty-first year and incorporates screenings, master classes, interviews and education events as well as the Light In Motion (LIM) Awards..

GERMAN FILM FESTIVAL

Web: www.germanfilmfestival.co.uk
Since 1997 this annual festival has been organised by the German Film Service to promote a range of German documentaries, feature and short films. Screenings are held at the Curzon in London, but for the last few years a selection of the films has been shown at the Irish Film Institute in Dublin.

GLASGOW FILM FESTIVAL

Web: www.glasgowfilmfestival.org.uk
The international Glasgow Film Festival, first held in 2005, includes a section featuring some of the best of classic and contemporary documentaries as well as feature films. Open to submissions.

HOTDOCS

Web: www.hotdocs.ca
Hot Docs Canadian International Documentary Festival is North America's largest documentary festival. Each year, the festival presents a selection of more than 100 cutting-edge documentaries from Canada and around the globe. Through its industry programmes, the Festival also provides a full range of professional development, market and networking opportunities for documentary professionals.

HUMAN RIGHTS WATCH INTERNATIONAL FILM FESTIVAL

Web: www.hrw.org/iff/2007/about.html

Fiction, documentary and animated films and videos with a distinctive human rights theme. Each year, the festival's programming committee screens more than 500 films and videos to create a programme that represents a range of countries and issues, with equal weight being given to artistic merit and human rights content, Screenings are held in London and New York and are generally followed by discussion.

IMAGE ET SCIENCE

Web: www.image-science.cnrs.fr
Established in 1988 and organised by CNRS (Centre National de la Recherche Scientifique) the international festival is held each year in Paris. The festival includes awards for international television science programmes.

IMAGES OF BLACK WOMEN FILM FESTIVAL

Web: www.imagesofblackwomen.com
An international festival, held annually in London, which aims to celebrate women of African descent in their roles both on and behind the screen

IMPERIAL WAR MUSEUM STUDENT FILM FESTIVAL

Web: http://london.iwm.org.uk/server/show/ConWebDoc.2310
Since 2000 the IWM has held an annual Student Film Festival. The Festival offers the opportunity to students who have made films and videos incorporating archive film from the Museum's collection or about its subject matter, to have their work screened publicly in the cinema. Each title

screened in the Festival is also eligible to be entered into a competition.

INTERNATIONAL FESTIVAL OF ETHNOGRAPHIC FILM

Web: www.raifilmfest.org.uk
Sponsored by the Royal Anthropological Institute since 1985, this biennial festival is an itinerant event, moving from one university host to another. The principal aims of the festival are: to promote cultural diversity and intercultural dialogue through ethnographic film; to screen outstanding recent work in ethnographic film and related documentary genres; to showcase the work of young film-makers in these genres; to explore new trends in these genres and their influence upon one another and on visual anthropology; to provide a marketing platform for both international and British productions.

INTERNATIONAL FILMMAKER FESTIVAL

Web: www.filmmakerfestival.com/
Aims to bring together industry figures and potential filmmakers.

INTERNATIONAL SCIENCE FILM FESTIVAL

Web: www.caid.gr/isffa/about.html
Established in 2006, the festival is held in Athens and organised by CAID (the Centre of Applied Industrial Design). Scientific films aimed at the general public are screened and the festival provides an informal forum in which topical and thought-provoking scientific issues can be discussed with scientists. Seven awards are presented during the festival.

INTERNATIONAL SCREENWRITERS FESTIVAL

Web: www.screenwritersfestival.com
Covering film, television and new media, this festival is based in Cheltenham and focuses on the art, craft, and business of writing for the screen and focuses on meetings with professionals rather than screenings.

INTERNATIONAL STUDENT ETHNOGRAPHIC FILM FESTIVAL

Web: www.goldsmiths.ac.uk/iseff/
A 2-day festival organised by the Anthropology Society, Goldsmiths, University of London. The festival promotes documentary films, videos and interactive media dealing with socio-cultural processes in the widest sense, and screenings are followed by discussion. Submissions are sought from students around the world and two awards of £200 are offered.

ITALIAN FILM FESTIVAL UK

Web: www.italianfilmfestival.org.uk
This annual event showcases Italian cinema, both new and old. Based in Edinburgh, its screenings are held all over the UK.

JUNGE STERNE MUNICH INTERNATIONAL SHORT FILM FESTIVAL

Web: www.muc-intl.de
Founded in 2006, the Munich Short Film Festival is held in June, immediately prior to the main Munich film festival. It showcases the world's best contemporary short films.

LEEDS INTERNATIONAL FILM FESTIVAL

Web: www.leedsfilm.com
Films are shown in three strands: Official Selection highlights some of the best new films of the year; Cinema Versa – dedicated to inspirational documentary filmmaking and the exploration of unconventional cinema; Fanomenon – screening the best horror, sci-fi, fantasy, anime and action films from around the world. The festival also includes UK Film Week, retrospectives and archive film. The Leeds Young People's Festival (see below) is incorporated within the Leeds nternational Film Festival.

LEEDS YOUNG PEOPLE'S FILM FESTIVAL

Web: www.leedsyoungfilm.co.uk/
Organised and run by Leeds City Council as part of the Leeds International Film Festival, the Leeds Young People's Film Festival features short and feature films from around the world that are aimed at young people, as well as a series of workshops and masterclasses to encourage talented young people to get involved in the film industry. Awards are also made in two age categories.

London Film Festival See **The Times BFI London Film Festival**

LONDON INTERNATIONAL ANIMATION FESTIVAL (LIAF)

Web: www.liaf.org.uk
The London International Animation Festival screens more than 200 of the world's best short animated films at four venues around London. It provides an opportunity to see an extensive line-up of recent films in competition and specially curated programmes. LIAF aims to challenge and inspire audiences with thematic, aesthetic and technical diversity from award winners, outstanding industry veterans and newcomers who are exploring their talent on screen for the very first time.

LONDON INTERNATIONAL DOCUMENTARY FESTIVAL: A CONVERSATION IN FILM

Web: www.lidf.co.uk
The LIDF is a collaboration with the American Museum of Natural History's Margaret Mead Film & Video Festival, covering innovative documentaries (10-120 minutes long) from the UK, Europe and USA. The main event is held in March and includes foyer events, Q & A sessions with the directors, and panel discussions with guest speakers and industry professionals, but there is now a rolling programme of events throughout the year.

LONDON SHORT FILM FESTIVAL

Web: www.shortfilms.org.uk/
Formerly known as the Halloween Short Film Festival, this festival screens drama, documentary, animation, music video, and experimental shorts at the Curzon, ICA and Roxy cinemas in London. Submissions invited.

THE MEDIA FESTIVAL

Web: http://themediafestival.com/
Launched in 2008 by Broadcast, Screen International and Shots, the Media Festival celebrates convergence in the digital content industries of television, film, online, gaming, mobile, music and advertising. Conference sessions explore creativity in a converging digital age and analyse current and future business models.

Munich International Short Film Festival See **Junge Sterne Munich International Short Film Festival**

NOISE FESTIVAL

Web: www.noisefestival.com/
An online festival that invites young creative people to submit stories about their subculture in the form of words, blogs, mobile phone pictures/ clips, photopgraphs, film/video, audio podcasts or animation.

ONEDOTZERO ADVENTURES IN MOTION

Web: www.onedotzero.com/home.php
A global network of film festivals which, since 1996, has been showcasing the best of new digital film and animation. Onedotzsero explores new ideas and innovation through curated compilation screenings, features, exhibitions, live audio-visual performances, club nights, presentations and panel discussions from internationally acclaimed artists and creatives at venues in over 60 cities worldwide.

ONE WORLD INTERNATIONAL HUMAN RIGHTS FILM FESTIVAL

Web: www.jedensvet.cz/ow/2007/ index_en.php?id=199
An annual international festival, based in Prague, of films on human rights issues, including investigative and activist films. The festival gives awards and includes a discussion forum, as well as having an educational brief to involve Czech schoolchildren and provide teaching

materials to accompany the use of the films in schools.

PALESTINE FILM FESTIVAL

Web: www.palestinefilm.org/
The Palestine Society at London's School of Oriental and African Studies (SOAS) organised the first London Palestine Film Festival in 1999 and subsequently established the Palestine Film Foundation as a body dedicated to the coordination of the festival. This two-week festival is the largest event of its kind in the world, showcasing over 35 films dealing with the subject of Palestine each year. Art, fiction, documentary, and experimental work by artists from across the world are screened alongside panel discussions, question and answer sessions, and book talks.

RAINDANCE

Web: www.raindance.co.uk/

This annual festival held at venues in central London celebrates the best of independent filmmaking worldwide, including feature films, shorts, documentaries and special events. Films must not have been previously released in the UK and be independently produced. Raindance also hosts the British Independent Film Awards.

RUSHES SOHO SHORTS FESTIVAL

Web: www.sohoshorts.com/
Now in its tenth year, this festival showcases the work of both new and established filmmakers. There is no entry fee and categories are documentary, short, animation, music video, broadcast design, and newcomers. Held over ten days at the Curzon, Soho.

RUSSIAN FILM FESTIVAL

Web: http://academia-rossica.org/en/film/russian-film-festival
The second Russian Film Festival, organised by Academia Rossica, provides British audiences with the opportunity see some of the best Russian films produced in the last year.

SCINEMA FESTIVAL OF SCIENCE FILM

Web: www.csiro.au/scinema
An annual international festival celebrating the science and the art of scientific filmmaking. Established in 2000 and originally based in Canberra, the festival was is intended to serve as a tool for communication between scientists and the public and forge links between the sciences and the arts.

SCOTTISH MENTAL HEALTH ARTS AND FILM FESTIVAL

Web: www.mhfestival.com
The multi-arts festival seeks to tackle stigma and promote positive attitudes towards mental health, mental illness, support and recovery, and to effect significant cultural change amongst opinion-formers and the public through the insights and influences of the creative arts.

SHEFFIELD DOC/FEST

Web: www.sheffdocfest.com
The UK's premiere documentary festival, first held in 1994. It is an international event celebrating the art and business of documentary during five days in November. Doc/Fest is a film festival, industry session programme and market place, offering pitching opportunities, controversial discussion panels and in-depth filmmaker masterclasses, as well as a wealth of inspirational documentary films from across the globe

SHORTFEST

Web: www.propellertv.co.uk/ShortFest.aspx
Held for the first time in 2008, ShortFest is a celebration of the best original shorts submitted by new filmmaking talent to television channel PropellerTV since its launch on Sky in 2006. Festival trailers and previews may be viewed online.

TELEVISUAL INTELLIGENT FACTUAL FESTIVAL

Web: www.televisual.com/festival

Founded in 2006, Televisual's Intelligent Factual Festival is devoted to the best of factual television and looks at the latest trends and the future for the genre. There are seminars, panel discussions, free workshops and master classes providing a hands-on overview of the latest production theories, techniques and technology.

TIMES BFI LONDON FILM FESTIVAL

Web: www.bfi.org.uk/lff/

The Festival showcases the best new films from around the world. Non-competitive, the LFF was originally conceived as a 'festival of festivals,' screening a selection of films from other European festivals. The Festival's aim is to bring film to the public and offer opportunities for people to see films that have never been screened before in the UK and may not go into distribution.

UK JEWISH FILM FESTIVAL

Web: www.ukjewishfilmfestival.org.uk

The UK Jewish Film Festival was inaugurated in 1997 in Brighton and seeks to promote cultural diversity and to explore issues relevant to the international Jewish community. It also administers The Pears Foundation UKJFF Short Film Fund Two which provides grants for the production of a short film or video – drama, animation or factual – with a Jewish theme of significance to both Jewish and general public audiences and a maximum length of ten minutes.

UNITED NATIONS ASSOCIATION FILM FESTIVAL

Web: www.unaff.org

An annual festival organised by Stanford University originally conceived to celebrate the fiftieth anniversary of the signing of the Universal Declaration of Human Rights. Films to be screened are selected from entries submitted from around the world.

VIDEOMED – INTERNATIONAL CONTEST OF MEDICAL, HEALTH AND TELEMEDICINE CINEMA

Web: http://videomed.dip-badajoz.es

The festival aims to boost the production of cinema and video relating to medicine and healthcare, with a particular emphasis on new communication techniques, medical imaging and telemedicine. Although based in Badajoz in Spain, Videomed has been held in many different cities over the years.

WILDSCREEN FESTIVAL

Web: www.wildscreenfestival.org

The Wildscreen Festival was founded 1982 in association with WWF-UK and is now a biennial fixture held in Bristol. Its aim is to encourage and applaud excellence in the production of moving images about the natural world, and so increase the global viewing public's awareness and understanding of nature and the need to conserve it. The centrepiece of every Wildscreen is the bestowing of its Panda Awards – the wildlife film industry's equivalent of the Hollywood Oscars.

WIMBLEDON SHORTS SHORT FILM FESTIVAL

Web: www.wimbledonshorts.com/index.html

Founded by the Wimbledon Film Club, this recently launched festival aims to promote and stimulate film production. Submissions must be under fifteen minutes in length.

Students of Anglia Ruskin University.

HE ACADEMY SUBJECT CENTRES

The Higher Education Academy was established in 2002, from a merger of the Institute for Learning and Teaching in Higher Education, the Learning and Teaching Support Network, and the TQEF National Co-ordination Team. Its mission is to help institutions, discipline groups and all staff to provide the best possible learning experience for their students. The HE Academy provides discipline-based support through its Subject Network of twenty-four Subject Centres. These are a mix of single-site and consortium-based centres located within relevant subject departments and hosted by higher education institutions. Each centre engages in a wide variety of activities to support practitioners, subject departments and discipline communities.

ART DESIGN MEDIA

Art Design Media Subject Centre, University of Brighton, Faculty of Arts & Architecture, 68 Grand Parade, Brighton, East Sussex BN2 9JY
Tel: 01273 643119 **Fax:** 01273 643429
E-mail: adm@heacademy.ac.uk
Web: www.adm.heacademy.ac.uk
Supporting and developing learning and teaching in Art, Design, Media, History of Art and the History of Design in higher education.

BIOSCIENCE

The Centre for Bioscience, the Higher Education Academy, Room 9.15, Worsley Building, University of Leeds, Leeds LS2 9JT
Tel: 0113 343 3001 **Fax:** 0113 343 5894
E-mail: heabioscience@leeds.ac.uk
Web: www.bioscience.heacademy.ac.uk
The Centre for Bioscience is the Subject Centre for the Life, Food, Agricultural and Biomedical Sciences. The Centre provides support for discussion, dissemination and innovation in all aspects of learning, teaching and assessment.

BUILT ENVIRONMENT (CEBE)

Centre for Education in the Built Environment (CEBE), Architecture, Landscape, Planning, Housing & Transport, Cardiff University, Bute Building, King Edward VII Avenue, Cardiff CF10 3NB
Tel: 029 2087 4600 **Fax:** 029 2087 4601
Construction, Surveying & Real Estate, University of Salford, Room 436, The School of The Built Environment, Maxwell Building, The Crescent, Salford M5 4WT
Tel: 0161 295 5944 **Fax:** 0161 295 5011
Web: www.cebe.heacademy.ac.uk
The Centre provides discipline-based support to enhance the quality of learning and teaching in the UK Higher Education Built Environment community.

BUSINESS, MANAGEMENT, ACCOUNTANCY AND FINANCE (BMAF)

BMAF, Oxford Brookes University, Business School, Wheatley Campus, Wheatley, Oxford OX33 1HX
Tel: 01865 485670 **Fax:** 01865 485829
E-mail: bmaf@brookes.ac.uk
Web: www.business.heacademy.ac.uk
The Centre aims to enhance the education experience of students by communicating and disseminating ideas and promoting good practice and innovations in higher education teaching and learning. It acts as a hub of information and resources across academic communities in Business, Management and Accountancy.

DANCE, DRAMA AND MUSIC (PALATINE)

PALATINE, The Great Hall, Lancaster University, Lancaster LA1 4YW
Tel: 01524 592614
E-mail: palatine@lancaster.ac.uk
Web: www.palatine.ac.uk
PALATINE is the Higher Education Academy Subject Centre for Dance, Drama and Music, established in 2000 to support and enhance learning and teaching in Performing Arts higher education across the UK.

ECONOMICS

The Economics Network, ILRT, University of Bristol, 8-10 Berkeley Square, Bristol BS8 1HH
Tel: 0117 331 4347 **Fax:** 0117 331 4396
E-mail: econ-network@bristol.ac.uk
Web: www.economicsnetwork.ac.uk
The Centre provides a range of services that support university teachers of Economics in the UK.

EDUCATION (ESCALATE)

ESCalate, 35 Berkeley Square, Bristol BS8 1JA
Tel: 0117 331 4291 **Fax:** 0117 925 1537
E-mail: heacademy-escalate@bristol.ac.uk
Web: http://escalate.ac.uk
The ESCalate partnership includes the universities of Bristol, St Martin's College and Stirling. Together these produce and disseminate resources for staff and students in higher and

further education involved in Education Studies, Continuing Education and Lifelong Learning and Initial Teacher Education. The Centre supports and advises on pedagogy, curriculum enhancement across foundation, undergraduate, masters, PhD and EdD programmes.

ENGINEERING

Engineering Subject Centre, Sir David Davies Building, Loughborough University, Leicestershire LE11 3TU
Tel: 01509 227 170 **Fax:** 01509 227 172
E-mail: enquiries@engsc.ac.u
Web: www.engsc.ac.uk
The Engineering Subject Centre's Mission is to improve the student learning experience in partnership with the UK engineering community. It is based in the Faculty of Engineering at Loughborough University. It draws upon the expertise of engineering academics and educationalists from across the higher education sector, and works closely with the engineering bodies.

ENGLISH

English Subject Centre, Royal Holloway, University of London, Egham, Surrey TW20 OEX
Tel: 01784 443 221 **Fax:** 01784 470 684
E-mail: esc@rhul.ac.uk
Web: www.english.heacademy.ac.uk
The English Subject Centre supports the teaching of English Literature, Language and Creative Writing in UK higher education.

GEOGRAPHY, EARTH AND ENVIRONMENTAL SCIENCE (GEES)

GEES Subject Centre, Buckland House, University of Plymouth, Drake Circus, Plymouth PL4 8AA
Tel: 01752 233 530 **Fax:** 01752 233 534
E-mail: info@gees.ac.uk
Web: www.gees.ac.uk
The aim of the Subject Centre is to support and enhance learning and teaching in these three disciplines in UK higher education.

HEALTH SCIENCES AND PRACTICE

Health Sciences & Practice Subject Centre,
King's College London, Room 3.12, Waterloo
Bridge Wing, Franklin-Wilkins Building,
150 Stamford Street, London SE1 9NN
Tel: 020 7848 3141 **Fax:** 020 7848 3130
E-mail: info-hsap@kcl.ac.uk
Web: www.health.heacademy.ac.uk
The Centre aims to promote the development of
good practices in Health Care through enhancing
the quality of learning, teaching and assessment,
both in higher education institutions and in
practice-based education.

HISTORY, CLASSICS AND ARCHAEOLOGY

The Subject Centre for History, Classics and
Archaeology, School of Archaeology, Classics and
Egyptology, Hartley Building, Brownlow Street,
University of Liverpool, Liverpool, L69 3GS
Tel: 0151 795 0343 **Fax:** 0141 330 5518
E-mail: hca.hea@liverpool.ac.uk
Web: www.hca.heacademy.ac.uk
The Centre aims to provide a comprehensive
framework for the support and development of
learning and teaching in History, Classics and
Archaeology, produce and disseminate resources
for staff and students, and advise on pedagogy and
curriculum enhancement.

HOSPITALITY, LEISURE, SPORT AND TOURISM (HLST)

Hospitality, Leisure, Sport & Tourism Network
(HLST), Oxford Brookes University, Wheatley
Campus, Wheatley, Oxford OX33 1HX
Tel: 01865 483861
E-mail: hlst@brookes.ac.uk
Web: www.hlst.heacademy.ac.uk
The Hospitality, Leisure, Sport & Tourism Net-
work aims to encourage and broker the sharing of
good learning and teaching practice across these
subject areas of UK higher education.

INFORMATION AND COMPUTER SCIENCES

Computer Science
Higher Education Academy, Room 16G28,
Faculty of Engineering, University of Ulster

at Jordanstown, Newtownabbey, Co. Antrim
BT37 0QB
Tel: 028 90368020 **Fax:** 028 90368206
E-mail: heacademy-ics@ulster.ac.uk

Information Science
Higher Education Academy – ICS, Research
School of Informatics, Loughborough University,
Hollywell Park, Loughborough, Leicestershire
LE11 3TU
Tel: 01509 635708
E-mail: A.S.McNab@lboro.ac.uk
Web: www.ics.heacademy.ac.uk

The primary aim is to enhance
the student learning experience
in ICS environments. This is done
by providing subject-based support to both ICS individuals and
departments to promote quality
learning and teaching by
stimulating the sharing of good
practice and innovation.

LANGUAGES, LINGUISTICS AND AREA STUDIES (LLAS)

Subject Centre for Languages, Linguistics and
Area Studies (LLAS), School of Modern
Languages, University of Southampton, Highfield,
Southampton SO17 1BJ
Tel: 023 8059 4814 **Fax:** 023 8059 4815
E-mail: llas@soton.ac.uk
Web: www.llas.ac.uk

The Centre's mission is to foster
world-class education in these
subject areas. It does this by
supporting stakeholders and
helping them to provide the best
possible learning experience for
students. LLAS is responsive to
the needs of its stakeholders and
also offers academic leadership
in promoting good practice and identifying
emerging issues.

LAW (UKCLE)

UK Centre for Legal Education – UKCLE,
University of Warwick, Coventry CV4 7AL
Tel: 024 7652 3117 **Fax:** 024 7652 3290
E-mail: ukcle@warwick.ac.uk

Web: www.ukcle.ac.uk

The UK Centre for Legal Education (UKCLE) supports effective practice in learning, teaching and assessment in Law.

MATERIALS (UKCME)

UK Centre for Materials Education,
2nd Floor, Brodie Tower, University of Liverpool, Liverpool L69 3GQ
Tel: 0151 794 5364 **Fax:** 0151 794 4466
E-mail: ukcme@liv.ac.uk
Web: www.materials.ac.uk

The UKCME supports high quality student learning in Materials Science and related disciplines. It promotes, encourages and coordinates the development and adoption of effective practices in learning, teaching and assessment.

MATHEMATICS, STATISTICS AND OPERATIONAL RESEARCH (MSOR)

Maths, Stats & OR Network (MSOR), School of Mathematics, The University of Birmingham, Edgbaston, Birmingham B15 2TT
Tel: 0121 414 7095 **Fax:** 0121 414 3389
E-mail: info@mathstore.ac.uk
Web: http://mathstore.ac.uk

Supporting lecturers in Mathematics, Statistics and Operational Research and promoting, disseminating and developing good practice in learning and teaching across the UK.

MEDICINE, DENTISTRY AND VETERINARY MEDICINE (MEDEV)

Higher Education Academy Subject Centre for Medicine, Dentistry and Veterinary Medicine (MEDEV), School of Medical Education Development, Faculty of Medical Sciences, Newcastle University, Newcastle upon Tyne NE2 4HH
Tel: 0191 222 5888 **Fax:** 0191 222 5016
E-mail: enquiries@medev.ac.uk
Web: www.medev.ac.uk

Working together with educators, communities and organisations to promote and enhance student learning in the health-related disciplines. Closely associated with the Health Sciences and Practice Subject Centre through the HEALTH Network Group (Higher Education Academy Learning and Teaching in Health).

PHILOSOPHICAL AND RELIGIOUS STUDIES (PRS)

The Subject Centre for Philosophical and Religious Studies (PRS), School of Theology and Religious Studies, University of Leeds, Leeds LS2 9JT
Tel: 0113 3434184 **Fax:** 0113 3433654
E-mail: enquiries@prs.heacademy.ac.uk
Web: http://prs.heacademy.ac.uk

The Centre's mission is to support and promote Philosophical, Theological and Religious Studies higher education in the UK, and to build on its culture of dialogue and reflection.

PHYSICAL SCIENCES

Higher Education Academy Physical Sciences Centre, Department of Chemistry, University of Hull, Hull HU6 7RX
Tel/Fax: 01482 465418
E-mail: psc@hull.ac.uk
Web: www.physsci.heacademy.ac.uk

Enhancing the student experience in Chemistry, Physics and Astronomy within the university sector.

PSYCHOLOGY

The Higher Education Academy Psychology Network, Department of Psychology,
1st Floor, Information Centre, Market Square, University of York, York YO10 5NH
Tel: 01904 433 154 **Fax:** 01904 433 655
E-mail: psychology@heacademy.ac.uk
Web: www.psychology.heacademy.ac.uk

The Centre exists to promote excellence in the learning, teaching and assessment of Psychology across the full range of curricula and activities relevant to UK higher education.

SOCIOLOGY, ANTHROPOLOGY AND POLITICS (C-SAP)

C-SAP, Nuffield Building, The University of Birmingham, Edgbaston, Birmingham B15 2TT
Tel: 0121 414 7919 **Fax:** 0121 414 7920
E-mail: enquiries@c-sap.bham.ac.uk
Web: www.c-sap.bham.ac.uk

C-SAP aims to promote a scholarly and disciplinary-specific approach to the innovation and reform of learning and teaching in the Social Sciences.

SOCIAL POLICY AND SOCIAL WORK (SWAP)

SWAP HE Academy Subject Centre,
Room 4125, Murray Building,
School of Social Sciences, University of
Southampton, Southampton SO17 1BJ

Tel: 02380 599 310 **Fax:** 02380 592 779
E-mail: swapteam@soton.ac.uk
Web: www.swap.ac.uk

SWAP, the Subject Centre for Social Policy and Social Work, aims to enhance the student learning experience by promoting high quality learning, teaching and assessment and by supporting Social Work and Social Policy.

Image courtesy of the University of East Anglia

MEDIA LEGISLATION AND REPORTS

This annotated bibliography comprises mainly government publications, but also diverse reports published by industry bodies and independent pressure groups. The documents cited here are those published since the previous edition of the BUFVC Handbook was prepared in July 2007, and are given in chronological order by publishing body or instititution. Please note that some of the web pages cited will open as PDF (.pdf) documents. Long website addresses are provided as TinyURLs.

The publishing bodies or institutions listed here are: BBC Trust; Centre for Intellectual Property and Information Law; Competition Commission; Department for Business, Enterprise & Regulatory Reform; Department for Children, Schools and Families; Department for Culture, Media and Sport; Department for Innovation, Universities & Skills; European Commission/Parliament; European Court of Justice; Intellectual Property Office; Ofcom; Olswang; Scottish Broadcasting Commission; UK Film Council; UK Legislation; UK Parliamentary Reports; World Intellectual Property Organization.

The full text of all legislation enacted by the UK parliament and delegated legislation (Statutory Instruments) is made available free of charge on the website: www.hmso.gov.uk/legislation/uk.htm – simultaneously or at least within twenty-four hours of its publication in printed form. The official revised edition of the primary legislation of the United Kingdom is made available through the UK Statute Law Database at: www.statutelaw.gov.uk.

BBC TRUST

2007 *From Seesaw to Wagon Wheel: Safeguarding Impartiality in the 21st Century*
Web: www.bbc.co.uk/bbctrust/research/
impartiality.html
On 18 June 2007 the BBC published a report on safeguarding its impartiality in the 21st century, together with extensive qualitative and quanti-

tative research on audience expectations and perceptions of impartiality. This report is the result of a project first commissioned by the BBC Board of Governors in conjunction with BBC management in November 2005 to identify the challenges and risks to impartiality. It contains 12 guiding principles to inform the BBC's approach to ensuring impartiality in the face of rapid technological and social change. These principles are complementary to the BBC's Editorial Guidelines on impartiality and do not replace them. The report also makes some recommendations to strengthen the BBC's delivery of impartiality throughout its broadcast output, all of which are being implemented.

2007 *Television Audience Perceptions of Innovation and Distinctiveness: Research Summary*
Web: www.bbc.co.uk/bbctrust/assets/files/pdf/consult/purpose_remits/audience_research.pdf
A summary of qualitative research conducted by Blinc Research for the BBC Trust following on from the BBC Trust's Purpose Remit Survey conducted in February 2007 which identified a clear 'innovation gap' and a perception that the BBC was not coming up with enough 'fresh and new ideas'. The overall objective was to understand in more detail what the public means by this, and the potential implications for the BBC.

2007 *Report of the Independent Panel for the BBC Trust on Impartiality of BBC Business*
Web: www.bbc.co.uk/bbctrust/research/impartiality/business_news.html

The report of an independent panel, led by Sir Alan Budd, into the impartiality of BBC news and factual coverage of business, with particular regard to accuracy, context, independence and bias, actual or perceived. The website also provides supporting documentation and BBC management's response to the report.

2007 *BBC High Definition Television Channel: Public Value Test Final Conclusions*
Web: www.bbc.co.uk/bbctrust/consult/closed_consultations/hdtv_consult.html
Following consultation via a BBC Trust Public Value Test and an Ofcom Market Impact Assess-

ment launched in May 2007, The BBC Trust in November 2007 gave broad approval to plans for a BBC high definition channel. The HDTV service description, the Public Value Assessment and provisional conclusions are also available on the website. Ofcom's Market Impact Assessment is available at www.ofcom.org.uk/research/tv/bbcmias/bbc_hdtv/bbc_hdtv.pdf

2007 *The BBC's Preparedness for Digital Switchover*
Web: www.bbc.co.uk/bbctrust/assets/files/pdf/review_report_research/vfm/switchover.pdf
This study, undertaken by the National Audit Office and presented to the BBC Trust's Finance and Strategy Committee in November 2007, looks at the BBC's preparations for digital switchover and, in particular, at how it plans to meet its obligations set out under the Royal Charter and Agreement.

2008 *Gaelic Digital Service: Public Value Test Final Conclusions*
Web: www.bbc.co.uk/bbctrust/
Following a full Public Value Test, the Trust has approved the Gaelic Digital Service to launch now on cable, satellite and broadband, but not Freeview at this time. In order to ensure both value for money for licence fee payers, and that the service meets the needs of the target audience in the best way, the Trust has decided that the service will be subject to review before digital switchover commences in central and northern Scotland in 2010.

The review will look at the actual performance of the service in achieving public value, including reaching a wider audience, and will consider launch on Freeview. In order to protect access for current users the Trust has concluded that the Gaelic Zone on BBC 2 will continue for the foreseeable future.

2008 *Children's Services – Public Consultation*
Web: www.bbc.co.uk/bbctrust/consult/open_consultations/childrens_services.html
This public consultation was launched on 12/5/2008 as part of a review of BBC services for children on television, radio and online, including full service reviews of the two dedicated children's

services, CBeebies and CBBC, in view of the opportunities and challenges offered by new technology. The review seeks the opinions of children, parents, other licence fee payers, schools, organisations in the media industry, children's charities and other groups with an interest in children's services from the BBC, and these will be considered in conjunction with other research. The consultation will run until 15/8/2008 and a report of the findings will be published by the end of the year. The BBC Executive will submit a response to the consultation alongside the BBC Trust's final report.

2008 *High Definition Services on Digital Terrestrial Television: Trust Interim Statement on BBC Non-service Application*
Web: www.bbc.co.uk/bbctrust/framework/ hd_services_on_dtt.html
In February the BBC Trust received a non-service application from the BBC Executive, in partnership with ITV, Channel 4 and Five, proposing an alternative way of rearranging the necessary spectrum to that suggested by Ofcom, to enable HD services on Freview. This interim statement issued by the BBC Trust on 3/4/2008 sets out the Trust's position to date and its course of action in the light of Ofcom's revised conclusions which are published simultaneously. It also explains the Trust's decision to suspend its consideration of the non-service application pending the outcome of the Ofcom process.

2008 *Service Review: bbc.co.uk*
Web: www.bbc.co.uk/bbctrust/framework/ bbc_service_licences/bbc_co_uk.html
Conclusions of a service review of bbc.co.uk carried out by the BBC Trust following a public consultation launched in July 2007. This is the first service review undertaken by the Trust as part of its ongoing programme of reviews of all BBC services under the terms of the new Charter and Agreement. The review's findings will inform the service's development over the next few years. The review considered how bbc.co.uk performed against its service licence, the service's governance and accountability, and whether its Service Licence needed to be developed in order to reflect changes in the market and users' needs.

Responses to the public consultation, commissioned research and a submission from the BBC Executive which informed the review are also available at www.bbc.co.uk/bbctrust/framework/ bbc_service_licences/bbc_co_uk_evidence.html

2008 *BBC Trust Report: Editorial Controls and Compliance*
Web: www.bbc.co.uk/bbctrust/research/ editorial_standards.html
In July 2007 the BBC Director General announced a 10-point action plan to address the editorial failings that had emerged in the course of the year. The Trust said it would review the impact of the action plan once it had been implemented. This review was completed in the spring of 2008 and contains the Trust's conclusions.

2008 *Economic Aspects of the Use of Premium Rate Services by the BBC*
Web: www.bbc.co.uk/bbctrust/assets/files/pdf/ review_report_research/prs_pwc_report.pdf
In October 2007, as part of its Fair Trading responsibilities, the BBC Trust commissioned an independent review of the BBC's financial and contractual arrangements for premium rate services. The report includes this review carried out by Pricewaterhouse Coopers, the Trust's conclusions in light of PwC's findings, and a response from the BBC Executive.

2008 *BBC Trust Report: On-screen and On-air Talent*
Web: www.bbc.co.uk/bbctrust/research/ value_for_money/talent_review.html
The BBC Trust commissioned an independent review, conducted by Oliver and Ohlbaum Associates Ltd, in November 2007 to provide an in-depth examination of the BBC's use of on-air and on-screen talent. This followed press reports about presenters' salaries during the course of 2006 which aroused industry and public concern. O&O were asked to investigate how the size and structure of the BBC's reward packages for talent compare with the rest of the market; what has been the impact of the BBC's policy on the talent market, particularly in relation to cost inflation; to what extent the BBC's policy and processes in relation to investment in, and reward of, talent

support value for money. The BBC management's response to the points raised and the BBC Trust's own judgements are published on the website alongside the report.

2008 *Study into the Economic Impact of the BBC on the UK*
Web: www.bbc.co.uk/bbctrust/research/ economic_impact/index.html
A wide-ranging study into the BBC's economic value to be conducted for the BBC Trust by PricewaterhouseCoopers, announced in November 2007. The terms of reference are to: identify the most important types of benefits and costs; provide evidence on the scale of these benefits and costs. The Trust will use the results of this study to help inform its judgements on future priorities and investment decisions. The study will focus on the BBC's operations alongside other broadcasters and creative businesses in the UK. The project will examine the economic impacts of the BBC's activities across all media, and in particular will consider new distribution channels (such as the internet) as well as the more traditional media of television and radio. It is the Trust's intention that the study will be published in early summer 2008.

2008 *BBC Trust Impartiality Report: BBC Network News and Current Affairs Coverage of the Four Nations*
Web: www.bbc.co.uk/bbctrust/research/ impartiality/nations.html
As part of the BBC Trust's routine research in 2007 it became apparent that some people felt the BBC was not covering the different policies of the nations in a way that enabled all audiences to understand fully what was happening in different parts of the UK. This is the BBC Trust's impartiality report and conclusions on this topic following an independent review by Professor Anthony King and extensive research by Cardiff University and the British Market Research Bureau (BMRB). The BBC's coverage was generally seen as being fair and impartial but the report recommends improvements be made to the range, clarity and precision of its network news coverage of what is happening in the different UK nations and regions, and this

coverage be made more relevant and interesting to all audiences. The report includes an initial plan of action and the Trust has asked for a final action plan by the summer. The Trust will track Management's progress and repeat the formal research within 18 months.

2008 *Local Video Public Value Test*
Web: www.bbc.co.uk/bbctrust/consult/ open_consultations/local_video_pvt.html
The BBC Trust's public value test (PVT) of the BBC's local video proposal began on 24/6/2008. The Trust published BBC management's application for a local video broadband service to complement existing BBC local websites, as well as supporting documents, a service description and a full timetable for the PVT, and invited responses from the public and the industry by 22/7/2008. The process includes two periods of public consultation. The first four-week consultation period allows contributions from interested parties about any relevant issues. A further period of consultation takes place after the Trust publishes its provisional conclusions in November 2008, with its final decision in February 2009. Alongside the BBC's PVT Ofcom is carrying out a four-week consultation prior to conducting its market impact assessment of BBC management's proposals.

2008 *The Operation of the Window of Creative Competition (WOCC): First Biennial Review by the BBC Trust*
Web: www.bbc.co.uk/bbctrust/research/wocc/ index.html
The BBC's Charter and Agreement sets out arrangements for the commissioning of network television programmes. It requires that 50% of programmes are reserved for in-house production and a statutory quota of 25% is reserved for the independent sector. In-house and external producers compete for the remaining 25% which is known as the Window of Creative Opportunity (WOCC). The Trust is obliged by the Charter and Agreement to review the WOCC at least every two years, and this review forms part of the Trust's published workplan for 2008/09. The review found that the WOCC is working well and commissioning decisions are being made on merit with no

obvious bias towards in-house teams or independent producers. Alongside the review are published an independent review by Pricewaterhouse Coopers of the processes and outputs that have resulted from the implementation for the WOCC; a survey of stakeholders conducted for the Trust by Larkhill Consultancy Ltd; and a substantive response to the public consultation from PACT.

2008 *BBC Annual Report 2007/2008*
Web: www.bbc.co.uk/annualreport/

Part of the BBC's Annual report is prepared by the BBC Trust. It assesses the performance of the BBC's management and its services. Part One provides the Trust's review of the year while part two gives the BBC Executive Board's review of the year, including performance and financial statements. The BBC Executive Board is responsible for the delivery of BBC services and the day-to-day running of the BBC.

CENTRE FOR INTELLECTUAL PROPERTY AND INFORMATION LAW

2008 *Review of the Economic Evidence Relating to an Extension of the Term of Copyright in Sound Recordings*
Web: www.hm-treasury.gov.uk/media/B/4/gowers_cipilreport.pdf
An independent report by the Centre for Intellectual Property and Information Law, University of Cambridge, commissioned to provide the Gowers Review with evidence on the economic consequences of extending the term of protection for sound recordings from the existing 50 years. In light of this evidence suggesting that an extension would negatively impact on consumers and industry, the Gowers Review recommended against an extension of the copyright term.

COMPETITION COMMISSION

2008 *Issues Statement on Commission Inquiry into Project 'Kangaroo': 'Video-on-demand'Jjoint Venture between BBC Worldwide Limited, Channel 4 Television Corporation and ITV plc*
Web: www.competition-commission.org.uk/inquiries/ref2008/kangaroo/index.htm
The Office of Fair Trading referred the proposed video on demand (Vod) joint venture between BBC Worldwide, ITV and Channel 4 – also known as Project 'Kangaroo' – to the Competition Commission (CC) to look into how the joint venture might affect the quality, price and amount of content for consumers and other VoD suppliers in the UK and overseas, as well as the acquisition of VoD content rights and advertising. The issues statement follows the initial process of gathering information, views and evidence, and identifies clearly for all interested parties the specific questions and areas the inquiry is examining. This will form the basis of the CC's analysis, with their report expected in January 2009.

DEPARTMENT FOR BUSINESS, ENTERPRISE & REGULATORY REFORM

2008 *Consultation on Legislative Options to Address Illicit Peer-to-peer (P2P) File-sharing*
Web: www.berr.gov.uk/files/file47139.pdf
This consultation is intended to set out and gather views on a proposal for a co-regulatory approach that could be adopted in order to facilitate and ensure co-operation between Internet Service Providers (ISPs) and rights holders to address the problem of illicit use of Peer-to-Peer (P2P) file-sharing technology to exchange unlawful copies of copyright material. This takes forward Recommendation 39 of the Gowers Review of Intellectual Property which addressed the issue of illicit use of P2P. The consultation also identifies and seeks views on other potential options and calls for evidence on issues related to illicit use of P2P. The consultation runs from 24/7/2008 – 30/10/2008.

DEPARTMENT FOR CHILDREN, SCHOOLS AND FAMILIES

2007 *Byron Review: Children and New Technology – Call for Evidence Document*
Web: www.dfes.gov.uk/byronreview/pdfs/
Byron%20Review%20Consultation%20Document
This document sets out the terms of the Byron Review, an independent review of the risks to children from exposure to potentially harmful or inappropriate material on the internet and in video games. This consultation, which ran from 9/10/2007 to 30/11/2007, called for evidence from all groups and individuals involved with the issues of the review. A separate version of the document inviting children and young people to contribute to the review is available at: www.dfes.gov.uk/byronreview/pdfs/Byron%20Review%20Children's%20Consultation%20Document.pdf

2008 *Safer Children in a Digital World: Report of the Byron Review*
Web: www.dfes.gov.uk/byronreview/pdfs/
Final%20Report%20Bookmarked.pdf

An independent report produced by Dr Tanya Byron for the Department for Children, Schools and Families and the Department for Culture Media and Sport, looking at the risks to children from exposure to potentially harmful or inappropriate material on the internet and in video games. The review concentrates on the needs of children and young people and preserving their right to take the risks that form an inherent part of their development, by enabling them to play video games and surf the net in a safe and informed way. Evidence provided by children and young people themselves was at the heart of the report, and a separate version of the document prepared for them is available at: www.dfes.gov.uk/byronreview/pdfs/A%20Summary%20for%20Children%20and%20Young%20People%20FINAL.pdf

2008 *The Byron Review Action Plan*
Web: www.dfes.gov.uk/byronreview/
actionplan/
A comprehensive plan for how the Government intends to make the internet and video games safer for children and young people by implementing recommendations made in Dr Tanya Byron's report *Safer Children in a Digital World*, published in March (see above).

DEPARTMENT FOR CULTURE, MEDIA AND SPORT (DCMS)

2007 *TV Licence Fee Settlement*
Web: www.culture.gov.uk/images/publications/
licenceFeeSettlementLetter.pdf
Letter from the Secretary of State to the BBC Trust on 16th June 2007 setting out the BBC's TV licence fee settlement. The letter confirmed the settlement announced by the Secretary of State to the House of Commons on 18th January 2007 and provided further details.

2007 *Future Broadcasting Regulation*
Web: www.culture.gov.uk/images/publications/
FutureBroadcastingRegulation.pdf
A report by Robin Foster commissioned by the DCMS to help stimulate and inform debate about future changes in the policy and regulatory framework for UK broadcasting and other electronic media. It develops four contrasting scenarios for the future of broadcasting in the UK, and examines some of the broad policy and regulatory implications which flow from those different scenarios. It focuses on the five to ten year time horizon rather than the near term, and on broad trends and challenges, rather than the detailed design of broadcasting regulations. The intention is to stimulate wide discussion and debate of the key issues, as part of the preparation for a potentially very different broadcasting environment in the UK after the completion of digital switchover.

2007 *New Media and the Creative Industries: Culture, Media and Sport Committee, Fifth Report of Session 2006-2007 (HC 509-I)*
TSO ISBN 9780215034014

Web: www.publications.parliament.uk/pa/
cm200607/cmselect/cmcumeds/509/50902.htm
The report *New Media and the Creative Industries*
surveys the new media technologies in the UK
today, examines the impact upon creators and
the links between creator and consumer, and
reports on the problem of piracy. The role of
government is also assessed, with the report
finding that there is a clear role in setting the
legal framework and enforcing it – particularly
to combat piracy – and that there should be
greater clarity in the law as to what is and is not
permitted. The accompanying *New Media and the
Creative Industries – Oral and Written Evidence*
(HC 509-II, ISBN 0215034007) is available
separately.

2007 *Government Response to the Culture, Media
and Sport Select Committee Report into New Media
and the Creative Industries*
TSO ISBN 9780101718622
Web: www.culture.gov.uk/images/publications/
375268_GovResponse.pdf
Response of the Department for Culture, Media
and Sport to the select committee's report on new
media and the creative industries.

2007 *Staying Ahead: the Economic Performance of
the UK's Creative Industries*
The Work Foundation for Department for Culture,
Media and Sport
Web: www.culture.gov.uk/reference_library/
publications/3672.aspx
A report analysing the economic importance of the
creative industries in the UK. Commissioned as
part of the Creative Economy Programme to
inform the drafting of a Green Paper.

2007 *Government Response to the Culture,
Media and Sport Select Committee Report on
Caring for Our Collections, Session 2006-07*
Cm 7233
TSO ISBN 9780101723329
Web: www.culture.gov.uk/images/publications/
Cm7233_GovResponseCaringCollections.pdf
Response of the Department for Culture, Media
and Sport to the select committee's report on
issues affecting museums, galleries, archives and
the audio-visual sector.

2007 *Creative Britain: New Talents for the New
Economy*
Web: www.culture.gov.uk/images/publications/
CEPFeb2008.pdf
A Green Paper for the creative industries,
produced by the DCMS in partnership with BERR
and DIUS. This strategy paper documents 26
commitments which outline how the Government
will take action to support the creative industries,
from the grassroots to the global marketplace,
including the creation of apprenticeships and steps
to protect intellectual property and deal with illegal
file sharing.

2007 *Digital Radio Working Group Interim Report*
Web: www.culture.gov.uk/images/publications/
DRWG2008-interimreport.pdf
The Digital Radio Working Group (DRWG) was
established in November 2007 by instruction of the
Secretary of State for Culture, Media & Sport. Its
purpose was to bring together senior figures from
the radio industry and related stakeholders, under
an independent Chair, to consider three questions:
What conditions would need to be achieved before
digital platforms could become the predominant
means of delivering radio?; What are the current
barriers to the growth of digital radio?; What are
the possible remedies to those barriers? The
DRWG was asked to report its findings to the
Secretary of State by the end of 2008 and this is its
interim report.

2007 *The Digital Switchover Help Scheme
(CM 7356)*
Web: www.culture.gov.uk/images/publications/
The_Digital_Switchover_Help_Scheme.pdf
A revision of the Government's Scheme Agree-
ment with the BBC which sets out the eligibility
criteria and governance rules under which the
Digital Switchover Help Scheme will operate. This
revision replaces CM 7118, published in May 2007.

2007 *Public Consultation on Implementing the EU
Audiovisual Media Services Directive*
Web: www.culture.gov.uk/reference_library/
consultations/5309.aspx
A consultation on how the UK should implement
the EU Audiovisual Media Services Directive which updates EU minimum standards on

scheduled television services. The Directive includes both compulsory and optional elements, some of which are expected to lead to new legislation. The consultation focuses on the Government's proposals on three specific issues in the Directive: product placement in television and video-on-demand services; introducing a system for regulating video-on-demand services in the UK; controls over the content of non-EU satellite channels which are uplinked from a ground station in the UK. The consultation runs for three months and closes on 31/10/2008.

2007 *Harmful Content on the Internet and in Video Games – HC 353-I, Tenth Report of the Culture, Media and Sport Select Committee Session 2007-08 – Volume I: Report, Together with Formal Minutes, Oral and Written Evidence*
TSO ISBN 780215523389
Web: www.publications.parliament.uk/pa/cm200708/cmselect/cmcumeds/353/353.pdf
Vol II: Oral and written evidence HC 353-II is also available from TSO (ISBN 9780215523372) and online at www.publications.parliament.uk/pa/cm200708/cmselect/cmcumeds/353/353ii.pdf

This report by the House of Commons, Culture, Media and Sport Committee addresses the growing public concern about offensive material on the Internet and the risks to children highlighted in the Government-commissioned report by Dr Tanya Byron. It recommends that proactive review of content should be standard practice for sites hosting user-generated content, and calls for provision of high profile facilities for reporting abuse or unwelcome behaviour directly to law enforcement and support organisations. It also addresses the confusion caused by there currently being two systems for labelling video games to indicate the nature of their content: the industry's own rating system and the British Board of Film Classification (BBFC) system.

2007 *Video Games Classification: A Consultation*
Web: www.culture.gov.uk/images/publications/VideoGames2008.pdf
As part of the Government's implementation of the Byron Review recommendations on children and new media, the DCMS is seeking views on the current classification system for video games. Currently there are both statutory and voluntary classifications systems for video games in the UK. The statutory system gives age-related classification and short content advice and is run by the British Board of Film Classification (BBFC). The non-statutory or voluntary system was set up by the industry and awards age classifications but also advises about content through pictograms. This latter system is called the Pan European Games Information (PEGI) system. The consultation sets out four options for consideration: Option 1 – Hybrid Classification System – BBFC ratings for all games for players over 12 and PEGI ratings for under 12s; Option 2 - Enhanced BBFC system; Option 3 – Enhanced PEGI system; Option 4 – Voluntary code of practice. Comments generated by this consultation will be used to develop the system in order to protect gamers from inappropriate content. The consultation runs until 20/11/2008.

DEPARTMENT FOR INNOVATION, UNIVERSITIES & SKILLS

2008 *Informal Adult Learning-Shaping the Way Ahead: Consultation Paper*
Web: www.adultlearningconsultation.org.uk/userfiles/DIUS_adu_lea_bro_an_05.8.pdf
A consultation designed to stimulate public debate and shape future government policy on informal adult learning, with particular emphasis on issues of access and the role of technology. Consultation ran from 15/1/2008 to 12/6/2008

2008 *Innovation Nation Cm 7345*
TS0 ISBN 9780101734523
Web: www.dius.gov.uk/docs/home/ScienceInnovation.pdf
This White Paper sets out the Government's aim of promoting innovation across society as a tool to develop and generate economic prosperity and improve the quality of life throughout the UK. It

includes a range of initiatives to help small businesses link up with universities and colleges to develop new products and services.

2008 *Harnessing Technology: Next Generation Learning 2008-14*
Web: http://publications.becta.org.uk/

Harnessing Technology was published by the Government in 2005 and set out a system-wide strategy for technology in education and skills. Three years on, much has changed in the education and skills system and in the ways learners of all ages use technology. The Department for Children, Schools and Families (DCSF) and Department for Innovation, Universities and Skills (DIUS) asked BECTA to revise *Harnessing Technology* and develop the strategy *Harnessing Technology: Next Generation Learning,* for the next six years. The revised strategy sets out a commitment to ensuring every school, college, university or training provider is 'technology confident'.

EUROPEAN COMMISSION / PARLIAMENT

2007 *Audiovisual Media Services without Frontiers Directive (Directive 2007/65/EC)*
European Parliament and the Council of the European Union
Web: http://eur-lex.europa.eu/en/index.htm
Tiny URL: http://tinyurl.com/5mr4ro

This Directive amends and renames the Television without Frontiers Directive, adopted in 1989 and subsequently revised in 1987. The amending directive entered into force on 19 December 2007 and Member States have two years to transpose the new provisions into national law, so that the modernized legal framework for audiovisual media services will be fully applicable by the end of 2009. The AVMSD offers a comprehensive legal framework that covers all audiovisual media services (including on-demand audiovisual media services), provides less detailed and more flexible regulation and modernises rules on TV advertising to better finance audiovisual content. The new rules respond to technological developments and create a level-playing field in Europe for emerging audiovisual media services. The Directive reaffirms the pillars of Europe's audiovisual model, which are cultural diversity, protection of minors, consumer protection, media pluralism, and the fight against racial and religious hatred. In addition to that, the new Directive aims at ensuring the independence of national media regulators.

2007 *Current Trends and Approaches to Media Literacy in Europe*
Web: http://ec.europa.eu/avpolicy/ media_literacy/studies/index_en.htm
The study, carried out in the second half of 2007 by the Universidad Autonoma de Barcelona for the European Commission, sets out to map current practices in implementing media literacy in the 27 Member States of the European Union and the EEA Member States. The specific aims were to: identify existing and possible approaches to media literacy; provide a description of emerging trends in this field throughout Europe; provide recommendations on measures to be implemented at EC level to help foster and increase the level of media literacy in Europe; outline the possible economic and social impact of European Union intervention in this field.

2007 *A European Approach to Media Literacy in the Digital Environment COM (2007) 833 final*
Web: http://ec.europa.eu/avpolicy/ media_literacy/docs/com/en.pdf

Following a period of consultation, in December the Commission adopted a Communication on media literacy in the digital environment as an integral part of its general policy to enhance the trust in, and take-up of, content online. The Communication adds a further building block to European audiovisual policy complementing the new Audiovisual Media Services Directive and the MEDIA 2007 support-programme. It is part of an initiative to build up better knowledge and understanding of how the media work in the digital world, who the new players in the media economy are, and which new possibilities and challenges digital media consumption may present. It is important for citizens to understand the economic and cultural dimension of media, and for discussion to take place on the importance for Europe's economy of having strong and competitive media at a global level, that deliver pluralism and cultural diversity. The results of the public media literacy consultation are available at: http://ec.europa.eu/avpolicy/media_literacy/consultation/index_en.htm

2007 *European i2010 Initiative on E-inclusion – to Be Part of the Information Society COM(2007) 694 final*
Web: http://ec.europa.eu/
http://tinyurl.com/63c9p6
Communication adopted by the European Commission on 8 November 2007.

It proposes a European Initiative on e-Inclusion comprising: an e-Inclusion campaign 'e-Inclusion, be part of it!' to raise awareness and connecting efforts during 2008, to be concluded by a Ministerial Conference, to demonstrate concrete progress and reinforce commitments; a strategic framework for action to implement the Riga Ministerial Declaration. Documents in support of this Communication are also available, including the statistical report on measuring e-Inclusion targets ('Riga dashboard'), and other relevant documents.

Further information on e-Accessibility is available in the report 'Measuring e-Accessibility in Europe' http:// ec.europa.eu/information_society/activities/einclusion/docs/meac_study/meac_report_06_11_final.pdf

2007 *Communication Extending the Current Rules on State Aid to Cinematographic and Other Audiovisual Works [OJ 2007/C 134/03]*
Web: http://europa.eu/
Tiny URL: http://tinyurl.com/5hbkxo
A European Commission Communication extending until 31/12/2009 at the latest the application of the current rules on state aid to cinematographic and other audiovisual works. This Cinema Communication extends the rules laid down in the 'Cinema Communications' of 2001, extended in 2004. This continuity aims to further encourage Europe's audiovisual industry by maintaining the current conditions and thereby helping the industry to face future challenges in a highly competitive market.

2008 *Directive on the Protection of Conditional-access Services: Commission Consultation of Interested Parties (IP/08/202)*
European Commission
Web: http://ec.europa.eu/internal_market/media/elecpay/index_en.htm
The rise of pay-TV has benefited from the EU-wide protection afforded by Directive 98/84/EC on conditional-access services. Now, 10 years after it was adopted, the European Commission wishes to compile a second report on how the Directive is being implemented in what is now a very different economic and technological climate. The Commission is therefore opening a consultation to run until 4/4/2008 to collect information before writing its report, which is due to be adopted by the end of 2008. An impact assessment of the Directive, carried out at the Commission's request by a consortium made up of KEA European Affairs and CERNA, was completed in December 2007 and is available on the Commission's website at the same URL as the consultation.

2008 *i2010 European Digital Libraries Initiative: Memorandum of Understanding on Diligent Search Guidelines for Orphan Works*
Web: http://ec.europa.eu/
Tiny URL: http://tinyurl.com/5zxg6x
The European Digital Libraries Initiative aims to provide a common multi-lingual access point to Europe's cultural heritage. This Memorandum, signed on 4/6/2008 by libraries, archives and

rights holders, will help bring Europe's literary and audiovisual heritage online, as it deals with the issue of orphan works – books, films, photographs or songs for which it is impossible to identify or locate the rightholders. It clarifies how searches for rightholders have to be handled for libraries and archives and representatives of publishers, photographers, authors, record and film companies. In relation to copyright issues, the High Level Group adopted a final report in which it endorsed a new model license for making works that are out of print or out of distribution accessible for all on the internet. It also gives guidance on copyright issues related to the preservation of web-content by cultural institutions.

2008 *Sector-specific Guidelines on Due Diligence Criteria for Orphan Works: Joint Report*
Web: http://ec.europa.eu/
Tiny URL: http://tinyurl.com/6xslac
Following a Stakeholder Conference held as part of the European Digital Libraries Initiative, four working groups (text, audiovisual, visual/ photography, and music/sound) were set up with a mandate to develop guidelines for cultural institutions seeking to find rightsholders of works that might be orphan in their specific areas. This is their joint report.

2008 *State Aid: Public Consultation on the Future Framework for State Funding of Public Service Broadcasting* IP/08/24
Web: http://europa.eu/
Tiny URL: http://tinyurl.com/6zyq9h
A consultation launched by the European Commission on 11/1/2008 applying to state funding of public service broadcasting. This consultation gives Member States and stakeholders the opportunity to submit their views at an early stage, before any Commission proposal, on the possible revision of the Broadcasting Communication – first adopted in 2001. Comments to be submitted by 10 March 2008. The consultation documents include an explanatory memorandum which gives an overview of the current rules, the relevant Commission decision-making practice and the possible scope for amendments. Key issues for discussion are the public service remit in the new media environment and control of overcom-

pensation. Replies to the consultation are published online at: http:// ec.europa.eu/comm/ competition/state_aid/reform/comments_ broadcasting/index.html.

Having reviewed the comments, the Commission may come forward later this year with a proposal for a revised Broadcasting Communication, with a view to its adoption in the first half of 2009.

2008 *Creative Content Online in the Single Market*
COM(2007) 836 final – *Communication from the Commission to the European Parliament, the Council, the European Economic and Social Committee of the Regions*
Web: http://ec.europa.eu/avpolicy/
other_actions/content_online/index_en.htm
The Communication issued on 3/2/2008 launched a public consultation on the challenges facing the market for online creative content in preparation for the adoption of a Recommendation by the Council and the European Parliament. The Commission intends to launch further actions to support the development of innovative business models and the deployment of cross-border delivery of diverse online creative content services. The four key areas to be addressed are: availability of creative content; multi-territory licensing; interoperability and transparency of Digital Rights Management systems; legal offers and piracy. Responses to the consultation which closed on 29/2/2008 are available on the website.

2008 *Public Consultation on Web Accessibility and Other E-accessibility Issues*
Web: http://ec.europa.eu/yourvoice/ipm/
forms/dispatch?form=accessibility&lang=en
On 2/7/2007 the European Commission launched a consultation on measures to make websites in Europe accessible. This public consultation takes place in the broader context of the European Commission's initiative for growth and jobs in the information society (IP/05/643). In 2005, the European Commission adopted a Communication on e-accessibility (IP/05/1144) and stressed the need to make many types of products based on ICT easier to use. In 2006, EU Member States committed to halve by 2010 the gap in internet usage by groups at risk of exclusion, such as older

people, people with disabilities, and unemployed persons (IP/06/769). In 2007 the Commission adopted a Communication urging renewed efforts to boost 'e-Inclusion', including efforts towards 'e-accessibility' (IP/07/1804). The consultation also addresses other technologies like digital television and is open until 27/8/2008. The study 'Measuring progress of eAccessibility in Europe' (MeAC) assesses the degree of compliance with the Web Content Accessibility Guidelines of the World Wide Web consortium. It is available at: http://ec.europa.eu/information_society/activities/eincl usion/library/studies/meac_study/index_en.htm

2008 *Proposal for a European Parliament and Council Directive Amending Directive 2006/116/EC of the European Parliament and of the Council on the Term of Protection of Copyright and Certain Related Rights* COM(2008) 464 final
Web: http://ec.europa.eu/internal_market/copyright/docs/term/proposal_en.pdf
The Commission adopted a proposal to extend the term of protection for performers and sound recordings to 95 years. The aim of the proposal is to bring performers' protection more in line with that already given to authors – 70 years after their death.

2008 *Consultation – Fair Compensation for Acts of Private Copying*
Web: http://ec.europa.eu/internal_market/copyright/levy_reform/index_en.htm
In order to deepen the Commission's understanding on the functioning of private copying levy schemes set up at national level, a 'call for comments' from stakeholders was held from mid-February to mid-April. Responses to the public consultation were published on the website in June. The aim was to inform future policy making on the role and impact of private copying levies in the digital environment; Member States' experience with private copying levies; what direction future policy on private copying levies should take.

2008 *Report on the Implementation of the Recommendation on Film Heritage and the Competitiveness of Related Industrial Activities*
Web: http://ec.europa.eu/avpolicy/docs/reg/cinema/report/swp_en.pdf

At the end of 2005, the European Parliament and the Council adopted a Recommendation to Member States on film heritage. This Recommendation highlights that the European film heritage has to be methodically collected, catalogued, preserved and restored, in order to ensure that is it can be passed on to future generations. Member States should inform the Commission every two years of action taken in response to the Film Heritage Recommendation. In July 2008 the Commission's Services adopted this report which describes the extent to which the measures set out in the Recommendation are working effectively. The report was drafted on the basis of Member States' reports received in reply to a questionnaire circulated by the Commission in October 2007.

2008 *Green Paper – Copyright in the Knowledge Economy European Commission COM(2008) 466/3*
Web: http://ec.europa.eu/
Tiny URL: http://tinyurl.com/6r3pdg7
The Green Paper focuses on how research, scientific and educational materials are disseminated to the public and whether knowledge is circulating freely in the internal market. It also looks at the issue of whether the current copyright framework is sufficiently robust to protect knowledge products and whether authors and publishers are sufficiently encouraged to create and disseminate electronic versions of these products. The Green Paper is an attempt to structure the copyright debate as it relates to scientific publishing, the digital preservation of Europe's cultural heritage, orphan works, consumer access to protected works and the special needs of the disabled to participate in the information society. It also encompasses the current legal framework in the area of copyright and the possibilities it can currently offer to a variety of users (social institutions, museums, search engines, disabled people, teaching establishments).

2008 *i2010: European Digital Libraries Initiative – Final Report on Digital Preservation, Orphan Works, and Out-of-Print Works*
Web: http://ec.europa.eu/
Tiny URL: http://tinyurl.com/6yqlcb

This report by the European Commission High Level Expert Group – Copyright Subgroup identifies priority areas to be dealt with as far as IPR challenges encountered by the Digital Library initiative are concerned: digital preservation of content, including via web-harvesting and the facilitation of clearances concerning rights on orphan and out-of-print works. It indicates what actions and arrangements could, if properly implemented, reduce the difficulties currently encountered in these areas. In the area of digital preservation, the report proposes several actions at the Member State level including the possibility of creating multiple digital copies for preservation purposes and of providing for web-harvesting under national legal deposit legislation.

2008 *i2010 European Digital Libraries Initiative: Final Report on Public Private Partnerships for the Digitisation and Online Accessibility of Europe's Cultural Heritage*
Web: http://ec.europa.eu/
Tiny URL: http://tinyurl.com/5k8zwq
The European Commission believes public private partnerships have an important role to play in helping achieve the Commission's strategy for digitisation, online accessibility and digital preservation of Europe's collective memory. Whilst libraries, archives, museums and galleries have preserved this collective memory and have experience of resource discovery and user requirements, private partners can bring to the table funding, technology, software and expertise required for large-scale digitisation. To make the most of these partnerships, case studies suggest that cultural institutions and private partners should take the following into account: the vision, mission and strategic objectives of all partners and the benefits for the citizen; the need for a formal, transparent, accountable partnership, which does not establish exclusive agreements that are not time-limited; the need to manage the partnership through a formal governance structure; the need of the partnership to operate within the framework of applicable copyright and intellectual property law, and the need for the ownership of such rights after digitisation to be clearly stated; the sustainability of the business model for the long-term.

2008 *MEDIA MUNDUS: Public Consultation*
Web: http://ec.europa.eu/information_society/media/mundus/index_en.htm
The Commission is currently exploring the benefits of adding to the EU's MEDIA programme – created in 1991 to promote the development and the distribution of European films across borders. A public consultation on the main features and priorities of a possible new MEDIA MUNDUS programme, to strengthen cultural and commercial relations between Europe's film industry and film-makers of third countries, closed on 15/6/2008. A summary of the outcome of the consultation is available on the website. This report will provide input for the impact assessment process and the drafting of the Communication, which the Commission plans to adopt in November 2008.

2008 *Communicating Europe through Audiovisual Media* SEC (2008) 506/2
Web: http://ec.europa.eu/commission_barroso/wallstrom/pdf/sec_2008_506-2_en.pdf
In this Communication, the Commission announced actions aimed at bringing more coverage of EU affairs to TV and radio channels and multimedia platforms. It will encourage audiovisual media professionals to create and take part in European audiovisual networks. In particular, it will propose a network of TV stations to complement the network of radio stations launched on 1/4/2008. The Commission will also increase the amount of raw audiovisual material which it already provides free of charge to audiovisual media professionals and will increase its own production of videos to illustrate or explain EU policies.

2008 *Directive on the Protection of Conditional-access Services: Commission Consultation of Interested Parties IP/08/202*
Web: http://ec.europa.eu/internal_market/media/elecpay/index_en.htm
Ten years after the adoption of EU Directive 98/84/EC on conditional access services such as pay-TV or video on demand, the European Commission is to compile a second report on how the Directive is being implemented in what is now a very different economic and technological

climate. To inform this report, due at the end of 2008, a public consultation was held from 11/02/2008 to 4/4/2008. An impact assessment of the Directive was completed in December 2007 and is available at the same URL as the consultation. The consultation focussed on six main areas: the development of cross-border services; how effectively the Directive is being implemented in the Member States; new services covered by the Directive; how the Directive has contributed to protecting copyright holders; digital rights management (DRM) systems; the use of conditional access for purposes other than to protect pay-services.

EUROPEAN COURT OF JUSTICE

2007 *Judgement of the European Court of Justice (Freedom to Provide Services – Television Broadcasting Activities – Directives 89/552/EEC and 97/36/EC – Definition of 'teleshopping' and 'television advertising' – Prize Game)*
IRIS Legal Observations of the European Audiovisual Observatory. IRIS 2008-1:4/2
Web: http://curia.europa.eu/
Tiny URL: http://tinyurl.com/5kc7bm
Judgement of the Court (Fourth Chamber) made on 18/10/2007 in Case C-195/06, Kommunikationsbehörde Austria (KommAustria) v Österreichischer Rundfunk (ORF).The Court laid down a number of criteria for the purposes of determining whether a prize game organised during the broadcast of a television programme can be classified as 'teleshopping' or 'television advertising' within the meaning of Article 1 of the Directive 89/552/EEC (Television Without Frontiers Directive).

INTELLECTUAL PROPERTY OFFICE

2007 *Copyright, Rights in Performances, Publication Right, Database Right – Unofficial Consolidated Text of UK Legislation to 3 May 2007*
Web: www.ipo.gov.uk/cdpact1988.pdf
This document is an unofficial consolidated text of the main UK legislation on copyright and related rights as amended up to 3/5/2007. (It does not include Statutory Instruments made under the Copyright, Designs and Patents Act 1988.) Produced by the IPO, this document has no legal authority, but it does detail the consider-

able number of changes made to the law in this area since the enactment of the Copyright, Designs & Patents Act 1988. Most of these have resulted from secondary legislation amending the 1988 Act in order to implement EC Directives.

2008 *Taking Forward the Gowers Review of Intellectual Property – Proposed Changes to Copyright Exceptions – Consultation Document*
Web: www.ipo.gov.uk/consult-copyright exceptions.pdf
In December 2006, Andrew Gowers reported his findings on the UK's Intellectual Property regime. While he concluded that the system was broadly satisfactory he identified a number of areas where improvements could be made. These included modifying copyright rules to improve access to, and use of, copyright material for private individuals, students and libraries. This consultation looks at how those adjustments might be made. Identifying where the boundaries should lie is critical in ensuring that the copyright system remains fit for today's world. A system of strong rights, accompanied by limited exceptions, will provide a framework that is valued by and protects right holders as well as being understood and respected by users. The consultation was launched by Lord Triesman in January and it ran to April 2008. A response by way of a second consultation is expected later in 2008.

2008 *Taking Forward the Gowers Review of Intellectual Property – Penalties for Copyright Infringement – Consultation Document*
Web: www.ipo.gov.uk/consult-gowers36.doc
Currently the maximum fine that Magistrates' Courts can award for online copyright infringement is £5,000. To reflect the commercial damage that large scale copyright infringement causes, the UK-IPO is consulting on increasing the level of fine handed down by a Magistrates' Court to a maximum of £50,000.

This consultation takes forward Gowers Review recommendation 36, which recommended matching penalties for online and physical copyright infringement by increasing sanctions for online infringements. Consultation runs from 11/8/2008 – 31/10/2008.

OFCOM

OFFICE OF COMMUNICATIONS

2007 *Signing on Television: New Arrangements for Low Audience Channels*
Web: www.ofcom.org.uk/consult/condocs/signing/statement/statement.pdf
A statement of Ofcom's decisions following a public consultation earlier in the year on how to better meet the needs of sign language users, particularly on low audience television channels.

2007 *New News, Future News: The Challenges for Television News after Digital Switch-over*
Web: www.ofcom.org.uk/research/tv/reports/newnews/newnews.pdf
An Ofcom discussion document setting out a framework for policy consideration ahead of the next full PSB review. The report examines the environment in which television news currently operates, and assesses how that may change in future (after digital switch-over and, in 2014, the expiry of current Channel 3 and Channel 5 licences).

It identifies particular issues that will need to be addressed and suggests some specific questions that may need to be answered. Responses to the document were published on the web later in the year at: www.ofcom.org.uk/research/tv/reports/newnews/responses.pdf

2007 *Market Impact Assessment of the BBC's High Definition Television Proposals*
Web: www.ofcom.org.uk/research/tv/bbcmias/bbc_hdtv/bbc_hdtv.pdf
A Market Impact Assessment (MIA) by Ofcom examining the BBC's plans to introduce a new High Definition channel. It finds that the BBC's plans are unlikely to have significant negative market impacts. The service can be expected to deliver consumer benefit through increased take up of HD which is likely to spread across all the major TV platforms including digital terrestrial television, satellite and cable. However, the MIA

made a few recommendations relating to certain aspects of the channel.

2007 *Consultation on the Future of Radio: The Next Phase*
Web: www.ofcom.org.uk/consult/condocs/futureradio07/nextphase.pdf
Following on from the *Consultation on the Future of Radio* earlier in the year, the Digital Radio Working Group was set up to carry forward certain aspects of the discussion. However, this document focuses on some specific issues that do not need to await resolution of the big digital question, and move in the direction of reducing regulation for analogue radio. The issues tackled here fall under four headings: commercial radio content regulation; commercial radio ownership rules, other radio spectrum issues and rules specifically applying to community radio. The consultation closed on 21/12/2007.

2007 *Guidance for Public Service Broadcasters in Drawing up Codes of Practice for Commissioning from Independent Producers*
Web: www.ofcom.org.uk/consult/condocs/cop/statement/statement.pdf
In the course of Ofcom's review of the Television Production Sector in 2005, both Public Service Broadcasters and producers highlighted to Ofcom that the area of new media rights needed to be revisited. In 2006 the two groups agreed new terms for the exploitation of these rights. Following consultation earlier in 2007 (www.ofcom.org.uk/consult/condocs/cop/cop.pdf) Ofcom published revised Guidance in light of these changes in June. PSBs must consider this Guidance when drawing up new Codes of Practice for commissioning from independent producers, which Ofcom will be asked to approve in due course.

2007 *Ofcom's Second Review of Public Service Broadcasting: Terms of Reference*
Web: www.ofcom.org.uk/tv/psb_review/psb_2review/psbreview2.pdf
On 11 September Ofcom published the terms of reference for its second review of public service television broadcasting (PSB). The review will examine the extent to which the public purposes of

PSB are being met and assess options for maintaining and strengthening the quality of PSB in future. It is expected to conclude in early 2009. Interested parties were invited to submit reponses to the terms of reference by the end of September. Ofcom also planned to hold seminars during the first phase of the review to gather further views from stakeholders.

2007 *The Future of Children's Television Programming: Discussion Paper*
Web: www.ofcom.org.uk/tv/psb_review/ psb_2review/psbreview2.pdf
On 3 October Ofcom published a discussion paper and research report (www.ofcom.org.uk/ consult/condocs/kidstv/kidstvresearch.pdf) on the future of children's television programming, assessing the current delivery and future prospects for a wide range of high-quality and original programming for UK children. Ofcom's review analyses the children's television market and for the first time provides a significant evidence base for an informed debate about the future delivery of public service broadcasting for children. Ofcom's analysis raises issues for children's television that reflect those facing UK public service broadcasting overall. The closing date for responses was 20/12/2007.

2007 *The Future of Digital Terrestrial Television: Enabling New Services for Viewers*
Web: www.ofcom.org.uk/consult/condocs/ dttfuture/dttfuture.pdf

An Ofcom consultation launched on 21/11/2007 outlining proposals for a significant upgrade of Digital Terrestrial Television that will offer more channels, including programmes broadcast in High-definition.The document sets out Ofcom's thoughts on how the DTT platform could evolve over the next few years and make best use of the valuable spectrum, while protecting viewers' access to the existing public service broadcast services. Consultation ends 20/1/2008.

2007 *Report of an Inquiry into Television Broadcasters' Use of Premium Rate Telephone Services in Programmes*
Web: www.ofcom.org.uk/tv/ifi/prsinquiry/ ayrereport/report.pdf
Results of an inquiry conducted by Richard Ayre for Ofcom looking into whether there were any systematic reasons behind the large number of apparent failures of compliance in the use of premium rate services (PRS) on television programmes. The inquiry was charged with making recommendations on actions needed to restore public confidence in the use of premium rate telephone services by television broadcasters.

2007 *Consulation on Participation TV: Protecting Viewers and Consumers, and Keeping Advertising Separate from Editorial*
Web: www.ofcom.org.uk/consult/condocs/ participationtv/consultation.pdf
An Ofcom consultation paper, published on 24/7/2007, examining how Participation TV should be regulated in order to protect viewers (particularly significant in view of the number of serious compliance and editorial failures in PTV that had recently come to light and were the subject of an inquiry by Richard Ayre), and to ensure that advertising is kept separate from programme content ('editorial') in accordance with European broadcasting legislation and UK regulation. Supporting documentation (an independent market overview and content analysis and viewer research on participation TV quizzes, adult chat and psychic readings) was also published online. Consultation closed 17/12/2007

2007 *Pay TV Market Investigation – Consultation document*
Web: www.ofcom.org.uk/consult/condocs/ market_invest_paytv/pay_tv.pdf
An Ofcom consultation document, published on 18/12/2007 investigating the pay TV market (including subscription and video-on-demand television services on all platforms: cable, digital terrestrial television (DTT), satellite and IPTV). The purpose of the consultation is to seek stakeholders' views on Ofcom's initial assessment of the operation of competition in the market and the outcome for consumers. Consultation closed

26/2/2008. Responses to the consultation were published on 13/5/2008 at: www.ofcom.org.uk/consult/condocs/market_invest_paytv/responses/. Ofcom intends to publish further consultation documents on separate aspects of the investigation simultaneously by the end of summer 2008.

2007 *Statement on the Digital Dividend*
Web: www.ofcom.org.uk/consult/condocs/ddr/statement/
A statement marking the end of the first phase of the Digital Dividend Review, launched in 2006 to look into how to award the spectrum freed up by digital switchover (the digital dividend) for new uses. It sets out a market-led approach to the release of the spectrum. The second phase of the review will study the detailed design of the award process and the licences.

2008 *Media Literacy Audit – Report on UK Children's Media Literacy*
Web: www.ofcom.org.uk/
Tiny URL: http://tinyurl.com/5d7w4g
The Media Literacy Audits are part of a wide programme of Ofcom research into Media Literacy in the UK. They provide the base of evidence to develop new policies and initiatives to facilitate access and use of digital media services and technologies. Awareness of online shops and free file sharing services is high, even among non-internet users, but most are not aware that downloading music or videos from some file-sharing services is illegal. There is also concern amongst children about the effect of violent video games on behaviour.

2008 *Media Literacy Audit – Report on UK Adult's Media Literacy*
Web: www.ofcom.org.uk/advice/media_literacy/medlitpub/medlitpubrss/ml_adult08/
The Media Literacy Audits are part of a wide programme of Ofcom research into Media Literacy in the UK. They provide the base of evidence to develop new policies and initiatives to facilitate access and use of digital media services and technologies. Concerns highlighted in the report include identity fraud, protecting children from unsuitable material on television and online, and the effect on behaviour of violent video games.

2008 *Social Networking: A Quantitative and Qualitative Research Report into Attitudes, Behaviours and Use*
Web: www.ofcom.org.uk/
Tiny URL: http://tinyurl.com/5wyxat
Extensive qualitative and quantitative research into adult and young children's use of social networking sites and their attitudes towards them. The research reveals just how quickly social networking sites have become parts of Britons' lives and suggests typical profiles of social networkers.

2008 *Statement on Participation TV Part 1: Protecting Viewers and Consumers*
Web: www.ofcom.org.uk/consult/condocs/
This Statement sets out new measures to protect consumers and to help restore confidence in programmes that invite members of the public to participate in them via telephony, the internet or any other form of communication. It details the outcomes of the Consultation 'Participation TV: protecting viewers and consumers, and keeping advertising separate from editorial' which followed the inquiry and recommendations made by Richard Ayre. The Consultation also considered, as a separate issue, the separation of editorial and advertising material in respect of programmes predicated on the promotion of PRS. That issue is not addressed in this Statement and is considered separately (as Participation TV Part 2) to be published later.

2008 *Statement on Digital Television: Enabling New Services*
Web: www.ofcom.org.uk/consult/condocs/dttfuture/statement/statement.pdf
A statement issued on 3/4/2008 that concludes Ofcom's consultation process initiated in November 2007, in response to a request by the Government for advice on how the MPEG-4 and DVBT2 technologies could be introduced to the digital terrestrial television platform, and the potential use of regulatory powers by the Government and Ofcom to bring this about. The statement describes how the huge potential of this technology can be realised without needing more spectrum, and at the same time protecting viewers' access to existing public service broadcasting services.

2008 *The Future of Children's Television Programming: Future Delivery of Public Service Broadcasting for Children*
Web: www.ofcom.org.uk/consult/condocs/ kidstv/statement/statement.pdf
A statement resulting from Ofcom's 2007 discussion paper and the subsequent feedback. The aim of the research was to create a firm foundation for debate by establishing a comprehensive body of evidence around current delivery and future prospects for public service broadcasting to children in the UK. Since the start of the children's review in February 2007, Ofcom has begun work on its second Review of Public Service Broadcasting (PSB Review) and it is proposed to integrate work on children's television with the wider and ongoing work of the PSB Review. Therefore this is the closing statement on The Future of Children's Television Programming. This statement is published simultaneously with the results of Phase One of the second Review of Public Service Broadcasting (PSB Review Phase 1: The Digital Opportunity) to which it is Annex 10.

2008 *The Future of Radio: Statement – Localness on Analogue Commercial Radio and Stereo and Mono Broadcasting on DAB*
Web: www.ofcom.org.uk/consult/condocs/ futureradio07/statement/
Ofcom's new guidelines, published on 7 February 2008, for the provision of local content on analogue (FM and AM) commercial radio. Ofcom's approach simplifies regulation for the commercial radio sector while protecting local content for listeners. Ofcom's statement follows a consultation on revised local content obligations and the regulation of stereo and mono broadcasting on Digital Audio Broadcasting (DAB).

2008 *What is Convergence?*
Web: www.ofcom.org.uk/media/speeches/ 2008/02/cttsubmission1.pdf
A paper submitted by Ofcom for a seminar held on 7/2/2008 by the Convergence Think Tank which was set up jointly by the Department for Culture, Media and Sport and the Department for Business, Enterprise and Regulatory Reform to

examine the implications of technological development for the media and communications industries, and the consequences for both markets and consumers. The paper highlights key themes and draws on Ofcom's existing research and policy work to understand convergence, its drivers, and its implications.

2008 *Participation TV Part 2: Keeping Advertising Separate from Editorial*
Web: www.ofcom.org.uk/consult/condocs/ participation2/
A consultation, published 9 April 2008, on new Broadcasting Code rules for the use and promotion of premium rate services (PRS) in programmes. The rules aim to make absolutely clear that such programmes must not in effect be vehicles for the promotion of PRS. This consultation follows Ofcom's consultation in July 2007 on 'Participation TV: Protecting Viewers and Consumers, and keeping Advertising separate from Editorial' and an important judgement by the European Court of Justice on 18 October 2007 regarding whether a quiz TV show where viewers call a Premium Rate Line line to take part could be classified as teleshopping. This consultation seeks feedback on proposed rules which, in view of responses to the 2007 consultation and ECJ judgment, are stricter than those originally put forward. Consultation closed 3 June 2008.

2008 *Ofcom's Second Public Service Broadcasting Review Phase One: The Digital Opportunity*
Web: www.ofcom.org.uk/consult/condocs/ psb2_1/
The review sets out alternative ways that public service broadcasting (PSB) can be funded in the future. The review covers all public service broadcasters, both publicly-owned (the BBC, Channel 4 and S4C) and commercial (ITV1, five and Teletext). In addition to the formal consultation, Ofcom launched an online blog for people to debate the issues in the review. Also available online are annexes to the consultation covering the audience's view on the future of PSB; PSB Review 2008 Research Findings; economic modelling of future scenarios for public service content; reviews on public service content online

and its value; future delivery of public service content for children; market failure in broadcasting. The consultation was published on 10/4/2008 and closed on 19/6/2008. A second report will be published in autumn 2008, to be followed by further consultation.

2008 *Regulation of Community Radio Services – A Consultation on the Procedure for considering Changes to a Station's Key Commitments*
Web: www.ofcom.org.uk/consult/condocs/regulation_cr/condoc.pdf
An Ofcom consultation, launched on 10/6/2008, on the criteria and process it proposes to use for considering changes to a community radio station's key commitments. Each community radio station has specific key commitments which form part of its licence and are based on the promises made in its application. Consultation closed 21/7/2008.

2008 *Ofcom Response to EU Consultation on Application of State Aid Rules to Public Service Broadcasting*
Web: www.ofcom.org.uk/tv/ifi/stateaidrules/ofcomresponse.pdf
Ofcom response to the European Commission consultation on the application of state aid rules to public service broadcasting. The Commission published a consultation paper on the future framework which applies to state funding of public service broadcasting in January 2008, exploring the possibility of revising the Broadcasting Communication first published in 2001.

2008 *Ofcom Fact Sheets relating to Digital Switchover*
Web: www.ofcom.org.uk/research/tv/reports/dsoind/factsheets/
Three fact sheets produced by Ofcom relating to the UK's digital switchover. They provide detailed information on digital terrestrial television coverage, as follows:
Fact Sheet 1: Digital terrestrial television coverage predictions. To assist the process of planning for switchover, computer models are used to predict coverage of the digital terrestrial television (Freeview) signal. This fact sheet explains how the predictions are worked out.

Fact Sheet 2: Coverage of the public service multiplexes after switchover. The coverage of the public service multiplexes has been designed to meet the same coverage level (98.5% of the population) as the existing analogue services after switchover. However, these multiplexes will not cover exactly the same 98.5% of households. This fact sheet sets out the reasons for the differences along with details on the ways in which different groups of households might be affected.
Fact Sheet 3: Why some people will receive more digital television channels than others. There are four different ways to get digital television: through an aerial (Freeview), by satellite, cable or broadband. This fact sheet sets out the different digital television options and explains why the number of television channels on Freeview differs in different parts of the UK.

2008 *The Nations & Regions Communications Market Review 2008*
Web: www.ofcom.org.uk/research/cm/cmrnr08/
The third of Ofcom's annual reviews of the markets for television, radio, and telecommunications, showing detailed data for the nations and regions across the UK. Its aim, like that of its predecessors, is to provide the context for Ofcom's own policy thinking and to inform debates and decisions taken by stakeholders in the public and private sectors. The 2008 review takes place against the background of significant policy debates on issues as diverse as the future of public service broadcasting and the future regulatory framework for high-speed broadband. Distinct versions of these debates are taking place in the regions of England and Northern Ireland, Scotland, and Wales. That is why Ofcom continues to seek to deepen the geographical detail of its research, as well as to reflect on new themes and patterns of consumer behaviour, brought about by the convergence between fixed and wireless communications technologies.

2008 *Digital Dividend Review: 550-630MHz and 790-854MHz. Consultation on Detailed Award Design*
Web: www.ofcom.org.uk/consult/condocs/clearedaward/condoc.pdf

This document launches the implementation phase of the digital dividend review (DDR). It set out detailed proposals for how the valuable spectrum that will be freed up as a result of the switchover to digital television will be released. The aim is to enable innovative services that will deliver significant benefits to UK citizens and consumers. The consultation ends on the 15/8/2008.

2008 *Digital Dividend Review: Geographic Interleaved Awards 470 – 550 MHz and 630 – 790 MHz. Consultation on Detailed Award Design*
Web: www.ofcom.org.uk/consult/condocs/ddrinterleaved/interleaved.pdf
Ofcom's second consultation on the spectrum that will be freed up as a result of digital switchover. It details proposals for the release of spectrum in the geographical 'white spaces' that will exist between digital television transmitters after digital switchover. This spectrum can be used for low power services including: new digital television services covering most of the UK, a UK region or nation; television services covering a city or a local area; services in support of programme making and special events; and possibly mobile television and mobile broadband. Consultation closes 21/8/2008.

2008: *Contract Rights Renewal Undertakings Review*
Web: www.oft.gov.uk/advice_and_resources/resource_base/register-orders-undertakings/reviews/CRR-review
The Office of Fair Trading (OFT) and Ofcom formally launched a review of the Contract Rights Renewal (CRR) undertakings in January 2008 that is expected to last around a year. The CRR undertakings were accepted by the Secretary of State in November 2003 following a finding by the Competition Commission (CC) that a proposed merger of Carlton and Granada to form ITV plc would be expected to be contrary to the public interest and have an adverse effect on competition for the sale of advertising airtime. The OFT is required to consider from time to time whether merger undertakings such as CRR should be varied, revoked or superseded in the light of any changes of circumstances. If the OFT considers that the CRR undertakings should be modified it

will make a reasoned recommendation to the Competition Commission, which will decide the outcome after consultation on its proposed decision.

2008 *Market Impact Assessment: New Local Video Proposals – Terms of Reference*
Web: www.ofcom.org.uk/research/tv/bbcmias/localvideo/
The Terms of Reference for Ofcom's Market Impact Assessment (MIA) of the BBC's proposed Local Video service, published 24/6/2008. The MIA will examine the likely impact of the service proposed by the BBC on similar and related products and services, particularly local newspapers, radio stations, television services and their associated online services, and look in particular at the extent to which the new service might affect innovation and investment in the commercial sector. The Local Video service would expand upon existing BBC Local websites on bbc.co.uk and focus on 60 areas across the UK. It would create bespoke local video news, sport and weather to complement the BBC's existing online provision. The consultation will run until 4/8/2008 and the results of the MIA will be published on 18 November, alongside those of the BBC Trust's concurrent Public Value Assessment.

2008 *Access Services Audio Description: Research into Awareness Levels*
Web: www.ofcom.org.uk/research/tv/reports/access_services_audio/
Independent research commissioned by Ofcom into UK Audio Description (AD) awareness levels. It measures awareness of the service both before and after the Ofcom-led Audio Description Awareness Campaign. It reveals that amongst people with visual impairments, awareness levels increased from 43 per cent to 72 percent following the campaign. Amongst the general UK population, awareness increased from 37 per cent to 60 per cent.

2008 *Ofcom Broadcast Bulletin Issue No 114 – Outcome of Investigation into THE GREAT GLOBAL WARMING SWINDLE*
Web: www.ofcom.org.uk/tv/obb/prog_cb/obb114/

The Bulletin details the outcome of Ofcom's investigation into THE GREAT GLOBAL WARMING SWINDLE, broadcast on Channel 4 on 8/3/2007. The programme sought to challenge the theory that human activity is the major cause of climate change and global warming. Ofcom says Channel 4 did not fulfil obligations to be impartial and to reflect a range of views on controversial issues. It also says the film treated interviewees unfairly, but did not mislead audiences 'so as to cause harm or offence'.

2008 *Public Service Broadcasting Review Phase 1 – Summary of Consultation Responses*
Web: www.ofcom.org.uk/consult/condocs/ psb2_1/responsesummary/
A summary of all 270 formal responses to Phase One of Ofcom's Public Service Broadcasting Review. A number of key themes emerged from the responses to the consultation document and the summary has been grouped within each theme. The subject groups include: long term models for delivery of public service content; prospects for children's programming; options for Channel 4, ITV, five and Teletext. Non-confidential versions of all responses can be viewed.

2008 *Citizens, Communications and Convergence – Discussion Paper*
Web: www.ofcom.org.uk/consult/condocs/ citizens/discussionpaper.pdf
Document published as part of a consultation running from 11/7/2008 – 8/10/2008 detailing how Ofcom serves its citizens' interests by ensuring that people have access to the communications services, content and skills needed to participate in society.

2008 *Code on the Scheduling of Television Advertising: Revised Rules on the Scheduling of Advertisements*
Web: www.ofcom.org.uk/consult/condocs/rada/ statement/statementcode.pdf
Following changes to the European framework of advertising regulation as set out in the Audio Visual Media Services (AVMS) Directive, Ofcom decided to carry out a comprehensive review of its Rules on the Amount and Distribution of Advertising (RADA) as part of its Review of Television Advertising and Teleshopping Regulation. Stage One of this review, published in March 2008, www.ofcom.org.uk/consult/condocs/rada/ invited comments on proposals for simplified and liberalised rules on the placing (or 'distribution') of television advertisements. This document sets out the conclusions of Stage One of the review and also describes the next steps in relation to Stage Two – a consultation to be published in the autumn dealing with the amount of advertising and teleshopping permitted on television, and how often advertising breaks should be allowed. Alongside the consultation on Stage Two of the review, a report on deliberative research into the attitudes of consumers towards possible changes to the frequency of television advertising will be published. Ofcom aims to conclude Stage Two of the review in time to allow any changes to the rules on the amount or frequency of television advertising to be incorporated in the new Code and implemented with effect from 1/1/2010.

OLSWANG

2007 *Olswang Convergence Consumer Survey 2007*
Web: www.olswang.com/convergence07/ default.asp

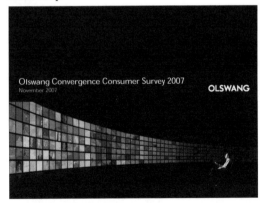

Olswang Convergence Consumer Survey 2007
November 2007

OLSWANG

The third annual independent survey conducted by Olswang in conjunction with YouGov. It reveals that, as consumers become increasingly connected using a range of connected devices at home and on the move, they are demanding more rich media content but are still reluctant to pay. To secure free content consumers are willing to tolerate online advertisements which they would normally go out of their way to avoid. Some are even willing to deliberately break the law to secure free content, while others simply don't understand the law.

SCOTTISH BROADCASTING COMMISSION

2008 *Scottish Broadcasting Commission: Interim Report on the Cultural Phase*
Web: www.scottishbroadcastingcommission.gov.uk/Resource/Doc/4/0000359.pdf
Since January, the Commission has been focusing its independent investigation on the cultural importance of Scottish broadcasting, looking at the main programme services and how well they meet the needs and aspirations of viewers. This interim report, together with evidence gathered during the investigation, was published in March.

2008 *Scottish Broadcasting Commission: Interim Report on the Democratic Phase*
Web: www.scottishbroadcastingcommission.gov.uk/Resource/Doc/4/0000393.pdf
Since March, the Commission has been gathering evidence on the democratic importance of broadcasting in Scotland. The interim report published in May reveals emerging issues in the role of news programmes in informing and engaging Scottish audiences, and in whether democracy in Scotland is being fully served by broadcasters. Evidence gathered during the investigation is also available on the SBC website.

2008 *Scottish Broadcasting Commission: Final Report*
Web: www.scottishbroadcastingcommission.com/about/documents
The Scottish Broadcasting Commission was established to conduct an independent investigation into the current state of television production and broadcasting in Scotland and define a strategic way forward for the industry. Since November 2007, the Commission has been gathering evidence in its investigation into the economic, cultural and democratic aspects of broadcasting in Scotland. Reports on the three phases of the enquiry as well as the oral and written evidence that informed the reports are published on the SBC website.

UK FILM COUNCIL

2007 *A Study of Feature Film Development and Screenwriter and Development Training in the UK: A Final Report for the UK Film Council and Skillset*
Web: www.ukfilmcouncil.org/media/research
Tiny URL: http://tinyurl.com/6q3jh6
Development_and_training_final_report_07.11.07
The final report of the study into feature film development and screenwriter and development training in the UK, conducted for the UK Film Council by Attentional (formerly David Graham and Associates).

2007 *The Economic Impact of the UK Film Industry*
Web: www.ukfilmcouncil.org/media/pdf/5/8/FilmCouncilreport190707.pdf
A report by Oxford Economics, supported by the UK Film Council and Pinewood Shepperton plc, which provides a comprehensive evaluation of the economic contribution of the UK film industry.

2007 *Digital & Physical Piracy in GB*
Web: www.ukfilmcouncil.org/media/pdf/g/m/Ipsos_Piracy_UK_2007.pdf

Research based on fieldwork conducted by IPSOS in November 2007 into the scale and impact of piracy and the motivations and behaviour of the people who engage in it. The survey explores the three types of piracy: physical piracy (buying counterfeit or home copied DVDs); digital piracy – electronic distribution downloading/streaming) from unofficial sources; secondary piracy (borrowing or viewing an illegal copy – as opposed to making or buying one).

2007 *Film Theft in the UK: An Analysis and Recommendations for Action*
Web: www.ukfilmcouncil.org/media/pdf/j/4/Film_theft_in_the_UK.pdf
A report from the Anti-Piracy Task Force covering both the scale and extent of copyright theft and means of countering this threat. Measures to combat piracy are reviewed under five headings: the legal framework; enforcement; security measures; education and consumer awareness; the development of new business models. As a result of this review, the Task Force makes 30 recommendations for Government, the industry and Government-backed and other stakeholders on how these measures could be improved.

UK LEGISLATION – STATUTORY INSTRUMENT

2008 *Statutory Instrument 1420: The Television Multiplex Services (Reservation of Digital Capacity) Order 2008*
TSO ISBN 9780110818290
Web: www.opsi.gov.uk/si/si2008/pdf/uksi_20081420_en.pdf
This Order makes provision enabling Ofcom to re-organise the broadcasting of digital terrestrial television services, in order to facilitate the introduction of new technologies. To achieve this, the Order modifies Part 1 of the Broadcasting Act 1996 and also makes provision for television multiplex services and digital television programme services. It is made under section 243(1) and (3) of the Communications Act 2003.

UK PARLIAMENTARY REPORTS

2007 *The Digital Switchover (Disclosure of Information) Bill – Revised January 2007*
TSO ISBN 9780108435805
Web: www.publications.parliament.uk/pa/cm200607/cmbills/003/07003.i-i.html
The Digital Switchover (Disclosure of Information) Bill permits social security and certain other information to be disclosed in connection with the delivery of the Digital Switchover Help Scheme, in order to identify people in the eligbile categories and maximise take-up levels. – see ACT in 2008.

2008 *The Ownership of the News Vol. 1: Report, 1st Report of Session 2007-2008. HL Paper 122-I*
TSO ISBN: 9780104013113
Web: www.publications.parliament.uk/pa/ld200708/ldselect/ldcomuni/122/122i.pdf
Report by the House of Lords Select Committee on Communications chaired by Lord Fowler. It examines the impact that media ownership can have on the news and the effect of consoli-dation on the newspaper, television and radio industries. *Volume 2* contains evidence (ISBN 9780104013120)

2008 *Preparations for Digital Switchover: Twenty-eighth Report of Session 2007-08 Report, together with Formal Minutes,Ooral and Written Evidence House of Commons Papers 416 2007-08*
TSO ISBN 9780215521279
Web: www.publications.parliament.uk/pa/cm200708/cmselect/cmpubacc/416/41602.htm
DCMS and BERR are jointly responsible for implementing digital switchover by 2012. The Departments have passed to the BBC respon-sibility for funding the public information cam-paign and delivering the help scheme, although the Departments have no means of holding the BBC to account for this use of licence fee money. This report by the House of Commons Public Accounts Commiteee points out that, to date, take-up of the help scheme has been significantly lower than the Departments expected, and they have not taken effective action to protect consumer interests.

WORLD INTELLECTUAL PROPERTY ORGANIZATION

2007 *Non-paper on the WIPO Treaty on the Protection of Broadcasting Organizations*
Web: http://www.wipo.int/meetings/en/doc_details.jsp?doc_id=77333
The World Intellectual Property Organization is a UN agency that creates international treaties governing intellectual property. Over the years, the Broadcasting Treaty has gone through several iterations, but it was originally created with the aim of granting broadcasters a property right in signals. This draft consultation document contains some controversial proposals in relation to new technologies and digital rights management.

This section offers a selection of organisations within the United Kingdom which are likely to be useful to those interested in audio-visual media in higher education and the work of the BUFVC. Further, comprehensive listings can be found in the Directory of British Associations, *or sector-specific publications such as the* Guardian Media Directory *and the* ASLIB Directory. *Organisations outside the UK are listed separately in the following section,* Organisations – International.

ADVERTISING ASSOCIATION

7th Floor North, Artillery House,
11-19 Artillery Row, London SW1P 1RT
Tel: 020 7340 1100 **Fax:** 020 7222 1504
E-mail: aa@adassoc.org.uk
Web: www.adassoc.org.uk

 A federation of twenty nine trade bodies and organisations representing the advertising and promotional marketing industries including advertisers, agencies, media and support services.

ADVERTISING STANDARDS AUTHORITY (ASA)

Mid City Place, 71 High Holborn,
London WC1V 6QT
Tel: 020 7492 2222 **Fax:** 020 7242 3696
E-mail: feedback@asa.org.uk
Web: www.asa.org.uk
The ASA was set up in 1962 to make sure that non-broadcast advertisements appearing in the UK are legal, decent, honest and truthful. The Authority protects the public by ensuring that the rules in the British Codes of Advertising and Sales Promotion are followed by everyone who prepares and publishes advertisements.

ALL PARTY PARLIAMENTARY COMMUNICATIONS GROUP (APCOMMS)

Office of John Robertson MP, House of Commons,
London SW1A 0AA
Tel: 020 7340 1420
Web: www.apcomms.org.uk/category/Home/
apComms was created in July 2007 following a merger between The All Party Parliamentary Group on Communications, The All Party Parliamentary Mobile Group (apMobile) and The All Party Parliamentary Internet Group (APIG). The new apComms group exists to provide a discussion forum between the communications industry and Parliamentarians for the mutual benefit of both parties. Accordingly, the group considers all communication issues as they affect society, informing current Parliamentary debate through meetings, informal receptions and reports.

ALLIANCE AGAINST IP THEFT

Riverside Building, County Hall, Westminster
Bridge Road, London SE1 7JA
Tel: 020 7803 1324, **Fax:** 020 7803 1310
E-mail: info@allianceagainstiptheft.co.uk
Web: www.allianceagainstiptheft.co.uk
The Alliance provides a single voice for trade organisations and enforcement organisations that

share an interest in preventing intellectual property theft in the UK.

ANIMATION RESEARCH CENTRE (ARC)

University for the Creative Arts at Farnham, Falkner Road, Farnham, Surrey GU9 7DS
Tel: 01252 892 806 **Fax:** 01252 892 787
E-mail: arcinfo@ucreative.ac.uk
Web: www.ucreative.ac.uk/

 The ARC aims to promote, contribute to and support the under-researched discipline of animation theory. The aims of the archive are to maintain and expand holdings of UK animation and to develop and produce teaching and other support materials for animation curricula and other disciplines affiliated with international archival institutions.

ART LIBRARIES SOCIETY (ARLIS)

The Business Manager, The National Art Library, V&A South Kensington, Cromwell Rd, London SW7 2RL
Tel. 0207 942 2317
E-mail: arlis@vam.ac.uk
Web: www.arlis.org.uk
ARLIS/UK & Ireland: the Art Libraries Society is the professional organisation for people involved in providing library and information services and documenting resources in the visual arts. It aims to promote all aspects of the librarianship of the visual arts, including architecture and design.

ARTS & HUMANITIES DATA SERVICE (AHDS)

Web: www.ahds.ac.uk
Until April 2008, the AHDS was a national service for the collection, preservation and promotion of electronic resources resulting from research and teaching in the arts and humanities. JISC has provided a further year's funding to keep the website available, to maintain and update the AHDS cross-search catalogue, and allow the Centres to continue to deliver AHDS collections. Despite the loss of central funding, the host institutions of the AHDS are committed to working separately and together to provide a revised set of services for the arts and humanities research community.

ARTS & HUMANITIES RESEARCH COUNCIL (AHRC)

Whitefriars, Lewins Mead, Bristol, BS1 2AE
Tel: 0117 987 6500 **Fax:** 0117 987 6600
E-mail: enquiries@ahrc.ac.uk
Web: www.ahrc.ac.uk

 The AHRC funds research and postgraduate study within the UK's higher education institutions. In addition, on behalf of the Higher Education Funding Council for England, it provides funding for museums, galleries and collections that are based in, or attached to, higher education institutions in England.

ARTS COUNCIL ENGLAND

14 Great Peter Street, London SW1P 3NQ
Tel: 0845 300 6200 **Fax:** 020 7973 6590
E-mail: enquiries@artscouncil.org.uk
Web: www.artscouncil.org.uk
Arts Council England is the national funding body for the arts in England. It is responsible for developing, sustaining and promoting the arts through the distribution of public money from central government and revenue generated by the National Lottery.

ARTS COUNCIL OF NORTHERN IRELAND

77 Malone Road, Belfast BT9 6AQ
Tel: 028 9038 5200 **Fax:** 028 9066 1715
Web: www.artscouncil-ni.org
E-mail: info@artscouncil-ni.org
The Council distributes government and National Lottery funds for the arts throughout Northern Ireland.

ARTS COUNCIL OF WALES

9 Museum Place, Cardiff CF10 3NX
Tel: 029 2037 6500 **Fax:** 029 2022 1447
Web: www.artswales.org.uk
The Council distributes government and National Lottery funds for the arts throughout Wales.

ASLIB – THE ASSOCIATION FOR INFORMATION MANAGEMENT

Holywell Centre, 1 Phipp Street, London EC2A 4PS

Tel: 020 7613 3031 **Fax:** 020 7613 5080
E-mail: aslib@aslib.co.uk
Web: www.aslib.co.uk
Aslib actively promotes best practice in the management of information resources, represents its members, and lobbies on all aspects of the management of and legislation concerning information at local, national and international levels.

ASSOCIATE PARLIAMENTARY MEDIA LITERACY GROUP (APMLG)

E-mail: APMLG@ofcom.org.uk
Web: www.apmlg.org.uk/index.htm
The Associate Parliamentary Media Literacy Group has been set up to promote a greater understanding of the importance of media literacy within Parliament and more widely.

ASSOCIATION FOR DATABASE SERVICES IN EDUCATION & TRAINING (ADSET)

The Business Exchange, Rockingham Road, Kettering, Northants NN16 8JX
Tel: 01536 526424
E-mail: info@adset.org.uk
Web: www.adset.org.uk
ADSET is a membership organisation which seeks to improve the quality, management, use and usefulness of information about learning opportunities, occupations and careers, student and client records, job vacancies, the labour market, and qualifications.

ASSOCIATION FOR LEARNING TECHNOLOGY (ALT)

ALT Administration, Gipsy Lane, Headington, Oxford OX3 0BP
Tel: 01865 484125 **Fax:** 01865 484165
E-mail: admin@alt.ac.uk
Web: www.alt.ac.uk
ALT is the leading UK body bringing together practitioners, researchers, and policy makers in learning technology.

ASSOCIATION FOR MEASUREMENT AND EVALUATION OF COMMUNICATION (AMEC)

Communications House, 26 York Street, London W1U 6PZ

Tel: 0208 675 4442
E-mail: Barryleggetter@amecorg.com
Web: www.amecorg.com
AMEC is the global trade body and professional institute for companies and individuals involved in research, measurement and evaluation in editorial media coverage and related communications issues.

ASSOCIATION FOR THE STUDY OF MEDICAL EDUCATION (ASME)

12 Queen Street, Edinburgh EH2 1JE
Tel: 0131 225 9111 **Fax:** 0131 225 9444
E-mail: info@asme.org.uk
Web: www.asme.org.uk
The Association seeks to improve the quality of medical education by bringing together individuals and organisations with interests and responsibilities in medical and healthcare education.

ASSOCIATION OF COMMONWEALTH UNIVERSITIES (ACU)

Woburn House, 20-24 Tavistock Square, London WC1H 9HF

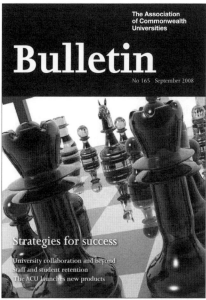

The September 2008 edition of the ACU Bulletin.

Tel: 020 7380 6700 **Fax:** 020 7387 2655
E-mail: info@acu.ac.uk

Web: www.acu.ac.uk

The ACU is a voluntary association of over 460 universities throughout the Commonwealth. Its aim is to promote contact and co-operation between member universities; to support the movement of academic staff and students between member universities; to provide information about Commonwealth universities; to host the consultancy, the Commonwealth Higher Education Management Service (CHEMS).

ASSOCIATION OF UK MEDIA LIBRARIANS (AUKML)

PO Box 14254, London SE1 9WL
E-mail: Chair@aukml.org.uk
Web: www.aukml.org.uk

AUKML was formed in 1986 to create links between librarians and information workers in all areas of the media industry. AUKML aims to improve the professional standing of information workers through exchanging knowledge and experience and by organising meetings, events and conferences to keep members up-to-date with emerging techniques in information management.

AUDIOBOOK PUBLISHING ASSOCIATION (APA)

Tel: 07971 280788
E-mail: info@theapa.net
Web: www.theapa.net

The APA is the UK trade association for the audiobook industry with membership open to anyone involved in the publishing of spoken word audio, including those working in BBC radio, cassette and CD duplication, actors' agencies, retail, producers and abridgers.

AUTHORS' LICENSING AND COLLECTING SOCIETY (ALCS)

The Writers' House, 13 Haydon Street,
London, EC3N 1DB
Tel: 020 7264 5700 **Fax:** 020 7264 5755
E-mail: alcs@acls.co.uk
Web: www.alcs.co.uk

The ALCS represents the interests of all UK writers and aims to ensure writers are fairly compensated for any works that are copied, broadcast or recorded.

THE BRITISH ACADEMY

10 Carlton House Terrace, London SW1Y 5AH
Tel: 020 7969 5200 **Fax:** 020 7969 5300
E-mail: secretary@britac.ac.uk
Web: www.britac.ac.uk

The British Academy was established by Royal Charter in 1902, under the full title of The British Academy for the Promotion of Historical, Philosophical and Philological Studies. It is an independent and self-governing fellowship of scholars. It is the national academy for the humanities and the social sciences, the counterpart to the Royal Society which exists to serve the natural sciences.

BRITISH ACADEMY OF FILM & TELEVISION ARTS (BAFTA)

195 Piccadilly, London W1J 9LN
Tel: 020 7734 0022 **Fax:** 020 7734 1792
Web: www.bafta.org

BAFTA is the UK's leading organisation promoting and rewarding the best in film, television and interactive media. A membership-led organisation, it runs a wide range of events covering topical issues on all areas which are not only open to Academy members but non-members as well. Based in central London, the Academy provides a meeting place for members as well as being a unique venue which hosts many prestigious events organised through its conference facilities department.

BRITISH AND IRISH SOUND ARCHIVES (BISA)

c/o Norfolk Record Office, The Archive Centre, Martineau Lane, Norwich, NR1 2DQ
Fax: 01603 761885
Web: www.bisa-web.org/

The purpose of BISA is to facilitate the exchange of information on all practical aspects of audio archiving in the United Kingdom, the Republic of Ireland, the Channel Islands and the Isle of Man, and to co-ordinate activity deemed by the membership to be in support of their professional interests. BISA members have online access to a list of sound archives organised by national, local, broadcasting and special collections.

BRITISH ASSOCIATION OF PICTURE LIBRARIES AND AGENCIES (BAPLA)

18 Vine Hill, London EC1R 5DZ
Tel: 020 7713 1780, **Fax:** 020 7713 1211
E-mail: enquiries@bapla.org.uk
Web: www.bapla.org.uk
BAPLA is the UK trade association for over 400 picture libraries and agencies in the UK. It is dedicated to fostering the picture library industry through promoting established best practice and standard contracts, providing information services and representing the industry through marketing and lobbying.

BRITISH BOARD OF FILM CLASSIFICATION (BBFC)

3 Soho Square, London W1D 3HD
Tel: 020 7440 1570 **Fax:** 020 7287 0141
E-mail: contact_the_bbfc@bbfc.co.uk
Web: www.bbfc.co.uk
The British Board of Film Classification is an independent, non-governmental body, which has classified cinema films since it was set up in 1912, and videos since the passing of the Video Recordings Act in 1984.

© Sander ten Brakel / SXC

BRITISH COMPUTER SOCIETY (BCS)

First Floor, Block D, North Star House,
North Star Avenue, Swindon, SN2 1FA
Tel: 01793 417417 **Fax:** 01793 417444
Web: www.bcs.org/
Established in 1957, the British Computer Society is the leading body for those working in IT. Its objects are to promote the study and practice of computing and to advance knowledge of and education in IT for the benefit of the public.

BRITISH COPYRIGHT COUNCIL

29-33 Berners Street, London W1T 3AB
Tel: 01986 788 122 **Fax:** 01986 788 847
E-mail: secretary@britishcopyright.org
Web: www.britishcopyright.org
The British Copyright Council is an umbrella organisation bringing together organisations which represent those who create or hold rights in literary, dramatic, musical and artistic works and those who perform such works. It functions principally as a liaison committee for its member associations, providing them with a forum for the discussion of matters of copyright interest. It also acts as a pressure group for changes in copyright law at UK, European and International level.

THE BRITISH COUNCIL

10 Spring Gardens, London SW1A 2BN
Tel: 0161 957 7755 **Fax:** 0161 957 7762
E-mail: general.enquiries@britishcouncil.org
Web: www.britishcouncil.org

Film Department:
Tel: 020 7389 3194 **Fax:** 020 7389 3199
E-mail: arts@britishcouncil.org
Web: www.britishcouncil.org/arts-film.htm
The British Council is the United Kingdom's international organisation for educational and cultural relations. The Council's Film Department promotes contemporary and innovative work from the UK to audiences around the world through the British Council's global network.

BRITISH EDUCATIONAL COMMUNICATIONS & TECHNOLOGY AGENCY (BECTA)

Milburn Hill Road, Science Park, University of Warwick, Coventry CV4 7JJ
Tel: 024 7641 6994 **Fax:** 024 7641 1418
E-mail: becta@becta.org.uk
Web: www.becta.org.uk
BECTa leads the national drive to improve learning through technology. It does this by working with industry to ensure the right technology for education is in place. It also supports the education sector to make the best use of technology so that every learner in the UK is able to benefit from its advantages and achieve their full potential.

BRITISH EDUCATIONAL SUPPLIES ASSOCIATION (BESA)

20 Beaufort Court, Admirals Way, London E14 9XL
Tel: 020 7537 4997 **Fax:** 020 7537 4846
E-mail: besa@besa.org.uk
Web: www.besanet.org.uk
BESA is a trade association promoting and providing information about its member companies which include manufacturers and distributors of equipment, materials, books, consumables, furniture, technology, ICT hardware and digital content to the education market.

BRITISH FEDERATION OF FILM SOCIETIES (BFFS)

Unit 315, The Workstation, 15 Paternoster Row, Sheffield S1 2BX
Tel: 0114 2210314
E-mail: info@bffs.org.uk
Web: www.bffs.org.uk/

 The BFFS is a national body which promotes voluntary film exhibition and represents the interests of film societies in the United Kingdom. It receives some financial support from the British Film Institute and works with other bodies such as local Arts Boards and the National Lottery Commission to support film societies.

BRITISH FILM INSTITUTE (BFI)

21 Stephen Street, London W1P 2LN
Tel: 020 7255 1444
Web: www.bfi.org.uk
The BFI promotes understanding and appreciation of Britain's rich film and television heritage and culture. Established in 1933, the BFI runs a range of activities and services: BFI Southbank (previously the National Film Theatre), the BFI IMAX Cinema, BFI Publishing, *The Times* BFI London Film Festival, the London Lesbian and Gay Film Festival, the BFI National Archive, video and DVD releases, film releases, the BFI National Library, BFI Education, and *Sight and Sound* magazine.

BRITISH INTERACTIVE MEDIA ASSOCIATION (BIMA)

Briarlea House, Southend Road, Billericay CM11 2PR

Tel: 01277 658107 **Fax:** 0870 051 7842
E-mail: info@bima.co.uk
Web: www.bima.co.uk
British Interactive Media Association is the trade association for the UK's interactive media sector. It provides its members with a forum for the exchange of information and views on the market, and promotes the sector to government, industry and education.

BRITISH INTERNET PUBLISHERS ALLIANCE (BIPA)

E-mail: your_comments@bipa.org.uk
Web: www.bipa.co.uk
The core purpose of the Alliance is to promote the growth and development of new Internet services in a way which permits a wide diversity of entrants to the market, on a free and fair competitive basis, in order to deliver a wide range of choice for the public and maximise the potential for British enterprise in e-commerce and other areas.

BRITISH KINEMATOGRAPH, SOUND & TELEVISION SOCIETY (BKSTS)

Pinewood Studios, Iver Heath, Bucks SL0 0NH
Tel: 01753 656656 **Fax:** 01753 657016
E-mail: info@bksts.com
Web: www.bksts.com
The BKSTS exists to encourage, sustain, educate, train and represent all those who, creatively or technologically, are involved in the business of providing moving images and associated sound in any form and through any media; to encourage and promote excellence in all aspects of moving image and associated sound technology; to promote these aims throughout the world, while remaining independent of all governments and commercial organisations.

BRITISH LIBRARY

96 Euston Road, London NW1 2DB
Tel: 0870 444 1500
E-mail: customer-services@bl.ac.uk
Web: www.bl.uk
The British Library is the national library of the United Kingdom and holds a copy of every UK and Irish publication.

BRITISH LIBRARY SOUND ARCHIVE

96 Euston Road, London NW1 2DB
Tel: 020 7412 7676 **Fax:** 020 7412 7441
E-mail: sound-archive@bl.uk
Web: www.bl.uk/soundarchive
The Sound Archive holds over a million discs, 185,000 tapes, and many other sound and video recordings. The collections come from all over the world and cover the entire range of recorded sound from music, drama and literature, to oral history and wildlife sounds. They range from cylinders made in the late 19th century to the latest CD, DVD and minidisc recordings.

BRITISH LITERARY AND ARTISTIC COPYRIGHT ASSOCIATION (BLACA)

Web: www.blaca.org.uk
BLACA is the UK national group of the International Literary and Artistic Association (ALAI). Since its foundation in 1981 BLACA has provided a forum for discussion of matters affecting the rights of authors and other copyright owners. Its members are mostly practising or academic lawyers and others interested in upholding the principles of copyright.

BRITISH MUSIC RIGHTS (BMR)

British Music House, 26 Berners Street, London W1T 3LR
Tel: 020 7306 4446 **Fax:** 020 7306 4449
E-mail: britishmusic@bmr.org
Web: www.ukmusic.org/page
BMR is an umbrella organisation which represents the interests of composers, songwriters and music publishers. Formed in 1996 by the British Academy of Composers & Songwriters, the Music Publishers Association (MPA), the Mechanical-Copyright Protection Society (MCPS) and the Performing Right Society (PRS), it provides a consensus voice promoting the interests of creators and publishers of music at all levels.

THE BPI

Riverside Building, County Hall, Westminster Bridge Road, London SE1 7JA
Tel: 020 7803 1300 **Fax:** 020 7803 1310
E-mail: general@bpi.co.uk
Web: www.bpi.co.uk
The BPI (formerly known as the British Phonographic Industry) is the British record industry's trade association. Its membership comprises hundreds of music companies including all four 'major' record companies, associate members such as manufacturers and distributors, and hundreds of independent music companies representing literally thousands of labels.

BRITISH SCREEN ADVISORY COUNCIL (BSAC)

13 Manette Street, London W1D 4AW
Tel: 020 7287 1111 **Fax:** 020 7287 1123
E-mail: bsac@bsacouncil.co.uk
Web: www.bsac.uk.com
The BSAC is an independent, advisory body to government and policy makers at national and European level. It is a source of information and research for the screen media industries. The BSAC provides a unique forum for the audio-visual industry to discuss major issues which affect the industry.

BRITISH UNIVERSITIES FILM & VIDEO COUNCIL (BUFVC)

77 Wells Street, London W1T 3QJ
Tel: 020 7393 1500 **Fax:** 020 7393 1555
E-mail: ask@bufvc.ac.uk
Web: www.bufvc.ac.uk
The BUFVC is a representative body which promotes the production, study and use of moving image, sound and related media in higher education and research. The Council is a related body of the Higher Education Funding Council for England and receives part funding as grant via the Joint Information Systems Committee.

BRITISH VIDEO ASSOCIATION (BVA)

167 Great Portland Street, London W1N 5PE
E-mail: general@bva.org.uk
Tel: 020 7436 0041 **Fax:** 020 7436 0043
Web: www.bva.org.uk
The BVA is the trade body that represents the interests of publishers and rights owners of video home entertainment. It liaises with government, the media, other industry bodies and carries out extensive market research.

BROADBAND STAKEHOLDER GROUP (BSG)

Russell Square House, 10-12 Russell Square, London WC1B 5EE
Tel: 020 7331 2163 **Fax:** 020 7331 2040
E-mail: peter.shearman@intellectuk.org
Web: www.broadbanduk.org
BSG is the industry-government forum tackling strategic issues across the converging broadband value chain.

BROADCAST JOURNALISM TRAINING COUNCIL (BJTC)

c/o 18 Miller's Close, Rippingale nr. Bourne, Lincolnshire, PE10 0TH
Tel: 01778 440025
E-mail: sec@bjtc.org.uk
Web: www.bjtc.org.uk
BJTC is a partnership of all the main employers in the UK broadcast industry. It develops training programmes to improve skills and knowledge across the broadcast journalism industry. It sets the criteria for course accreditation and then sends teams of professional journalists and tutors to inspect courses and provide advice.

THE BROADCAST TRAINING & SKILLS REGULATOR (BTSR)

C/o Ofcom, Contents & Standards Administrative Office, Fifth Floor Riverside House, 2A Southwark Bridge Road, London SE1 9HA
Tel: 0844 5611675
E-mail: info@btsr.org.uk
Web: www.btsr.org.uk/

Created by and for the broadcasting industry, the BTSR's aim is to ensure the industry is providing its employees with training and development opportunities that are relevant, inclusive and cost-effective. It identifies common issues, evaluates the funding options, shares good practice and looks for any gaps between what the industry might need and what broadcasters and training organisations are providing.

BROADCASTERS' AUDIENCE RESEARCH BOARD (BARB)

E-mail: enquiries@barb.co.uk
Web: www.barb.co.uk
BARB is responsible for providing estimates of the number of people watching television. This includes which channels and programmes are being watched, at what time, and the type of people who are watching at any one time within the UK. The data is available for reporting nationally and at ITV and BBC regional level and covers all analogue and digital platforms.

BROADCASTING, ENTERTAINMENT & CINEMATOGRAPH TECHNICIANS UNION (BECTU)

373-377 Clapham Road, London SW9 9BT
Tel: 020 7346 0900 **Fax:** 020 7346 0901
E-mail: info@bectu.org.uk
Web: www.bectu.org.uk
BECTU is the independent union for those working in broadcasting, film, theatre, entertainment, leisure, interactive media and allied areas. The union represents permanently employed, contract and freelance workers who are primarily based in the United Kingdom.

THE BROADCASTING TRUST

Web: http://freespace.virgin.net/local.tv/ TV%20Trust%20for%20Scotland.html
Formed in 2004 from the merger of The Television Trust for Scotland and the Association of Scottish Small-scale Broadcasters. The Broadcasting Trust's brief is to focus on all electronic community media developments – radio, television and Internet – and to continue to support training and other initiatives which increase awareness of community broadcasting opportunities.

BUFVC/CBA COMMITTEE FOR AUDIOVISUAL EDUCATION (CAVE)

c/o BUFVC, 77 Wells Street, London W1T 3QJ
Tel: 020 7393 1507 **Fax:** 020 7393 1555
E-mail: cathy@buvc.ac.uk
CAVE exists to promote the use of audio-visual materials in the teaching of archaeology at all levels. Members are drawn from the educational,

media and archaeology sectors. CAVE administers the Channel 4 Awards, part of the biennial British Archaeological Awards.

CAMPAIGN FOR PRESS AND BROADCASTING FREEDOM (CPBF)

2nd Floor, Vi & Garner Smith House,
23 Orford Road, Walthamstow, London E17 9NL
Tel: 020 8521 5932
E-mail: freepress@cpbf.org.uk
Web: www.cpbf.org.uk
The Campaign for Press and Broadcasting Freedom is an independent voice for media reform. Since 1979 it has been working for a more accountable, freer and diverse media.

CHANNEL 4 BRITISH DOCUMENTARY FILM FOUNDATION

E-mail: info@britdoc.org
Web: https://www.britdoc.org/
The Foundation runs multiple projects dedicated to securing the creative future of British documentary and developing new funding and distribution models for the digital age. Activities involve the funding of short and feature films, organising the annual Britdoc Festival, holding conferences and running training programmes.

CHARTERED INSTITUTE OF LIBRARY AND INFORMATION PROFESSIONALS (CILIP)

7 Ridgmount Street, London WC1E 7AE
Tel: 020 7255 0500 **Fax:** 020 7255 0501
E-mail: info@cilip.org.uk
Web: www.cilip.org.uk
Provides access to knowledge, information and resources to support members in their continuing professional development. Membership is open to anyone working with knowledge, information or in library services.

CILT – THE NATIONAL CENTRE FOR LANGUAGES

3rd Floor, 111 Westminster Bridge Road,
London SE1 7HR
Tel: 020 7379 5101 **Fax:** 020 7379 5082
E-mail: info@cilt.org.uk
Web: www.cilt.org.uk

CILT, the National Centre for Languages, is the Government's recognised centre of expertise on languages. The organisation's mission is to promote a greater capability in languages amongst all sectors of the UK population.

CIMTECH

Cimtech Limited, Innovation Centre, University of Hertfordshire, College Lane, Hatfield AL10 9AB
Tel: 01707 281060 **Fax:** 01707 281061
E-mail: c.cimtech@herts.ac.uk
Web: www.cimtech.co.uk
Cimtech is the UK's centre of expertise on all aspects of information management and technology. It was established in 1967 and numbers amongst its members and clients over 1,000 of the UK and Europe's leading organisations in both the public and private sectors.

CLEARCAST

2nd Floor, 4 Roger Street, WC1N 2JX
Tel: 0207 339 4700
Web: www.clearcast.co.uk/clearcast/
Clearcast (formerly known as The British Advertising Clearance Centre) is the company responsible for the pre-transmission examination and clearance of television advertisements. All advertisements being transmitted as a national television campaign on UK terrestrial and satellite channels should be submitted to Clearcast for approval. Clearcast is funded by commercial broadcasters who pay a quarterly copy clearance fee.

COMMONWEALTH BROADCASTING ASSOCIATION (CBA)

17 Fleet Street, London EC4Y 1AA
Tel: 020 7583 5550 **Fax:** 020 7583 5549
E-mail: cba@cba.org.uk
Web: www.cba.org.uk
The CBA is an association of more than 100 broadcasting organisations in Europe, Asia, Africa, the Caribbean, Australasia, the Pacific, North and South America.

COMMONWEALTH INSTITUTE

New Zealand House, 80 Haymarket,
London SW1Y 4TE

Tel: 020 7024 9822 **Fax:** 020 7024 9833
E-mail: info@commonwealth-institute.org
Web: www.commonwealthfoundation.com/
about/CA/CDP/Commonwealth%20Institute/
The primary object of the Commonwealth Institute
is to advance education in the Commonwealth,
specifically primary and secondary education and
teacher training across the Commonwealth. Its
initiatives include the Centre for Commonwealth
Education, which is a joint venture with
Cambridge University.

COMMUNITY MEDIA ASSOCIATION (CMA)

The Workstation, 15 Paternoster Row,
Sheffield S1 2BX
Tel: 0114 279 5219 **Fax:** 0114 279 8976
E-mail: cma@commedia.org.uk

CMA Scotland:
E-mail: scotland@commedia.org.uk
Web: www.commedia.org.uk
CMA is the UK representative body for the community media sector and is committed to promoting access to the media for people and communities. It aims to enable people to establish and
develop community based communications media
for empowerment, cultural expression, information and entertainment.

COMMUNITY TV TRUST (CTVT)

10 Denman Road, London SE15 5NP
Tel: 020 7701 0878
E-mail: chris@communitytrust.org
Web: www.communitytvtrust.org
CTVT promotes the use of media and new media
in local organisations and schools in the belief that
self esteem and general personal empowerment
come from participating in local media making,
and that it also aids cross-cultural understanding in
communities. CTVT provides a forum for debate,
as well as supplying information and promoting
local initiatives, talent and needs.

CONVERGENCE THINK TANK (CTT)

DCMS, 2-4 Cockspur Street, London
SW1Y 5DH
Tel: 020 7211 6443 **Fax:** 020 7211 6339
E-mail: convergence@culture.gsi.gov.uk

Web: www.culture.gov.uk/convergence/
index.html
The CTT was set up jointly by the Department
for Culture, Media and Sport (DCMS) and the
Department for Business, Enterprise and Regulatory Reform to examine the implications of
technological development for the media and
communications industries, and the consequences
for both markets and consumers. It is envisaged
that the CTT will have a key role in helping to
shape future policy development in relation to
these sectors, which include TV, radio, mobile and
fixed telecoms and online services. It is seeking
the views of stakeholders and will produce a report
to Government in early 2009.

COPYRIGHT LICENSING AGENCY (CLA)

Saffron House, 6-10 Kirby Street,
London EC1N 8TS
Tel: 020 7400 3100 **Fax:** 020 7400 3101
E-mail: cla@cla.co.uk
Web: www.cla.co.uk
The CLA is the UK's Reproduction Rights
Organisation. It was set up in 1983 by the Authors'
Licensing and Collecting Society and the Pub-
lishers' Licensing Society to perform collective
licensing on their behalf. It provides a fair and
effective way of collecting fees due to authors and
publishers for the reproduction of their work.

COUNCIL FOR BRITISH ARCHAEOLOGY (CBA)

St Mary's House, 66 Bootham, York YO30 7BZ
Tel: 01904 671417 **Fax:** 01904 671384
E-mail: info@britarch.ac.uk
Web: www.britarch.ac.uk
The CBA works to improve and promote public
interest in and understanding of Britain's past and
concerns itself with conservation, information,
research, publishing, education and training in
archaeology. The CBA Education Department
works with the BUFVC on a joint Working Party to
review and co-ordinate the listing of films, videos
and new media on archaeology suitable for use in
education. The CBA also runs, again in conjunction with the BUFVC, the biennial Channel 4
Awards for the best ICT project and television or
radio programme on an archaeological subject.

CYFLE

33-35 West Bute Street, Cardiff CF10 5LH
Tel: 029 2046 5533 **Fax:** 029 2046 3344
E-mail: Cyfle@cyfle.co.uk
Web: www.cyfle.co.uk
Cyfle is the training company for the Welsh television, film and interactive media industry. The organisation was originally formed in order to train Welsh speaking technicians for the television industry which grew as a result of the creation of S4C. In 2000 the Company became a Skillset (Sector Skills Council) accredited Training Partner and became a national provider for the industry across Wales.

DEPARTMENT FOR CHILDREN, SCHOOLS AND FAMILIES (DCSF)

Sanctuary Buildings, Great Smith Street,
London SW1P 3BT
Tel: 0870 000 2288 **Fax:** 01928 794248
E-mail: info@dcsf.gsi.gov.uk
Web: www.dcsf.gov.uk
The Department for Children, Schools and Families (DCSF) is responsible for improving the focus on all aspects of policy affecting children and young people, as part of the Government's aim to deliver educational excellence.

DEPARTMENT FOR CULTURE, MEDIA AND SPORT (DCMS)

2-4 Cockspur Street, London SW1Y 5DH
Tel: 020 7211 6200
E-mail: enquiries@culture.gov.uk
Web: www.culture.gov.uk
The DCMS is responsible for Government policy on the arts, sport, the National Lottery, tourism, libraries, museums and galleries, broadcasting, creative industries including film and the music industry, press freedom and regulation, licensing, gambling and the historic environment.

DEPARTMENT FOR INNOVATION, UNIVERSITIES AND SKILLS (DIUS)

Castle View House, East Lane, Runcorn WA7 2GJ
Tel: 020 7215 5555 or 01928 794666
E-mail: info@dius.gsi.gov.uk
Web: www.dius.gov.uk
This Department brings together functions from the former Department of Trade and Industry, including responsibilities for science and innovation, with further and higher education and skills, previously part of the Department for Education and Skills. It aims to bring together the nation's strengths in science, research, universities and colleges to build a dynamic, knowledge-based economy.

DESIGN AND ARTISTS COPYRIGHT SOCIETY (DACS)

33 Great Sutton Street, London EC1V 0DX
Tel: 020 7336 8811 **Fax:** 020 7336 8822
Web: www.dacs.org.uk
DACS is the UK's copyright and collecting society for artists and visual creators. It exists to promote and protect the copyright and related rights of artists and visual creators.

DIGITAL CONTENT FORUM (DCF)

131-151 Great Titchfield Street,
London, W1W 5BB
Tel: 020 766 58440
E-mail: info@dcf.org.uk
Web: www.dcf.org.uk
The DCF works in an advisory and collaborative capacity with government departments, in delivering policy and strategy for the digital content sector. The DCF collaborates with groups such as the Broadband Stakeholders Group, the Information Age Partnership and HMSO's Crown Copyright Advisory Panel, and actively engages with government consultations, UK and EU legislation and its implementation.

DIGITAL CURATION CENTRE

University of Edinburgh, Appleton Tower,
Crichton Street, Edinburgh EH8 9LE
Tel: 0131 651 1239
E-mail: info@dcc.ac.uk
Web: www.dcc.ac.uk/
Funded by the JISC and the e-Science core programme, the Digital Curation Centre advises scientists, researchers and scholars at UK institutions on the storage, management and preservation of digital data, to help ensure their enhancement and continuing long-term use. Advice is offered on creating adequate docu-

© Daniela Martina / SXC

mentation for the data, and dealing with problems of technology obsolescence and the fragility of digital media.

DIGITAL PRESERVATION COALITION

Innovation Centre, York Science Park, Heslington, York YO10 5DG
Tel: 01904 435362 **Fax:** 01904 435 135
E-mail: info@dpconline.org
Web: www.dpconline.org
The Digital Preservation Coalition was established in 2001 to foster joint action to address the urgent challenges of securing the preservation of digital resources in the UK and to work with others internationally to secure our global digital memory and knowledge base.

DIGITAL RADIO DEVELOPMENT BUREAU

The Radiocentre, 77 Shaftesbury Avenue, London W1D 5DU
Tel: 020 7306 2630 **Fax:** 020 7470 0062

E-mail: info@drdb.org
Web: www.drdb.org/
DRDB is a trade body funded and supported by the BBC and commercial radio multiplex operators. It is the central industry communicator on DAB digital radio, working directly with broadcasters, manufacturers and retailers to encourage more and different products, heightened consumer and high street awareness, and improved understanding of DAB technology and co-ordination of brand usage.

DIGITAL RADIO WORKING GROUP (DRWG)

c/o Radio & Media Markets Branch, DCMS, 2-4 Cockspur Street, London SW1Y 5DH.
E-mail: DRWG@culture.gsi.gov.uk
Web: www.culture.gov.uk/what_we_do/broadcasting/4014.aspx
The DWRG was established in November 2007 by instruction of the Secretary of State for Culture,

Media & Sport. Its purpose was to bring together senior figures from the radio industry and related stakeholders, under an independent Chair, to consider three questions: what conditions would need to be achieved before digital platforms could become the predominant means of delivering radio; what are the current barriers to the growth of digital radio; what are the possible remedies to those barriers? The DRWG was asked to report its findings to the Secretary of State by the end of 2008.

DIGITAL TELEVISION GROUP (DTG)

Nine Elms Lane, Vauxhall, London, SW8 5NQ
Tel: 020 7501 4300
E-mail: office@dtg.org.uk
Web: www.dtg.org.uk
The Digital TV Group is the industry association for digital television in the UK. The group is currently focussed on digital switchover and the rich media services and products it will help enable, including high definition television, mobile television, video-on-demand, broadband television and television metadata.

DIRECTORS GUILD OF GREAT BRITAIN (DGGB)

4 Windmill Street, London W1T 2HZ
Tel: 020 7580 9131 **Fax:** 020 7580 9132
E-mail: info@dggb.org
Web: www.dggb.co.uk
DGGB is an organisation representing directors in all media: film, television, theatre, radio, opera, commercials, corporate, multimedia and new technology. It is a Craft Guild, offering training and opportunities for its members to share and exchange expertise and skills at a wide variety of events.

DIRECTORS UK

20-22 Bedford Row, London WC1R 4EB
Tel: 020 7269 0677 **Fax:** 020 7269 0676
E-mail: info@dprs.org
Web: www.directorsuk.com
Directors UK (formerly the Directors' and Producers' Rights Society) is the collecting society which represents British film and television directors. It collects and distributes money due to directors for the exploitation of their work. The Society is also a campaigning organisation, working to establish and protect directors' rights in the UK and abroad.

DOCHOUSE

Riverside Studios, Crisp Road, Hammersmith, London W6 9RL
Tel: 020 8237 1220 **Fax:** 020 8237 1001
E-mail: info@dochouse.org
Web: www.dochouse.org
DocHouse was formed to support and promote documentary in the UK. It aims to increase participation and develop new audiences for documentaries in the cinema, on television and emerging media; create faster and easier access to UK and international documentary; promote the use of documentary through education at all levels; and nurture and encourage new talent for the future.

DOCSPACE

Scottish Documentary Institute, 74 Lauriston Place, Edinburgh EH3 9DF
Tel: 0131 221 6245/6125 **Fax:** 131 221 6100
E-mail: docspaceprod@eca.ac.uk
Web: www.docspace.org.uk
Docspace brings the power and art of documentary into the spotlight, forging partnerships with venues and digital technology. It works in the public domain, introducing new audiences to documentaries. It carries out research on audiences, and hosts master classes with feature documentary directors.

DOCUMENTARY FILMMAKERS GROUP (DFG)

4th Floor, Shacklewell Studios, 28 Shacklewell Lane, London E8 2EZ
Tel: 020 7249 6600
E-mail: info@dfgdocs.com
Web: www.dfgdocs.com
DFG, founded in 2001, is an organisation providing a comprehensive resource for documentary filming. Its aim is to encourage, stimulate, promote and support the growth of a strong community of documentary filmmakers and film audiences. DFG's work falls into three main strands: training, the running of screenings, festivals and forums, and production.

E-LEARNING FOUNDATION

3000 Hillswood Drive, Hillswood Business Park, Chertsey Surrey KT16 0RS
Tel: 01932 796036 **Fax:** 01932 796660
E-mail: info@e-learningfoundation.com
Web: www.e-learningfoundation.com/
Cms.aspx?link=e4338a2a-cd7f-4465-9594-eb9897745520
The e-Learning Foundation aims to significantly increase access to ICT for education, and specifically to ensure that every child in the UK should have home access to technology for learning when and where they want to learn. The Foundation proides a free advisory and support service for schools, acts as a fundraiser and grant provider, and campaigns at government level to keep the digital divide at the forefront of public consciousness.

EDINA

Causewayside House, 160 Causewayside, Edinburgh EH9 1PR
Tel: 0131 650 3302 **Fax:** 0131 650 3308
E-mail: edina@ed.ac.uk
Web: http://edina.ac.uk
EDINA, based at Edinburgh University Data Library, is one of the two JISC-funded national data centres. It offers the UK tertiary education and research community networked access to a library of data, information and research resources.

EDUCATIONAL RECORDING AGENCY (ERA)

New Premier House, 150 Southampton Row, London WC1B 5AL
Tel: 020 7837 3222 **Fax:** 020 7837 3750
E-mail: era@era.org.uk
Web: www.era.org.uk

On behalf of its members, ERA operates a Licensing Scheme for educational use of copyright material. The scheme permits staff at educational establishments to record, for non-commercial educational purposes, broadcast output of ERA's members. Most educational establishments in the UK are covered by an ERA licence.

ENTERTAINMENT RETAILERS ASSOCIATION (ERA)

Colonnade House, 1st Floor, 2 Westover Road, Bournemouth, Dorset BH1 2BY
Tel: 01202 292063 **Fax:** 01202 292067
E-mail: admin@eraltd.org
Web: www.bardltd.org
The ERA is a UK trade organisation formed specifically to act as a forum for the retail and wholesale sectors of the music, video, DVD and multimedia products industry.

EQUITY

Guild House, Upper St Martins Lane, London WC2H 9EG
Tel: 020 7379 6000 **Fax:** 020 7379 7001
E-mail: info@equity.org.uk
Web: www.equity.org.uk
Equity is a trade union representing artists from across the entire spectrum of arts and entertainment including actors, singers, dancers, choreographers, stage managers, theatre directors and designers, variety and circus artists, television and radio presenters, walk-on and supporting artists, stunt performers and directors and theatre fight directors.

ESDS QUALIDATA

Economic and Social Data Service, UK Data Archive, University of Essex, Wivenhoe Park, Colchester, Essex CO4 3SQ
Tel: 01206 873058 **Fax:** 01206 872003
E-mail: qualidata@esds.ac.uk
Web: www.qualidata.essex.ac.uk
ESDS Qualidata is a specialist service of the ESDS led by the UK Data Archive at the University of Essex. The service provides access and support for a range of social science qualitative datasets, promoting and facilitating increased and more effective use of data in research, learning and teaching.

FEDERATION AGAINST COPYRIGHT THEFT (FACT)

Europa House, Church Street, Old Isleworth, Middlesex TW7 6DA
Tel: 020 8568 6646 **Fax:** 020 8560 6364

E-mail: contact@fact-uk.org.uk
Web: www.fact-uk.org.uk/index.htm
FACT is the leading representative trade body committed to protecting the interests of the audio-visual industry in the fight against pirate film and DVDs and the increasing threat from online piracy.

FEDERATION AGAINST SOFTWARE THEFT (FAST)

York House, 18 York Road, Maidenhead, SL6 1SF
Tel: 01628 622121 **Fax:** 01628 760338
E-mail: info@fast.org
Web: www.fast.org.uk
FAST was created in 1984 by the software industry to lobby Parliament for changes to the copyright law. It works on behalf of the software industry, and addresses the misuse, overuse and theft of software intellectual property.

FEDERATION OF COMMERCIAL AUDIO-VISUAL LIBRARIES (FOCAL)

Pentax House, South Hill Avenue, Northolt Road, South Harrow, Middlesex HA2 0DU
Tel: 020 8423 5853 **Fax:** 020 8933 4826
E-mail: info@focalint.org
Web: www.focalint.org

FOCAL was formed in 1985 as an international, non-profit making, professional trade association limited by guarantee. It represents commercial film/audio-visual, stills and sound libraries as well as interested individuals such as facility houses, professional film researchers and producers working in the industry.

FILM ARCHIVE FORUM (FAF)

c/o Linda Kaye, c/o British Universities Film & Video Council, 77 Wells Street, London W1T 3QJ
E-mail: linda@bufvc.ac.uk
Web: www.bufvc.ac.uk/faf
Established in 1987, the Film Archive Forum represents all of the public sector film and television archives which care for the UK's moving image heritage. It represents the UK's public sector moving image archives in all archival aspects of the moving image, and acts as the advisory body on national moving image archive policy.

FILM DISTRIBUTORS' ASSOCIATION

22 Golden Square, London W1F 9JW
Tel: 020 7437 4383 **Fax:** 020 7734 0912
E-mail: info@fda.uk.net
Web: www.launchingfilms.com
FDA is the trade body for theatrical film distributors in the UK - the companies that release films for UK cinema audiences. Originally established in London in 1915, FDA represents a distribution stance in regular representations to and consultations with the UK Film Council, the government and other trade organisations in the film industry.

FILM EDUCATION

21-22 Poland Street, London W1F 8QQ
Tel: 020 7851 9450 **Fax:** 020 7439 3218
E-mail: postbox@filmeducation.org
Web: www.filmeducation.org

Film Education is a registered charity funded by the film industry in the UK. Its aim is to encourage and promote the use of film and cinema within the National Curriculum.

FILM LONDON

Suite 6.10, The Tea Building, 56 Shoreditch High Street, London E1 6JJ
Tel: 020 7613 7676 **Fax:** 020 7613 7677
E-mail: info@filmlondon.org.uk
Web: www.filmlondon.org.uk
Film London is the capital's film and media agency. It supports the growth and development of all the screen industries based in the capital – film, television, video, commercials and new interactive media. Its aim is to sustain, promote and develop London as a major international film-making and film cultural capital.

FOUNDATION FOR INFORMATION POLICY RESEARCH (FIPR)

10 Water End, Wrestlingworth, Sandy, Bedfordshire SG19 2HA
Tel: 01223 334733
E-mail: chair2006@fipr.org
Web: www.fipr.org
The FIPR is the leading think tank for Internet policy in Britain. It studies the interaction between IT, Government, business and civil society. It

researches policy implications and alternatives, and promotes better understanding and dialogue between business, Government and NGOs across Europe.

FREE CULTURE UK

Web: www.freeculture.org.uk

Free Culture UK is a grassroots movement with an online network and locally-based groups of members working for an open, participatory culture, believing that individuals and communities should be empowered to be creative, and that this can be done by legal, social and political means by defending and promoting cultural spaces such as Free Software, Creative Commons and the public domain.

GRIERSON TRUST

c/o Ivan Sopher & Co, 5 Elstree Gate, Elstree Way, Borehamwood, Hertfordshire WD6 1JD
Web: www.griersontrust.org

The 2007 Grierson Awards ceremony.

The Grierson Trust commemorates the pioneering Scottish documentary maker John Grierson and the man widely regarded as the father of the documentary. Each year the Trust recognises the best documentary filmmaking from Britain and abroad through the Grierson Awards. Throughout the year the Grierson Trust organises and collaborates in activities for the promotion and celebration of the best in documentary film and television production.

HIGHER EDUCATION WALES (HEW)

2 Caspian Point, Caspian Way, Cardiff Bay, Cardiff CF10 4DQ

Tel: 029 2044 8020
E-mail: t.evans@wales.ac.uk
Web: www.hew.ac.uk

Higher Education Wales (HEW) provides an expert resource on higher education in Wales, with membership encompassing the heads of all the Welsh universities and higher education institutions. HEW represents the interests of its members to the National Assembly, to Parliament, political parties, European institutions and bodies, and negotiates on behalf of Welsh higher education.

INCORPORATED SOCIETY OF MUSICIANS (ISM)

10 Stratford Place, London W1C 1AA
Tel: 020 7629 4413 **Fax:** 020 7408 1538
E-mail: membership@ism.org
Web: www.ism.org

The UK's professional body for musicians. The ISM promotes the art of music and the interests of professional musicians and aims to raise standards in the profession and give its members the best available advice on issues ranging from education to ethics, and from intellectual property to broadcasting.

INDEPENDENT CINEMA OFFICE

3rd Floor, Kenilworth House, 79-80 Margaret Street, London W1W 8TA
Tel: 020 7636 7120 **Fax:** 020 7636 7121
E-mail: info@independentcinemaoffice.org,uk.
Web: www.independentcinemaoffice.org.uk

The Independent Cinema Office is a national organisation that aims to develop and support independent film exhibition throughout the UK. It works in association with independent cinemas, film festivals, film societies and the regional and national screen agencies.

INDEPENDENT FILM PARLIAMENT (IFP)

Web: www.filmparliament.org.uk

Launched in July 2003, the IFP offers an opportunity for those involved in the production, distribution and exhibition of independent films to share ideas on structures and policy in an open, public forum.

INDUSTRY TRUST FOR IP AWARENESS

E-mail: info@copyrightaware.co.uk
Web: www.copyrightaware.co.uk/index.asp
In 2004 the major DVD distributors joined forces with retail and rental outlets in the UK and formed the Industry Trust for Intellectual Property Awareness to combat DVD piracy.

INSTITUTE FOR LEARNING (IFL)

Bracton House, 34-36 High Holborn,
London WC1V 6AE
Tel: 0844 815 3202
E-mail: enquiries@ifl.ac.uk
Web: www.ifl.ac.uk/
IFL is the professional body for teachers, trainers, tutors and student teachers in the Learning and Skills sector, representing the the needs of its members by continuing to raise the status of teaching practitioners across the sector.

INSTITUTE FOR PUBLIC POLICY RESEARCH (IPPR)

30-32 Southampton Street, London WC2E 7RA
Tel: 020 7470 6100 **Fax:** 020 7470 6111
Web: www.ippr.org.uk

The UK's leading progressive think tank, producing cutting edge research and innovative policy ideas for a just, democratic and sustainable world.

INSTITUTE OF MEDICAL ILLUSTRATORS (IMI)

29 Arboretum Street, Nottingham, NG1 4JA
Tel: 020 7731 7962
Web: www.imi.org.uk
Founded in 1968 to bring together the several disciplines of medical illustration, for over thirty years IMI has set and maintained standards for the profession. For its membership, IMI provides a rich network of fellow professionals, working together to improve and develop medical illustration by means of conferences, courses and regional meetings.

INSTITUTE OF PRACTITIONERS IN ADVERTISING (IPA)

44 Belgrave Square, London SW1X 8QS

Tel: 020 7235 7020 **Fax:** 020 7245 9904
E-mail: info@ipa.co.uk
Web: www.ipa.co.uk
The IPA is the industry body and professional institute for leading advertising, media and marketing communications agencies in the UK.

INTELLECTUAL PROPERTY AWARENESS NETWORK

1st Floor, 36 Great Russell Street, London
WC1B 3QB
Tel: 020 7436 3040 **Fax:** 020 7323 5312
Email: ipi@ip-institute.org.uk
Web: www.ipaware.net/
The Network was formed in 1993 aiming to bring together the separate IP awareness activities and concerns of a wide range of professional, educational and business organisations. There are currently about forty member organisations and the UK Intellectual Property Office has observer status.

INTELLECTUAL PROPERTY INSTITUTE (IPI)

1st Floor, 36 Great Russell Street,
London WC1B 3QB
Tel: 020 7436 3040 **Fax:** 020 7323 5312
Email: ipi@ip-institute.org.uk
Web: www.ip-institute.org.uk/
The IPI exists to promote awareness and understanding of intellectual property law and its contribution to economic and social welfare through high quality, independent research. It aims to provide knowledge and expertise for industry, policy makers, professionals and the general public, in order to foster a legal, social and regulatory climate that supports an innovation-based economy.

INTERNATIONAL BROADCASTING TRUST (IBT)

CAN Mezzanine, 32-6 Loman Street, London
SE1 0EH
Tel: 020 7922 7940
E-mail: mail@ibt.org.uk
Web: www.ibt.org.uk
The IBT is an educational and media charity working to promote high quality television coverage of

the developing world through lobbying Government, regulators and broadcasters; conducting research on television coverage of the developing world; developing innovative programme ideas.

INTERNATIONAL VISUAL COMMUNICATIONS ASSOCIATION (IVCA)

19 Pepper Street, Glengall Bridge, Docklands, London E14 9RP
Tel: 020 7512 0571 **Fax:** 020 7512 0591
E-mail: info@ivca.org
Web: www.ivca.org
The IVCA exists to promote effective business and public service communications of the highest ethical and professional standards. It aims to be a centre of excellence for best communication practice and works with production companies, freelancers, support service providers and clients of the industry to represent their interests and help maximise their competitiveness and professionalism.

INTERNET SERVICES PROVIDERS ASSOCIATION (ISPA UK)

28 Broadway, London SW1H 9JX
Tel: 0870 050 0710 **Fax:** 0871 594 0298
E-mail: admin@ispa.org.uk
Web: www.ispa.org.uk
ISPA UK is the UK's Trade Association for providers of Internet services. It was established in 1995 and promotes competition, self-regulation and the development of the Internet industry.

JANET (UK)

Lumen House, Library Avenue, Harwell Science and Innovation Campus, Didcot, Oxfordshire OX11 0SG
Tel: 01235 822200 **Fax:** 01235 822399
E-mail: service@ja.net
Web: www.ja.net

 JANET is the network dedicated to the needs of education and research in the UK. It connects the UK's education and research organisations to each other, as well as to the rest of the world through links to the global Internet. Formerly known as UKERNA.

JOINT INFORMATION SYSTEMS COMMITTEE (JISC)

JISC Secretariat, Northavon House, Coldharbour Lane, Bristol BS16 1QD
Tel: 0117 931 7317 **Fax:** 0117 931 7255
E-mail: info@jisc.ac.uk
Web: www.jisc.ac.uk
JISC's activities support education and research by promoting innovation in new technologies and by the central support of ICT services.

KRASZNA-KRAUSZ FOUNDATION

c/o Angela English, 3 Downscourt Road, Purley, Surrey CR8 1BE
E-mail: info@kraszna-krausz.org.uk
Web: www.kraszna-krausz.org.uk/
The Kraszna-Krausz Awards, sponsored by the Kraszna-Krausz Foundation, are made annually, with prizes for books on still photography alternating with those for books on the moving image. Entries in each year cover books published in the previous two years. The winning books are those which make original and lasting educational, professional, historical, technical, scientific, social, literary or cultural contributions to the field.

LEARNING & TEACHING SPACES MANAGERS GROUP (LTSMG)

Web: http://ltsmg.org.uk
The group consists of managers, technical supervisors and senior technicians within higher education, responsible for managing and delivering audio visual facilities and equipment within lecture theatres and teaching space throughout higher education.

LIBRARIES AND ARCHIVES COPYRIGHT ALLIANCE (LACA)

c/o CILIP, 7 Ridgmount Street, London WC1E 7AE
Tel: 020 7255 0500 **Fax:** 020 7255 0501
E-mail: info@cilip.org.uk
Web: www.cilip.org.uk/policyadvocacy/copyright/about
LACA monitors and lobbies in the UK and Europe about copyright and related rights on behalf of its member organisations and all users of copyright

works through library, archive and information services.

MCPS-PRS ALLIANCE

Copyright House, 29-33 Berners St, London W1T 3AB
Tel: 020 7580 5544 **Fax:** 020 7306 4455
Web: www.mcps-prs-alliance.co.uk
Formed in 1997 by two royalty collection societies (MCPS and PRS), the MCPS-PRS Alliance exists to collect and pay royalties to its members when their music is recorded and made available to the public (MCPS); and when their music is performed, broadcast or otherwise made publicly available (PRS).

© Andrzej Pobiedzinski / SXC

MEDIA, COMMUNICATION & CULTURAL STUDIES ASSOCIATION (MECCSA)

Web: www.meccsa.org.uk
MeCCSA is the subject association for the field of media, communication and cultural studies in UK Higher education. Membership is open to all who teach and research these subjects in HE institutions, via either institutional or individual membership. The field includes film and television production, journalism, radio, photography, creative writing, publishing, interactive media and the web; and it includes higher education for media practice as well as for media studies.

MEDIA EDUCATION ASSOCIATION (MEA)

c/o 2nd Floor, 21-22 Poland Street, London W1F 8QQ
E-mail: info@mediaedassociation.org.uk

Web: www.mediaedassociation.org.uk
Founded in June 2006 to provide media teachers in England and Wales with their own professional association to support media teachers, promote media literacy and work to raise the status of media education.

MEDIA LITERACY TASK FORCE

Tel: 020 8305 8006
E-mail: info@medialiteracy.org.uk
Web: www.medialiteracy.org.uk/taskforce/
The Media Literacy Task Force is an informal grouping of stakeholders, set up and supported by the Secretary of State for Culture, Media and Sport, which exists to help bring strategic cohesion to the development of media literacy in the UK. The founding members of the Media Literacy Task Force are the UK Film Council and Channel 4, the British Film Institute, the BBC and Skillset.

MEDIA MARCH

PO Box 244, Malvern WR14 9AY
Tel: 020 8467 6452
E-mail: mediamarch@gmail.com
Web: www.mediamarch.org.uk
A multi-faith protest movement, founded in 1999, to campaign for a strengthening of the country's obscenity laws to reduce the harmful effects of the media, particularly broadcasting and the internet, on children, families and society. They engage in peaceful public protest, particularly the organisation of marches, and lobbying of the government.

MEDIA SOCIETY

Administrator, Dorothy Josem,
Flat 1 24 Park Road, London NW1 4SH
E-mail: Dorothy@themediasociety.co.uk
Web: www.themediasociety.co.uk
The Media Society stands for freedom of expression and the encouragement of high standards in journalism. The Society holds meetings and receptions through the year to discuss topics of current interest to its members, such as communications legislation, privacy and the press, the future of public service broadcasting, political reporting and the development of digital services.

MEDIA TRUST

Riverwalk House, 157-161 Millbank,
London SW1P 4RR
Tel: 020 7217 3717 **Fax:** 020 7217 3716
E-mail: information@mediatrust.org
Web: www.mediatrust.org
Media Trust's aim is to help charities communicate by providing an advice service, training courses on media production, and volunteering opportunities for media professionals.

MEDIAWATCH-UK

3 Willow House, Kennington Road, Ashford,
Kent TN24 0NR
Tel: 01233 633936 **Fax:** 01233 633836
E-mail: info@mediawatchuk.org
Web: www.mediawatchuk.org
Launched in 2002, mediawatch-UK is the successor to the National Viewers and Listeners Association, which was founded by Mary Whitehouse in 1965 with the purpose of putting pressure on the broadcasting authorities to improve their public accountability and to explain their policies on standards of taste and decency.

MENTAL HEALTH MEDIA

356 Holloway Road, London N7 6PA
Tel: 020 7700 8171 **Fax:** 0171 686 0959
E-mail: info@mhmedia.com
Web: www.mhmedia.com
The aim of Mental Health Media is to bring together media and the fields of mental health and learning difficulties to challenge discrimination. It works to help journalists print and broadcast the voices of people who have experienced mental health problems. Through video journalism training it helps people with learning difficulties record their own stories, wishes and demands.

MIMAS

Manchester Computing, Kilburn Building,
University of Manchester, Oxford Road,
Manchester M13 9PL
Tel: 0161 275 6109
E-mail: info@mimas.ac.uk
Web: www.mimas.ac.uk

MIMAS is a JISC- and ESRC-supported national data centre providing the UK higher education, further education and research community with networked access to key data and information resources to support teaching, learning and research across a wide range of disciplines. MIMAS also offers specialist support and training, and data sharing and gateway services.

MUSEUMS, LIBRARIES AND ARCHIVES COUNCIL (MLA)

Grosvenor House, 14 Bennetts Hill,
Birmingham B2 5RS
Tel: 0121 345 7300 **Fax:** 0121 345 7303
E-mail: info@mla.gov.uk
Web: www.mla.gov.uk
MLA is the government agency for museums, libraries, galleries and archives. It is part of the wider MLA Partnership, working with the nine regional agencies to raise professional standards and champion better services for all users and readers.

MUSIC PUBLISHERS ASSOCIATION (MPA)

6th Floor British Music House, 26 Berners Street,
London W1T 3LR
Tel: 020 7580 0126 **Fax:** 020 7637 3929
E-mail: info@mpaonline.org.uk
Web: www.mpaonline.org.uk
The MPA looks after the interests of all music publishers based or working in the UK and exists to safeguard and improve the business and legal environment within which its members operate.

MUSICIANS UNION

33 Palfrey Place, London SW8 1PE
Tel: 020 7840 5504 **Fax:** 020 7840 5599
E-mail: info@musiciansunion.org.uk
Web: www.musiciansunion.org.uk
The trade union for musicians in the UK.

THE NATIONAL ARCHIVES (TNA)

Kew, Richmond, Surrey, TW9 4DU
Tel: 020 8876 3444
Web: www.nationalarchives.gov.uk
The National Archives is at the heart of information policy – setting standards and supporting

The National Archives

innovation in information and records management across the UK, and providing a practical framework of best practice for opening up and encouraging the re-use of public sector information. The National Archives is also the UK government's official archive.

NATIONAL COMPUTING CENTRE (NCC)

Oxford House, Oxford Road, Manchester
M1 7ED
Tel: 0161 228 3444 **Fax:** 0161 242 2499
E-mail: info@ncc.co.uk
Web: www.ncc.co.uk
NCC champions the effective deployment of IT by providing independent and impartial advice and support, best practice and standards, personal and professional development, managed service delivery, awareness raising and experience sharing.

NATIONAL COUNCIL ON ARCHIVES (NCA)

Ruskin Avenue, Kew, Richmond, Surrey TW9 4DU
Tel: 020 8392 5347 **Fax:** 020 8487 1987
E-mail: nca@nationalarchives.gov.uk
Web: www.ncaonline.org.uk
The National Council on Archives was established in 1988 to bring together the major bodies and organisations, including service providers, users, depositors and policy makers, across the UK concerned with archives and their use. It aims to develop consensus on matters of mutual concern and provide an authoritative common voice for the archival community.

NATIONAL FILM & TELEVISION SCHOOL (NFTS)

The Registry, Beaconsfield Studios, Station Road, Beaconsfield, Buckinghamshire HP9 1LG
Tel: 01494 671234 **Fax:** 01494 674042
E-mail: info@nfts.co.uk
Web: www.nftsfilm-tv.ac.uk
The NFTS is one of the leading European centres for professional training in the screen entertainment and media industries. NFTS courses are predominantly practical and geared to the needs of people who plan to make their careers in the screen industries. The school's unique partnership with government and industry – both in funding and in liaison and consultation – ensures that its courses meet the present and future needs of the industry.

NATIONAL INSTITUTE OF ADULT CONTINUING EDUCATION (NIACE)

Renaissance House, 20 Princess Road West, Leicester LE1 6TP
Tel: 0116 204 4200/4201 **Fax:** 0116 285 4514
E-mail: enquiries@niace.org.uk
Web: www.niace.org.uk
NIACE is the national, independent organisation for adult learning in England and Wales. As a registered charity, NIACE both represents and advances the interests of all adult learners and potential learners – especially those who have benefited least from education and training. In 2007 the Basic Skills Agency merged with NIACE, and the resulting Alliance for Lifelong Learning, together with Tribal, forms the country's leading concentration of expertise in literacy, language and numeracy across all age ranges.

NATIONAL MEDIA MUSEUM

Bradford, West Yorkshire BD1 1NQ
Tel: 0870 7010200 **Fax:** 01274 723155
Web: www.nationalmediamuseum.org.uk
The National Media Museum (formerly the National Museum of Photography, Film and Television) exists to engage, inspire and educate by promoting an understanding and appreciation of photography, film, television, radio and the web; using its collection and knowledge to deliver a cultural programme accessibly and authoritatively.

NATIONAL RESOURCE CENTRE FOR DANCE (NRCD)

University of Surrey, Guildford, Surrey GU2 7XH
Tel: 01483 689 316 **Fax:** 01483 689 500
E-mail: nrcd@surrey.ac.uk
Web: www.surrey.ac.uk/NRCD
The NRCD is a non-profit national archive, centre for research, and information service for dance and movement. It aims to preserve the nation's dance heritage and enables, supports, and enhances the study, research, and teaching of dance. It has an extensive film and video archive.

NATIONAL SCHOOLS RADIO NETWORK

Vision Charity/Schools Radio, PO Box 729, Aylesbury HP229AS
Tel: 01296 655227
E-mail: info@schoolsradio.com
Web: www.schoolsradio.com/
The Network, launched at the end of 2007, is a school-based audio project that encourages schoolchildren aged up to 18 to create their own radio broadcasts, with suitable classroom guidance, on subjects and issues that are important to them. Teachers are then encouraged to post the programmes onto a responsible social networking website and log the details on the Network's site to allow students across the country to share their broadcasts.

NATIONAL STUDENT TELEVISION ASSOCIATION (NASTA)

Tel: 0116 2231088
E-mail: nasta@le.ac.co.uk
Web: www.nasta.org.uk
NaSTA exists to bring together all the student TV stations from across the UK, to help them communicate as a community and overcome problems, to offer advice, and to help new stations set up. It organises an annual conference and awards ceremony to showcase the best in student television and raise the profile of student television in the industry.

NEW PRODUCERS ALLIANCE (NPA)

7.03 Tea Building, 56 Shoreditch High Street, London E1 6JJ

Tel: 020 7613 0440 **Fax:** 020 7729 1852
E-mail: queries@npa.org.uk
Web: www.npa.org.uk
The NPA is the UK's national membership and training organisation for independent new producers and filmmakers.

OFCOM

2a Southwark Bridge Road, London SE1 9HA
Tel: 020 7981 3000 **Fax:** 020 7981 3333
Web: www.ofcom.org.uk

The Ofcom offices in London.

Ofcom is the independent regulator and competition authority for the UK communications industries, with responsibilities across television, radio, telecommunications and wireless communications services. Ofcom has inherited the duties of the five previous regulators it replaced: the Broadcasting Standards Commission, the Independent Television Commission, Oftel, the Radio Authority and the Radiocommunications Agency.

OFFICE OF THE QUALIFICATIONS AND EXAMINATIONS REGULATOR (OFQUAL)

Spring Place, Coventry Business Park, Herald Avenue, Coventry CV5 6UB
Tel: 0300 303 3344 **Fax:** 0300 303 3348
E-mail: info@ofqual.gov.uk
Web: www.ofqual.gov.uk/default.aspx
Ofqual began its interim work in April 2008. The government will be bringing in legislation to establish Ofqual as the regulator of qualifications,

exams and tests in England but until this legislation is passed it will operate as part of the Qualifications and Curriculum Authority. Ofqual monitors awarding organisations and exam fees.

OFFICE OF THE TELECOMMUNICATIONS OMBUDSMAN (OTELO)

PO Box 730, Warrington WA4 6WU
Tel: 0845 050 1614 or 0330 440 1614
Fax: 0330 440 1615
E-mail: enquiries@otelo.org.uk
Web: www.otelo.org.uk
Opened in January 2003, Otelo is a free, independent service designed to offer residential and small business consumers a way to settle unresolved disputes with their telecommunications providers. It is funded by member companies which have agreed to abide by the decisions of the Ombudsman on complaints referred by their customers.

ONE WORLD BROADCASTING TRUST (OWBT)

CAN Mezzanine, 32-36 Loman Street,
London SE1 0EH
Tel: 020 7922 7941 **Fax:** 020 7922 7706
E-mail: oneworld@owbt.org
Web: www.owbt.org
Established in 1987, the Trust was set up to promote greater understanding between the developed and developing countries of the world through broadcasting and related educational activities. It aims, through encouraging the effective use of media, to promote a clear and balanced awareness of human rights and global development issues among the UK public - from poverty and debt to education and good governance.

OPEN KNOWLEDGE FOUNDATION

37 Panton Street, Cambridge, CB2 1HL
Tel: 07795 176 976
E-mail: info@okfn.org
Web: www.okfn.org
The Open Knowledge Foundation exists to promote more equitable access to knowledge, which has become a possibility due to the technological revolution.

ORAL HISTORY SOCIETY

c/o Department of History, Essex University,
Colchester C04 3SQ
Tel: 020 7412 7405
E-mail: rob.perks@bl.uk
Web: www.ohs.org.uk
The Oral History Society is a national and international organisation dedicated to the collection and preservation of oral history.

PPL

1 Upper James Street, London W1F 9DE
Tel: 020 7534 1000 **Fax:** 020 7534 1111
E-mail: info@ppluk.com
Web: www.ppluk.com
PPL (formerly Phonographic Performance Ltd) is a music industry organisation working on behalf of its performer and record company members by collecting and distributing royalties from the use of sound recordings and music videos in broadcast, public performance and new media.

PRESS COMPLAINTS COMMISSION (PCC)

Halton House, 20/23 Holborn, London EC1N 2JD
Tel: 020 7831 0022 **Fax:** 020 7831 0025
E-mail: complaints@pcc.org.uk
Web: www.pcc.org.uk
The Press Complaints Commission is an independent body which deals with complaints from members of the public about the editorial content of newspapers and magazines.

PRODUCERS ALLIANCE FOR CINEMA & TELEVISION (PACT)

Procter House, 1 Procter Street, Holborn,
London WC1V 6DW
Tel: 020 7067 4367 **Fax:** 020 7067 4377
E-mail: enquiries@pact.co.uk
Web: www.pact.co.uk
Pact is the UK trade association that represents and promotes the commercial interests of independent content producers in the feature film, television, animation and interactive media sectors.

PRODUCTION MANAGERS' ASSOCIATION

Ealing Studios, Ealing Green, London W5 5EP
Tel: 020 8758 8699

E-mail: pma@pma.org.uk
Web: www.pma.org.uk

The PMA is a professional body of film, television, corporate and multi-media production managers, both freelance and permanently employed.

PUBLISHERS' LICENSING SOCIETY (PLS)

37-41 Gower Street, London WC1E 6HH
Tel: 020 7299 7730 **Fax:** 020 7299 7780
E-mail: pls@pls.org.uk
Web: www.pls.org.uk

The PLS was established in 1971 by the UK publishing industry. Its role is to oversee a collective licensing scheme in the UK for book, journal, and magazine copying; stimulate innovation and good practice in rights management; clarify the relationship between traditional copyright management practices and those needed in the digital age.

QUALIFICATIONS & CURRICULUM AUTHORITY (QCA)

83 Piccadilly, London W1J 8QA
Tel: 020 7509 5555 **Fax:** 020 7509 6666
E-mail: info@qca.org.uk
Web: www.qca.org.uk

QCA maintains and develops the national curriculum and associated assessments, tests and examinations, and accredits and monitors qualifications in colleges and at work.

QUALITY IMPROVEMENT AGENCY (QIA)

Friars House, Manor House Drive, Coventry CV1 2TE
Tel: 0870 1620 632 **Fax:** 0870 1620 633
Web: www.qia.org.uk

The QIA was set up to spark fresh enthusiasm for innovation and excellence in the adult and lifelong learning sector. It supports teachers, trainers and lecturers by running a series of programmes to inspire a culture of self-improvement.

RADIO ACADEMY

5 Market Place, London W1W 8AE
Tel: 020 7927 9920 **Fax:** 020 7636 8924
Web: www.radioacademy.org

The Radio Academy is a registered charity dedicated to the encouragement, recognition and promotion of excellence in UK broadcasting and audio production.

RADIO INDEPENDENTS GROUP (RIG)

c/o Electric Airwaves Ltd, Essel House, 29 Foley Street, London W1W 7JW
Tel: 020 7079 2082 **Fax:** 020 7079 2080
E-mail: chair@radioindependentsgroup.org

RIG is a membership body that represents the interests and needs of the UK's independent radio production industry in negotiations with the BBC, commercial radio groups and the Government, as well as offering support, resources, information, access and training.

© Antonio Jiménez Alonso / SXC

THE RADIOCENTRE

77 Shaftesbury Avenue, London W1D 5DU
Tel: 020 7306 2603 **Fax:** 020 7306 2505
E-mail: info@radiocentre.org
Web: www.radiocentre.org

The RadioCentre formed in July 2006 from the merger of the Radio Advertising Bureau (RAB) and the Commercial Radio Companies Association (CRCA). Its role is to maintain and build a strong and successful commercial radio industry, in terms of both listening hours and revenues.

RADIO JOINT AUDIENCE RESEARCH (RAJAR)

Paramount House, 162-170 Wardour Street, London W1F 8ZX
Tel: 020 7292 9040 **Fax:** 020 7292 9041
E-mail: info@rajar.co.uk
Web: www.rajar.co.uk

Wholly owned by the RadioCentre and the BBC, RAJAR was established in 1992 to operate a single audience measurement system for the radio industry - BBC, UK licensed and other commercial stations.

RADIO SOCIETY OF GREAT BRITAIN (RSGB)

3 Abbey Court, Fraser Road, Priory Business Park, Bedford MK44 3WH
Tel: 01234 832700 **Fax:** 01234 831496
E-mail: postmaster@rsgb.org.uk
Web: www.rsgb.org
Founded in 1913, the RSGB is the national membership organisation for amateur radio enthusiasts.

RAINDANCE

81 Berwick Street, London W1F 8TW
Tel: 020 7287 3833 **Fax:** 020 7287 3833
E-mail: info@raindance.co.uk
Web: www.raindance.co.uk
Raindance is dedicated to fostering and promoting independent film in the UK and around the world, spanning the full spectrum of the art, craft and business of independent movies.

RESEARCH INFORMATION NETWORK (RIN)

96 Euston Road, London NW1 2DB
Tel: 020 7412 7946 **Fax:** 020 7412 7339
Web: www.rin.ac.uk
The Research Information Network's role is to undertake evidence-based research into information and data issues that relate to professional researchers – and particularly academic researchers – and to develop policy, guidance and advocacy on that basis.

THE ROYAL ANTHROPOLOGICAL INSTITUTE (RAI)

50 Fitzroy Street, London W1P 5HS
Tel: 020 7387 0455 **Fax:** 020 7388 8817
E-mail: admin@therai.org.uk
Web: www.therai.org.uk
The RAI is the world's longest-established scholarly association dedicated to the furtherance of anthropology (the study of humankind) in its broadest and most inclusive sense.

THE ROYAL SOCIETY

6-9 Carlton House Terrace, London SW1Y 5AG
Tel: 020 7451 2500 **Fax:** 020 7930 2170
Web: www.royalsoc.ac.uk
The Royal Society is the independent scientific academy of the UK and the Commonwealth dedicated to promoting excellence in science. The Society plays an influential role in national and international science policy and supports developments in science, engineering and technology in a wide range of ways.

ROYAL TELEVISION SOCIETY (RTS)

5th Floor, Kildare House, 3 Dorset Rise, London EC4Y 8EN
Tel: 020 7822 2810 **Fax:** 020 7822 2811
E-mail: info@rts.org.uk
Web: www.rts.org.uk
The RTS is the leading forum for discussion and debate on all aspects of the television community.

SATELLITE AND CABLE BROADCASTERS GROUP (SCBG)

Gainsborough House, 81 Oxford Street, London W1D 2EU
Tel: 0789 420 6515 **Fax:** 020 7637 0419
E-mail: info@scbg.org.uk
Web: www.scbg.org.uk
The SCBG is the trade association for satellite and cable programme providers.

SCOTTISH ARTS COUNCIL

12 Manor Place, Edinburgh EH3 7DD
Tel: 0131 226 6051 **Fax:** 0131 225 9833
E-mail: help.desk@scottisharts.org.uk
Web: www.sac.org.uk
The Scottish Arts Council is the lead body for the funding, development and advocacy of the arts in Scotland.

SCOTTISH BROADCASTING COMMISSION

5 Atlantic Quay, Glasgow G2 8LU
Tel: 0141 228 7328
E-mail: reply@scottishbroadcastingcommission. gov.uk
Web: www.scottishbroadcastingcommission. gov.uk/

The Scottish Broadcasting Commission was established by the First Minister to conduct an independent investigation into the current state of television production and broadcasting in Scotland and define a strategic way forward for the industry. Taking account of the economic, cultural and democratic importance of broadcasting, the Commission's brief is to: make recommendations for Scottish government action; focus attention on issues where other organisations have responsibility and encourage action to address these issues; identify matters for further consideration and debate in the Scottish Parliament. The Commission will publish its report in 2008.

SCOTTISH SCREEN

249 West George Street, Glasgow G2 4QE
Tel: 0845 300 7300
E-mail: info@scottishscreen.com
Web: www.scottishscreen.com
Scottish Screen is the national development agency for the screen industries in Scotland.

SCREEN HERITAGE NETWORK

Attn. Michael Harvey, National Media Museum, Bradford, West Yorkshire BD1 1NQ
Tel: 01274 203374
E-mail: michael.harvey@nationalmediamuseum.ac.uk
Web: http://screenheritage.wordpress.com/
The Screen Heritage Network was established in 2005 by the National Media Museum, the BUFVC, the BKSTS and the Film Archive Forum with start-up funding from the Museums Libraries and Archives Council. The Network is a group of national and regional museums and archives, educational institutions and organisations connected with the UK screen sector, interested in advancing the concept of screen heritage.

SHOOTING PEOPLE

P.O. Box 51350, London N1 6XS
Web: www.shootingpeople.org
Shooting People is an online community of film-makers, sharing resources, skills and experience. Members post to and receive daily e-mail bulletins covering all aspects of filmmaking. Members can also fill in online searchable profile cards.

SKILLSET

Focus Point, 21 Caledonian Road, London N1 9GB
Tel: 020 7713 9800 **Fax:** 020 7713 9801
E-mail: info@skillset.org
Web: www.skillset.org

Skillset is the sector skills council for creative media which comprises TV, film, radio, interactive media, animation, computer games, facilities, photo imaging and publishing. It exists to encourage the delivery of informed training provision so that the British broadcast, film, video and multimedia industry's technical, creative and economic achievements are maintained and improved. Skillset is a strategic, all-industry organisation and is supported by key employers and unions.

SOCIETY FOR RESEARCH INTO HIGHER EDUCATION (SHRE)

76 Portland Place, London W1B 1NT
Tel: 020 7637 2766 **Fax:** 020 7637 2781
E-mail: srheoffice@srhe.ac.uk
Web: www.srhe.ac.uk
SHRE is an independent society which aims to improve the quality of higher education through the encouragement of debate and publication on issues of policy, on the organisation and management of higher education institutions and on the curriculum, teaching and learning methods.

SOCIETY OF ARCHIVISTS

Prioryfield House, 20 Canon Street, Taunton, Somerset TA1 1SW
Tel: 01823 327030 **Fax:** 01823 271719
E-mail: societyofarchivists@archives.org.uk
Web: www.archives.org.uk
The Society of Archivists is the principal professional body for archivists, archive conservators and records managers in the United Kingdom and Ireland. The society exists to promote the care and preservation of archives and the better administration of archive repositories, to advance the training of its members and to encourage relevant research and publication.

SOCIETY OF AUTHORS

84 Drayton Gardens, London SW10 9SB
Tel: 020 7373 6642 **Fax:** 020 7373 5768
Web: www.societyofauthors.net
A membership organisation serving the interests of professional writers, including academics and broadcasters, by offering business and legal advice, holding meetings, publishing a journal and administering a range of prizes.

SOCIETY OF COLLEGE, NATIONAL AND UNIVERSITY LIBRARIES (SCONUL)

102 Euston Street, London NW1 2HA
Tel: 020 7387 0317 **Fax:** 020 7383 3197
E-mail: info@sconul.ac.uk
Web: www.sconul.ac.uk

SCONUL promotes excellence in library services in higher education and national libraries across the UK and Ireland. All universities in the United Kingdom and Ireland are SCONUL members: so too are many of the UK's colleges of higher education.

STAFF & EDUCATIONAL DEVELOPMENT ASSOCIATION (SEDA)

SEDA Administration Office, Woburn House, 20-24 Tavistock Square, London
WC1H 9HF
Tel: 020 7380 6767 **Fax:** 020 7387 2655
Web: www.seda.ac.uk
SEDA is the professional association for staff and educational developers in the UK, promoting innovation and good practice in higher education.

STANDING CONFERENCE FOR HEADS OF MEDIA SERVICES (SCHOMS)

Selly Wick House, 59-61 Selly Wick Road, Selly Park, Birmingham B29 7JE
Tel: 0121 415 6803 **Fax:** 0121 415 6809
E-mail: info@schoms.ac.uk
Web: www.schoms.ac.uk
SCHoMS is the professional body for heads of services working within UK Higher education. Its purpose is to provide a forum for discussion of strategic issues and a mechanism for the exchange of good practice.

STRATEGIC ADVISORY BOARD FOR INTELLECTUAL PROPERTY (SABIP)

Harmsworth House, 13-15 Bouverie Street, London EC4Y 8DP
Tel: 020 7596 6533
Web: www.sabip.org.uk/home.htm
SABIP is a Non-Departmental Public Body, with the UK Intellectual Property Office (UK-IPO) as its sponsor department. Its role is to advise Ministers and the UK-IPO Chief Executive on the development of intellectual property (IP) policy. In formulating this advice, SABIP will: provide an overview of IP policy; provide independent input into Government policy-making; advise on the UK's stance in international negotiations.

STUDENT RADIO ASSOCIATION (SRA)

c/o The Radio Academy, 5 Market Place, London, W1W 8AE.
E-mail: chair@studentradio.org.uk
Web: www.studentradio.org.uk
The association covers all aspects of student radio, producing publications and factsheets and presenting awards at their AGM.

TASI – TECHNICAL ADVISORY SERVICE FOR DIGITAL MEDIA

Institute for Learning & Research Technology, University of Bristol, 8-10 Berkeley Square, Bristol BS8 1HH
Tel: 0117 331 4447
E-mail: info@tasi.ac.uk
Web: www.tasi.ac.uk
TASI, the Technical Advisory Service for Digital Media is a service funded by the JISC set up to advise and support the academic community on the digital creation, storage and delivery of image-related information.

TECHDIS

The Higher Education Academy, Innovation Way, York Science Park, York YO10 5BR
Tel: 01904 717580 **Fax:** 01904 717505
E-mail: helpdesk@techdis.ac.uk
Web: www.techdis.ac.uk
TechDis aims to be the leading educational advisory service, working across the UK, in the fields of accessibility and inclusion. Its mission is

to support the education sector in achieving greater accessibility and inclusion by stimulating innovation and providing expert advice and guidance on disability and technology.

TECHNOLOGY EXEMPLAR NETWORK

E-mail: feskills@becta.org.uk
Web: http://feandskills.becta.org.uk/display.cfm?page=2019
Jointly led by Becta and the Learning and Skills Council, Technology Exemplar Network is a new approach to supporting learning providers in further development of their e-maturity. Providers from across the country will support each other and share effective practice.

UK DATA ARCHIVE (UKDA)

University of Essex, Wivenhoe Park, Colchester, Essex CO4 3SQ
Tel: 01206 872143 **Fax:** 01206 872003
E-mail: help@esds.ac.uk
Web: www.data-archive.ac.uk
The UKDA is a centre of expertise in data acquisition, preservation, dissemination and promotion; and is curator of the largest collection of digital data in the social sciences and humanities in the UK.

UK FILM COUNCIL

10 Little Portland Street, London W1W 7JG
Tel: 020 7861 7861 **Fax:** 020 7861 7862
E-mail: info@ukfilmcouncil.org.uk
Web: www.ukfilmcouncil.org.uk

The UK Film Council is the Government-backed strategic agency for film in the UK. Its main aim is to stimulate a competitive, successful and vibrant UK film industry and culture, and to promote the widest possible enjoyment and understanding of cinema throughout the nations and regions of the UK.

UK INTELLECTUAL PROPERTY OFFICE

Concept House, Cardiff Road, Newport, South Wales NP10 8QQ
Tel: 0845 9 500 505 **Fax:** 01633 817777
E-mail: enquiries@ipo.gov.uk

Web: www.ipo.gov.uk
The official government body responsible for granting Intellectual Property (IP) rights in the United Kingdom. These rights include patents, designs, trade marks and copyright.

UK MEDIA

c/o UK Film Council, 10 Little Portland Street, London W1W 7JG
Tel: 020 7861 7511 **Fax:** 020 7861 7950
E-mail: England@mediadesk.co.uk
Web: www.mediadesk.co.uk
MEDIA is a support programme of the European Union to strengthen the competitiveness of the European film, television and new media industries and to increase the international circulation of European audio-visual product. MEDIA 2007 commenced on 1 January 2007 and will run to 31 December 2013. With a budget of 755 million euros, MEDIA 2007 supports professional training (screenwriting, business and new technologies), project development, and the distribution and promotion of European audio-visual works.

UK OFFICE FOR LIBRARY & INFORMATION NETWORKING (UKOLN)

The Library, University of Bath, Bath BA2 7AY
Tel: 01225 826580 **Fax:** 01225 826838
E-mail: ukoln@ukoln.ac.uk
Web: www.ukoln.ac.uk
UKOLN is a national centre for support in network information management in the library and information communities. It provides awareness, research and information services.

UNIVERSITIES' COLLABORATION IN E-LEARNING (UCEL)

University of Cambridge, 16 Mill Lane, Cambridge CB2 1SB
Tel: 01223 765363 **Fax:** 01223 765505
E-mail: info@ucel.ac.uk
Web: www.ucel.ac.uk
UCeL was founded in 2002 by a group of UK universities to collaboratively produce and share high quality interactive multimedia resources for health-professional education.

UNIVERSITIES UK

Woburn House, 20 Tavistock Square, London
WC1H 9HQ
Tel: 020 7419 4111 **Fax:** 020 7388 8649
E-mail: info@UniversitiesUK.ac.uk
Web: www.universitiesuk.ac.uk
Universities UK is the major representative body
and membership organisation for the higher
education sector. Its members are the executive
heads of UK universities. Together with Higher
Education Wales and Universities Scotland,
Universities UK works to advance the interests of
universities and to spread good practice through-
out the higher education sector.

UNIVERSITIES SCOTLAND

53 Hanover Street, Edinburgh EH2 2PJ
Tel: 0131 226 1111 **Fax:** 0131 226 1100
E-mail: info@universities-scotland.ac.uk
Web: www.universities-scotland.ac.uk/
Universities Scotland exists to represent and
promote Scotland's higher education sector and
campaign on its behalf.

VEGA SCIENCE TRUST

Sussex Innovation Centre, Science Park Square,
Brighton BN1 9SB UK.
Tel: 01273 678726 **Fax:** 01273 234645
E-mail: vega@vega.org.uk
Web: www.vega.org.uk
Vega produces programmes for network television
which treat science as cultural activity, so complementing present media coverage of science. It
aims to bridge the gap between professional and
public understanding of science by creating programmes in which the state-of-the-art understanding of leading scientists is made more accessible.

VERA MEDIA

30-38 Dock Street, Leeds LS10 1JF
Tel: 0113 242 8646 **Fax:** 0113 242 8739
E-mail: vera@vera-media.co.uk
Web: www.vera-media.co.uk
This video/multimedia production and training
organisation produces programmes for education,
arts, voluntary and public sector, and community
documentaries with women's, youth and similar
groups.

VIDEO STANDARDS COUNCIL (VSC)

Kinetic Business Centre, Theobald Street,
Borehamwood, Hertfordshire WD6 4PJ
Tel: 020 8387 4020 **Fax:** 020 83874004
E-mail: vsc@videostandards.org.uk
Web: www.videostandards.org.uk
Established 1989 as a non-profit making body to
develop and administer a Code of Practice
designed to promote high standards within the
video industry. In 1993 its brief was expanded to
include the computer games industry.

VOICE OF THE LISTENER & VIEWER (VLV)

101 King's Drive, Gravesend, Kent DA12 5BQ
Tel: 01474 352835 **Fax:** 01474 351112
E-mail: info@vlv.org.uk
Web: www.vlv.org.uk
The VLV is an independent body that speaks for
listeners and viewers on the whole range of broadcasting issues. It is concerned with the regulation,
funding, structures and institutions which underpin the British broadcasting system, and supports
the principles of public service broadcasting.

VPL

1 Upper James Street, London W1F 9DE
Tel: 020 7534 1400
E-mail: info@vpluk.com
Web: www.ppluk.com/en/About-Us/
Who-we-are/What-is-VPL/
VPL is the collecting society set up by the record
industry in 1984 to license the broadcast and
public performance of music videos on behalf of
its members, in the same way that PPL had
already been doing for recorded music. VPL and
PPL work alongside each other, sharing admini-
stration.

WRITERS GUILD OF BRITAIN

15 Britannia Street, London WC1X 9JN
Tel: 020 7833 0777 **Fax:** 020 7833 4777
E-mail: erik@writersguild.org.uk
Web: www.writersguild.org.uk
The Writers' Guild of Great Britain is the trade
union working on behalf of writers in television,
radio, theatre, books, poetry, film and video
games.

This is a small selection of international organisations working in audio-visual media in a broadly educational context. Most either have associations with the BUFVC or share in one or other of its interests. A number belong to the International Association for Media in Science (IAMS), of which the BUFVC is a founder member.

ACTION COALITION FOR MEDIA EDUCATION (ACME)

2808 El Tesoro Escondido NW, Albuquerque, NM 87120, USA
Tel: +1 505 839 9702 **Fax:** + 1 505 828 3142
Web: www.acmecoalition.org
ACME is a USA-based, independent strategic network linking media educators, health advocates, media reformers, independent media makers, community organisers and others.

LA ASOCIACIÓN ESPAÑOLA DE CINE CIENTÍFICO (ASECIC)

C/Vitruvio, 8, 28006 Madrid, Spain
Tel/Fax: +34 91 564 69 12
Web: www.asecic.org
ASECIC was founded in 1966 by Dr Guillermo Fernandez Zúñiga. Since then it has promoted the work of audio-visual Spanish scientists and scientific cinema internationally, and the use of scientific film as an educational tool.

ASSOCIATION OF MOVING IMAGE ARCHIVISTS (AMIA)

1313 N. Vine Street, Hollywood, CA 90028, USA
Tel: +1 323 463 1500 **Fax:** +1 323 463 1506
E-mail: amia@amianet.org
Web: www.amianet.org

A US-based non-profit professional association established to advance the field of moving image archiving by fostering co-operation among individuals and organisations concerned with the acquisition, preservation, exhibition and use of moving image materials.

AUDIOVISUEEL CENTRUM VRIJE UNIVERSITEIT (AVC)

V.d. Boechorststraat 7-9, 1081 BT Amsterdam, The Netherlands
Tel: +31 20 598 9161 **Fax:** +31 20 598 9160
E-mail: avc@dienst.vu.nl
Web: www.audiovisueelcentrum.nl
The audio-visual services department of Vrije Universiteit, Amsterdam, specialising in videoconferencing, webcasting, streaming video services, video lectures, and medical imaging.

AVNET

K.U.Leuven, Kapeldreef 62, B-3001 Heverlee (Leuven), Belgium
Tel: +32 16 32 82 00 **Fax:** +32 16 32 82 70
E-mail: info@avnet.kuleuven.be
Web: www.avnet.kuleuven.be
AVNet (Audio-Visual and New Educational Technologies) is a new structure incorporating K.U.Leuven Audiovisual Services AVdienst, eLink,

and the Open University Study Centre. For several years K.U.Leuven has been a major player in the field of ICT and media-supported higher education, through projects implemented at the university as well as in an international context. AVNet acts as a central department for educational support, provided more specifically by using audio-visual media and interactive multimedia in education, in networked e-learning and distance education.

CENTRE NATIONALE DE LA RECHERCHE SCIENTIFIQUE (CNRS)

E-mail: webcnrs@cnrs-dir.fr
Web: www.cnrs.fr
CNRS is a government-funded research organisation, under the administrative authority of France's Ministry of Research. Founded in 1939 by governmental decree, CNRS has the following missions: to evaluate and carry out all research capable of advancing knowledge and bringing social, cultural, and economic benefits for society; to contribute to the application and promotion of research results; to develop scientific information; to support research training; to participate in the analysis of the national and international scientific climate and its potential for evolution in order to develop a national policy.

CERIMES (CENTRE DE RESSOURCES ET D'INFORMATION SUR LES MULTIMÉDIAS POUR L'ENSEIGNEMENT SUPÉRIEUR)

6, avenue Pasteur 92170 Vanves, France
Tel: +33 1 41 23 08 80 **Fax:** +33 1 45 29 10 99
E-mail: info@cerimes.fr
Web: www.cerimes.education.fr
CERIMES exists to facilitate access for teachers, researchers and students to audio-visual resources suitable for use in higher education. It locates, describes and distributes such materials, with particular emphasis on resources produced by higher education and research institutions. Previously known as Service du film de recherche scientifique (SFRS).

COALITION FOR NETWORKED INFORMATION (CNI)

21 Dupont Circle, Suite 800, Washington, DC, 20036, USA

Tel: +1 202 296 5098 **Fax:** +1 202 872 0884
E-mail: info@cni.org
Web: www.cni.org
The CNI is an organisation dedicated to supporting the transformative promise of networked information technology for the advancement of scholarly communication and the enrichment of intellectual productivity. Some 200 institutions representing higher education, publishing, network and telecommunications, information technology, and libraries and library organisations make up CNI's members.

DIMA – THE DIGITAL MEDIA ASSOCIATION

1029 Vermont Ave, NW, Suite 850, Washington, DC 20005, USA
Tel: +1 202 639 9509
Web: www.digmedia.org
The DiMA promotes pro-consumer competitive opportunities that will contribute to the growth, production and enjoyment of digital content; supports the development and use of responsible measures to protect intellectual property rights underlying digital media, and the payment of fair and reasonable royalties associated with such rights; and opposes technical and legal barriers that inhibit innovation or adoption of new digital technologies, products and services.

DIVERSE

Web: www.diverse-video.net
DIVERSE stands for Developing Innovative Video Resources for Students Everywhere. It began life as a Teaching and Learning Technology Programme Phase 3 project, funded by the UK government through the Higher Education Funding Council for England. It has developed to become an international community of international practitioners in both video production and videoconferencing, with an annual conference. The focus is on developing alternative modes of learning and teaching to complement the asynchronous text-based formats that predominate within e-learning.

EURODOC

4, rue Astruc, F- 34000, Montpellier, France
Tel: +33 4 67 60 23 30 **Fax :** +33 4 67 60 80 46

E-mail: eurodoc@wanadoo.fr
Web: www.eurodoc-net.com

 EURODOC is a training programme designed for European professionals in the documentary field developing a specific project, either independent producers of documentary projects with international potential, or commissioning editors from the documentary departments of the broadcasters or from partners in the sector, bankers, distributors etc.

EUROPEAN AUDIOVISUAL OBSERVATORY

76 allée de la Robertsau, 67000 Strasbourg, France
Tel: +33 3 88 14 44 00 **Fax:** +33 3 88 14 44 19
E-mail: obs@obs.coe.int
Web: www.obs.coe.int
Set up in December 1992, the purpose of the European Audiovisual Observatory is to gather and circulate information on the audio-visual industry in Europe. The Observatory is a European public service body with thirty-six member States and the European Community, represented by the European Commission.

EUROPEAN BROADCASTING UNION (EBU)

L'Ancienne-Route 17A, CH-1218 Grand-Saconnex, Switzerland
Tel: + 41 22 717 2111 **Fax:** + 41 22 747 4000
E-mail: ebu@ebu.ch
Web: www.ebu.ch
The EBU is the largest professional association of national broadcasters in the world. It negotiates broadcasting rights for major sports events, operates the Eurovision and Euroradio networks, organises programme exchanges, stimulates and coordinates co-productions, and provides a full range of other operational, commercial, technical, legal and strategic services.

EUROPEAN BUREAU OF LIBRARY, INFORMATION AND DOCUMENTATION ASSOCIATIONS (EBLIDA)

PO Box 16359, NL-2500 BJ The Hague,
The Netherlands

Tel: +31 70 309 05 51 **Fax:** +31 70 309 05 58
E-mail: eblida@debibliotheken.nl
Web: www.eblida.org
An independent umbrella association of national library, information, documentation and archive associations and institutions in Europe. Subjects on which EBLIDA concentrates are European information society issues, including copyright and licensing, culture and education and EU enlargement. EBLIDA promotes unhindered access to information in the digital age and the role of archives and libraries in achieving this goal.

EUROPEAN DIGITAL MEDIA ASSOCIATION (EDIMA)

Tel: +32 2 626 1990 **Fax:** +32 2 626 9501
E-mail: info@europeandigitalmedia.org
Web: www.europeandigitalmediaassociation.org
EDiMA is an alliance of digital media and technology companies that distribute audio and audio-visual content on line. The main business of EDiMA revolves around two different areas: the formation of EU legislation and the licensing regime in the EU for the distribution of content online. The association is involved in developments relating to copyright issues, music licensing, competition law, taxation of digital music sales and a range of other market and legislative issues which impact on the way in which online content distributors do business in the EU.

EUROPEAN TELEVISION HISTORY NETWORK (ETHN)

E-mail: Sonja.deLeeuw@let.uu.nl
Web: www.birth-of-tv.org/birth/pages/static/research/Research.jsp
The ETHN was founded in April 2005 by the Media Studies department of Utrecht University. It is a European network of academics and institutions active in the field of European television history to facilitate international research co-operation. The ETHN has a dedicated section on the BIRTH Television Archive website which disseminates information, hosts a discussion forum and provides space for academics to post their CVs and research interests.

FÉDÉRATION INTERNATIONALE DES ARCHIVES DU FILM (FIAF)

1 Rue Defacqz, B-1000 Brussels, Belgium
Tel: +32 2 538 3065 **Fax:** +32 2 534 4774
E-mail: info@fiafnet.org
Web: www.fiafnet.org

FIAF brings together institutions dedicated to rescuing films both as cultural heritage and as historical documents. Founded in Paris in 1938, FIAF is a collaborative association of the world's leading film archives whose purpose has always been to ensure the proper preservation and showing of motion pictures. Today, more than 120 archives in over sixty-five countries collect, restore, and exhibit films and cinema documentation spanning the entire history of film. They also publish the Journal of Film Preservation.

FIAT/IFTA

c/o Oesterreichischer Rundfunk, Documentation & Archives, Wuerzburggasse 30, A-1136 Wien, Austria
Tel: +43 1 87878 12380 **Fax:** +43 1 87878 12739
E-mail: office@fiatifta.org
Web: http://fiatifta.org

The International Federation of Television Archives is an international professional association established to provide a means for co-operation amongst broadcast and national audiovisual archives and libraries concerned with the collection, preservation and exploitation of moving image and recorded sound materials and associated documentation.

HUMANITARIAN MEDIA FOUNDATION (HMF)

E-mail: pr@humanitarianmedia.org
Web: http://humanitarianmedia.ning.com/

Founded in 2008, the HMF is a non-partisan, non-sectarian entity in the United States that employs multiple forms of media (film, television, journalism, photojournalism, new media, art, photography, music) to explore aspects of domestic and international humanitarian crises, issues and histories; raise awareness of humanitarian matters; encourage collaboration among media entities and international stakeholders; and facilitate change in areas where it is most needed.

INSTITUT FÜR DEN WISSENSCHAFTLICHEN FILM (IWF)

Nonnenstieg 72, D-37075 Göttingen, Germany
Tel: +49 551 5024 0 **Fax:** -400
E-mail: iwf-goe@iwf.de
Web: www.iwf.de

IWF – Knowledge and Media is the German federal and states' service facility for multimedia communication in a scientific context. It promotes science and education through its development and transfer services in the field of audio-visual media. Its core task is to acquire scientific audio-visual media, to optimise it and to make it available for teaching and research in the long-term.

INTERNATIONAL ASSOCIATION FOR MEDIA AND HISTORY (IAMHIST)

Box 1216, Washington, CT 06793, USA
E-mail: info-contact@iamhist.org
Web: www.iamhist.org

The International Association for Media and History is an organisation of filmmakers, broadcasters, archivists and scholars dedicated to historical inquiry into film, radio, television, and related media. It encourages scholarly research into the relations between history and the media as well as the production of historically informed documentaries, television series, and other media texts.

INTERNATIONAL ASSOCIATION FOR MEDIA IN SCIENCE (IAMS)

c/o CERIMES, 6, avenue Pasteur 92170 Vanves, France
Tel: +33 1 41 23 08 80 **Fax:** +33 1 45 29 10 99
Web: http://iams.cerimes.fr

Established in 1992 as the successor to the International Scientific Film Association, IAMS promotes the production, documentation, preservation, distribution and use of audio-visual media and materials for the growth and communication of knowledge in the natural and human sciences, technology and medicine. Its members come from the major national associations for scientific media, numerous audio-visual centres of universities, production houses, and individual experts from all over the world.

INTERNATIONAL ASSOCIATION OF SOUND & AUDIOVISUAL ARCHIVES (IASA)

Web: www.iasa-web.org

IASA was established in 1969 in Amsterdam to function as a medium for international co-operation between archives that preserve recorded sound and audio-visual documents. The organisation is concerned with the development of good practice and the dissemination of information on collection development and access, documentation and metadata, copyright and ethics, and conservation and preservation.

INTERNET2

1000 Oakbrook Drive, Suite 300, Ann Arbor
MI 48104, USA
Tel: +1 734 913 4250 **Fax:** +1 734 913 4255
E-mail: info@internet2.edu
Web: www.internet2.edu

Internet2 is the foremost US advanced networking consortium. Led by the research and education community since 1996, Internet2 promotes the missions of its over 300 members by providing both leading-edge network capabilities and unique partnership opportunities that together facilitate the development, deployment and use of revolutionary Internet technologies.

MOTION PICTURE ASSOCIATION

1600 Eye Street, NW, Washington, DC 20006, USA
Tel: +1 202 293 1966 **Fax:** +1 202 296 7410
Web: www.mpaa.org

The Motion Picture Association of America (MPAA) and its international counterpart, the Motion Picture Association (MPA) serve as the voice and advocate of the American motion picture, home video and television industries, domestically through the MPAA and internationally through the MPA. Main areas of concern to the association are educating young people about copyright theft, promoting copyright protection, and working with the technology sector to find innovative ways of delivering entertainment.

NATIONAL SCIENCE FOUNDATION (NSF)

4201 Wilson Boulevard, Arlington, Virginia
22230, USA
Tel: +1 703 292 5111
Web: www.nsf.gov

The NSF is an independent federal agency created by Congress in 1950 'to promote the progress of science; to advance the national health, prosperity, and welfare; to secure the national defense ...' With an annual budget of about $5.91 billion, it is the funding source for approximately twenty percent of all federally supported basic research conducted by America's colleges and universities. In many fields such as mathematics, computer science and the social sciences, NSF is the major source of federal backing.

ONLINE/MORE COLOUR IN THE MEDIA (OLMCM)

PO Box 672, 3500 AR Utrecht, The Netherlands
Tel: +31 30 239 9035 **Fax:** +31 30 230 2975
E-mail: info@olmcm.org
Web: www.olmcm.org

Online/More Colour in the Media is a network of minority organisations and multicultural NGOs, local and national broadcast media, training institutes and media education organisations, aiming to improve the representation of ethnic minorities in the media.

SURFFOUNDATION

Hojel City Center, building D (5th floor),
Graadt van Roggenweg 340, 3531 AH Utrecht,
The Netherlands
Tel: + 31 30 234 66 00 **Fax:** + 31 30 233 29 60
E-mail: info@surf.nl
Web: www.surffoundation.nl

SURF is the collaborative organisation for higher education institutions and research institutes aimed at breakthrough innovations in ICT. SURF provides the foundation for the excellence of higher education and research in the Netherlands. It has published several reports and *Surf*, its own magazine.

UNIVERSITY FILM AND VIDEO ASSOCIATION (UFVA)

c/o Peter J. Bukalski, Box 1777 Edwardsville, IL 62026, USA
E-mail: ufvahome@aol.com
Web: www.ufva.org
An association for universities – predominantly but not exclusively American and Canadian – with an interest in the making and teaching film, video and other media arts.

VIDEO ACTIVE

Kromme Nieuwegracht 29, 3512 HD Utrecht, Netherlands
Tel: +31 (0)30 2536526
E-mail: Sonja.deLeeuw@let.uu.nl
Web: www.videoactive.eu
A consortium of archives, academic institutions and ICT developers whose aim is to create access to television archives across Europe. Video Active is funded by the eContentPlus programme of the European Commission.

VIDEO DEVELOPMENT INITIATIVE (VIDE)

Web: www.vide.net
ViDe is an international professional organisation built around the development and deployment of digital video and collaborative technologies. ViDe is open to all people studying or engaged in digital video or collaborative research and services within the education community, government agencies, and non-profit organisations.

WORLD ASSOCIATION OF MEDICAL AND HEALTH FILMS (WAMHF)

E-mail: WAMHF@ammonite.nl
Web: www.ammonite.nl/WAMHF.htm

The WAMHF was founded in 1990 in Spain. Its objectives are: to promote medical and health audio-visual media; to promote the circulation and distribution of medical and health audio-visual productions throughout the world; to develop an approved index of all medical films; to develop an international data bank of medical and health films, available to all the members of the Association from anywhere in the world; to facilitate co-operation among existing festivals; to defend and harmonise copyright laws in the medical and health fields.

WORLD INTELLECTUAL PROPERTY ORGANISATION (WIPO)

PO Box 18, CH-1211 Geneva 20, Switzerland
Tel: +41 22 338 91 11 **Fax:** +41 22 733 54 28
Web: www.wipo.int/

WIPO, founded in 1967, is a specialised agency of the United Nations. It is dedicated to developing a balanced and accessible international intellectual property system, which rewards creativity, stimulates innovation and contributes to economic development while safeguarding the public interest.

PODCASTING

Podcasts are digital media files available over the Internet, which can be downloaded for later use through an iPod or computer. Podcasts can be audio or video (vodcasts). The BUFVC's Moving Image Gateway (www.bufvc.ac.uk/gateway) includes podcasting and vodcasting services in its classified listing of websites relating to moving images and sound for use in higher education. Below is a small selection of the rapidly growing number of relevant sites that offer podcasts, with an emphasis on those available from universities.

BATH POD

Web: www.bath.ac.uk/podcast
Podcasts from the University of Bath's public lecture series where leading names from the worlds of science, humanities and engineering talk about the latest research in their field.

BBC RADIO PODCASTS

Web: www.bbc.co.uk/radio/podcasts/
A large selection of radio programmes are available from this site and can be searched by radio station, genre and through an alphabetical title listing.

BERKELEY GROKS SCIENCE SHOW

Web: www.groks.net/groks.rss
Berkeley Groks Science Show is a weekly science programme broadcast on radio stations throughout the USA. Each programme provides an in-depth look at recent developments in the world of science and technology and examines the effects of these discoveries on our daily lives. Each new show is available as a podcast and past episodes are archived as MP3 files on the Internet Archive (www.archive.org).

BIZ/ED

Web: www.bized.co.uk/homeinfo/podcasting.htm
Biz/ed broadcasts regular podcasts for students and educators in business studies, economics, accounting, leisure, sport and recreation, and travel and tourism in the UK.

© Michal Ferák / SXC

CUSP-BLUESCI PODCASTS

Web: www.sciencelive.org/content/view/100/76/
Popular science broadcasts produced by Cambridge University's *BluSci* science magazine,

including the Darwin Lectures series from 2006 and 2007.

DEEP (DIGITAL EDUCATION ENHANCEMENT PROJECT)

Web: www.open.ac.uk/deep/Public/web/about/deepBriefings.html

The Open University's DEEP project is a research and development programme investigating the use of new information and communications technology (ICT) for teaching and learning, working in schools serving disadvantaged communities in different parts of the world. Its 'DEEP Briefings' are podcasts giving quick introductions to the ideas, contexts and practices of the project.

ECS VIDEO PODCASTS

Web: www.ecs.soton.ac.uk/about/podcasts.php

Electronics and Computer Science (ECS), University of Southampton, was the first academic institution in the UK to offer a video podcast news service, providing coverage of a wide range of activities in the School.

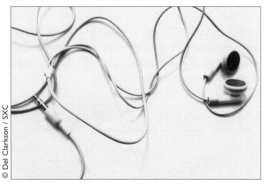

© Del Clarkson / SXC

EDUCATION PODCAST NETWORK

Web: http://epnweb.org

Mainly American schools-oriented directory of podcast programming that may be helpful to teachers looking for content to teach with and about, and to explore issues of teaching and learning in the 21st century.

ENLIGHTENMENT IN THE 21ST CENTURY

Web: www.ed.ac.uk/explore/av/enlightenment2006

In partnership with Scottish Power, the University of Edinburgh hosted a series of lectures and seminars examining aspects of the Enlightenment's legacy in the context of our own fraught and hectic times.

GUARDIAN

Web: www.guardian.co.uk/podcasts

Daily news podcasts and weekly single-subject ones on aspects of sport, media culture, film & music, science & technology, and books. Ricky Gervais' exclusive podcasts proved to be enormously successful.

IMPALA

Web: www.impala.ac.uk/

IMPALA (Informal Mobile Podcasting and Learner Adaptation) is a Higher Education Academy-funded project researching into the use of podcasts in university teaching and learning. It has produced its own series of podcasts offering guidance for staff on how to use this resource. There is also a blog providing up-to-date information on the project. A linked project, IMPALA 2, is investigating the impact of podcasting on student learning in Geography, Earth and Environmental Sciences (GEES), and IMPALA4T investigates the use of 'student created' podcasts to support the transition of students into higher education.

IMPERIAL COLLEGE LONDON – PUBLIC LECTURES

Web: www3.imperial.ac.uk/aboutimperial/events/onlinelectures

Video podcasts of public lectures from Imperial College London, including guest lecturers such as Trevor Phillips, Professor Sir Harry Kroto and Lord Robert Winston.

INSTITUTE FOR PUBLIC POLICY RESEARCH (IPPR)

Web: www.ippr.org/podcasts

The IPPR launched a podcasting programme in March 2007 to provide information on the organisation's latest research developments and events programmes, as well as web reports, books and broadcast media. The IPPR is the UK's leading progressive think tank, producing cutting edge research and innovative policy ideas for a just, democratic and sustainable world. Topics include prison populations in the UK, the failings of ASBOs, and Home Office reform.

ITUNES U

Web: http://www.apple.com/education/itunesu_mobilelearning/itunesu.html
Video and audio recordings of lectures from leading universities in the UK, USA and Europe available to students and the wider public. Initially US-dominated, content is now provided by an increasing number of UK universities including Oxford, Cambridge, UCL, and the OU.

MICROBIOLOGYBYTES

Web: www.microbiologybytes.com/podcasts/help.html
The latest news on microbiology, from the University of Leicester, with detailed supporting textual information.

NOVA

Web: www.pbs.org/wgbh/nova/rss/podcasting.html
Wide range of podcasts and vodcasts on the world of science, from the US science television channel.

OPENCULTURE

Web: www.oculture.com/2007/07/freeonlinecourses.html
Listing of free online courses and lectures (via podcast and MP3) from leading universities including Berkeley UCLA and Stanford, covering all subject areas.

PBS

Web: www.pbs.org/podcasts/
The American Public Service Broadcaster has several regular podcasts that users can subscribe to, linking to their television transmissions.

PODCAST ALLEY

Web: www.podcastalley.com/
A podcast portal, searchable by genre.

PODCASTS FOR EDUCATORS, SCHOOLS AND COLLEGES

Web: http://recap.ltd.uk/podcasting
A UK-based directory of podcasts for education, predominantly those aimed at children and young people at school, but including some suitable for universities and colleges. Includes a section on video podcasts. Provides an RSS feed, weblog and educators' tips.

PODCATS

Web: www.podcats.co.uk
Professional service providing podcasts for charities and commercial organisations. Clients (whose podcasts are available from the Podcats site) include the Royal Shakespeare Company, the Royal Society for the Protection of Birds, and the Philharmonia Orchestra.

PODDFEED.NET

Web: www.podfeed.net/
A podcast directory that helps you find podcasts, read and write podcast reviews, listen to podcasts and share your podcast with others.

PROJECT XIPHOS

Web: http://blogs.talis.com/xiphos/category/podcast/
Project Xiphos is run by the software company Talis which specialises in semantic web technologies. It provides an information and discussion forum, using blogs and podcasts, for how education might make use of this web 2 technology over the next few years.

PUBLIC SERVICE REFORM INTERVIEWS

Web: www.bris.ac.uk/Depts/CMPO/audio/main.htm
Series of interviews from the University of Bristol's Centre for Market and Public Organisation discussing current research.

REGIONAL SUPPORT CENTRE NORTHWEST

Web: www.rsc-northwest.ac.uk/content/blogcategory/194/262/

The JISC Regional support centre for the North West highlights cases of good practice of e-learning from FE colleges, sixth forms, and other learning providers in the region.

RESEARCH AT CHICAGO

Web: http://research.uchicago.edu/highlights
Audio and video interviews with staff at the University of Chicago on a variety of research topics.

THE ROYAL SOCIETY

Web: http://royalsociety.org/page.asp?id=3966
A selection of the lectures recorded at the Royal Society are available as video or audio podcasts. A broad range of scientific subjects is covered including biology, climate science, chemistry, geology, mathematics and physics. Lecturers include Lisa Jardine, Steve Jones and Bill Bryson.

© Renato Benicio / SXC

SCIENTIFIC AMERICAN PODCASTS

Web: www.sciam.com/podcast
A weekly audio report by Steve Mirsky discussing the latest developments in science and technology through interviews with leading scientists and journalists. Also a series of daily, one-minute commentaries and reports on the world of science.

SHAKESPEARECAST.COM

Web: www.shakespearecast.com
A project that aims eventually to provide the complete works of William Shakespeare, podcast act by act. Recordings made by the Antioch

Classical Theatre Company, Los Medanos College, and Antioch High School in the USA.

SNOWMAIL

Web: www.channel4.com/news/watchlisten/more4snowmail.jsp
Channel 4 News presenter Jon Snow's alternative take on the news, broadcast every Saturday on More4 and available online or via iTunes.

THE SOUTH BANK SHOW

Web: www.itv.com/Entertainment/chatandtalent/SouthBankShow/podcast/default.html
This site includes podcasts and vodcasts of interviews from recent programmes in this long-running arts series.

STANFORD ON ITUNES U

Web: http://itunes.stanford.edu
Provides access to a wide range of Stanford-related digital audio content via iTunes. The public site includes Stanford courses, faculty lectures, event highlights, music, sports, etc.

STARTINGUNI

Web: www.le.ac.uk/beyonddistance/startinguni/
StartingUni.info podcasts are recordings of students talking about their experiences of starting university. It features a range of topics which new students will find useful, such as accommodation, money management, the first few days at university, assessments, etc. Although the recordings are mostly of students studying biological sciences at the University of Leicester, most of what they say will apply to any course at any university.

TEACHERS' TV

Web: www.teachers.tv/help/podcasting
Video podcasts of selected programmes from Teachers' TV, the UK digital television channel for teachers. Delivered via iTunes.

UNIVERSITY CHANNEL (AKA UCHANNEL)

Web: http://uc.princeton.edu/main/index.php?option=com_frontpage&Itemid=1

A collection of public affairs lectures, panels and events from academic institutions across the world. Participating universities contribute video and audio recordings of lectures, seminars, panels and interviews to a virtual pool of academic content; these are made available as podcasts and vodcasts, as downloadable MP3 or MP4 files, or as streaming audio/video.

UNIVERSITY OF CAMBRIDGE: PROFESSIONAL ENGLISH ONLINE

Web: www.cambridge.org/elt/resources/professional/podcast.htm
A series of podcast and vodcast interviews with leading professional English writers and practitioners. Topics include teaching political English, English for legal purposes, social and communication skills, how to network, cultural awareness in ESP, etc.

UNIVERSITY OF ULSTER PUBLIC AFFAIRS AUDIO ARCHIVE

Web: http://news.ulster.ac.uk/podcasts
Audio files from the life and work of the University of Ulster, its staff, students, partners and visitors.

VIDEO PODCASTS

Web: www.videopodcasts.tv
A directory of video podcasts, organised by category such as new technology, history and business, that encourages contributions from its users.

WARWICK PODCASTS

Web: www2.warwick.ac.uk/newsandevents/audio
University of Warwick experts commenting on important issues, their research and events. Includes Will@Warwick, featuring academic thoughts on William Shakespeare (www2.warwick.ac.uk/newsandevents/audio/more/will).

WOLVERHAMPTON RADIOPHONIC INSTITUTE

Web: www.radiophonic.org.uk
A weekly radio show on culture, politics and philosophy from the University of Wolverhampton. Broadcast on 101.8 WCR FM and available as a podcast.

Z-AXIS: HISTORY OF ANIMATION IN COURT

Web: http://podcasts.zaxis.com/pac
A continuing series of video podcasts of some of the computer animations that have been used in USA courtrooms over the last twenty years. Z-Axis Corporation was a pioneer in the creation of animated trial exhibits in the late 1980s and has continued to develop new ways to present visual information to judges and juries. This collection includes some of the landmark cases to use computer animation over the years as well as other less famous, but still innovative and interesting applications of computer graphics.

REGIONAL SUPPORT CENTRES

JISC RSCs (Regional Support Centres) exist to advise the learning providers of designated sectors in the deployment of Information and Communications Technologies (ICT) to achieve their organisational mission. The various RSCs are based regionally across the UK, with staff usually located within host institutions, although some operate on a distributed model. RSCs give advice to key contacts within the learning providers that they support. Usually such contacts comprise a senior management contact, a teaching and learning contact, a learning resources contact and an IT technical contact. The overall aim of the RSCs is to advise, with customers then responsible for any actions taken.

JISC RSC UK

2nd Floor Beacon House, Queens Road,
Clifton, Bristol, BS8 1QU
Tel: 0117 331 0656
Angela Harvey,
RSC UK Services
Coordinator
E-mail: a.harvey@jisc.ac.uk
Web: www.jisc.ac.uk/rsc

JISC RSC EASTERN

Anglia Ruskin University, CU House,
Southernhay, Basildon, Essex SS14 1EZ
Tel: 01268 273277 **Fax:** 01268 293145
E-mail: support@rsc-eastern.ac.uk
Web: www.rsc-eastern.ac.uk

JISC RSC EAST MIDLANDS

Loughborough College, Radmoor Road,
Loughborough LE11 3BT
Tel: 01509 618110
E-mail: support@rsc-em.ac.uk
Web: www.rsc-east-midlands.ac.uk

JISC RSC LONDON

University of London Computing Centre,
20 Guilford Street,
London WC1N 1DZ
Tel: 020 7692 1637 **Fax:** 020 7692 1601
E-mail: admin@rsc-london.ac.uk
Web: www.rsc-london.ac.uk

JISC RSC NORTHERN

Sunderland Enterprise Park West,
Wessington Way (A1231), Colima Avenue,
Sunderland SR5 3XB
Tel: 0191 515 3456
E-mail: support@rsc-northern.ac.uk
Web: www.rsc-northern.ac.uk

JISC RSC NORTHERN IRELAND

Queen's University Belfast, Riddel Hall,
185 Stranmillis Road, Belfast BT9 5EE
North West Institute of Further and
Higher Education, Strand Road,
Londonderry BT48 7AL
Tel: 028 9097 5611 **Fax:** 028 9097 4264

E-mail: support@rsc-ni.ac.uk
Web: www.rsc-ni.ac.uk

JISC RSC NORTHWEST

2nd Floor, Bailrigg House, Lancaster University,
Lancaster LA1 4YE
Tel: 01253 503180 **Fax:** 01253 503182
E-mail: support@rsc-northwest.ac.uk
Web: www.rsc-northwest.ac.uk

JISC RSC SCOTLAND NORTH & EAST

Edinburgh's Telford College, 350 West Granton
Road, Edinburgh EH5 1QE
Tel: 0131 559 4112
E-mail: www.rsc-ne-scotland.ac.uk/contact.php
Web: www.rsc-ne-scotland.ac.uk

JISC RSC SCOTLAND SOUTH & WEST

1 Todd Campus, West of Scotland Science Park,
Acre Road, Glasgow G20 0XA
Tel: 0141 585 0022/0023 **Fax:** 0141 585 0020
E-mail: support@rsc-sw-scotland.ac.uk
Web: www.rsc-sw-scotland.ac.uk

JISC RSC SOUTH EAST

D Block, Keynes College, University of Kent,
Canterbury, Kent CT2 7NP
Tel: 01227 827 091 **Fax:** 01227 824 225
E-mail: support@rsc-southeast.ac.uk
Web: www.rsc-southeast.ac.uk

JISC RSC SOUTH WEST

University of Plymouth, Babbage Room 316,
Drake Circus, Plymouth PL4 8AA
Tel: 01752 233 899
E-mail: rsc-advice@rsc-south-west.ac.uk
Web: www.rsc-south-west.ac.uk

JISC RSC WALES

Regional Support Centre Wales,
Library and Information Services,
Swansea University, Singleton Park,
Swansea, SA2 8PP
Tel: 01792 295959
E-mail: support@rsc-wales.ac.uk
Web: www.rsc-wales.ac.uk

JISC RSC WEST MIDLANDS

Technology Centre,
Wolverhampton Science Park,
Stafford Road, Wolverhampton
WV10 9RU
Tel: 01902 518 982 **Fax:** 01902 824 345
E-mail: support@rsc-wm.ac.uk
Web: www.rsc-westmidlands.ac.uk

JISC RSC FOR YORKSHIRE AND HUMBER

University of Leeds, 44 Clarendon Road, LS2 9PJ
Tel: 0113 343 1000 **Fax:** 0113 343 4652
E-mail: support@rsc-yh.ac.uk
Web: www.rsc-yh.ac.uk

UNIVERSITY AUDIO-VISUAL CENTRES

This is a listing of the main universities that promote their audio-visual production facilities as being central services, rather than simply supporting particular academic courses in media production. Details of videoconferencing facilities are also included, where known. Some universities make these services available for commercial hire by users outside the university, and details are generally given on the unit's website.

UNIVERSITY OF ABERDEEN: DEPARTMENT OF MEDICAL ILLUSTRATION

Polwarth Building, Foresterhill, Aberdeen
AB25 2ZD
Tel: 01224 553813 **Fax:** 01224 554635
E-mail: i.harold@abdn.ac.uk
Web: www.abdn.ac.uk/clsm/services/
medillustration/
Provides photographic, graphic and television/audio-visual services for the Medical School and Aberdeen Royal Hospital Trusts and other departments within the university. Services include programme planning and production for clinical and non-clinical applications; standards conversion; video and audio dubbing; video editing; voice-over recording/editing; live interactive video for teaching/symposia within the medical faculty; teaching room equipment servicing within the medical faculty.

UNIVERSITY OF ABERTAY DUNDEE: INFORMATION SERVICES

Bell Street, Dundee, DD1 1HG
Tel: 01382 308816
E-mail: itdesk@abertay.ac.uk
Web: www.abertay.ac.uk/About/Facilities/
IT.cfm

Television and video equipment and a video-conferencing studio are available for use by outside clients as well as within the university.

ANGLIA RUSKIN UNIVERSITY: INFORMATION SYSTEMS & MEDIA SERVICES

East Road, Cambridge CB1 1PT
Tel: 0845 271 3333 ex 2221
E-mail: answers@anglia.ac.uk
Web: www.anglia.ac.uk/ruskin/en/home/
central/isms.html

Students using the media facilities at Anglia Ruskin University.

The Media Production team provides a full range of audio-visual, media production and graphic design services across the university. It also provides videoconferencing facilities and classroom support.

ASTON UNIVERSITY: ASTON MEDIA

Birmingham B4 7ET
Tel: 0121 204 4237 **Fax:** 0121 359 6427
E-mail: media@aston.ac.uk
Web: www1.aston.ac.uk/from-business/
business-services/astonmedia/
Aston Media provides multimedia production, equipment and expertise within the university and also to private and public sector clients. It offers a full range of services including production management, studio and location video recording, post-production editing, graphic design, multimedia authoring, web design and streamed video delivery, as well as audio-visual technical support.

UNIVERSITY OF BATH: AUDIO VISUAL UNIT

Audio Visual Unit, Claverton Down, Bath BA2 7AY
Tel: 01225 384846
E-mail: a.v.bookings@bath.ac.uk
Web: www.bath.ac.uk/bucs/services/
audiovisual/
Provides audio-visual equipment to assist with all university activities. The Audio Visual service is normally free of charge to University of Bath staff and students, but some services are open to external customers for a fee. The recording studio is equipped with three high quality Sony 3 chip colour cameras, lighting grid and an assortment of radio and floor microphones. Video and audio post production facilities and portable audio and video recording equipment for location work are also available.

UNIVERSITY OF BIRMINGHAM: MEDIA CENTRE

Edgbaston, Birmingham B15 2TT
Tel: 0121 414 3344 **Fax:** 0121 414 3971
E-mail: comtempdagger@adf.bham.ac.uk
Web: www.mediacentre.bham.ac.uk/
The Media Centre has comprehensive studio facilities and offers a full script to screen service.

The editing suite has a full range of facilities – editing, duplication, caption generation and audio production and the studio is fully equipped with state-of-the-art cameras, microphones and lighting. The studio and equipment are available for hire by internal and external users, with technical advice being available. Radio broadcast facilities enable live radio interviews to be held directly from the university. Multimedia programmes are also produced, from simple text and graphics CD-ROMs with simple step-through instructions, to video, audio and animation with more complicated search and option facilities.

UNIVERSITY OF BIRMINGHAM: VISUAL AND SPATIAL TECHNOLOGY CENTRE (VISTA)

Institute of Archaeology and Antiquity, Edgbaston, Birmingham B15 2TT
Tel: 0121 414 5513
E-mail: vista@contacts.bham.ac.uk
Web: www.vista.bham.ac.uk/
VISTA supports academic research and application development for spatial analysis, visualisation and imaging, using state-of-the-art technology in one of the best-equipped archaeological visualisation laboratories in Europe. Centre staff use VISTA facilities for research, postgraduate and professional training in archaeology, the Humanities and associated sciences. Separate divisions specialise in 3D laser scanning, GIS, remote sensing, marine and terrestrial geophysics, and visualisation.

BOURNEMOUTH UNIVERSITY: MEDIA SERVICES

Library and Learning Centre, Talbot Campus, Poole Dorset BH12 5BB
Tel: 01202 965515 **Fax:** 01202 966955
E-mail: itservicedesk@bournemouth.ac.uk
Web: www.bournemouth.ac.uk/itservices/
Media Services looks after the media equipment for lecture theatres and centrally booked teaching rooms on both campuses. Staff and students are able to borrow from an extensive range of media equipment including: DV cameras, digital stills cameras, projectors, analogue and digital audio recording devices.

UNIVERSITY OF BRADFORD: LEARNER SUPPORT SERVICES

Bradford, West Yorkshire BD7 1DP
Tel: 01274 233343
E-mail: lsshelp@bradford.ac.uk
Web: www.brad.ac.uk/lss/it-services/index.php
The Interactive Learning Centre provides students and staff with a large room with multimedia networked PCs, all with DVD players and CD writers; three study rooms for group work or quiet study all with video playback facilities; audio-visual teaching and learning equipment, video editing facilities and scanner. Other services provided include CD-ROM writing and videoconferencing.

UNIVERSITY OF BRIGHTON: MEDIA CENTRES

Information Services, Moulescombe Media Centre, Brighton BN2 4GJ
Tel: 01273 642767
E-mail: mcm9@brighton.ac.uk
Web: www.brighton.ac.uk/is/cms/index.php?option=com_content&task=
A range of media services is available at each site for staff and students including audio, video and IT equipment for loan, as well as video editing suites and media conversion facilities, an animation suite and a television studio. The media streaming service can convert video and audio materials into appropriate digital formats and serve them via the web from centrally-managed servers for delivery to students via the VLE or other web pages. The video and audio studios and editing suites are available for outside hire when not in use by students and staff. Duplication of videotapes and DVDs is also available to non-members of the university.

BRUNEL UNIVERSITY: MEDIA SERVICES

Computer Centre, John Crank building, Kingston Lane, Uxbridge UB8 3PH
Tel: 01895 274 000 **Fax:** 01895 255614
E-mail: colin.burgess@brunel.ac.uk
Web: www.brunel.ac.uk/life/study/computing/media
Media Services provides a range of services and facilities to support teaching, learning and research: supplying audio-visual presentation facilities in lecture rooms; offering creative and technical expertise to produce photographic, video and multimedia projects; teaching video and radio production modules within the university's degree programme; providing a central off-air recording service (television and radio, including satellite/digital) to enable staff to use broadcast material for teaching purposes.

CAMBRIDGE UNIVERSITY SCIENCE PRODUCTIONS (CUSP)

E-mail: enquiries@bluesci.org
Web: www.bluesci.org/index.php?option=com_content&task=view&id=471&Itemid=483
Cambridge University Science Productions is a society founded by students and members of the University of Cambridge with the aim of helping people who are interested in science communication, in all media. It produces multi-media packages such as podcasts and webcasts and training in science communication and 'how the media works' for all its members. CUSP produces webcasts for the annual BA Festival of Science and a regular science magazine entitled *BlueSci*.

CARDIFF UNIVERSITY: MEDIA RESOURCES CENTRE

University Hospital of Wales (UHW Unit), Block A-B link corridor, Cardiff University, Heath Park, Cardiff CF14 4XN
Tel: 029 2074 3305
E-mail: Med-Res@cardiff.ac.uk
Web: www.cardiff.ac.uk/insrv/graphicsandmedia/mediaresources
Responsible for the design, production and provision of media and resources to support teaching, research and clinical documentation in the Wales College of Medicine, Biology, Life and Health Sciences and the Cardiff and Vale NHS Trust, Heath Park Cardiff. The Video Unit is based at the Media Resources Centre, in the University Hospital Wales building. The Video Unit also offers video solutions and professional advice on procurement and production to commercial clients.

UNIVERSITY OF CHESTER: MEDIA SERVICES

Learning Resources, Parkgate Road,
Chester CH1 4BJ
Tel: 01244 375444
E-mail: david.evans@chester.ac.uk
Web: www.chester.ac.uk/lr/media.html
Provides a range of services to support academic
staff and students. These services include: audio-
visual support; graphic design; photography;
printing and reprographics; video production;
video streaming; video compression archiving and
transfer service for broadcast (webcast) over the
Intranet or Internet (copyright-enabled).

CITY UNIVERSITY: AUDIO-VISUAL SERVICES

Computing Services, Northampton Square,
London EC1V OHB
Tel: 020 7040 8181
E-mail: response-centre@city.ac.uk
Web: www.city.ac.uk/it-staff/
audio_visual_services.html
Responsible for: equipment loans; a studio
equipped with a two-camera Panasonic system
controlled via a vision and audio production mixer,
fed into an industrial SVHS video recorder,
autocue and talk-back facilities; audio and video
transfers; digital editing facilities consisting of a
non-linear G4 Macintosh editing system running
Adobe Premiere Software. Analogue editing room
facilities consist of two Panasonic industrial SVHS
linear editing systems and a title generator.

UNIVERSITY OF DUNDEE: VIDEO PRODUCTION SERVICE

Information & Communication Services,
Computing Centre, Park Place, Dundee DD1 4HN
Tel: 01382 384140 **Fax:** 01382 385505
E-mail: avsupport@dundee.ac.uk
Web: www.dundee.ac.uk/ics/services/
videoprod
Services include production of television (video)
material for teaching, promotional and other
purposes; a digital non-linear video editing suite;
consultancy in video production; specialist
services in the video area; transfer of video
between different formats; titling, music and voice-
over services for video editing; tape to DVD

copying; production of clips for VLE Blackboard.
These services are also available for outside
commercial use.

DURHAM UNIVERSITY: AUDIO VISUAL SERVICE

Information Technology Services, Old Elvet,
Durham DH1 3HP
Tel: 0191 334 1185
E-mail: it-av@durham.ac.uk
Web: www.dur.ac.uk/its/services/audio_visual
There are two professional videoconferencing
rooms based on the Sony and Polyspan equipment
which gives excellent audio and video quality (up
to 384 Kbps on ISDN6 and up to 1024 Kbps on the
campus network). There is a video editing PC
containing a Pinnacle DV500 Plus video capture
card and a copy of Adobe Premiere 6.0. Audio-
visual/IT equipment and technical support are
available for occasional hire for external meetings
and conferences.

UNIVERSITY OF EAST ANGLIA: AUDIO VISUAL SERVICES

Information Services, University of East Anglia,
Norwich NR4 7TJ
Tel: 01603 592488
E-mail: C.Browne@uea.ac.uk
Web: www1.uea.ac.uk/cm/home/services/
units/is/avs

University of East Anglia

AVS supports four main activities within the university: television studio and video production, lecture room support, and videoconferencing. Production services include studio recording, video and audio copying, video standards conversion, location audio recording, voice-over recording, off-air recording, media training, post production facilities and equipment hire. Videoconferencing is provided by Access Grid. The facilities are available for hire by outside clients.

UNIVERSITY OF EAST LONDON: LEARNING RESOURCE CENTRES

Docklands Campus, 4-6 University Way, London E16 2RD
Tel: 020 8223 3434
E-mail: hamilton@uel.ac.uk
Web: www.uel.ac.uk/students/being_student/lrc.htm
There are six Learning Resource Centres across the university's different campuses. Video playback machines for individual and group viewing are provided in all LRCs. In the Barking LRC there are video production and editing suites. A range of equipment can be borrowed including camcorders, cameras and audio cassette recorders.

EDGE HILL UNIVERSITY: LEARNING SERVICES

St Helens Road, Ormskirk Lancs L39 4QP
Tel: 01695 584286
Web: www.edgehill.ac.uk/ls/EquipFac/mediafac.htm
Learning Services provides a range of presentation and media equipment within its resource centres for use by students and staff. Media facilities include a fully equipped television studio, linear and non-linear editing, sound production and off-air recording facilities.

UNIVERSITY OF ESSEX: AUDIOVISUAL & MEDIA SERVICES

Wivenhoe Park, Colchester, Essex CO4 3SQ
Tel: 01206 873220 **Fax:** 01206 873216
E-mail: avs@essex.ac.uk
Web: www.essex.ac.uk/avms

AVMS advises University of Essex staff and technical staff at other HE institutions on the use of multimedia and audio-visual technologies for teaching and learning. AVMS is also responsible for audio-visual equipment in seminar and lecture rooms and hire of portable equipment. For videoconferencing, the university has a centrally provided system (Tandberg 990) in the Multi Media Centre that uses digital telephone lines (ISDN 6) or an Internet connection (IP). Staff of the university and external users can book the service.

UNIVERSITY OF EXETER: IT SERVICES

Academic Services, Main Library, Stocker Road, Exeter, Devon EX4 4PT
Tel: 01392 263939
E-mail: itsreception@exeter.ac.uk
Web: www.its.ex.ac.uk/services
Provides technical support for audio-visual facilities in centrally-bookable teaching and meeting rooms; co-ordination of audio-visual facilities throughout the university; support for videoconferencing in teaching and meeting rooms; support for desktop videoconferencing systems; management of the ongoing programme for upgrade/replacement of audio-visual equipment and infrastructure in centrally-bookable teaching and meeting rooms. Audio-visual support is available for external clients using university facilities for conferences and events.

UNIVERSITY COLLEGE FALMOUTH: MEDIA CENTRE

Tremough Campus, Penryn TR10 9EZ
Tel: 01326 370400
Web: www.falmouth.ac.uk/index.php?option=com_content&task=view&id=299&Itemid=138
The Media Centre houses industry-standard facilities including a recording studio, a well-equipped newsroom with an IRN news feed and forty-five workstations with professional scriptwriting and editing software, three radio control rooms and a talk studio with three radio control rooms, four dedicated Pro-Tools audio post-production rooms with 5.1 surround sound capability and a new animation studio. Other facilities include a television studio, fourteen AVID

© 'Jean Scheijen / SXC

edit suites, a well-stocked equipment store with a range of cameras and related items, an IT Suite with audio editing and graphics software, and a 106-seat cinema. The facilities are available for use by local businesses.

UNIVERSITY OF GLAMORGAN: MEDIA SERVICES

Learning Resources Centre, Pontypridd CF37 1DL
Tel: 01443 482610
E-mail: avslrc@glam.ac.uk
Web: http://lcss.glam.ac.uk/lrc/media/
Media Services supports the effective use of audio and visual media in teaching, learning and research by providing facilities, equipment, production services, advice and training. It assists staff in producing and acquiring audio-visual content and in delivering it in the classroom or online. It helps with the production of video, audio and photographic materials to support teaching, learning, and research. Media Services has two fully equipped videoconferencing studios, which are part of the Welsh Video Network that supports over eighty similar studios throughout the Welsh HE and FE sectors.

UNIVERSITY OF GLASGOW: LEARNING & TEACHING CENTRE

Southpark House, 64 Southpark Avenue G12 8LB
Tel: 0141 330 4864/3870 **Fax:** 0141 330 5674
E-mail: learn@admin.gla.ac.uk

Web: www.gla.ac.uk/services/learningteaching/mediaproduction
The media production team provide innovative and cost-effective teaching aids, mixed media, consultancy and training. They offer a comprehensive script to screen service from script development to completed programme, plus creative preparation of materials for multi-format delivery. Production facilities include top of the range filming and editing crews and equipment, well equipped television studio, sound suite, video transfers between all major professional formats, video encoding, DVD and CD authoring, VHS, CD and DVD duplication, and off-air recording.

GLASGOW CALEDONIAN UNIVERSITY: AUDIO-VISUAL SERVICES

William Harley Building, Cowcaddens Road, Glasgow G4 0BA
Tel: 0141 273 1234
E-mail: ithelp@gcal.ac.uk
Web: www.learningservices.gcal.ac.uk/avs
Audio-Visual Services provide a range of support for teaching and learning within the university, including videoconferencing, off-air recording, classroom resources, audio-visual equipment hire, sound and video production facilities and expertise. There is broadcast-quality camera and editing equipment, a fully-equipped sound studio, and open-access video editing facilities for use by staff and students.

UNIVERSITY OF HULL: AUDIO-VISUAL SERVICES

Scarborough Campus, Filey Road, Scarborough YO11 3AZ
Tel: 01723 362392
E-mail: ithelp-scar@hull.ac.uk.
Web: www.hull.ac.uk/scarborough/support/IT/AVService.html
In addition to the core IT support, there are staff dedicated to providing support for audio-visual equipment. Services provided include: loaning equipment such as digital projectors, cameras and video cameras to staff and students; producing the Scarborough Campus graduation DVD; recording assessments for departments, events on campus and field trips; providing assistance with production of professional-style CD printing; producing multimedia and radio projects for promotional activities. The campus also has two videoconferencing suites which are available to staff and also businesses.

UNIVERSITY OF HULL: HULL IMMERSIVE VISUALIZATION ENVIRONMENT (HIVE)

Cottingham Road, Hull HU6 7RX
Tel: 01482 465016 **Fax:** 01482 465823
E-mail: hive@hull.ac.uk
Web: www.hive.hull.ac.uk
HIVE provides state-of-the-art visualisation, interaction and computing technology and related support for both university departments and industry. Facilities include stereoscopic vision (using immersive workwall or desktop PCs); virtual and augmented reality; virtual prototyping; collaborative design reviews; development of virtual environment trainers; simulation of urban development and terrain; scientific and medical visualisation scene capture and reverse engineering using stereo cameras, motion tracking, CMM; haptic interaction with visualisations; high performance computing.

UNIVERSITY OF KEELE: MEDIA AND COMMUNICATIONS CENTRE

Chancellors Building, Keele,
Staffordshire ST5 5BG
Tel: 01782 583377
Fax: 01782 714832

E-mail: info@mediaandcomms.co.uk
Web: www.mediaandcomms.co.uk/
The Media and Communications Centre has a large range of audio visual equipment for hire; purpose built studio space with the latest Tandberg videoconferencing equipment; multimedia and video facilities including video production and digital edit suites, CD, VHS and DVD duplication and standards conversion, and television and radio off-air recording. The facilities are available for commercial hire by organisations outside of the university.

UNIVERSITY OF KENT: AUDIO VISUAL SERVICES

Computing Services, Cornwallis South Building, Canterbury CT2 7NF
Tel: 01227 824666
E-mail: avs@kent.ac.uk
Web: www.kent.ac.uk/itservices/avs/
Audio Visual Services aims to enhance learning and teaching through the use of interactive and digital technology. It provides videoconferencing facilities for internal and external use, lecture recording in web-ready format for putting online so that students can download and listen to them, an off-air recording service, and equipment loan for use in lecture rooms.

LANCASTER UNIVERSITY TELEVISION

Round House, Lancaster University,
Lancaster LA1 4YW
Tel: 01524 593984
E-mail: lutv@lancaster.ac.uk
Web: www.lancs.ac.uk/users/lutv
Lancaster University Television provides a wide range of television and video production services to staff and students at the University. Most of these services are also available to commercial companies, organisations and government agencies in the UK and overseas. Services range from off-air recording and multiple copying to high quality programme production and the provision of production skills workshops. LUTV is able to produce and distribute video materials on DVD, VHS, MPEG files for use in PowerPoint presentations and web video for streaming media servers.

UNIVERSITY OF LEEDS: MEDIA SERVICES

Roger Stevens Building, Leeds LS2 9JT
Tel: 0113 3432668
E-mail: mediaservices@leeds.ac.uk
Web: http://mediant.leeds.ac.uk/A2a.html
Media Services supports the academic, student and administrative communities at the university with a full range of audio-visual and print solutions. It offers a full script-to-screen service and has a purpose-built multi-camera studio, broadcast quality location recording unit, graphic design unit, linear and non-linear editing suites, and a sound studio. There are also facilities for producing 2D and 3D graphics and images, webcasting, video and audio copying and off-air recording. Many of the unit's video productions are available for sale to other institutions.

LEEDS METROPOLITAN UNIVERSITY: TECHNOLOGY SERVICES

Room C520 Civic Quarter, Leeds LS1 3HE
Tel: 0113 812 5965
E-mail: j.lynch@leedsmet.ac.uk
Web: http://helpzone.leedsmet.ac.uk/staff_video_recording.htm
Video recordings can be made in the television studios or on location in classrooms, lecture theatres, labs and off campus. The Media Production Support Service (http://helpzone.leedsmet.ac.uk/media_production_support.htm) offers video recording and video editing support for students working on media projects. Camcorders and audio recorders are available for loan and there are edit suites on both campuses.

LEEDS TRINITY & ALL SAINTS: MEDIA SERVICES

Brownberrie Lane, Horsforth, Leeds,
West Yorkshire LS18 5HD
Tel: 01132 283 7249
E-mail: a.clifford@leedstrinity.ac.uk
Web: www.leedstrinity.ac.uk/services/media_services
The Media Centre is housed in purpose-built accommodation offering television and radio production and training services. Studio facilities and a wide range of production equipment allow realistic broadcasting, recording and editing to take place. Both domestic and broadcast quality video and audio equipment is available for loan from the Media Centre.

UNIVERSITY OF LEICESTER: MULTIMEDIA SERVICE

Maurice Shock Building, University Road,
Leicester LE1 9HN
Tel: 0116 252 2914
E-mail: jems1@le.ac.uk
Web: www.le.ac.uk/avs/video.html

Still from the University of Leicester production, MR KIRBY'S STORY.

The Multimedia Service provides facilities and expertise to support the presentation needs of the university, as well as undertaking some outside work. Equipped to broadcast standards, it produces video, audio and multimedia materials for teaching, promotion and research. A complete range of services is offered from copying, digitising and editing to full production facilities. Equipment support, video and telephone conferencing, and television/radio off-air recording are also undertaken.

LIVERPOOL HOPE UNIVERSITY: LIBRARY, LEARNING & INFORMATION SERVICES (LLIS)

Hope Park, Liverpool L16 9JD
Tel: 0151 291 2100
E-mail: itshelp@hope.ac.uk
Web: www.hope.ac.uk/it-services/welcome-to-information-services.html
LLIS supports the learning, teaching, research and administrative activities of the university. Its responsibilities include IT and AVA support and videoconferencing.

BIRKBECK, UNIVERSITY OF LONDON: ESTATES AND FACILITIES

Malet Street, Bloomsbury, London WC1E 7HX
Tel: 020 7631 6271 **Fax:** 020 7631 6019
E-mail: roombookings@bbk.ac.uk
Web: www.bbk.ac.uk/ef/roombookings/audiovisual/index.shtml
Recently refurbished lecture theatres and meeting rooms with state-of-the-art technology are available for external hire as well as internal use. This service also includes video and audio editing.

GOLDSMITHS, UNIVERSITY OF LONDON: MEDIA SERVICES CENTRE

Rutherford Building, New Cross,
London SE14 6NW
Tel: 020 7919 7546
E-mail: media-services@gold.ac.uk
Web: www.goldsmiths.ac.uk/media-services/
The Media Services Centre provides materials, facilities, support and services to help with all media requirements from video to audio, and from photography to photocopying. There are non-linear digital 'Casablanca' suites with opportunities for special effects; a linear tape-to-tape suite for quicker tasks; multi-format video-copying facilities with capacity for making high quality video stills; equipment for fast and real-time audio copying and simple audio mixing.

IMPERIAL COLLEGE, UNIVERSITY OF LONDON: COMMUNICATIONS DIVISION

5th Floor, Sherfield Building, London SW7 2AZ
Tel: 020 7594 8135 or 020 7594 8136
E-mail: c.grimshaw@imperial.ac.uk or m.sayers@imperial.ac.uk
Web: www3.imperial.ac.uk/communications/digitalmedia
The Video Production section of Digital Media, now part of the Communications Division, provides professional video and DVD production, web streaming and podcasting services to Imperial College and external clients. They offer location recording, post-production and VHS and DVD duplication as well, using high end computer technology to encode video content for storing on the server and streaming out onto the Internet.

The Queen's Tower at the South Kensington campus of Imperial College.

Imperial College

INSTITUTE OF EDUCATION, UNIVERSITY OF LONDON: INFORMATION SERVICES

20 Bedford Way, London WC1H 0AL
Tel: 020 7612 6700
E-mail: media.enq@ioe.ac.uk
Web: http://ioewebserver.ioe.ac.uk/ioe/cms/get.asp?cid=8869&8869_0=9580
The Media section of IS provides facilities and help with the creation of print, audio and video materials; facilities for audio and video copying/editing in a variety of analogue and digital formats; a playback area for viewing multimedia materials.

KING'S COLLEGE, UNIVERSITY OF LONDON: AUDIO VISUAL SERVICES

Information Services & Systems, Room 23B, Main Building, The Strand, London WC2R 2LS
Tel: 020 7848 2386 **Fax:** 020 7848 2790
E-mail: avsu@kcl.ac.uk
Web: www.kcl.ac.uk/iss/av
Provides audio-visual support for lectures and conferences and also carries out the following work for both staff and students within the college and external clients: videoconferencing; video and audio recording of events and lectures; video and audio dubbing; digital video editing; off-air and satellite recording. There is a small television studio equipped for basic video recording onto DV or mini-DV tape. This can then be edited on PC using a range of video editing software. Captions and voice-overs can be added and the edit written to DVD disk. The filmed material can also be pro-

cessed by ISS staff for web streaming etc. Audio Visual Services also has location equipment including portable DV and mini-DV digital camcorders, audio mixer, microphones, and more.

KING'S COLLEGE LONDON: KING'S VISUALISATION LAB

King's Visualisation Lab, Centre for Computing in the Humanities, 26-29 Drury Lane, London WC2B 5RL
Tel: 020 7848 2684/ 01926 885 083
E-mail: kvl@kcl.ac.uk
Web: www.kvl.cch.kcl.ac.uk/index.html

 KVL specialises in visual representation for archaeology, historic buildings, cultural heritage organisations, and academic research. The team of modellers, artists and designers can turn a vision into moving or still images, combined with a web presence, interactive displays, video, CD-ROM or DVD products.

ROYAL HOLLOWAY, UNIVERSITY OF LONDON: AUDIO VISUAL SERVICE

Room AG 01 Arts Building, Egham Hill, Egham TW20 0EX
Tel: 01784 443319/443232
E-mail: audiovisual@rhul.ac.uk
Web: www.rhul.ac.uk/Information-Services/Audio-Visual

The Audio Visual Service is responsible for providing teaching room support; satellite and terrestrial off-air recording; language lab support; videoconferencing; video and audio duplication; maintaining and running the video codec and associated equipment which provides the Livenet interactive video network links to other colleges in London University.

ROYAL VETERINARY COLLEGE, UNIVERSITY OF LONDON: ELECTRONIC-MEDIA UNIT

Room F17, Royal College Street, London NW1 0TU
Tel: 020 7468 5175 **Fax:** 020 7383 0615
E-mail: nshort@rvc.ac.uk

Web: www.rvc.ac.uk/AboutUs/Services/eMedia/Index.cfm

The e-Media Unit was set up to develop multimedia learning resources, and staff have experience of graphics, video, animation, instructional design and web development. The Unit's activities include: filming, editing and streaming all college digital videos; developing podcasts, wikis and blogs including collaborative projects with other institutions; developing and supporting the Blackboard Academic Suite VLE; providing technical and pedagogic support to the RVC e-CPD programme.

ST GEORGE'S, UNIVERSITY OF LONDON: TELEVISION PRODUCTION UNIT

4th Floor Hunter Wing, Cranmer Terrace, London SW17 0RE
Tel: 020 7825 5087 **Fax:** 020 8725 0075
E-mail: television@sgul.ac.uk
Web: www.sgul.ac.uk/depts/academic-services/tv.cfm

Still from the virtual reality scenarios created by the St Georges. e-learning unit for the Paramedic Science degree course as part of the PREVIEW project.

The Television Production Unit is responsible for video programme development, multi-camera production, digital and slide imaging, fully equipped studio and editing facilities, off-air broadcast recording, video duplication, audio production. In terms of television graphics it offers: 3-D modelling for animated sequences and still frames, anatomical 'wire-frame' library, titling and special effects. Some of the programmes produced by St George's Media Services are available for sale for patient or medical staff education, and the CLINICAL SKILLS ONLINE series of video titles has been developed for web distribution by the e-learning Unit at St George's. An advanced videoconferencing unit is available for use in various locations.

UNIVERSITY COLLEGE LONDON: MULTIMEDIA UNIT

Windeyer Building, Cleveland Street,
London W1T 4JF
Tel: 020 7679 9257
E-mail: c.nalty@ucl.ac.uk
Web: www.ucl.ac.uk/mediares/av
The Multimedia Unit within Media Services is responsible for the provision and support of video communications across UCL including networked multimedia, video production, streaming, and digitisation of media, as well as the development of multimedia software and web applications in support of teaching and learning. The section is also involved in the research and development of systems to further support teaching and learning within UCL. Delivery mechanisms include CD-ROMs, DVDs, the Web, streaming servers and also through the university wide VLE (Virtual Learning Environment), Moodle.

LONDON METROPOLITAN UNIVERSITY: MEDIA SERVICES

166-200 Holloway Rd, London N7 8DB
Tel: 020 7133 2315
E-mail: d.coles@londonmet.ac.uk
Web: www.londonmet.ac.uk/services/sas/
service-man/media/home.cfm
Media Services offers advice, resources and production facilities in various media to enhance and support teaching and learning. Among these are equipment and technical support for teaching and presentations in classrooms and lecture theatres; creative facilities, assistance and advice on the production of teaching materials; off-air recording service for radio and television broadcasts; photographic services for the production of teaching aids, promotional work and publications.

LOUGHBOROUGH UNIVERSITY: MEDIA SERVICES

Loughborough, Leicestershire LE11 3TU
Tel: 01509 222197 **Fax:** 01509 610813

E-mail: television@lboro.ac.uk
Web: www.lboro.ac.uk/mediaservices/
multimedia/index.html
Among the services offered are video editing, video production, video encoding, websites, CD-ROM mastering and duplication, on face printing and video transfer and standard conversions to the format of your choice. The video production service offers a professional service from initial concepts and storyboards, location or studio filming, to a final high-quality master in a choice of formats. The unit delivers innovative multimedia solutions for a wide array of markets including promotional, educational, training, technical and informative.

MANCHESTER METROPOLITAN UNIVERSITY: INFORMATION AND COMMUNICATION TECHNOLOGY SERVICES

Ormond Building, Lower Ormond Street,
Manchester M15 6BX
Tel: 0161 247 6905
E-mail: a.fraser@mmu.ac.uk
Web: www.mediaservices.mmu.ac.uk
ICTS Services include multimedia and video production and editing; videoconferencing; television and radio off-air recording; supply and maintenance of audio-visual equipment. Full length video productions or short sequences can be produced for use on VHS, DVD, CD-ROM or incorporated into a website.

UNIVERSITY OF MANCHESTER: MEDIA CENTRE

Tel: 0161 275 2521
E-mail: media-centre@manchester.ac.uk
Web: www.campus.manchester.ac.uk/
mediacentre/
The Media Centre has a range of audio and video production facilities using broadcast standard technology to support course requirements. Facilities are available for requests ranging from simple CD duplication to video programme creation. Cutting edge technology in audio, video and graphic design is available to service all audio-visual requirements. The professional staff are always willing to give help and advise on any aspect of audio-visual equipment, production, or

problem. The Audio Visual Support section provides equipment and technical support for teaching and off-air recording of terrestrial television programmes.

MIDDLESEX UNIVERSITY: LEARNING RESOURCES

Information and Learning Resources, Cat Hill Campus, Barnet EN4 8HT
Tel: 020 8411 5798
E-mail: p.dade@mdx.ac.uk
Web: www.lr.mdx.ac.uk/av/index.htm
Audio-visual facilities include videoconferencing, television and photographic studios, darkrooms, video editing suites and various kinds of equipment for loan, such as cameras and camcorders.

UNIVERSITY OF NEWCASTLE UPON TYNE: TELEVISION SERVICES

William Leech Building, The Medical School, Framlington Place, Newcastle upon Tyne NE2 4HH
Tel: 0191 222 6633
E-mail: urwin.wood@ncl.ac.uk
Web: www.ncl.ac.uk/iss/tvservices
Television Services provides a comprehensive range of audio, video and film services to both internal and external clients, including: research and script writing; broadcast quality camera recording; analogue/digital broadcast editing; DVD authoring; digital conversion of audio and video files; off-air recording of Freeview television programmes; ISDN and IP videoconferencing; broadcast quality radio interview recording; video streaming. Many of the unit's productions are available for sale to other institutions.

NORTHUMBRIA UNIVERSITY: IT SERVICES

Room 128, Northumberland Building, Newcastle upon Tyne NE1 8ST
Tel: 0191 232 6002 ext 4242
E-mail: it.helpline@northumbria.ac.uk
Web: www.northumbria.ac.uk/sd/central/its/staff_info/audio_visual_info/
IT Services provide fixed audio-visual equipment in classrooms, lecture theatres and meeting rooms, including PCs with connection to the network, LCD projectors and screens; loan of equipment to staff for use on university premises; portable videoconferencing facilities; streaming media service.

UNIVERSTY OF NOTTINGHAM: TELEVISION AND VIDEO PRODUCTION UNIT

IS Learning Team, Kings Meadow Campus, Lenton Lane, Nottingham NG7 2NA
Tel: 0115 846 7809
E-mail: IS-Video-Production-Group@ nottingham.ac.uk
Web: www.nottingham.ac.uk/is/services/video/index.phtml
The Unit (part of the IS Learning Team) based at the King's Meadow Campus (previously Carlton Television Studios), produces broadcast quality educational and promotional material for academic, medical and commercial audiences. These include filming (location and studio); creation of video 'still' images as well as MPEG, AVI and QuickTime movies; offline and online video editing; sound recording and editing; live event coverage; media streaming – live and on-demand; digital media encoding/compression (video, audio and stills); DVD authoring/ production; CD/DVD duplication and printing; videotape duplication and standards conversion; off-air recording; video archive; audio broadcasting; equipment loan/hire; advice and consultancy; videoconferencing.

OXFORD BROOKES UNIVERSITY: AUDIO VISUAL PRODUCTION

F1/17 Harcourt Hill Campus, Oxford OX2 9AT
Tel: 01865 48 8382
E-mail: avharcourthill@brookes.ac.uk
Web: www.brookes.ac.uk/avproduction
Provides a service for recording lectures, studio or location filming, video editing in PC-based suites, tape copying and international standards conversion, off-air recording, and making training videos. Advice and consultancy is offered in matters concerning video production, from concept through to duplication. All these services can be hired by external customers, subject to availability. Audio visual equipment loan and facilities in teaching rooms are handled by Audio Visual Services.

Joe Carr, producer of BrookesTV, interviewing George Osbourne MP.

UNIVERSITY OF OXFORD: MEDIA PRODUCTION UNIT

5 Worcester Street, Oxford OX1 2BX
Tel: 01865 289980
E-mail: lisa.wiggins@admin.ox.ac.uk
Web: www.ox.ac.uk/publicaffairs/mpu
The Media Production Unit has the facility to produce broadcast quality video. The crew can be hired to produce programmes to support teaching and to promote university or college activities, or for commercial activities outside the university. The unit offers professional digital editing as well as an iMac suite where customers may edit their own video footage, tape duplication and standards conversion, and video-conferencing facilities for up to 100 people. There is a small amount of audio-visual equipment for hire.

UNIVERSITY OF PAISLEY: ICT MEDIA SERVICES

High Street, Paisley PA1 2BE
Tel: 0141 848 3824
E-mail: charlie.hunter@paisley.ac.uk
Web: www.paisley.ac.uk/schoolsdepts/ICT/media/index.asp
Facilities include a colour television studio, video-conferencing suite, television and radio off-air recording from all the UK national terrestrial networks plus the majority of satellite channels broadcast in the western hemisphere, tape duplication, and loan of a range of media services equipment to students and staff.

UNIVERSITY OF PLYMOUTH: TELEVISION AND BROADCAST SERVICES

Information & Communication Systems, Drake Circus, Plymouth PL4 8AA
Tel: 01752 233640
E-mail: d.hurrell@plymouth.ac.uk
Web: www.plymouth.ac.uk/pages/view.asp?page=2525
Services include live television broadcasting; satellite services supporting broadcasting and research experiments; video production; television presentation training; video recording of lectures; location recording; specialist graphic facilities; video editing; videoconferencing ISDN2 and ISDN6 for meetings and specialist lectures; advice on all aspects of television production; satellite installation site surveys and advice; video-transfer; web streaming. Technical advice, facilities hire and video production are also available to external clients.

UNIVERSITY OF PORTSMOUTH: E-LEARNING CENTRE

Town Mount, Hampshire Terrace, Portsmouth PO1 2QG
Tel: 023 9284 6510
E-mail: richard.hackett@port.ac.uk
Web: www.port.ac.uk/departments/services/dcqe/eLearningCentre/
The Media Production team is part of the e-Learning Centre which draws together the university's central resources for e-learning, media production (including video streaming and podcasting) and editorial print-based publishing. The Media Producion team can guide colleagues through the production process and advise on using different techniques or the many pedagogical issues that may arise. Services offered include: script development; location filming; television studio production; blue screen; post-production/editing; media encoding; podcasting; recording of lectures; videoconferencing.

QUEENS UNIVERSITY BELFAST: MEDIA SERVICES

Information Services Learning & Teaching Division, Science Library, Chlorine Gardens, Belfast BT9 5EQ

Tel: 028 90974293
E-mail: avs@qub.ac.uk
Web: www.qub.ac.uk/is/MediaServices
In addition to teaching room support, Media Services is responsible for portable videoconferencing facilities; photographic and graphic design services; video and audio digitisation for Powerpoint, multimedia or web streaming applications; video duplication and systems conversion. Video production at all levels is supported, from 'self-drive' VHS and digital editing for staff and students, to broadcast quality recording and post production. A multimedia production service is available for producing digital files for use in PowerPoint presentations, media streaming or CD-ROM format.

UNIVERSITY OF READING:
MEDIA PRODUCTION

IT Services Centre, Whiteknights P.O. Box 220 Reading RG6 6AF
Tel: 0118 378 8771
E-mail: its-media@reading.ac.uk
Web: www.reading.ac.uk/its/info/services/media.htm
Media Production provides low cost, quality digital and traditional media components for teaching, learning, and research, including: single camera video (digital); video digitisation and encoding; basic video editing (digital and traditional); VHS and digital video copying; off-air terrestrial and satellite recordings; audio recording and copying (digital and traditional); 35mm and medium format stills photography; slide digitisation.

ROBERT GORDON UNIVERSITY:
EDUCATIONAL MEDIA SERVICES (EMS)

Department for the Enhancement of Learning, Teaching and Assessment (DELTA), Blackfriars Building, Schoolhill, Aberdeen AB10 1FR
Tel: 01224 263349
E-mail: emsvideo@rgu.ac.uk
Web: http://www2.rgu.ac.uk/celt/ems/index.html
EMS supports learning and teaching needs across the university through the provision of video and multimedia production, digital photography and imaging, and audio-visual hardware. It offers a comprehensive range of services includ-

ing educational DVD video production; digital video encoding; interactive multimedia design and production; audio programmes production; audio-visual presentation programmes; graphic design; digital media files; screen graphics design; still video animation; video frame capture; CD/DVD replication; media production training.

ROEHAMPTON UNIVERSITY: TELEVISION
ROEHAMPTON (TVR)

Information Services, Television Centre, Digby Stuart, Roehampton Lane, London SW15 5PH
Tel: 020 8392 3590
E-mail: tvr@roehampton.ac.uk
Web: http://studentzone.roehampton.ac.uk/media/index.html
The facilities of TVR include four studios (a small presentation studio, a sound studio for audio recording, interviews and voice-overs, and two small production studios); VHS, digital, linear and non-linear editing; location and studio-based production; off-air recording from terrestrial and satellite broadcasts. The Multimedia section of Media Services provides and supports the facilities for sound editing from audio cassette, VHS and CD digitised to computer, edited and transferred to audio cassette or CD in conjunction with TVR voice recordings, as well as video editing for multimedia projects.

ST ANDREWS UNIVERSITY: SALTIRE

Hebdomadar's Block, St Salvator's Quad, 75 North Street, St Andrew
Fife KY16 9AJ
Tel: 01334 462141
E-mail: learning@st-andrews.ac.uk
Web: www.st-andrews.ac.uk/saltire
SALTIRE was established to enhance the development of traditional as well as innovative approaches to learning and teaching. One of SALTIRE's six main areas of activity is supporting the delivery of study skills. This includes assisting schools to create and maintain learning and teaching materials in order to enhance teaching via both traditional and innovative methods, including online approaches using a virtual or managed learning environment (VLE or MLE). The Psychology Department provides audio and video production and editing services, as well as

off-air recording, video copying and standards conversion.

UNIVERSITY OF SALFORD: AUDIO VISUAL SERVICES

Information Services Division, Chapman Building, Salford, Greater Manchester M5 4WT
Tel: 0161 2955000
E-mail: avs-cars@salford.ac.uk
Web: www.ils.salford.ac.uk/audiovisual/
AVS supports the teaching and learning environment across the university campus. It provides audio, video and DVD duplication and transfer, and a broadcast quality filming, editing and DVD authoring service. Facilities and services are available to users outside the university via the Conference Office.

UNIVERSITY OF SHEFFIELD: LEARNING DEVELOPMENT AND MEDIA UNIT

5 Favell Road Sheffield S3 7QX
Tel: 0114 222 0400
E-mail: ldmu@shef.ac.uk
Web: www.shef.ac.uk/ldmu
LDMU has a skilled production team comprising designers, programmers and educational advisers that work with academic staff to produce high quality resources to support student learning. Their involvement ranges from offering advice at the beginning of projects and allowing staff to produce their own material using the DIY facilities suite, providing equipment and a television studio, to producing bespoke videos as stand-alone programmes or as video clips embedded into a larger learning resource, and to producing large interactive multimedia teaching packages and networked learning courses for WebCT. Other services offered include media conversion and copying, off-air recording and standards conversion.

UNIVERSITY OF SOUTHAMPTON: E.MEDIA

Information Systems Services, Building 35-3003, Highfield SO17 1BJ
Tel: 023 8059 7626
E-mail: emedia@soton.ac.uk
Web: www.southampton.ac.uk/emedia/
e.media is the university's specialist multimedia production team for interactive CD-ROMs, DVDs, websites and videos. Services offered include video and audio encoding and streaming; video duplication and off-air recording. e.media also provides a complete range of media production services, from the straightforward videoing of lectures or demonstrations, to writing, filming, editing and bulk-copying promotional material and complete educational packages.

UNIVERSITY OF STRATHCLYDE: LEARNING SERVICES

Alexander Turnbull Building, 155 George Street, Glasgow G1 1RD
Tel: 0141 548 2712
E-mail: ls-visualresources@strath.ac.uk
Web: www.strath.ac.uk/learningservices/video/

The video production service produces resources ranging from simple lecture recordings to complex projects produced in studio or in other locations, for delivery via the web, CD-ROM, DVD and use in PowerPoint presentations. A campus-wide 24/7 video streaming service is provided as well as live video streaming to provide enhanced access to lectures and conference presentations. Learning Services also provides teaching room audio-visual equipment, support for the VLE and e-learning, IT training, special needs IT support, design, Internet copyright clearance and multimedia production.

UNIVERSITY OF SUNDERLAND: AUDIO VISUAL TEAM

Learning Development Services, Room 008, Prospect Building, Sir Tom Cowie campus at St. Peter's, St. Peters Way, Sunderland SR6 0DD
Tel: 0191 515 1177
E-mail: paula.devlin@sunderland.ac.uk
Web: http://microsites.sunderland.ac.uk/lds/audio-visual
The audio-visual team is responsible for equipping the theatres and managing the audio-visual facilities; promoting the use of new equipment and technology; evaluating new and emerging audio-visual technology and equipment; WebCT support; offering audio-visual support, advice and expertise to special events.

UNIVERSITY OF SURREY:
UNIS TELEVISION

Guildford, Surrey GU2 7XH
Tel: 01483 879991
E-mail: b.johnson@surrey.ac.uk
Web: www.surrey.ac.uk/tv

UniS Television offers professional production and facilities house services including two fully equipped studios, DVC Pro and Betacam Edit Suite, DVC pro and Betacam SP ENG facilities, AVID online suite, SVHS Edit Suite, voice-over recording and a sound booth. It also offers video copying and industrial standards conversion that can master from DVC pro DvCam, Umatic and VHS formats via TBC and VDA ADA distribution amps to quality Panasonic HiFi VHS machines. Audio-visual equipment support for teaching rooms is provided by the Audio Visual Services section of IT Services.

UNIVERSITY OF SUSSEX:
MEDIA SERVICES UNIT

Education Development Building, EDB 252,
Falmer, Brighton BN1 9RG
Tel: 01273 678022
E-mail: msu@sussex.ac.uk
Web: www.sussex.ac.uk/its/msu

Multimedia services include providing audio-visual equipment and staff for teaching rooms and conferences, and a consultancy service for advice on purchase and installation; audio and video copying and standards conversion; digital video editing using industry-standard Avid DV Xpress and digital audio editing using Adobe Audition software; professional-quality audio and video programme production and post-production facilities for academic and commercial clients; a videoconferencing facility using ISDN and other technologies on other networks via the JVCS service.

UNIVERSITY OF ULSTER:
MEDIA TECHNOLOGY SUPPORT

IT User Services, South Building, Cromore Road,
Coleraine BT52 1SA
Tel: 028 9036 6777
E-mail: helpdesk@ulster.ac.uk
Web: www.ulster.ac.uk/isd/itus/media

Services include teaching and space support; a range of room-based, roll-about and personal videoconferencing systems; video streaming; video and sound production team to enable staff to create, edit and produce video and audio recordings on video cassette, CD-ROM and DVD for incorporation into lectures and tutorials or digitisation for online learning via download or on-demand video streaming.

UNIVERSITY OF WALES, ABERYSTWYTH:
SEE3D LTD

See3D, The Visualisation Centre, Penglais Campus, Aberystwyth, Ceredigion SY23 3BF
Tel: 01970 628428
E-mail: info@see3d.co.uk
Web: www.see3d.co.uk

The See3D Visualisation Centre.

See3D uses a Silicon Graphics Prism machine for developing specialist visualisations and software, providing motion tracking, stereo 3D, and true perspective imagery. The facilities are available for use by outside academic and commercial institutions as well as by staff at Aberystwyth. Videoconferencing, off-air recording, lecture recording, video streaming, and video duplication and conversion services within the university are provided by Media Services (www.inf.aber.ac.uk/mediaservices).

UNIVERSITY OF WALES, BANGOR:
MEDIA CENTRE

Hen Goleg, College Road, Bangor,
Gwynedd LL57 7PX
Tel: 01248 382412
E-mail: R.P.Wood@bangor.ac.uk

Web: www.bangor.ac.uk/itservices/av/ mediacentre.php.en

The Media Centre houses radio and television facilities, together with video and audio editing suites. It has a range of portable video and audio equipment for use by staff and students, a broadcast radio studio with analogue and digital facilities, video editing facilities, television studio, and three videoconferencing studios.

UNIVERSITY OF WALES, NEWPORT: IT AND MEDIA SERVICES

Library and Information Services, Room C1A41 Lodge Road, Caerleon Newport NP18 3NT
Tel: 01633 432172 ext. 2172
E-mail: rob.hyde@newport.ac.uk
Web: http://lis.newport.ac.uk/av

The television studio can produce material with up to five cameras simultaneously and record on to S-VHS video tape or semi-professional Mini-DV format. The Control Room has the facility for caption camera, a video playback machine and audio playback. The studio has a Panasonic vision and effects mixer, which provides a range of luminance and 'chroma-keying' facilites. A videoconferencing suite, with facilities to conference by both IP and ISDN, is available for university and external use. Other services include off-air recording, equipment loan and teaching room support.

UNIVERSITY OF WALES, SWANSEA: MEDIA RESOURCES

Room 15 Keir Hardie Building, Singleton Park, Swansea SA2 8PP Wales
Tel: 01792 295010
E-mail: aamedia@swan.ac.uk
Web: www.swan.ac.uk/acu/MediaResources

Media Resources is a central service providing a wide range of facilities to the university, some of which include television and video, language laboratory, audio-visual facilities and videoconferencing.

UNIVERSITY OF WALES INSTITUTE, CARDIFF: AUDIO VISUAL SUPPORT

Howard Gardens Campus, Cardiff CF24 0SP
Tel: 029 2041 7107
E-mail: AVsupportHG@uwic.ac.uk

Web: www2.uwic.ac.uk/UWIC/Departments/ FacilitiesManagement/technical/teaching/

Audio-visual offices are situated at all four teaching sites. The core functions of the service are: provision of audio-visual support services to general teaching areas; equipment loan service; supporting a videoconferencing facility.

UNIVERSITY OF WARWICK: AUDIO VISUAL CENTRE

IT Services Building, Gibbett Hill Road, Coventry CV4 7AL
Tel: 02476 522463
E-mail: audio-visual@warwick.ac.uk
Web: www2.warwick.ac.uk/services/its/ servicessupport/av

The multimedia production service offers analogue and digital copying between formats, and basic editing. The filming service provides digital camera recording of lectures given in centrally timetabled teaching rooms. The Audio Visual Centre also supports the equipment needs of teaching rooms; operates a short-term equipment loan scheme for staff; provides videoconferencing facilities; and runs the off-air recording scheme.

UNIVERSITY OF WESTMINSTER: COMPUTING AND AUDIO VISUAL

E-mail: mrav@wmin.ac.uk
Web: www.wmin.ac.uk/sabe/page-942

Each of the four campuses provides a range of audio-visual equipment from data projectors, cameras and video camcorders to flip chart stands and microphones for use by staff and students. Audio-visual equipment, a CCTV studio and video editing suite, together with technical support, are available for outside hire from the university's Estates and Facilities Department (www.wmin. ac.uk/ page-6661).

UNIVERSITY OF WINCHESTER: IT & COMMUNICATION SERVICES DEPARTMENT

Winchester SO22 4NR
Tel: 01962 841515
E-mail: ITCentre@winchester.ac.uk
Web: www.winchester.ac.uk/?page=7856

ITCS provides a wide range of equipment and support for IT, audio, video and photographic activities. A loan service offers photographic, video, lighting and audio equipment, supported by advice on its choice and use. Staff also provide training and support in the use of the video editing suites and video copying facilities which are available for post-production work.

UNIVERSITY OF WORCESTER: DIGITAL ARTS CENTRE

Henwick Grove, WR2 6AJ
Tel: 01905 855445
E-mail: d.james@worc.ac.uk
Web: www.worc.ac.uk/digitalmedia
Offers studio facilities, consultancy, courses and content creation to the local community as well as students attending courses at the university. Users are able to draw on a central bank of digital multimedia facilities such as computers running industry-standard digital media software and smaller spaces for digital media experimentation, research, production and development work. There is a 48-track digital recording studio, a digital video production studio with full lighting rig and blue screen technology, digital video editing facilities and web servers.

UNIVERSITY OF YORK: AUDIO-VISUAL CENTRE

Directorate of Facilities Management, Heslington, York YO10 5DD

Tel: 01904 43 3031
E-mail: pas118@york.ac.uk
Web: www.york.ac.uk/campusservices/avcentre

The Tandberg 990 MXP unit is used at the University's videoconferencing facility.

Responsible for providing equipment and technical staff to support teaching in term-time and conference business in vacation. The Centre consists of colour television and sound studios, control room and full editing suite for the production of high band video recordings. It can also offer a three-camera outside recording unit. The university has a closed circuit television network capable of transmitting four programmes simultaneously across the campus. The videoconferencing facility is equipped with a Tandberg 990 MXP unit and can use either ISDN channels providing from 128Kbs (ISDN 2) to 384Kbs (ISDN 6) bandwidth, or a network connection to provide IP connectivity up to 2Mbps.

WEBSITES

All of these websites, and over 1,000 more, can be found on the BUFVC's Moving Image Gateway (www.bufvc.ac.uk/gateway). The MIG collects together sites that relate to moving images and sound and their use in higher and further education. The sites are classified by academic discipline, some forty subjects from Agriculture to Women's Studies, collected within the four main categories of Arts & Humanities, Bio-Medical, Social Sciences and Science & Technology. Each site is evaluated and described by the BUFVC's Information Service. The selection of sites given below all offer video or audio content, and provide an indication of the great variety of specialist sites delivering audio-visual materials online.

ARCHAEOLOGY CHANNEL

Web: www.archaeologychannel.org/
A site run by the Archaeological Legacy Institute, a US-based non-profit organisation. It streams videos of archaeological interest in their entirety at a choice of connection speeds. American archaeology is strongly represented, but the extensive collection contains programmes covering archaeology worldwide. There is also a series of audio interviews with archaeologists and another of archaeologists commenting on topics of particular interest to them.

ARTS ON FILM ARCHIVE

Web: http://artsonfilm.wmin.ac.uk/
The archive offers a complete database and online video streaming of all 450 films made by the film department of Arts Council England between 1953 and 1998 and several films produced before 2003 by the Dance Department of ACE. The films are available in digital form as the result of a three-year project by the University of Westminster, and access is free of charge to UK further and higher

Image from RICHARD HAMILTON (1969) by James Scott, available to view through the Arts On Film Archive.

education institutions. The collection provides a unique record of British and international post-war art, as well as of documentary filmmaking in the UK.

BBC MOTION GALLERY

Web: www.bbcfootage.com/customer/index.jsp
Part of the BBC's commercial arm, the BBC

Motion Gallery includes footage from its archives as well as those of CBS in the United States, and is primarily a footage resource for companies in the commercial sector. However, the site also features hundreds of streamed samples of its wares, which can be searched by subject and viewed freely via Windows Media Player. The advanced search, using the criteria of keyword (title or elsewhere), programme genre, collection and date range, effectively operates as an index to the whole BBC archive. Registration is required but is free and all clips feature BBC digital onscreen graphics as watermarks. In Nov 2007 a new online service was launched in partnership with JISC, to give UK FE and HE institutions access to a selection of footage for use in an educational setting, via the password-protected site www.jiscmotiongallery.com

BBC PROGRAMMES
Web: www.bbc.co.uk/programmes/
A new project, which aims to ensure that every television and radio programme the BBC broadcasts has a permanent, findable web presence. Starting from October 2007, this website will grow and change as its functionality and data are tested and improved. At the moment the programme information offered is limited to current schedules. When programmes are available to watch or listen to the video is on the page or a link is given to iPlayer Radio. The site is searchable by title, genre or transmission channel/date. A selection of older programmes is available for viewing or listening to via the BBC archives.

BFI YOUTUBE CHANNEL
Web: http://uk.youtube.com/user/BFIfilms

Germaine Greer as seen in DARLING, DO YOU LOVE ME (1968).

As of October 2008 close to 200 titles from the British Film Institute Archive are available to view from this site, ranging from silent obscurities from the 1920s to counter-culture student films from the 1960s, such as DARLING, DO YOU LOVE ME featuring a young Germaine Greer. The quality of the encoding is generally very high and includes copious selections from the Mitchell and Kenyon Collection and Friese-Greene's recently restored THE OPEN ROAD.

BRANDREPUBLIC.TV
Web: www.brandrepublic.tv/
BrandRepublic.tv is an online video channel of video productions aimed at people who work in the advertising, media and marketing industries. It is part of BrandRepublic.com, which is a news, views and jobs website with a thriving online community. An archive of video webchats with influencial figures in the industry, recorded during the last year, are available for online viewing or download. A new programme of talks is planned and these will also be available via podcast.

DOCUMENTARY FILM NETWORK
Web: www.documentary-film.net/
The Documentary Film Network bridges the gap between filmmakers and their audience and provides a home for many controversial, political documentaries that are not available elsewhere. Free registration allows users to view some of the 100+ films free, in full and at high quality, buy them on DVD, or download others very cheaply. Filmmakers can upload their own films free on to the site's servers, make money when viewers pay to watch their film, have a free directory listing, and post announcements on a notice-board.

EBST ONLINE
Web: www.ebst.co.uk/shop/
EBST Online is the new home and access point for the vocational training programmes produced by the Educational Broadcasting Services Trust and consortia of further and higher education institutions, with input from business and industry. The Skillset, Shotlist and Maths for Engineers series cover areas including biology, engineering,

interpersonal skills, maths, plumbing, psychology, brickwork, and carpentry & joinery. Previously distributed on video, these programmes are now available for online preview, download or purchase on DVD.

FILM AND SOUND ONLINE

Web: www.filmandsound.ac.uk/

Still from THE BATTLE OF THE SOMME (1916), available to view at Film and Sound Online.

Film and Sound Online is a JISC-funded set of collections of film and video that have been cleared and digitised for use in UK higher education by the Managing Agent and Advisory Services which was based at BUFVC. The films are of high quality and downloadable, either in full or as segments, and can be used freely in learning, teaching and research. Collections available include: Amber Films, Anglia Television, Biochemical Society, ETV, Films of Scotland, Healthcare Productions, IWM, IWF, Logic Lane, Open University, Performance Shakespeare, St George's Hospital Medical School, and Sheffield University Learning Media Unit. The collection was previously known as Education Media Online.

FRANCE24.COM

Web: www.france24.com/en/
France 24 is the first French international news channel to broadcast on a 24/7 basis. Launched in December 2006 and broadcast in French, English and Arabic, it offers a French perspective on world events. The channel is characterized by respect for diversity and attention to political and cultural differences and identities. As well as being available via the various digital television platforms and podcasting, the Internet is at the heart of its strategy, with a trilingual site as of its launch. In addition to online viewing of the live broadcast schedule, there is an extensive video archive of programmes and special reports available for on-demand viewing.

HOWARD HUGHES MEDICAL INSTITUTE

Web: www.hhmi.org/biointeractive/
The Howard Hughes Medical Institute is a non-profit medical research organisation, whose activities include promoting science education at all levels. The 'Biointeractive' section of the website includes interactive virtual laboratories, as well as video clips and animations organised under the headings stem cells, evolution, obesity, cancer, neuroscience genomics & chemical genetics, sex determination, biological clocks, infectious diseases, cardiovascular, immunology, DNA, and RNA. There are also live webcasts and a webcast archive of the 'Holiday Lectures on Science' programme.

IDEASFORLIFE.TV

Web: www.ideasforlife.tv/
Launched in 2008, ideasforlife.tv is an online video channel showcasing innovative science-based business and research taking place across the Birmingham Science City region. It is a collaborative project run by the University of Warwick and Maverick Television. Videos focus on the core themes of energy, medicine & health, digital media, automotive and materials science and feature inspiring projects which improve our everyday lives, and encourage more people to get involved with science. The goal is to promote and de-mystify science and enterprise by providing a forum for communication catering for different levels of interest and knowledge – satisfying needs ranging from mild curiosity through to serious academic debate. The over fifty video titles on the site have been produced by Maverick, Warwick University or scientific video archives.

THE ISLAM CHANNEL

Web: www.islamchannel.tv/
The Islam Channel is the first free-to-air, English language, Islamic-focused television channel available globally via the Internet and digital television platforms. It aspires to be an alternative channel that advances unbiased and accurate images of Islam and Muslims and endeavours to bring about cultural understanding and awareness for a peaceful and harmonious co-existence amongst communities.

MATHS FOR ECONOMISTS

Web: www.lifesign.ac.uk/portal/
version2.asp?gid=36
Maths for Economists Enhancing Teaching and Learning is a UK Higher Education funded project that integrates interactive video with online learning resources and question banks for academics and students. Interactive video production is provided by StreamLearn in association with the Department of Economics at the University of Portsmouth. This site consists of a considerable collection of short video clips, which present problems in economics, with accompanying animations explaining the mathematics involved in solving the problems. Free streaming or download to UK HE and FE institutions.

NASA

Web: www.nasa.gov/multimedia/index.html

The *Eagle* in lunar orbit. It landed on the moon on 20 July 1969.

The Multimedia section of the NASA website features an extensive video archive for on-demand streaming that includes Hubble Space Telescope animations, videos from the Mars Climate Orbiter, Space Shuttle launches, Apollo video clips, and an archive of NASA webcasts; an image gallery; and audio and video podcasts for news of the latest missions. NASA TV also has an education channel showing programmes for various educational levels in addition to a more general public channel.

OPEN STUDENT TELEVISION NETWORK

Web: www.ostn.tv/OSTNWebsite/OSTNuk/
OSTNuk.html
Open Student Television Network is a 24–hour global channel devoted exclusively to student-produced programming. It originated in the United States but in 2007, with support from JANET, OSTN UK was launched. This channel features content produced by students on film, media and journalism courses throughout the UK, as well as by student unions. JANET-member institutions also have access to the rest of OSTN's educational, foreign language, news, and entertainment IPTV content. The programming schedule includes a variety of genres such as college-themed soap operas, student-produced dating shows, controversial talk shows, cutting edge digital animation, and documentaries from a number of National Student Television Association (NASTA) member institutions.

OUVIEW

Web: www.youtube.com/ou
The Open University has launched a YouTube channel featuring over 300 videos, with educational content in the OULearn section, and videos from staff, students and alumni in the OULife section. OULearn (www.youtube.com/oulearn) showcases extracts of video learning materials from Open University courses and television broadcasts, covering languages, arts & humanities, and science. OULife (www.youtube.com/oulife) contains video blogs, graduation ceremonies, etc uploaded by OU staff and students. A Youtube research channel is planned for launch in 2009. OU educational resources are

also available for download as free audio or video podcasts at www.open.ac.uk/ itunes

PEACE CHANNEL

Web: www.peacechannel.tv/about.php?pid=7
The Peace Channel is a global online TV website containing videos about peace and conflict issues, as well as a picture gallery, debate forums, and an interactive zone. It was launched in Norway in September 2008 by Point of Peace, an independent media and human rights organisation based in Norway, and Ten Alps, a factual media company based in the UK and founded by Bob Geldof. The videos are in three categories: impartial videos produced by the Peace Channel editorial team; videos from organisations; and videos sent in by people from around the world.

POLICY REVIEW TV

Web: www.policyreview.tv/
This website offers access to speeches, discussions, question and answer sessions and interviews with senior figures from government, politics and business, captured at policy-related conferences and events across the country. Users can view streamed video and download podcasts and documents from an event, including Power-Point presentations and speaker notes. Some content is free, but the majority is available either on a subscription basis or one-off payment per item/event. The content is grouped in themes, such as business, education and skills, environment etc, although you can also search by speaker. RSS feeds are available to alert users to new content in their field of interest.

ROYAL SOCIETY IPTV

Web: http://royalsociety.tv/dpx_royalsociety/dpx.php?dpxuser=dpx_v12
This extensive resource offers well encoded video and audio recordings and podcasts of lectures held at the Royal Society on a broad range of scientific subjects including biology, climate science, chemistry, geology, mathematics, physics and history of science. The archive is very well catalogued and organised. The lecturers include such luminaries as David Attenborough, Bill Bryson, Ben Okri and Tim

Berners-Lee. RealOne and Windows Media Player required.

RSA VISION

Web: www.thersa.org/events/vision

Professor Michael Young of the University of London opens the first RSA Edge lecture, 'What are schools for?'

The RSA (Royal Society for the Encouragement of Arts, Manufactures & Commerce) works to remove the barriers to social progress. It drives ideas, innovation and social change through an ambitious programme of projects, events and lectures. These lectures, available as live webcasts, streamed video or audio, and podcasts, feature some of the world's most influential thinkers such as Steven Pinker, and cover a wide range of topics such as whether scientists get the media they deserve, the science of persuasion, secularism, and restructuring the global economy for a sustainable future. There is also a series of podcast interviews with Royal Designers.

RUSSIA TODAY

Web: www.russiatoday.com/news/news/31148
Russia Today is the first 24/7 English-language television news channel to present the Russian point of view on events happening in Russia and around the globe. The channel was established in April 2005 by TV-Novosti. RT provides viewers with breaking news, stories on politics, business, and public affairs, particularly relating to events in Russia, Eastern Europe and Central Asia. A

selection of the best news reports, stories and programmes can be viewed on YouTube (http://uk.youtube.com/russiatoday), and news bulletins from the current day are available on the RT website.

UK STUDENT FILMS

Web: www.ukstudentfilms.co.uk/
UK Student Films is an online promoter and showcase for short, independent films made by UK students and aspiring young filmmakers. To ensure quality it sources material direct from individual filmmakers, who are invited to post in their work, or from film festivals and events around the country. The site also contains useful information on filming and provides a forum for students to discuss their film ideas, experiences and exploits with fellow film students.

VETS.TV

Web: www.vets.tv/
Vets.tv is a new web TV service from the British Veterinary Association offering vets and all those who work with animals help and support in all aspects of their working life. It is being launched as a pilot to test the level of response and whether it will be an effective method of communication for continuing professional development. The short videos that are streamed on demand are in four broad categories: CPD – support and help on clinical skills and related areas; practice issues – help on managing a practice, including customer-care; general issues – reports on major issues affecting vets across the country; information on a range of commercial products and services.

WHY DEMOCRACY?

Web: www.whydemocracy.net/
In October 2007, ten one-hour films focusing on

Electioneering in Bolivia in LOOKING FOR THE REVOLUTION, from the 'Why Democracy?' website.

contemporary democracy were broadcast around the world. Running alongside the ten documentaries, and integral to the outreach component of *Why Democracy?* is a collection of short films made by emerging filmmakers from around the world. The films produced by the project have a common reference beyond the thematic. Both the global broadcast and the debates arising from the films were intended to lead to a greater understanding concerning conditions of governance facing people in different societies and cultures, as well as a broader understanding of democracy. The twenty short films available online deal with personal, political and rights issues around the theme 'What does democracy mean to me?'

INDEX